Leaving
Springfield

Contemporary Approaches to Film and Television Series

*A complete listing of the books in this series
can be found online at wsupress.wayne.edu*

General Editor
Barry Keith Grant
Brock University

Advisory Editors
Patricia B. Erens
Dominican University

Lucy Fischer
University of Pittsburgh

Peter Lehman
Arizona State University

Caren J. Deming
University of Arizona

Robert J. Burgoyne
Wayne State University

Tom Gunning
University of Chicago

Anna McCarthy
New York University

Peter X. Feng
University of Delaware

Leaving Springfield

The SIMPSONS
and the POSSIBILITY
of OPPOSITIONAL CULTURE

Edited by
JOHN ALBERTI

Wayne State University Press
Detroit

Copyright © 2004 by Wayne State University Press,
Detroit, Michigan 48201. All rights are reserved.
No part of this book may be reproduced without formal permission.

Manufactured in the United States of America.
ISBN-13: 978-0-8143-2849-1 ISBN-10: 0-8143-2849-0

Library of Congress Cataloging-in-Publication Data

Leaving Springfield : the Simpsons and the possibility of oppositional
culture / [edited by] John Alberti.
      p.   cm. — (Contemporary film and television series)
Includes bibliographical references and index.
     ISBN 0-8143-2849-0 (pbk. : alk. paper) 0-8143-2848-2 (cloth : alk. paper)
  1. Simpsons (Television program) I. Alberti, John. II. Series.
    PN1992.77.S58L43 2003
    791.45'72—dc21   2002156592

∞ The paper used in this publication meets the minimum requirements of the American National Standard for Information Sciences—Permanence of Paper for Printed Library Materials, ANSI Z39.48-1984.

"Bart Simpson: Prince of Irreverence" is from *Media Virus! Hidden Agendas in Popular Culture* by Douglas Rushkoff, copyright © 1994. Used by permission of Ballantine books, a division of Random House, Inc.

Material in "*The Simpsons* and Hanna-Barbera's Animation Legacy" originally appeared in "*The Flintstones* Then and Now: The Long Life of American Television's First Cartoon Sitcom" by Megan Mullen, which appeared in the *Mid-Atlantic Almanack* 7, 1998.

To Martha,
who knows her way around Springfield
better than I do.

CONTENTS

ACKNOWLEDGMENTS

Like all good television programs, essay collections are truly collaborative efforts, and obviously *Leaving Springfield* could not exist without the creativity, cooperation, patience, and good humor of the contributors. Equally indispensable to the appearance of this book has been the unflagging support and advice of my editor at Wayne State University Press, Jane Hoehner, who from the beginning has believed in the value of this project and has seen this collection through from initial proposal through the revision process to its completion. Jennifer Gariepy provided able supervision through the final publication process, and Tom Ligotti was an attentive, scrupulous, and insightful copyeditor. Thanks as well to the outside reviewers and editorial board members who read the manuscript versions and offered suggestions for revision that have helped focus and deepen the strength of the collection. Research on this project was greatly facilitated as well by the legion of dedicated *Simpsons* fans on the world wide web who have painstakingly compiled episode lists, synopses, and catalogues of references to the program. Finally, this project would not exist without the partnership and love of Kristin and Martha, my companions in life and *Simpsons* viewing, and especially Martha, who helped with the proofreading and fact-checking. I raise a can of Duff and say "Woo-hoo!" to all of you.

INTRODUCTION

JOHN ALBERTI

During the spring 1987 television season, The Tracy Ullman Show, a variety series on the then new start-up "fourth network," Fox, began to run a series of brief animated shorts before and after commercial breaks. These short cartoons featured a yellow-skinned, boggle-eyed dysfunctional nuclear family named Simpson, and in the heart of the Reagan era, these films took satirical aim at the pieties of suburban American family life. "The Pagans," for example, from spring of 1988, focuses on the reluctance of the two oldest Simpson children, Bart and Lisa, to attend church services. Instead, rejecting what they see as their parents' mindless conformity to a religion based on guilt and repression, they cast off their clothes, proclaim themselves pagans, and conduct their own nature-worshiping rituals, much to the fury of their dictatorial, if inept, father Homer and the consternation of their indulgent but conventional mother Marge.[1] Few previous television shows had ever so boldly made fun of such a sensitive topic, especially to suggest, as Bart and Lisa's playfulness does, that paganism might be a healthier alternative to Christianity.

The characters had been created by an alternative comics artist named Matt Groening, known for his *Life in Hell* comic strip which features the existential dilemmas of a one-eared rabbit named Binky. Groening was invited to create the cartoon by *Tracy Ullman* producer and long-time television comedy writer, director, and producer James L. Brooks. It was Brooks's clout—along with the leeway offered by a new network willing to tolerate a certain amount of experimentation in order to attract younger viewers—that allowed Groening's biting satire on the spiritual hollowness and mindless conformity of suburban Christianity to appear on prime-time television (on Sunday night, no less). These short films quickly led to a Christmas special in late 1989 and finally to the appearance, in early 1990, of *The Simpsons*, which was to become the first successful prime-time network cartoon since *Wait Till Your Father Gets Home* and eventually the longest-running situation comedy in television history.[2] *The Simpsons* has achieved iconic status, and the various members of the Simpson family are now easily recognized features of contemporary U.S. pop culture.

From the beginning, a key attraction for many fans of the show has been the sense of "getting away with something," a delight in the idea that a program could become one of the most popular shows on television while dealing in and even promoting the subversive and the transgressive. Rather than becoming a cult program that appeals only to viewers belonging to a demographically small subculture, *The Simpsons* has entered fully into the mainstream, even while apparently embracing ideas (e.g., the promotion of paganism; the critique of Christianity) that conventional wisdom would see as fatal to mass public acceptance. It is this phenomenon—the enduring popularity of *The Simpsons* either in spite or because of its potentially countercultural elements—that is the focus of *Leaving Springfield:* The Simpsons *and the Possibility of Oppositional Culture.* In the process of exploring the subversive potential of *The Simpsons,* the essays collected here reveal the inventiveness, creativity, and richness of "America's most nuclear family."[3]

I

Not surprisingly, the success of *The Simpsons* has proved enormously influential in shaping television programming, as evidenced by the season-long appearance on ABC in the mid-nineties of *The Critic,* also produced by Brooks, and the raft of prime-time animation that has appeared on cable television since then: *Beavis & Butt-head, Daria, Ren and Stimpy, Dr. Katz: Professional Therapist,* and, more recently, *South Park* and *Celebrity Deathmatch.* Indeed, with *The Simpsons, Futurama* (also created by Groening), and *King of the Hill,* prime-time animation has become a staple of the Fox programming strategy.

Before *Who Wants to Be a Millionaire* launched a retro-game show craze among the major networks in the fall of 1999, animation had become the biggest trend in prime-time television programming. Widely seen among the networks as a hedge against the increasing loss of audience-share to the expanding cable market, especially among the coveted young adult male demographic group, the incentives driving the move to prime-time animation were not hard to determine. Economically speaking, animation has never been cheaper to produce. The use of drawings and clay figures means low studio overhead: few lights, no sets, no studio audience, no three-camera set-up, no crew, and a relatively small group of voice actors who can play multiple characters. Compared with live-action television programs, costs are drastically cut for rehearsal time, since the voice parts for an entire season can be recorded without significant time-lapse between episodes. The use of computer animation (as evidenced, for example, by *Dr. Katz: Professional Therapist*) as well as outsourcing to Asian studios has driven down the biggest cost factor, the labor-intensive graphic artwork.[4]

There are creative benefits to cartoons as well, benefits that have defined the history of animation. Not bounded by the physical laws governing 3-D space, animated programs can feature casts of hundreds and take place in any geographic or historical time frame. In the case of the animated prime-time television series, this "cartoon for grown-ups" inhabits a cultural space between children's television and prime-time programming. This ambiguous cultural space allows producers and writers to take advantage of the resulting uncertainty regarding generic expectations from this mixing of the childlike and the adult, the supposedly trivial and the serious, by being able to treat serious and even controversial issues under the cover of being "just a cartoon." As Megan Mullen points out in her essay on the history of prime-time animation, this cultural space was first opened by Hanna-Barbera Productions in the early sixties with *The Flintstones* and *The Jetsons,* and this latest wave of prime-time animation represents a reemergence of this trend by a generation of television artists who grew up watching these earlier shows.

Prime-time cartoons for grown-ups also have their counterparts on television for children with the rise of cable outlets such as Nickelodeon and Cartoon Network (the latter itself a hybrid aimed at both young and adult fans of animation), and they along with *The Simpsons* thrive on this blurred distinction between programming aimed at children and that created exclusively for adults. Beginning with *Sesame Street* and continuing in contemporary programs such as *Rugrats, Hey Arnold,* and *The Power-puff Girls,* characters and plot situations geared for children are combined with pop culture references and an ironic style meant to appeal to the adults watching with (or perhaps instead of) the presumed target audience.[5] The result of this new cultural form for both prime-time cartoons and the latest animation for children is the potential for the representation and treatment of social issues and concerns in ways that violate the norms and traditions of the standard television genres.

Again, however, what is especially significant and surprising about the success of *The Simpsons,* and what is the impetus behind this collection, is not just its pioneer status in reintroducing the prime-time cartoon and the reopening of this cultural space but in using this space to allow the emergence of an underground-comics sensibility on network television. The chief characteristics of that sensibility are a postmodern self-referentiality and cultural/political satire from a generally leftist/liberal perspective. So *The Simpsons* is not just a popular sitcom and cartoon show; it also represents some of the most daring cultural and political satire in television history, beyond even the groundbreaking *Saturday Night Live* in 1974. Perhaps *Roseanne,* premiering in 1988 at the same time *The Simpsons* was first appearing, comes closest in recent network programming history in terms of using the traditional sitcom format to ridicule powerful cultural, social, and political institutions with anything like a coherent political vision.

While cultural politics is often the subject of television comedy, the approach taken by most sitcoms usually represents the given issue as a matter of individual lifestyle or personality (what David Marc refers to as the sitcom's "unflappably centrist political psychology").[6] When feminism is broached, for example, gender relations are taken seriously usually as a matter of interpersonal dynamics, often focused on ironing out conflicts within heterosexual romantic relationships. Feminist leaders—that is, characters seen as pursuing a specific feminist political agenda as part of a social movement—are often dismissed as shrill dogmatists. This narrow focus on the personal allows for easy jokes, usually stemming from traditionally misogynist forms of humor, but it also enables a sitcom to recognize and then work through the real gender conflicts experienced by viewers in ways that provide comfort rather than confrontation (the popular *Home Improvement,* for example, poked fun at the main character's pretensions to traditional male dominance in order to suggest that all tensions resulting from gender inequality can be ameliorated within a traditional heterosexual nuclear family).

The same individualist approach can be seen in the way television comedy deals with race relations and other social issues, even in supposedly "progressive" ways, as Matthew Henry's essay in this collection demonstrates in relation to the politics of sexuality and the recent appearance of "gay-themed" programs such as *Ellen* or *Will and Grace*. Even when actual political figures are named, the tendency in television comedy is to reflect the logic of contemporary political campaigns, where ideological and structural political differences are presented as questions of personality. Hence, *Saturday Night Live,* for all its irreverence, bases much of its political satire on the telling impersonation of given political personalities. Thus, Dana Carvey could perform his George Bush the Elder impersonation at the White House, since it was understood that the impersonation was more about poking fun at physical and verbal mannerisms than political critique, while Will Ferrell's potentially devastating portrayal of George W. Bush as a simple-minded frat boy has been crucially distanced from suggesting any fundamental challenge to Bush's legitimacy as president, particularly following September eleventh.

While incorporating this life-style based approach to social satire (as in "Two Bad Neighbors," in which Homer engages in an irreverent if largely apolitical feud with new neighbors George and Barbara Bush), *The Simpsons* also consistently works at connecting the personal to the political, in the classic sense, by taking advantage of the creative freedoms offered by animation to place the behavior of individual characters in social and historical context. Consider "Lisa the Vegetarian," where Lisa's decision to forego the eating of meat is treated not just as evidence of a sentimental fondness for animals but in the light of the ideological marketing campaign staged by the meat and advertising industries. To take a longer example, in "Last Exit to Springfield," Homer unwittingly becomes union president and leads a strike against nuclear plant owner J. Montgomery Burns. The episode shows Homer's relationship to labor organizing as essentially rooted in personal concerns over how he can pay for Lisa's braces (for Homer, the ethical dilemma is reduced to deciding whether to accept Burns's offer of free beer in lieu of a dental plan). In a characteristic borrowing/parody of film technique, the episode also uses a flashback to give a brief, albeit cynical history of labor organizing. As a turn-of-the-century worker is arrested for theft, he challenges the owner of the plant, Burns's grandfather: "You can't treat the working man this way. One day, we'll form a union and get the fair and equitable treatment we deserve! Then we'll go too far, and get corrupt and shiftless, and the Japanese will eat us alive." Here we see some of the typical ways satire operates on *The Simpsons*. While affirming the inherent justice of the labor rights movement, the final joke about the erosion of American economic dominance seems to retreat into a conventional neo-liberal assessment that unions "went too far" and thus are equally guilty as management for the current state of U.S. economic productivity (a "balanced" position that represents a kind of political thinking parodied in "The Crepes of Wrath" when Homer attempts good parenting in an effort to resolve a political argument between Lisa and an Albanian exchange student/spy: "Maybe Lisa's right about America being the land of opportunity, and maybe Adil has a point about the machinery of capitalism being oiled with the blood of the workers"). The fact that this assessment is a kind of conventional political sound bite draws attention to the very glibness of the joke, just as the worker's anachronistic summation points to the media tendency towards simplistic historical generalizations.

Still, the interpretive possibility remains that the program merely intends to reinforce an utterly cynical, and therefore politically "neutral," position towards the mock labor struggle represented in the episode. In the end, however, Burns capitulates, not as a result of Homer's bumbling or the actions of any individual character, but because the plant workers maintain solidarity. Lisa Simpson even concludes the episode by singing, in her trademark earnest style, a labor song she has composed for the occasion. The cynicism expressed in the parodic labor history is featured in the middle verse of the song, when Lisa sings

> We'll march 'til we drop
> the girls and the fellas
> we'll fight 'til the death
> or else fold like umbrellas.

This cynicism seems to vanish, however, in the final verses, which Lisa sings with heartfelt sincerity:

> So we'll march day and night
> by the big cooling tower
> They have the plant
> but we have the power.

Corporate capitalism, organized religion, the Republican Party as political wing of the dominant economic classes, education as part of the ideological state apparatus—all have figured as targets of satire on *The Simpsons*. Yet the show also relies on mainstays of the sitcom—the incompetent, infantile father, a well-meaning but neurotically overprotective mother, two smart aleck kids (one a trickster, one a brain), goofy neighbors—even as *The Simpsons* self-consciously acknowledges and thereby parodies these clichés. While seeming to operate from sociopolitical positions subversive to mainstream U.S. cultural practices, the show itself has become a part of mainstream American culture, which brings us again to the central questions motivating this collection: can *The Simpsons* be both mainstream and oppositional? How do we understand the politics of a show that consistently holds corporate capitalism and consumer culture up to ridicule at the same time that it is the flagship program of a multinational media conglomerate? Does *The Simpsons* make television safe for satire or vice versa, and what does this say about the possibilities for the legacy of *The Simpsons* in particular and the idea of oppositional mass media in general? In short, what, if anything, is *The Simpsons* getting away with?

The title of this collection, *Leaving Springfield,* relates to these questions in three main ways. In the style of *The Simpsons,* the title alludes to a popular culture text—Mike Figgis's film *Leaving Las Vegas*—that achieved high middlebrow status, the kind of pop cultural capital that *The Simpsons* mocks with regularity (e.g., "22 Short Films About Springfield," an episode playing off the title of François Girard's film, *Thirty Two Short Films About Glenn Gould*) while at the same time claiming another kind of the cultural capital that accrues from embedding such a reference in a cartoon show in the first place. After all, it's a reference only a specific segment of the audience for *The Simpsons* is likely to get. This simultaneous parody/homage is indicative of the desire to both belong to and make fun of a cultural elite, to be both of and above television, an unstable relationship with intellectual culture that is also inherent in cultural studies itself, which can oscillate between claiming high artistic status for popular culture materials and using these materials to understand the very concepts of "high" and "low" culture.

Taken as metaphor, *Leaving Springfield* questions the relationship between the fictional, almost mythic town of Springfield and the U.S. culture that *The Simpsons* both makes fun and is now an integral part of, a relationship the show consistently highlights through episodes devoted to the self-referential treatment of its own status as prime-time sitcom. The main vehicle for this self-referential quality of *The Simpsons* may be the cartoon-within-a-cartoon *Itchy & Scratchy* show (itself discussed in many of the essays in this collection), a *Tom and Jerry/Roadrunner* parody that consistently features titles involving clever plays on pop culture texts (e.g., "My Dinner with Itchy," "Four Funerals and a Wedding," "Foster Pussycat! Kill! Kill!") and ultra-violent plots. *The Simpsons* has used *Itchy & Scratchy* to focus on various aspects of the cultural work of television programs, from the debates about the effects of media violence on children (the subject of William Savage's essay) to the corporate decision-making processes that go into the development of a television program, to the continuing viability of *The Simpsons* itself as contemporary satire (the focus of Rob Sloane's analysis in this collection).

Finally, *Leaving Springfield* raises the question of what, if any, utopian gesture is involved in *The Simpsons* as social satire, a question that goes to the heart of the problematic nature of *The Simpsons*'s status as "subversive" mainstream media. As Fredric Jameson has pointed out, "the effectively ideological is also, at the same time, necessarily Utopian," suggesting that if *The Simpsons* is "ideological, whether subversively or not," then we should have a sense of where we might be going if we leave Springfield.[7] Do we understand *The Simpsons*, finally, as being about leaving Springfield, or is *The Simpsons* the latest version yet of the co-optation of the subversive, where a critical point-of-view is turned from being the basis for political action to a kind of attitude, coping mechanism, and ultimately consumer profile?

At this point, we may be tempted to ask if this is not too much cultural significance to bring to bear on what is, after all, a cartoon show. It is a question, of course, that betrays its own cultural bias. In a sense, to pose the question is to answer it. If the case needs to be made that *The Simpsons* deserves the kind of close reading it will receive in these pages, the essays included all testify to the richly allusive quality of the show, its multifaceted construction, and the sheer density of the cultural references that make a VCR an essential piece of viewing equipment for many fans of the show. (In fact, the writers of the show deliberately include gags and jokes only available by using the "pause" button.) Indeed, it is probably the case that no television program has ever been more about television—its history, formal conventions, and social impact—than *The Simpsons*, nor has any program made such extensive, detailed, and meticulous use of the visual field.

The main purpose of this collection, however, is not simply to make the claim that *The Simpsons* is worthy of serious appreciation as conventionally understood; that is, that *The Simpsons* is "better" than most television and therefore rises above the generally mediocre fare that defines the medium. The point is not that *The Simpsons* is "not like other television," for this argument reproduces the standard hierarchical construction of contemporary culture, an issue addressed by both Kurt Koenigsberger and David Arnold in this collection. One of the premises informing this collection is not, therefore, to see how *The Simpsons* is unlike television but to understand the program *as* television, and highly influential television as well. As has been noted, one of the remarkable features of *The Simpsons* as opposed to other "cult" television shows (such as *Twin Peaks, The X-Files,* or the various incarnations of *Star Trek*) is its very popularity across a wide spectrum of viewers, and it is this popularity as a mass media text that makes *The Simpsons* especially significant. From this perspective, the postmodern self-referentiality of *The Simpsons* can be taken not just as a marker of the "intelligence" of the show and thereby of the viewer discerning enough to appreciate this aspect of the program, but as a kind of action, an attempt to make an impact in society beyond the function of simple entertainment. In other words, the very popularity of *The Simpsons* raises the stakes of the social satire that is the hallmark of the show from a series of "in-jokes" for the cognoscenti to a potential kind of political action itself. It is this uneasy boundary between *The Simpsons* as television entertainment and *The Simpsons* as political intervention that invites scholarly attention and study.

If *The Simpsons* is an act of cultural intervention, then what is the nature of this intervention? What is *The Simpsons* saying about U.S. culture and society, and to what ends? The essays in this collection are meant to provide the context and some starting points for the exploration of these questions. Roughly speaking, these starting points can be broken down into a series of primary areas of concern related to the nature of a postmodern satirical animated television program: the problematics of "postmodern" satire; the relation of the cultural specificity inherent in satire to the global distribution network of contemporary mass media; the semiotics of television comedy; and the complexities of viewer reception and interaction with the program. These areas of concern can also be read in terms of John Fiske's classic definition of the foci of television studies: "the formal qualities of television programs and their flow; the intertextual relations of television within itself, with other media, and with conversation; and the study of socially situated readers and the processes of reading."[8]

The "postmodern" status of *The Simpsons* troubles both the ideas of cultural oppositionality and cultural satire. As critics from Jean-François Lyotard to Frederick Jameson have famously noted, the fragmented, self-conscious nature of postmodern culture tends to undermine, often deliberately, the idea of a sustained, coherent, and activist political worldview or critique informing any cultural text. Definitions of the "postmodern" are of course legion, but for our purposes we can locate the postmodernity of *The Simpsons* in the program's relentless self-referentiality, a consistent foregrounding of itself as a television program and media construct that functions as an operative principle and satirical strategy of the show, not just as an occasional rhetorical gesture. Thus, *The Simpsons* uses satire not only to undermine the pretensions to cultural significance of various texts from both "high" and "low" culture, it includes itself as part of that mockery, potentially undercutting the cultural critique in which the program seems to be engaged. Such a cultural stance that operates through the destabilizing of the concepts of positionality, identity, and referentiality creates perhaps insurmountable problems when we try to determine the focus, direction, and purpose of its satirical operation.

As Jane Feuer points out, "Television presents a further problem for theorists of the postmodern . . . in that TV is not 'post'-anything. There was no modernist TV."[9] In other words, whether discussing the self-referentiality or pastiche-quality of television, we cannot do so in relation to some earlier, precapitalist or pretechnological formation of television about which we can construct a nostalgic model of plenitude, referentiality, or sincerity, as has been the case in literary, art, and music criticism. Instead, television has been a quintessential "postmodern" medium from the very beginning. Like film and radio, television was developed as a mass medium in an industrially based, capitalist mass society. Like all broadcast media, television can therefore be understood as a "corporate" art form in two senses.

From the perspective of economic structure, television is a product of the corporation as economic entity (as opposed to, say, the novel, the development of which predated the emergence of corporate capitalism). As a result, we can understand the artistic production of television programs as a thoroughly "corporate" activity, with a creative process that takes place within and is directed by corporate management structures (like film, television production involves just as many vice-presidents as it does writers, directors, and actors). The idea of the artistic text as commodity is not a manifestation of changing modes of production in relation to television; it is instead definitive of the form, as most early television programs did not just sell advertising time within the shows but were in fact produced by the sponsoring corporations. Thus, in the case of U.S. television, the concept of the auteur is an even shakier idea than in film. When auteur theory is used in television, as Vincent Brook points out in his essay in this collection, the attention significantly is paid more to producers (Norman Lear, Aaron Spelling, Steven Bochco) than to directors and writers.[10]

Prime-time animation in general and *The Simpsons* in particular are significant in that they seem to buck this corporate trend, in part because the drawing style that defines each animated show acts as a visible signifier of an identifiable artist, thus suggesting a personal vision that does in fact hearken back to "modernist" constructions of culture, with their Romantic insistence on the importance of the unique consciousness and style of the individual artist. As a consequence, television animation has seen the rise of the artist as cultural celebrity and video auteur, whether Matt Groening in the case of *The Simpsons* and *Futurama*, Mike Judge (*Beavis & Butt-head, King of the Hill*), or Matt Stone and Trey Parker (*South Park*). Television journalists regularly identify *The Simpsons* as Groening's show, although he has only written or co-written a handful of episodes once the program became a series. Clearly, in his role as executive producer, Groening is an important part of the creative team, but it is probably safe to say that the identification with Groening is most strongly maintained by the visual look of the program, a style that extends to the level of orthography, as it is even possible to install a *Simpsons*/Groening font on word processing programs.

Groening himself actively promotes the connection of the show with himself not just in terms of artistic style but general political outlook as well. His ongoing comic strip *Life in Hell* makes occasional reference to Groening's work on *The Simpsons*. In a cartoon from 1994, for example, Groening depicts himself at his laptop logging onto the alt.tv.Simpsons listerv to distract him from a vague depression. He comes across (and reprints in the cartoon) a right-wing diatribe occasioned by the airing of "Sideshow Bob Roberts," a *Simpsons* episode that takes specific aim at the Republican party, whose local Springfield brain trust is depicted as praying to Satan and whose candidate, the former children's television personality and ex-con Sideshow Bob, threatens Bart and Lisa with the imprecation, "No children ever meddled with the Republican party and lived to tell about it." The listerv contributor urges his fellow viewers not to "let the sleaziest, least ethical elements of the left wing in television get away with slandering the Republican party" and fantasizes about "seeing Groening writhing in pain as he dangled by a section of his intestine from a tree." Throughout the cartoon Groening is pictured staring impassively at the screen before looking up in the final panel and asking, "Why do I feel so suddenly refreshed?"[11] (Of course, the fact that *The Simpsons*'s viewership includes the politically conservative previews the complexities of understanding the reception dynamics of the program).

Still, if *The Simpsons* can be seen as Groening's show it is just as obviously a product of Rupert Murdoch's Fox network, a relationship the program does not try to hide. On the contrary, in good postmodern fashion the program regularly foregrounds its status as Fox corporate product, often while denigrating the Fox network and its corporate holdings, to the point even of suggesting viewers turn to other networks as soon as *The Simpsons* is over. One obvious reading of this strategy is to resist or at least dilute the perception that *The Simpsons* has been co-opted by the corporate media empire of which it is a lucrative part. These mocking references to Fox can function at the same time as signifiers of both the independence of *The Simpsons* and the supposed hipness of Fox, meanings that can work together in the marketing of the show as "alternative" oppositional television and the marketing of Fox as a "renegade" network. This complicated relationship between *The Simpsons* and Fox encapsulates the potentially circular logic plaguing the idea of "oppositional" mass media: are Groening et al. using Fox, or is Fox using them?

II

From further considerations of postmodern satire and irony, to the history of efforts to create politically relevant pop culture, to reception theory and the multiple nature of television viewership, the essays in *Leaving Springfield* wrestle with the question of oppositionality in regards to *The Simpsons* across the wide range of theoretical issues touched on in this introduction. The collection opens with two essays that directly address the function of *The Simpsons* in relation to the cultural politics of mass and elite cultures. David Arnold's essay "'Use a Pen, Sideshow Bob': *The Simpsons* and the Threat of High Culture" situates *The Simpsons* within the twentieth-century debate among critics from both the right and the left over the value (or lack thereof) of popular mass culture, a debate frequently featured as part of the program's social satire, particularly as it involves Springfield's most notorious criminal and high culture vulture, Sideshow Bob, the erudite former sidekick on the Krusty the Klown Show. Bob's hatred for and running feud with Bart suggests the antagonism between the high and the low in a manner signaling the program's awareness of and strategic deployment of its own "vulgarity." In the end, though, Arnold argues that Bob's

> irrational hatred of Bart suggests that the central structure of the show is more than a contest of the highbrow against the low. Rather, this narrative describes the forces at work within a single medium, the pull of the conservative and the revolutionary. Bob's disruptions are the show's, are the medium's, recollections of its own history, excoriated as a subversive, culturally corrosive force, praised as a teacher, a democratizer,

an ambiguity that points to the cultural instability of television itself as perhaps its most oppositional characteristic.

In "Commodity Culture and Its Discontents: Mr. Bennett, Bart Simpson, and the Rhetoric of Modernism," Kurt Koenigsberger compares two strategies for bridging the gulf between low and high cultures at the opposite ends of the twentieth-century and on opposite sides of the cultural ideology and rhetoric of Modernism: the novels and essays of Arnold Bennett and *The Simpsons*. In both cases, he considers the necessity for the social critic and satirist to construct a totalized concept of society as a whole in order to mount an effective and focused critique, a project frustrated in both its pre-Modernist and Modernist manifestations by the complexity and fragmentation of industrialized consumer society, a frustration that has resulted in the postmodern embrace of or retreat into pastiche, chaos, and irony. In the end, Koenigsberger argues for the "recentering" function of a show like *The Simpsons,* a concept of postmodern totality that replaces the idea of oppositionality with the more provisional, Foucault-like notion of "resistance" as a way of understanding the subversive function of *The Simpsons*.

Megan Mullen's essay "*The Simpsons* and Hanna-Barbera's Animation Legacy" brings the examination of the cultural project of *The Simpsons* into the specific field of television history by examining the development of the prime-time cartoon from *The Flintstones* to the present. Mullen draws parallels between *The Simpsons* and the development of both *The Flintstones* and *The Jetsons,* not only the first two prime-time animated sit-coms developed specifically for network television but also programs that pioneered the strategy of combining a medium, animation, typically regarded by many television viewers as children's programming, with top-ical social references and even political satire.

The next essays then extend the contemporary discussion of the the-oretical implications and possibilities of postmodern satire. Kevin Dettmar's "Countercultural Literacy: Learning Irony with *The Simpsons*" undertakes a close reading of "The Cartridge Family" episode on gun con-trol and the NRA to argue for a didactic function of the show. Instead of locating this didactic effect in any particular message or political point of view, Dettmar concludes that *The Simpsons* works to educate its viewers in the interpretation of ironic discourse. In keeping with Douglas Rushkoff's argument later in the collection about the media savviness of the television generations, Dettmar makes the claim for the subversive function of the show as consisting in how well it helps attune viewers to the operation and critical value of postmodern irony.

Valerie Weilunn Chow then draws on Marxist-influenced poststruc-turalist critical theory to make the case for *The Simpsons* as self-decon-structing artifact. In "Homer Erectus: Homer Simpson as Everyman . . . and Everywoman," Chow considers how *The Simpsons* operates as a critique of consumerism and commodity capitalism, specifically through the ways Homer's narcissistic obsession with himself on the show becomes emblem-atic of how television constructs the consumer subject; specifically, through the iconic representation of Homer's body parts. The potential result is an eerie self-awareness on the part of the viewers, who in their con-structed identities as consumers are themselves the objects of the gaze of advertisers and networks: "We as *Simpsons* viewers are left with the uncomfortable notion that we are somehow both Bart's *us* and *they*. We are the voyeurs watching the Simpson family, yet we are also like the Simpson family, ourselves watched as commodities within the televisual system."

While both Dettmar and Chow provide alternative versions of the pro-oppositional argument for *The Simpsons,* Rob Sloane introduces a more skeptical point of view in "Who Wants Candy? Disenchantment in *The Simpsons.*" Focusing his attention on three shows from the eighth season that specifically address the production of mass media and fan culture, a frequent self-reflective topic of *The Simpsons,* Sloane speculates about the relationship between fans of the show and the creative staff, particularly as manifested in the increasing interactivity between producer and consumer afforded by cyberculture. Sloane thus directly engages the subject of viewer reception in the Internet age, a crucial question in the development of cultural studies in general and television studies in particular.

Sloane's essay explores the question of the hyperinfluence of the cyberfan, computer-literate viewers of the show who populate the many listervs, chatrooms, and Web sites devoted to *The Simpsons,* by suggesting that the three shows under consideration reveal an increasingly cynical and caustic representation of the show's audience. Sloane points out the danger of the writers and creators of the show growing frustrated with the perceived lack of political awareness or interest on the part of cyberfans, an audience that the writers may see as having expected too much and benefited too little from *The Simpsons.*

Vincent Brook's essay "Myth or Consequences: Ideological Fault Lines in *The Simpsons*" extends the discussion of the concerns raised by Sloane through a thick description and analysis of the responses of a group of non-fan viewers to "Lisa the Iconoclast," an episode in which Lisa faces an ethical dilemma over whether to debunk the wholly false myth surrounding the supposedly heroic pioneer founder of Springfield. An episode featuring Lisa is an apt choice for an analysis of viewer reception. In a sense, all of the Simpson family members function as representations of different potential audiences for the program, from the bright but pretentious Lisa to the thrill-seeking Bart, from morally anxious Marge to gullible Homer, subject positions we can expand by considering the entire fictive population of Springfield. These multiple subject positions for viewers have implications for analyses of the show itself. Who, for example, is the "hero" of the show? Even if we mold this question to fit the interests of this collection and ask which character best represents the voice of satirical intent in the show, we are caught between Bart, the classic, anti-authoritarian male trickster figure (think Huck Finn or Tom Sawyer) whose politics seem more a matter of instinct than intent, and Lisa, the thoughtful social critic whose stated political and social opinions come the closest to defining the moral viewpoint of the show. Indeed, Al

Jean admits that "the writers empathize with her more than any other character. She has a more intellectual reaction to how disquieting her life has become."[12] This empathy is made clear in the show's portrayal of her: while her earnestness and sense of superiority is often made fun of, the moral logic of her opinions, from feminism to vegetarianism, never seems seriously questioned.

Brook's essay in a sense brings the theoretical discussion of the possibilities of postmodern mass media satire full circle by connecting his survey of the ambivalent reactions of his test audience to the decisions Lisa makes (in the end, she decides not to expose the truth about the town's founder, explicitly claiming that the founding myth provides a sense of pride for the population. The circumstances of the plot, however, also suggest her fear of the repercussions involved should she follow through on her iconoclast role). Rather than using the ambivalence of his test audiences' reactions to suggest the ultimate futility of reading *The Simpsons* in terms of specific political outcomes or opinions, Brook instead argues that the program's habit of consistently upsetting formal expectations of sitcom closure exposes areas of ideological instability—the ideological fault lines of Brook's title. If it is difficult to make definitive claims about any unilateral or even polylateral political effect of *The Simpsons* on its audience, we can document the ways in which the plot structure of the program disturbs these fault lines enough to cause tremors in the ideological landscape of Springfield and beyond.

The concluding essays in the collection include case studies that chart some of these specific tremors and aftershocks. They range from considerations of media censorship to representations of sexuality, from the place of *The Simpsons* as part of nuclear culture to the dynamics of cross-cultural reception and interpretation. "'So Television's Responsible!': Oppositionality and the Interpretive Logic of Satire and Censorship in *The Simpsons* and *South Park*" by William J. Savage, Jr., considers the two most famous oppositional prime time cartoons in the context of the history of attempts to control mass public exposure to "dangerous" cultural influences. By looking at episodes of *The Simpsons* and *South Park* that focus on the production of mass media cartoons, Savage demonstrates how these shows consistently thematize cartoons in order to demonstrate the parallel (though often conflicting) interpretive logics of censorship and satire in ways that addresses the fundamentally elitist assumptions that have governed even leftist critiques of mass media.

Matthew Henry's "Looking for Amanda Hugginkiss: Gay Life on *The Simpsons*" examines the exploration of gay identity on *The Simpsons* and by extension the potential of the show to offer a critique of homophobia in U.S. culture. Focusing on the character of Waylon Smithers and situating his analysis in the context of the much-publicized development of "gay-friendly" shows such as *Ellen* and *Will and Grace,* Henry argues that *The Simpsons* "is rearticulating 'gayness' for its audience," overtly enacting the same reading that gay men and women have done covertly for years and "thereby making mainstream what is still derisively referred to as an 'alternative' lifestyle." In many ways, the fact that *The Simpsons* are only drawings makes it extremely effective in terms of exposing ambiguities and anxieties about gender and sexuality.

Mick Broderick then situates *The Simpsons* within the discourses of nuclear culture in "Releasing the Hounds: *The Simpsons* as Anti-Nuclear Satire." An expert on and critic of the propaganda and popular culture created by the nuclear technology and weapons industry, Broderick examines the ways *The Simpsons* both ventriloquizes and parodies the discourses of nuclearism, primarily though not exclusively through the portrayal of the Springfield Nuclear Power Plant and its nefarious owner, J. Montgomery Burns. Broderick demonstrates the high degree of detail and allusion permeating *The Simpsons* in relation to the history of nuclear culture and searches for the boundaries that delimit the range of the show's satirical nerve, boundaries he argues that have to do with representations of inspectors from government nuclear regularity agencies who periodically appear to menace if never shut down Burns's power plant. For Broderick, the "Realpolitik of avoiding a serious critique (or even of lampooning) a federal bureaucracy such as the NRC or EPA appears, for *The Simpsons,* to be the ideological barrier at which its sense of oppositional culture must retreat" for fear of losing the mass popularity which makes the program effective satire in the first place.

Duncan Stuart Beard's "Local Satire With a Global Reach: Ethnic Stereotyping and Cross-Cultural Conflicts in *The Simpsons*" looks at the portrayal of ethnicity and foreignness on *The Simpsons* as a means of addressing the question of the possibility and paradoxes of cross-cultural satire. That cultural specificity is central to satire is a commonplace; the teaching of literature demonstrates the difficulty of recreating the sociopolitical context for, and thus having access to the rhetorical strategies of, historically distant satirical texts. The same is especially true for the broadcast media, where the ability to respond quickly to transient historical events is definitive of their development, in many ways their very reason for existence. While *The Simpsons* is unusual in television comedy for the historical range of its cultural allusions, it is also highly topical, as any good satire should be.

The issue of cultural specificity is complicated by the increasingly global nature of mass media. The Fox Broadcasting Company itself bears the name of a legendary U.S. movie studio but is part of the tabloid empire built by Australian-born Rupert Murdoch, and the corporation may be better understood as international rather than national, as English-language based rather than American, English, or Australian. As a result, Fox tends to avoid overly "local" programming in favor of creating shows that can be distributed globally in a variety of languages and cultures. Animation fits this bill particularly well, since the same cost benefits that accrue from using one voice actor to play multiple roles carry over into the ease of dubbing cartoons into different languages.

In his essay, Beard discusses the uproar that surrounded the airing in Australia of "The Simpsons Down Under," an episode that sent the Simpsons to Australia and which indulged in a variety of American stereotypes about Australian culture and politics. While much of the popularity of *The Simpsons* in Australia stems from the perception, especially among college-age viewers, that the show consistently undermines American claims to cultural superiority in ways that are presumed to go over the head of the average U.S. viewer, "The Simpsons Down Under" came in for a barrage of criticism for apparently embodying the very nationalistic chauvinism that the program was usually taken to satirize. Beard uses this episode and the resulting controversy to consider the relationship between the diversity of global cultures versus the globalizing mass media. *The Simpsons* thus becomes a test case to "teas[e] out the ramifications of the globalization of culture upon the localization of satire"; in particular how the representation of ethnic, racial, and national others both does and does not work as a means of satirizing U.S. society in the context of a global viewing public.

Finally, the collection ends with the strong case for seeing *The Simpsons* as oppositional mass media made by Douglas Rushkoff in his influential book *Media Virus! Hidden Agendas in Popular Culture*. Rushkoff is a journalist, novelist, and leading commentator on the interactive pop culture of the computer age. In *Media Virus!*, he makes the argument for how a program such as *The Simpsons* "gets away with it," managing to function at once as both mainstream and oppositional. His concept of the "media virus" exploits the metaphorical cross-linking of biology and computer science found in the current usage of the term "virus" to create a kind of ecological analysis of contemporary electronic mass media.

Put briefly, Rushkoff starts with the metaphor of "mediaspace," of understanding the vast global matrix of electronic mass media both in spatial terms as the arena where contemporary issues of cultural, social, and political power are contested and as an almost organic entity, or at least such a complex system that the most useful analogies to make are to the equally complex, interactive, and non-linear systems of ecology and biology. He argues that a combination of increasing accessibility to this mediaspace through the variety of consumer technologies, from the Internet to home video, along with the increasing media savvy of people raised in the era of electronic mass media, suggest that it is time we understand and even "appreciate the media as facilitator rather than hypnotizer."[13] His book focuses on the activities of "a new generation of media activists" who make use of what he calls "media viruses," or "media events provoking real social change."[14] Like biological viruses, which use the cover and protection of a protein shell to inject rogue DNA into the cells of the host organism, media viruses use the "protein shell" of a media event, whether spontaneous or manufactured—Rodney King and OJ Simpson or a show such as *The Simpsons*—to inject "ideological code" into the mediaspace.[15] As in a biological host, the virus starts with a single cell but eventually affects the entire system along what we might call, using Vincent Brook's term, "ideological fault lines," or, in Rushkoff's words, places where "our societal 'code' is faulty," in ways that are not fully controllable or predictable but subversively powerful (as, for example, in the discussions about race, privilege, and gender that emerged around the OJ Simpson spectacle.[16] In extending this biological analogy to consider *The Simpsons* as a media virus, Rushkoff's argument suggests that the show is not simply a commentary on culture but an intervention into culture, changing the very mediaspace it comments upon, thus creating a new space that includes *The Simpsons* as part of the territory to be contested by those in search of cultural power. As a powerful argument for the oppositional potential of *The Simpsons*, Rushkoff's essay is a fitting summation to *Leaving Springfield*. Given the many references to his idea of the media virus in this collection, his essay would also serve as a useful entry point to the other essays.

III

As of this writing, *The Simpsons* may be at the height of its cultural influence, if no longer a major source of notoriety. As is the case with popular cultural texts, almost from the beginning fans have anxiously and in some cases fatalistically charted evidence of the program's artistic "decline," especially as new writers are introduced to the show, fears that increased with Matt Groening's involvement in the production of *Futurama*. Meanwhile, the future of prime-time animation as a source of cultural critique and satire is mixed. While *South Park* gives evidence of having exhausted its satiric energy (in spite of the surprising success, both commercially and critically, of the film version, *South Park: Bigger, Longer, and Uncut*), *King of the Hill* is still producing some of the subtlest insights into the construction of American masculinity in television history.

The long-term influence of *The Simpsons* has as much to do with the current instability of network television as with the popularity of the show. As network viewership continues to decline, particularly among young people, network programming has focused more and more on recapturing the young adult (preferably 15–35) viewer, with the result being a decrease in the diversity of characters represented according to age, race, and class level. As has been seen, this trend both whets the desire for animated programming and discourages innovation and risk-taking, further fueling the desire to transform satire into simple, often reactionary outrageousness, as in the case of Comedy Central's *The Man Show*. The imitative logic of the mass media clings to the belief that form or genre alone holds the key to popularity, so that as long as a prime-time show is animated, it must be popular. Inevitably, the network rush to animation has faded, as this logic proved hollow in the wake of programs that lacked the imagination and attention to detail that are the hallmarks of *The Simpsons*.

Yet *The Simpsons* has forever changed expectations for television satire. In a manner reminiscent of *Mad* magazine, that key media virus of the fifties and sixties, *The Simpsons* has helped educate a generation of fans in what Linda Hutcheon calls "complicitous critique" as well as worked to restore a sense of the need for broad historical and cultural awareness and facility in the cause of cultural critique and subversion. Through syndication, videotape and videotaping, and web distribution, *The Simpsons* has ensured itself a pop cultural lifespan that will extend far beyond its eventual end of production. For the time being, at any rate, we do not seem to be in any danger of leaving Springfield soon. The essays in this collection can help further a discussion of why we enjoy staying so much and where we might go from here.

NOTES

1. Both a complete chronological listing of all episodes of *The Simpsons* as well as an alphabetical listing of those episodes referred to in this collection, along with production code numbers, original airdates, and credits for writers and directors, can be found in the appendix.

2. Stephen Bochco's abortive *Fish Police* notwithstanding.

3. Caption from *Simpsons* postcard.

4. The current drive among the broadcast networks to lower production costs while holding onto a shrinking share of the viewing public links the reemergence of prime time animation to both the post-*Millionaire* game show trend and the *Survivor*-influenced proliferation of so-called "reality" programming, both of which represent substantial production savings in terms of writing, on-air talent, and other costs associated with conventional sitcoms and dramas.

5. Not coincidentally, one of the leading producers of cable television animation, Klasky-Csupo studios (*Rugrats, The Wild Thornberrys, Rocket Power*), was also the home of *The Simpsons* from its beginning on *The Tracy Ullman Show* to the end of the third season.

6. David Marc, *Comic Visions: Television Comedy and American Culture,* 2nd ed. (Malden, MA: Blackwell Publishers, 1997), 20.

7. Frederic Jameson, *The Political Unconscious: Narrative As A Socially Symbolic Act* (Ithaca, NY: Cornell University Press, 1981), 286.

8. John Fiske, *Television Culture* (London and New York: Methuen, 1987), 16.

9. Jane Feuer, *Seeing Through The Eighties: Television And Reaganism* (Durham: Duke UP, 1995), 6.

10. This situation is somewhat different in countries with large government-subsidized networks, such as the BBC, where television series are sometimes identified as the work of a particular writer. The advent of cable television may suggest a similar development in U.S. television, where so-called "premium" channels such as HBO will sponsor a series featuring the work of a particular writer or performer (e.g., Gary Shandling's *The Larry Sanders Show,* Tom Fontana's *Oz,* David Chase's *The Sopranos,* or Allan Ball's *Six Feet Under*).

11. Matt Groening, "Life in Hell," cartoon, Acme Features Syndicate, October 28, 1994.

12. Quoted in Douglas Rushkoff, *Media Virus! Hidden Agendas in Popular Culture* (New York: Ballantine Books, 1996), 111.

13. Rushkoff, *Media Virus!* 6.

14. Rushkoff, *Media Virus!* 6, 9.

15. Rushkoff, *Media Virus!* 10.

16. Rushkoff, *Media Virus!* 10.

"Use a Pen, Sideshow Bob": The Simpsons and the Threat of High Culture

DAVID L. G. ARNOLD

We can learn a lot about ourselves by watching *The Simpsons* watch television. This television family spends a lot of time consuming television, and their habits reveal a great deal about how our society uses culture. In "Marge on the Lam," for instance, we find them watching a public television fund-drive. A Garrison Keillor look-alike is reading a monologue in the "Prairie Home Companion" vein. The television audience laughs politely at the gentle, homespun humor, but *The Simpsons* are baffled. "What the hell's so funny about that," Homer asks. "Maybe it's the TV," Bart suggests. Homer gets up and whacks the television, scolding it: "Stupid TV! Be more funny!"

Later Homer is horrified when Marge contributes thirty dollars to the public television telethon, but he seems appeased when she says she will receive two tickets to the ballet. "The ballet!" he says, "Woo-hoo!" "You like the ballet?" Marge asks, incredulous. "Marjorie please," Homer retorts, "I enjoy all the meats of our cultural stew. Ah, ballet," he says, and we see that he is imagining a bear in a fez driving a little Shriners car around in circles under a circus big top.

This scene suggests several directions for a discussion of *The Simpsons* and its relationship to the larger culture. It raises questions about per-ceived differences between high and low culture and about how we and the Simpson family respond to both. Homer's conception of ballet is a good index of the family's relationship to culture. He clearly has no idea what ballet is all about, but he knows that it represents high culture and that high culture is somehow a value. Furthermore, his comparison of cultural

1

diversity to a stew, while bathetic, nonetheless reveals an awareness that culture can function on different levels. Their response to the Garrison Keillor sequence is also illuminating as it suggests that the family has no real idea where cultural artifacts come from or how they are produced. Subtle humor like Keillor's has little meaning for them, and it interrupts their access to television and other forms of entertainment they find more meaningful. Nonetheless, despite the profound mystery surrounding its sources, Homer at least imagines an interactive relationship with his culture, one in which he can alter currents of media taste and production by the simple, direct expedient of scolding his television set.

For Homer, though, and for the rest of the family (except perhaps the precocious Lisa), culture functions at a very low level. They have acquired this minimally functional culture, the show suggests, as a result of a slipshod educational system, an all-encompassing environment of consumerism and commodification, careless and misguided parenting, and, of course, television. If this evacuated, smilingly ignorant, and militantly banal sense of culture seems familiar, it is because literary and cultural critics have been warning us about it for generations. In *The Simpsons* we find, digested and realized, the worst fears of mass culture theorists from Matthew Arnold to the Frankfurt School and beyond. In general, these theorists decry the effects of democratization, urbanization, and industrialization on culture, arguing that if common people are allowed to define culture, it becomes common. People with more refined taste and sensibilities, they insist, must assume stewardship of culture before it is lost in the moil of popular music, trashy romance novels, and television sitcoms.

The subject of this essay is the battle of culture(s) enacted in *The Simpsons,* the gap between high and low culture, between the intellectual elite and the "mass," the perceived struggle between self-appointed defenders of culture and the entropic forces of consumerism, degeneration of community, and intellectual sloth. I focus my examination of this struggle on Sideshow Bob, a second-string television clown with an Ivy-League education and a passionate, indeed murderous, desire to elevate culture in Springfield. In the rhetoric of the show he stands in direct opposition to Bart, proud underachiever and product of a mass-culture upbringing, and for the most part Bob's portrayal on the show invites us to label him as simply a bad guy, as Bart's nemesis. But in terms of an examination of cultural conflict and of the role of television in such a conflict, assessing Bob's character becomes more complicated. How does such a figure, a crusader for high-cultural values, function in an animated television sitcom? Of what significance is Bob's choice of television specifically not only as the target of his protests but also their chief vehicle? Is Bob a laughable snob or an emblem of the possibilities of truly oppositional television? Before examining Bob's career and assessing the threat he poses, we need to review, briefly and generally, how cultural theorists of this century and the last have set up the differences between high, low, and mass culture, and what kinds of social and political forces they see underlying the creation of a mass society.

WHAT THE MASS CULTURE THEORISTS WARNED US ABOUT

In *Culture and Anarchy* (first published as a single volume in 1868), Matthew Arnold defines culture as a process of distillation and education. Being cultured, he stipulates, amounts to a "pursuit of our total perfection by means of getting to know, on all the matters that most concern us, the best which has been thought and said in the world."[1] As an investigator of English schools Arnold was professionally concerned with the democratization of education enacted by the Education Act of 1870, which mandated basic education for all citizens. He argues that the "difficulty for democracy is, how to find and keep high ideals," and he voices the need for a cultural hierarchy, implemented by the state, to ensure that English culture will not suffer what he calls "Americanization," the situation that comes from "the multitude being in power, with no adequate ideal to elevate or guide the multitude."[2] Maintaining a focus on "the best which has been thought and said," in other words, requires that the elite assume stewardship of culture.

By the early twentieth century, what Arnold had expressed as a mild concern was becoming (high-) cultural hysteria as literary critics and cultural theorists responded against the perceived deadening of culture brought on by industrialism and growing urbanization. F. R. Leavis, for example, envisions an organic society run by a natural oligarchy as a cure for the cultural desiccation brought on by the shift to an industrial society. While he insists, like Arnold, on the centrality of the concept of democracy in an enlightened society, he decries the attendant decline in educational and cultural standards. He argues that "In any period it is upon a very small minority that the discerning appreciation of art and literature depends: it is (apart from cases of the simple and familiar) only a few who are capable of unprompted, first-hand judgment."[3] Defending the need for a cultural elite to guide society and condemning the suggestion that his argument promotes his own class interests, he argues:

> The word "elitism" is a product of ignorance, prejudice, and unintelligence. It is a stupid word, but not for that the less effective in its progressivist-political use, appealing as it does to jealousy and kindred impulses and motives. It is stupid, and perniciously so, because there must always be elites, and, mobilizing and directing the ignorance, prejudice, and unintelligence, it aims at destroying the only adequate control for "elites" there could be.[4]

His tone notwithstanding, Leavis's argument implies a split from an earlier, Arnoldian conception of culture; Leavis suggests that the appreciation of literature and art itself comprises culture, where before this was merely a step toward a harmonious, "cultured" existence. An advocate, though guardedly, of democratized education, Arnold also suggested that everyone should have access to culture, where Leavis seems to contend that it is the purview only of an elite, discerning minority.

Q. D. Leavis takes this same kind of stand, suggesting that for an intellectual and cultural elite determined to stem the tide of ignorance, "all that can be done . . . must take the form of resistance by an armed and conscious minority." Education, though not the kind Arnold envisioned, is central to Q. D. Leavis's plan of attack, specifically "the training of a picked few who would go into the world equipped for the work of forming and organizing a conscious minority," a cadre of guerrillas, it seems, who would then undertake an ambitious "training of taste."[5] The Leavises, like Arnold, see literature and art not just as expressions of ethical and cultural values but in particular of the universal values for which they and their university-trained colleagues speak. They view academicians and intellectuals as an embattled minority whose responsibility it is to take charge of the cultural well-being of the masses.

The Leavises and theorists like them worked on the premise that with the rise of urban industrialism and mass media, a new, atomized, homogenized social class was taking shape, one less burdened by the necessity of constant work but still bound by taste, education, and predilection to the lower classes. While this new class had only limited access to the resources of "high" culture, neither had they any longer a connection with the organic or "folk" culture associated with older, more cohesive, agrarian societies. Where before a "natural" distinction had existed between high and low or folk culture, now only an amorphous "mass" culture obtained. Arguing that part of the effect of mass culture is the regrettable effacement of the distinction between high and low culture, Dwight Mac-Donald suggests that:

> Like nineteenth-century capitalism, Mass Culture is a dynamic, revolutionary force, breaking down the old barriers of class, tradition, taste, and dissolving all cultural distinctions. It mixes and scrambles everything together, producing what might be called homogenized culture, after another American achievement, the homogenization process that distributes the globules of cream evenly throughout the milk instead of allowing them to float separately on top. It thus destroys all values, since value judgments imply discrimination. Mass culture is very, very democratic: it absolutely refuses to discriminate against, or between, anything or anybody. All is grist to its mill, and all comes out finely ground indeed.[6]

For MacDonald, the democratization of culture is a threat, an indication that contemporary society is in danger of losing sight of its highest cultural traditions (the "cream" floating to the top). More serious than this, perhaps, is the dangerous influence of mass production and mass media on the collective consciousness. Members of the mass society have a certain amount of spending power, a certain amount of leisure time, and a measurable effect on the way society consumes culture. But can they deploy real social power? Does the culture they consume reflect their own, organic sense of values or values manufactured for them by unscrupulous purveyors of leisure? Focusing on the relationship that mass production and mass media imply between its producers and consumers, MacDonald argues:

> Mass Culture is to some extent a continuation of the old Folk Art which until the Industrial Revolution was the culture of the common people, but here, too, the differences are more striking than the similarities. Folk Art grew from below. It was a spontaneous, autochthonous expression

of the people, shaped by themselves, pretty much without the benefit of
High Culture, to suit their own needs. Mass Culture is imposed from
above. It is fabricated by technicians hired by businessmen; its audiences
are passive consumers, their participation limited to the choice between
buying and not buying. The Lords of kitsch, in short, exploit the cultural needs of the masses in order to make a profit and/or to maintain
their class rule. . . . Folk Art was the people's own institution, their private little garden walled off from the formal park of their masters' High
Culture. But Mass Culture breaks down the wall, integrating the masses
into a debased form of High Culture and thus becoming an instrument
of political domination.[7]

Note MacDonald's conception of the "natural" relationship obtaining
between the classes before the onset of industrialism, a relationship that
defined not only appropriate social position but appropriate art and
leisure as well. In this shrill condemnation of mass culture, MacDonald
suggests that capitalism and industrialism are not only to blame for the
degeneration of culture but that this degeneration is a conscious attempt
on the part of the producers of culture or of kitsch to secure a market and,
more significantly, to reinforce class domination.

We hear these same fears echoing in the work of Frankfurt School
social theorists such as Theodor Adorno and Max Horkheimer, who
specifically develop the idea of the masses as victims and suggest, in their
conception of the "Culture Industry," that cultural commodities are
imposed on society by forces of production and that consumers are passive recipients of these cultural suggestions. Adorno says that the imposition of commodified culture

is made possible by contemporary technical capabilities as well as by economic and administrative concentration. The culture industry intentionally integrates its consumers from above. To the detriment of both it forces
together the spheres of high and low art, separated for thousands of years.
The seriousness of high art is destroyed in the speculation about its efficacy; the seriousness of the lower perishes with the civilizational constraints imposed on the rebellious resistance inherent within it as long as
social control was not yet total. Thus, although the culture industry undeniably speculates on the conscious and unconscious state of the millions
towards which it is directed, the masses are not primary but secondary,
they are an object of calculation, an appendage of the machinery.[8]

Here as well we see a "top-down" stratification of culture and consumption, in which commercial hierarchy functionally supplants class hierarchy. In this atmosphere high art is dismissed as inefficient, and low art is prevented from functioning meaningfully in people's lives or from mounting meaningful opposition. The consumer of culture, Adorno suggests, is stripped even of the agency to lower the standards of taste. Through the mechanism of the culture industry, market forces in the form of conscious, profit-motivated decisions of industry and media wholly determine the shape of culture. For this culture to be produced efficiently, it must be standardized. Conformity, the heart of mass-production, becomes the central value, and for this reason opportunities for oppositional expression dry up. Consumers of this culture are "arrested at an infantile stage . . . their primitivism is not that of the undeveloped, but of the forcibly retarded."[9] Adorno calls this kind of cultural consumerism "regressive," because through it consumers lose their ability to make discerning cultural judgments or to think oppositionally. Capitalism finds, in the culture industry, a tool for promoting social stability at the expense of cultural richness.

Of special interest is the focus theorists such as Adorno place on the role of mass media in the formation of mass culture. As Adorno suggests above, we can see mass media not only as products of the culture industry, but as its chief tools, pervasive, powerfully suggestive voices which create and fulfill consumer/cultural needs. In this way, producers can use mass media to create the illusions of freedom and choice while in reality they limit the development of individual cultural expression. In one summary of this idea, Bernard Rosenberg says,

> There can be no doubt that the mass media present a major threat to man's autonomy. To know that they might also contain some small seeds of freedom only makes a bad situation nearly desperate. No art form, no body of knowledge, no system of ethics is strong enough to withstand vulgarization. A kind of cultural alchemy transforms them all into the same soft currency. Never before have the sacred and the profane, the genuine and the specious, the exalted and the debased, been so thoroughly mixed that they are all but indistinguishable. Who can sort one from the other when they are built into a single slushy compost?[10]

Here Rosenberg emphasizes both the power of mass media to influence culture and also the apparently helpless inability of society to resist such incursions. Later he suggests even more explicitly that the goal of mass media is to take over society, arguing, "At its worst, mass culture threatens not only to cretinize our taste, but to brutalize our senses while paving the way to totalitarianism."[11]

Moving the idea of mass society as victim one step further, Raymond Williams claims that the masses are not even necessarily a separate class but an artificial distinction established by the elites to hierarchize society. The masses, he argues, can affect society only through market demands, not through informed participation in governance. Thus, the market can be used as a tool to shape the desires of the masses and ultimately to manipulate them.[12]

Less pessimistic about the potential of mass society than some earlier cultural theorists, Williams focuses on mass society's capacity to define a vigorous sense of culture and to resist the manipulations of the elite. He maps the struggle among different elements of a hierarchized culture by plotting the relationships between an "effective dominative culture" and "residual" and "emergent" cultural elements. While artists typically focus on rifts and changes within mainstream culture, they nonetheless reproduce structures that reinforce the dominative culture, which Williams defines as "the central, effective, and dominant system of meanings and values, which are not merely abstract but which are organized and lived."[13] For Williams, the potential for a truly oppositional art that functions meaningfully in the lives of average people is greatly reduced in a hierarchized cultural market. Effective dominative culture corresponds to "tradition," common wisdom, and high culture, the ideas that define a society and proscribe the behaviors of its members. Williams insists, however, on the potential of the masses to shake off this cultural proscription in a "Long Revolution." This type of change involves "the conviction that men can direct their own lives, by breaking through the pressures and restrictions of older forms of society, and by discovering new common institutions."[14]

Like Williams, Richard Hoggart insists on the potential for a vital mass culture, though he is still suspicious about the influence of mass media. In his landmark book, *The Uses of Literacy*, Hoggart suggests, based on his experience as a former member of the lower middle class, that a simpler life still provides the potential for a sense of community and values that the Leavises eulogize. However, Hoggart is still concerned with the commodification of the cultural object. This commodification can lead, he argues, to a dilution or leveling of culture. While he does not condemn mass culture outright, he sees some danger and says,

> Most mass-entertainments are in the end what D. H. Lawrence described as "anti-life." They are full of a corrupt brightness, of improper appeals and moral evasions. To recall instances: they tend towards a view of the world in which progress is conceived as a seeking of material possessions, equality as a moral leveling, and freedom as the ground for endless irresponsible pleasure.[15]

Here again we see the suggestion that the media and those who control them represent the chief threat to the quality of culture because they encourage materialism, cheap good times, and "moral leveling."

It would be a mistake, though, to equate Hoggart's comments on "mass-entertainments" with those of the other theorists we have heard from. Despite his critical attitude toward the "corrupt brightness" of such cultural products, his formulation of the relationship between mass culture and high culture is a sensitive one. In an appreciative, though not uncritical, reading of Hoggart's book that uses it as a template for contemporary television studies, John Hartley says,

> Hoggart wanted to apply to [the media of popular entertainment] the language of literary appreciation, but was also critical of them for *not* often enough bringing their readers and audiences "the best that has been thought or said," as Matthew Arnold's term was then understood. So to the question "what are the *uses* of literacy?" Hoggart made two answers simultaneously—he was able to show that popular literacy *had* uses, which were as he pointed out rooted in the culture of the people whose lives were under investigation, not under the control of those who taught them the literacy; and at the same time he was able to maintain a critical, independent eye on the media products themselves, to see what their "use" was from that perspective. In the internal tension of his book, the dialogue between the "cultural" use and the "critical" use, both understood to have political consequences, lies the origin of cultural studies.[16]

In addition to clarifying Hoggart's position on the politics of literacy, Hartley makes the important points that cultural studies must adopt a language of "literary appreciation" as a method for examining the artifacts of mass culture and that such an examination should focus on consumers rather than the producers of these artifact. Mass entertainments (such as television) ought to be studied as texts "rooted in the culture of the people whose lives were under investigation." "Cultural studies," Hartley says,

> has begun to forget its commitment to ordinariness as a positive civic goal. Hoggart is one route back to that "usefulness"; TV studies is useful as a systematic inquiry into the personal, ordinary sense-making practices of modern democratizing society. It links textmakers and readers, high and popular culture, in a way that Hoggart himself couldn't have predicted even as he embodied it. . . . He thought, like other professionalized knowledge-class writers, that the way to "bridge" the gap would be to have "laymen" cross over to the "expert" side. In fact the movement has not been all one-way, and the popularization (populism) of the knowledge professions has not been disastrous.[17]

Hartley's own program explores the uses of television and the ways its consumers understand its function in their culture. He concludes that television is a "transmodern teacher," a medium that informs and persuades through many different modes, and that it functions in "the formation of cultural citizenship." "The 'usefulness' of TV studies," he says, "is that by means of its very specific history, television can let us meditate on the processes in the 'expansion of difference' in contemporary culture."[18]

Hartley's book represents a significant advance in the examination of the forces in front of as well as behind television. We should remember, though, that the intellectual chagrin television and mass culture caused (and continue to cause) among the cultural elite is an equally important part of their history. Our study of *The Simpsons* takes this chagrin as its starting point. Though this survey of ideas about mass culture is necessarily brief and incomplete, it demonstrates that over the course of many years cultural theorists and critics experienced a growing sense of panic. The rise of industrialism, the changing shapes of urban societies, improvements in communications and other technologies, and shifting political ideologies all combined to threaten the conception of a stable, organically hierarchized cultural landscape. In many of these sound bites we hear the first strains of a self-conscious elegy for high culture, self-conscious because the singers suspect that no one in their audience knows what an elegy is anymore. We note also in the tone of many of these outcries the unmistakable sounds of intolerance and elitism. The members of mass-cultural society are either to be pitied because they are the passive dupes of political and commercial forces they cannot understand or reviled because their torpor contributes to the deracination of culture. In a society thus cheerfully committed to cultural decline, what place is left for the intellectual? Of what use are taste, refinement, and an expensive education?

"NO ONE WHO SPEAKS GERMAN CAN BE AN EVIL MAN"

With these kinds of questions in mind, we can begin our examination of Sideshow Bob, the role he plays in Springfield society, and the kind of society Springfield represents. As I mentioned above, Bob (whose full name is Robert Onderdonk Terwilliger) is by profession a clown, a secondary figure in the cast of the more famous Krusty the Klown's TV show. Krusty himself is an esteemed figure in the world of Springfield culture, and we will examine his status as an "artist" at some length below. Bob's frustration at playing second fiddle, his sense of himself as an embattled intellectual, is first highlighted in "Krusty Gets Busted." As do many others in *The Simpsons* canon, this episode foregrounds the power of television in shaping a society's attitudes, but here we see an especially clear and articulated distinction between high and low culture, a distinction that mounts into a lethal struggle. In this episode, Sideshow Bob frames Krusty in a holdup of the Kwik-E-Mart so he can take over Krusty's television show.

We should look first at the complex status accorded Krusty's show by Springfield society. Its popularity with children is profound. The show opens each day with a litany of adoration: Krusty asks, "How much do you love me?" and the children in the studio audience reply, en masse, "With all our hearts!"

> KRUSTY: "What would you do if I went off the air?"
> AUDIENCE: "We'd kill ourselves!"

The scene shifts during this second response to Bart and Lisa echoing the chant in their living room, indicating that love of Krusty is spread, via television, throughout Springfield. Bart expresses his devotion plainly: in response to Krusty firing Sideshow Bob out of a cannon, Bart reverently intones, "Comedy, thy name is Krusty." The role played by the show and of television in general in the formation of Bart's intellect becomes clear when he says, "I've based my whole life on Krusty's teachings."

These comments suggest a different status for the "Krusty the Klown Show" than we might have expected for a children's TV program, and snippets from other *Simpsons* episodes bear this out. In "Bart of Darkness," reruns of "classic" Krusty episodes depict a shorthaired, business-suited Krusty interviewing AFL-CIO chairman George Meany on the subject of labor relations. Another "classic" episode features Krusty in love beads and a dashiki hosting Ravi Shankar. Krusty is a versatile and venerable performer, hip to serious intellectual and political matters and to artistic cultural diversity. His role in Springfield society apparently transcends that of a kid's show personality; he is major celebrity, as suggested by the many television extravaganzas he hosts, such as the "Krusty Komedy Klassic" and "A Krusty Kinda Kristmas," and an important figure in Springfield's cultural pantheon ("Simpsoncalifragilisticexpiala[Annoyed Grunt]cious").

The character of Krusty represents an obvious jab at the quality of television in general and at the level of culture found in Springfield: how much can we expect when a television clown represents any kind of artistic pinnacle? In this context, Sideshow Bob's efforts to elevate his society's culture appear even more plainly as the struggle of high against low culture, of refinement besieged by encroaching crudity. Frustrated by his role as a "sideshow," as a stooge in Krusty's cheap gags (gags which include firing Bob out of a cannon), Bob frames Krusty and usurps his role as don of Springfield's cultural life. Interestingly, despite his self-serving motives in deposing Krusty, Bob seems genuinely committed to a program of artistic and intellectual enlightenment. He changes the name of the show to "Sideshow Bob's Cavalcade of Whimsy" and replaces the traditional clown show shenanigans with readings from classic literature, Cole Porter tunes, and segments that examine issues of social and emotional importance to pre-teens.

By all accounts, except perhaps Bart's, Sideshow Bob's elevated approach to entertainment is a success. The kids in the audience cheer just as loudly for Bob, and even Lisa comments that he's "much less condescending" than Krusty. Signing autographs and chatting with producers about marketing rights, Bob comments, "I'm glad we finally dispelled the myth that I'm too 'uptown' for the tots." Bob sees Krusty's brand of culture as "lowbrow" and assumes that children and people in general will respond to more sophisticated fare. Exposure to high culture, he believes, will enhance the lives of his audience. In this he takes a Leavis-like stand: he becomes the embattled intellectual fighting to preserve society's values.

The paradox, of course, is that despite what Matthew Arnold might say about the salubrious effects of "the best that has been thought and said," Bob's own conscience and morality are clearly unaffected by the high culture he represents. In addition to being an armed robber and a snob, he is, as subsequent episodes reveal, a multiple-attempted-murderer, a terrorist, an election fixer, a Republican, and other heinous things. Furthermore, in his attempt to gain control of the media and impose his values upon the masses, he sets himself up as an intolerant and ruthless opponent of their culture. He represents a new iteration of the typical formulation in which a medium such as television is used to manipulate the tastes of the masses. The power relationship between producer and audience implied in Bob's manipulation of the children's market, his knowledge and exploitation of audience demographics, becomes a discourse with which media producers exert power. The difference, of course, has to do with motives. Rather than a least-common-denominator sales pitch, Bob seems to offer something substantial. In his aggressive play to get the word out, though, he exposes a darker side to the proselytizing of culture. He is not merely a snob, but a murderous snob, and he gives high culture a dangerous name.

The grudge against Bart that begins in "Krusty Gets Busted" develops through "Black Widower," in which Bob plots to marry Aunt Selma and murder her as a way of exacting revenge, and beyond. These confrontations point up a deeper, structural conflict between Bart and Bob. We can read Bart as an avatar of the kind of culture available in and defined by Springfield, and Sideshow Bob's persistent attempts to kill him represent an attack on, and a defense against, the gradual evacuation of high-cultural taste and values. We can get a clearer picture of the explicit threat Bob's cultural campaign poses in another episode of *The Simpsons* that focuses specifically on his role as an intellectual in society. "Cape Feare" parodies the Martin Scorsese remake of *Cape Fear* released in 1991, with Sideshow Bob as the parolee who terrorizes the family and ultimately tries to kill Bart. In addition to important developments in Bob's character, "Cape Feare" posits a number of brief and troubling suggestions about the relationships among culture, politics, and the media. The episode opens with Bart and Lisa watching a television talk show called "Up Late with McBain." McBain is the movie hero character played by Ranier Wolfcastle, a parody of Arnold Schwarzenneger. The show is announced by an old man wearing a Nazi uniform whose last name is also Wolfcastle, a not-too-subtle suggestion that there are political skeletons in Ranier's closet. Ranier begins the show by introducing the house musicians and commenting to one, "that's some outfit . . . it makes you look like a homosexual." The audience hoots and boos, and Wolfcastle turns on them: "Maybe you're all homosexuals, too." Bart comments: "This is horrible," and Lisa adds, "The Fox network has sunk to a new low."

Without having introduced the main theme of the episode, these comments focus our attention on the idea of oppositional television and the connection between television and hegemony. The talk show clearly has an ideological agenda to promote, the presence of the Nazi announcer suggesting that its function is to disseminate totalitarian propaganda. The audience's reaction to Wolfcastle's un-PC comments (which allude to Johnny Carson's frequent homophobic baiting of band leader Doc Severinson on the *Tonight Show*) and his hostile rejoinder makes clear that this show is testing some kind of limits. Bart and Lisa's comments also establish the discourse as a critique of television, with Lisa's comment about the Fox network (the network on which *The Simpsons* airs) enhancing the moment's reflexivity. Furthermore, these images provide an appropriately chilling introduction to the reappearance of Sideshow Bob, whose initial grab for power was also an act of television demagoguery.

At this point, Marge walks in and hands Lisa a letter. "It's from my pen-pal, Anya!" Lisa says. As she reads, we hear Anya's voice: "Dear Lisa, as I write this I am very sad. Our president has been overthrown and. . . ." At this point the voice changes abruptly. We hear an adult male with an eastern-European accent pick up where Anya has left off: " . . . replaced by the benevolent General Krull. All hail Krull and his glorious new regime! Sincerely, Little Girl." Lisa is visibly downcast. Bart receives a letter as well, one evidently written in blood, which reads "I'M GOING TO KILL YOU." Bart gasps, and the scene jumps to a hand holding a dagger. Scary music plays, and, pricking an index finger to draw blood, the unseen villain composes a new threatening note, this one reading, "DIE BART, DIE." Then, as the ominous music mounts, the hands put away the note and bring out a "Things to Do" list, also evidently written in blood. First on the list is "Threaten Bart." Next is "Do Laundry." The villain checks off these two items and adds (still using blood), "Get corn holders." The scene lingers here for several beats as the blood from the letters runs down the page.

The juxtaposition of Bart and Lisa's letters and the introduction of the threats on Bart's life set up a context in which we can begin to understand Bart's relationship to Sideshow Bob and Bob's self-appointed role as the scourge of mass culture. Lisa's letter appears to have come out of an area troubled by political instability, one in which a totalitarian military regime has just seized power. This regime's efforts to spread propaganda have gone as far as the censorship, even the (apparently forcible) emendation, of children's letters out of the country. The appearance earlier of the television announcer in the Nazi uniform reinforces the parallel relationship between the media and totalitarian propaganda.

The letter from Lisa's pen pal sets the tone for our reception of Bart's death threat. In this context, Sideshow Bob's plan to murder Bart begins to look like an act of cultural cleansing. Note though, that Bob is not associated with the forces of cultural totalitarianism. Quite the opposite. Bart is, for Bob, the manifestation of all of the evils of mass culture, the victim of the kind of cultural totalitarianism we saw decried by Rosenberg, Williams, and Hoggart. Bob, then, has assumed the Leavis-esque role of a cultural savior, one who would reverse the damage to culture that decades of television have caused. Bart is thus a victim twice, almost. He is quite clearly the victim of television, and only his native wit keeps him from becoming a victim of high culture as well.

In the next several sequences, the tension and Bart's fears for his safety mount, and we finally hear him moan, "You're out there somewhere, but where?" The camera pulls away and pans stylistically across town and through ominous clouds to Springfield State Prison, where we see Bart's nemesis, Sideshow Bob, writing a final greeting which reads "SEE YOU SOON BART." He laughs maniacally, then puts the note aside and begins a more pleasant, more intellectual letter (still written in blood): "Dear 'Life in These United States,' a funny thing happened to me. . . ." At this point he becomes woozy, apparently from loss of blood, and passes out, prompting his cellmate Snake to suggest, "Use a pen, Sideshow Bob."

Here Bob's status as an intellectual is reinforced, if somewhat ironically, by the focus on his act of writing. After composing the threatening note, he begins a contribution to a collective cultural memoir, an act at once personally reflective and culturally conscious. Even though the intellectuality of this act is lampooned a bit by the fact that he's writing to *Reader's Digest,* it demonstrates that Bob is an active participant in his society's culture. Despite the lowbrow audience he targets here, he clearly understands himself to be a cut above the moil. As he is about to go before the Parole Board, Bob says to Snake, "Take care, Snake. May the next time we meet be under more felicitous circumstances." Visibly confused, Snake says, "Gah?" Bob simplifies: "Take care." Snake understands now and replies warmly, "Bah." This exchange is a brief example of Bob's interaction with Springfield society at large. He thinks and communicates over the heads of average people (or at least of average convicted criminals), and must here, as elsewhere, dumb down his discourse to engage with them. For the Parole Board, on the other hand, his intelligence is clearly a plus. Asked about the tattoo on his chest that reads, "DIE BART, DIE," he quickly explains that it's German for, "The Bart, The." The Parole Board members are visibly impressed, and one comments, "No one who speaks German can be an evil man." For people with college degrees and foreign language credits, this may seem like acceptable reasoning, but we must recall also that this episode opens with a Nazi media-propagandist.

Once out of prison, Bob begins stalking the Simpson family. Terrorized, they enter the Witness Protection Program and are relocated to Terror Lake, but Bob follows, intent on killing Bart. As Bob finally closes in on Bart, his status as a cultural maven is brought to the fore. He asks, "Any last requests?" Bart stalls for time, luring Bob in by complimenting him on his beautiful singing voice, and requests that he sing the entire score from *H.M.S. Pinafore*. Bob is too vain, and too cultured, to refuse, and by this ruse Bart again saves himself and sends Bob back to prison.

This episode tells us a number of important things about Bob and his relationship to Springfield society. His hatred of Bart stems not only from his desire for revenge, but from his disgust at the debasement of cultural values the Simpsons represent. Bob perceives himself as an intellectual, and his conception of the role of intellectuals in society recalls Q. D. Leavis's call for "resistance by an armed and conscious minority" against the incursions of mass culture. This episode's portrayal of television both as oppositional voice and hegemonic propaganda also reminds us that Bob's actions represent broadly influential cultural forces and a large-scale struggle for control over the attention of the masses.

Bob's motives and his relationship to Springfield culture assume a more straightforwardly political aspect in "Sideshow Bob Roberts." In this episode, Bob uses his media savvy and showmanship in the service of the Republican party. At the instigation of Rush Limbaugh-look-alike Birch Barlow, Bob is released from jail and set up as a candidate for mayor. Overall this episode is an excoriation of society's lazy, uninformed attitude about the electoral process, as evidenced by Homer's admission that he finds people who vote "kind of fruity." Beyond this, though, we find a comment on the role in society of a cadre of elites (the Republican party) who see themselves as naturally suited to lead. Initially, it seems as if they may be correct in this assumption. Bob wins by a landslide over Mayor Quimby, only to be accused later of election fraud. In court he rants to the townspeople, "Your guilty consciences force you to vote Democratic, but secretly you want someone who'll cut taxes, brutalize criminals, and rule you like a king! You *need* me, Springfield!" This comment provides an important clue to Bob's character and his motives. He considers himself a member of the social elite, and neither he nor his cohorts are shy about using criminal means to acquire and exercise power. Clearly more intelligent than average people such as Homer, Bob assumes not only that it is his right and responsibility to lead but also that the masses actually want his kind of leadership. His criminal past certainly proves no obstacle. As Lisa says after Bob's election, "It's not that I have trouble believing a convicted felon got so many votes, but that another convicted felon [Mayor Quimby] got so few."

Interestingly, most of the energy in this episode goes to condemning lazy voters and the ignorance of the masses. Both liberal and conservative viewpoints take some hits, especially conservatives, who are characterized as thugs and vampires. At one point, Bob and a couple of henchman kidnap Bart, and Bob warns him, "No child has ever meddled with the Republican party and lived." As the episode closes, though, we are reminded that at the heart of Springfield's relationship with Bob lies a fundamental mistrust of social elites. Foiled again by his own arrogance, Bob is returned to prison, this time a minimum-security establishment (more in keeping, we suppose, with his new status as a political powerhouse), where he is identified specifically as a "Yalie" and asked to join the crew team to compete against the "Princeton alums." The crew chief's upper-class, east coast drawl and the prisoners' participation in uppercrusty sports such as crewing solidify a connection between social standing and criminal tendencies.

THE CHATTERING CYCLOPS

"Krusty Gets Busted," "Cape Feare," and "Sideshow Bob Roberts" all suggest that the push to elevate culture and to redefine society to reflect "natural" social and cultural hierarchies is inherently dangerous. For Springfielders, at

least, these impulses pose a significant threat. If we see Bart as a representative of mass cultural interests, this threat is specific and lethal:
Sideshow Bob wants to kill Bart. This may be because Bart can consistently
thwart him, or simply because Bart represents all that he sees as wrong
with society. Like Homer, Bart watches too much television, scoffs at learning, and represents the intellectual lowest common denominator. While
Homer is both intellectually and physically slothful, however, Bart is ener-
getic, and, in a youthful, skateboarding, cherry-bomb-flushing, under-
achieving kind of way, pursues a vigorous course of cultural leveling. Bob
sees in Bart, we imagine, the threat of creeping mass culture hegemony, a
kind of cartoon Snopesism that threatens his more refined vision of the
world.

While in his earlier crime sprees Bob directs his energies for the most
part against Bart, his apt avatar of low culture, he increases the scope of
his cultural critique in "Sideshow Bob's Last Gleaming." We are always
aware in *The Simpsons* of an underlying critique of television culture, and
here we see it merge with Bob's own, more aggressive social agenda. Once
again in jail and irritated at the way his fellow prisoners fritter away their
time watching television, Bob lashes out specifically at the medium, which
he describes as an "omni-directional sludge pump" and a "chattering
Cyclops." No longer content to elevate the quality of Springfield's culture
by simply co-opting television, as he does in "Krusty Gets Busted," or by
doing away with Bart, he does away with television altogether and brings
society to its knees.

Besides highlighting Bob's nefariousness and his disdain for low culture, this episode reminds us of the centrality of television in Springfield
society and as a motif in *The Simpsons* in general. After Bob broadcasts his
threat to blow up Springfield with a purloined nuclear bomb if television
is not eliminated, Mayor Quimby holds an emergency meeting in an
underground bunker, to which he invites "the esteemed representatives
of television," who include Krusty the Klown, Kent Brockman, Dr. Who,
and others. When the mayor suggests that they must accede to Bob's
demands, an alarmed Krusty asks, "Would it really be worth living in a
world without television? I think the survivors would envy the dead!"
The mayor overrides this objection and maintains, "TV must go," concluding in a tense whisper, "May God have mercy on our souls."

Panic ensues as the community moves to comply with the anti-television edict. Among those most deeply affected are television professionals

themselves, including Kent Brockman, who in a soulful on-the-air good-bye intones, "As my final broadcast draws to a close I'm reminded of a few of the events that brought me closer to you: the collapse of the Soviet Union; premium ice cream price wars; dogs who were mistakenly issued major credit cards, and others who weren't so lucky." Krusty is so desperate to remain on the air that he breaks into an Emergency Broadcast System shack where he vows to continue producing (unscripted, unrehearsed) television twelve hours a day. Both of these sequences suggest not only the self-importance of television personalities, but also the disturbing proximity of television to monumental social upheavals. Brockman's bathetic juxtaposition of the end of the Cold War and ice cream prices suggests that television can homogenize experience, rendering widely disparate events with more or less the same intensity and sense of importance. Further, even as it levels, television sensationalizes, transforming the serious and the trivial alike into tabloid pabulum. Krusty's gesture is perhaps more chilling. The Emergency Broadcast System is a holdover from an era when the threat of nuclear attack was (we were told) a real daily concern, and when the only warning we might expect of global annihilation would come from the faithful, vigilant television. By invoking the EBS, Krusty not only elevates losing television to the level of global thermonuclear war, but reminds us of the sad, earnest way Americans were brought together by that threat, and by the familiar, piercing signal tone that carried it into our homes.

Krusty's co-optation of this culturally significant medium is appropriate here because Bob is threatening nuclear devastation. It is also important to remember that as we watch Bob's status as a threat to society escalate, we grow more and more aware of how intimately Springfield's culture (Bob's target, it seems, as well as his intended beneficiary) is wrapped up with television. Bob indicates an awareness of this relationship at the beginning of the episode when he admits that his "foolish capering [on the Krusty the Klown Show] destroyed more young minds than syphilis and pinball combined." More interesting, his broadcast threats remind us of his own and the show's meta-televisual acuity when he comments, "By the way, I'm aware of the irony of appearing on television in order to decry it, so don't bother pointing that out." With this comment he situates us in a debate about the possibilities of a critiquing a medium from within that same medium, and invites us to evaluate him as a figure in that debate.

CONCLUSIONS: SIDESHOW BOB
AS MEDIA VIRUS?

What do Bob's efforts, and his failures, to keep Springfielders from watch-ing too much television and to enhance their appreciation of the finer things, tell us about Springfield and about the show's comment on high and low culture? The most overt message is that this society mistrusts high culture, regarding it at best as a laughable eccentricity, at worst as a dan-gerous threat.

In one sense we must read "Sideshow Bob's Last Gleaming" and the show's running commentary on television as a straightforward condem-nation of the medium and its effects on mass culture: intellectual, social, and family values suffer when television replaces quality parenting and when it supersedes reasoned public debate. Its influence on society is so pervasive, so fundamental, that it is often represented as a kind of heavy industry: in one instance, we see a factory, complete with belching smoke-stacks, as the site of television production; in another we see cartoons being produced by row upon row of hunched workers in a sweatshop. In these images, we see the collusion of industry and culture identified by members of the Frankfurt School. Herbert Marcuse, for instance, makes the comment that the industrial "apparatus" (the complex of technologies employed in producing consumer goods) and its needs come to define the society it was intended to serve. A person in such a society "learns to transfer all subjective spontaneity to the machinery" he serves, to subor-dinate his life to the "matter-of-factness" of a world in which "the machine is the factor and he is the factum."[19]

We see this reversal of priorities in *The Simpsons,* an inversion of per-spective in which the narratives and structures we create to entertain our-selves become, through our intellectual, emotional, and monetary investments in them, more significant than the reality we created them to reflect. Commenting on the state of humanity in such a society, Marcuse says: "The free economic subject . . . has developed into the object of large-scale organization and coordination, and individual achievement has been transformed into standardized efficiency."[20] In a situation such as this, Marcuse suggests, an important distinction arises between the masses and a community. In a society dominated by the logic of industry, "Rational-ity is . . . transformed from a critical force to one of adjustment and com-pliance. Autonomy of reason loses its meaning in the same measure as the thoughts, feelings and actions of men are shaped by the technical requirements of the apparatus which they themselves have created."[21] Marcuse's critique reminds us, among other things, of Homer's relationship with television: he willingly allows it, or those who control it, to set the parameters of his life, and his limited opportunities to enjoy power come only at television's convenience. Marcuse reflects this kind of situation when he notes, "Modern mass society quantifies the qualitative features of individual labor and standardizes the individualistic elements in the activities of intellectual culture."[22] Rather than a vehicle for culture, television in Springfield, like Marcuse's industrial apparatus, has become the central defining element of culture.

This said, it becomes possible to speculate that the real threat faced by the masses of Springfield comes not specifically from members of the cultural or social elite, but from those who control, as it were, the means of production, the forces behind the creation of television. Paradoxically, what makes Bob such an attractive candidate for mayor, for instance, is his experience with television and his ability to fit his discourse to the medium and its audience. Furthermore, his short-lived success as star of his own show rests in part on his ability to collect and exploit audience demographics. In a fascinating study of responses to the television drama *Dallas*, Ien Ang makes a similar observation about the media's acquisition of knowledge about and power over audiences, the better to exploit the immense economic potential of television's centrality. Ang says,

> What is at stake here is a politics of knowledge. In the way television institutions know the audience, epistemological issues are instrumental to political ones: empirical information about the audience such as delivered by audience measurement could become so important only because it produces a kind of truth that is more suitable to meet a basic need of the institutions: the need to control.[23]

Audiences in this way become part of a discourse of power, power derived in a specifically information-oriented, consumerist society. On the receiving end, television is a dispenser of culture, a staggeringly effective educator and inculcator. On the producing end, it is a conduit to an enormous array of different markets, a means both of creating and exploiting markets for consumer products among mass society. Springfield is a society enslaved by these processes, and whatever his more highfalutin' motives,

Sideshow Bob represents forces in society that seek to profit by manipulating the tastes and values of the masses.

It is important to remember, however, that for all of its obvious power, television is a two-edged sword, with perhaps as much potential to empower Springfielders as to subjugate them. In the conclusion of "Homer Badman," access to the airwaves, no matter how primitive or mediated, enables Homer to clear his name. A thoughtless devotion to television defines most aspects of Springfielders' lives, but despite this they are able occasionally to wield social power, particularly when they can co-opt the power of television and begin to create culture themselves.

We see this suggested frequently. For instance, in "The Front," Bart and Lisa decide, after watching "a rather lifeless" episode of "Itchy & Scratchy," that they could write better cartoons themselves. Although they have to use Grandpa as a "front" because the producer of "Itchy & Scratchy" will not take the work of children seriously, their cartoons are acute and popular enough to win awards. In Bart and Lisa's success at infiltrating the world of mass media production, we can glimpse possibilities of cultural participation beyond a slavish devotion to television and the manipulations by the social elite who control it. Here Bart and Lisa display what television critic David Bianculli calls "teleliteracy," an awareness of and facility with powerful cultural codes disseminated through television.[24] What Bart and Lisa accomplish in "The Front" is a full-scale co-optation of the mechanisms of television. Their competition at Itchy & Scratchy Studios consists of a gaggle of Ivy League graduates, none of whom can see real life clearly enough to write a compelling (cartoon) narrative reflecting it. This episode reminds us that even when it is not posing a deadly threat, high culture and its stewards are fundamentally disconnected from mass society. Bart and Lisa are storming the citadel: they are challenging high-cultural hegemony, the control of important cultural media by a narrowly self-interested elite. They are co-opting the means of cultural production and creating their own vital cultural artifacts. By naturalizing some of the methods of high culture, they neutralize its threat, turning its tactics to their own cultural purposes.

This episode suggests that television viewers may not be the passive dupes that mass cultural theorists have labeled them, and that the medium itself, if properly understood and exploited, can deliver appreciable social power into the hands even of "Joe Six-Pack." According to Douglas Rushkoff, a steady diet of television has turned us all into budding "media theorists" who have the capacity to critique and to shape the media that define us: "Having been raised on a diet of media manipulation," he contends, "we are all becoming aware of the ingredients that go into these machinations."[25] For Rushkoff, this kind of media knowledge can lead eventually to revolutionary social power when young people who have grown up on television disseminate heterodox ideas through what he calls "media viruses." The children of the 50s and 60s are now in a position to control television's "techniques of thought control, pattern recognition, and neurolinguistic programming . . . to create television that changes the way we view reality and thus reality itself."[26] Although this sounds like just the kind of sinister threat to an unsuspecting public that mass culture theorists foretold, Rushkoff is optimistic, suggesting that

> This is not so much a conspiracy against the viewing public as it is a method for getting the mainstream media to unwittingly promote countercultural agendas that can actually empower the individuals who are exposed to them. The people who run network television or popular magazines, for example, are understandably unwilling to run stories or images that directly criticize the operating principles of the society that its sponsors are seeking to maintain. Clever young media strategists with new, usually threatening ideas need to invent new nonthreatening forms that are capable of safely housing these dangerous concepts until they have been successfully delivered to the American public as part of our daily diet of mainstream media.[27]

In "The Front," Bart and Lisa employ exactly this strategy, though less with the aim of promoting cultural change. Their goal is for television to reflect their values as regards the constitution of quality entertainment, but the sophistication they display and the power they derive from this display are significant, suggesting the possibility, whether subversive or not, of meaningful interaction between the producers and consumers of mass culture and of the potential for television itself to comment on its own function in society. This possibility should also seem familiar to us because it is, essentially, the same strategy for promoting cultural change we see employed by Sideshow Bob. Like Bart and Lisa, Bob tries to change how television is used by mass society. The difference, of course, is that where Bart and Lisa are motivated by their love of and dependence on television, Bob is motivated by intolerance, and his methods are mostly violent. He is blinkered and ultimately foiled by his social and cultural arrogance, his insistence that his taste represents a valuable standard, his need to identify himself as elite.

Whatever our opinions of Cole Porter, Dumas, or Gilbert and Sullivan, it is clear that Sideshow Bob is a crank. By using him as such, the writers of *The Simpsons* seem cheerfully to disdain the puffery and snobbishness of high culture, but we must remember that the show has other dimensions besides a celebration of "lowest common denominator" society. It also excoriates lowbrow thoughtlessness and the dominance of television. We see in Homer and in Bart the depths to which democracy and the deterioration of high cultural values will allow us to fall if we let them. Homer and Bart, however, are not the only Simpsons. Lisa, we must also recall, is a reliable index of cultural values and functions as a kind of still center of truth in the family. She is mostly misunderstood or ignored, but usually right, and good for a sensitive evaluation of the situation. She is also educated (well beyond what either we or her school system expect for a second grader) and has access to high-cultural artifacts like literature and jazz. She too, though, is a richer signifier than this description might suggest, and her reactions are not always predictable. She is a young child, and her behavior is often childish. This is clear especially when we see her laughing alongside Bart at "Itchy & Scratchy" cartoons. How do these get by her sensors, we wonder? How can she not recognize them for the signature examples of mass-culture manipulation they are? Her reactions complicate her status as a cultural index and complicate the show's comment on high and low culture in our society. And what are we to make of Marge's painting of Mr. Burns, or the idea that Bart, as he grows insane in "Bart of Darkness," begins to write a play? Or Homer's appreciation of ballet? Are these examples of high culture consumption by the Simpsons an indication of the availability of culture to common people, or of the lowering of the standards of high art to a mass culture lowest common denominator?

How we answer this question determines how we receive the show, and, to an extent, our behaviors as members of its audience. After noting with amusement the suggestion that high culture, as Sideshow Bob manifests it, is some kind of threat, we begin to suspect that something more is going on, that this easy joke is perhaps too easy. Lurking behind the joke is the suspicion that the show still depends for its impact on access to high culture. In "Oh! Streetcar," for instance, we appreciate the send up given to both the Williams play and its bathetic juxtaposition to Broadway musicals, but we realize guiltily that were we never to have seen, read, or at least heard of the play, the jokes would not work on as many levels. We need access to high culture ourselves to appreciate the fun the show makes of high culture and its devotees.

Part of the show's strategy, part of its complexity as satire, is that it sells itself to smart viewers, viewers, perhaps, who read Tennessee Williams, know enough about art to recognize the Venus de Milo, and perhaps occasionally think probingly about their relationship to their culture. Self-satisfaction that we get the jokes is certainly one of our responses to *The Simpsons,* one invited not only by the show's submerged sophistication but also by its overt nose-thumbing at television viewers (such as Homer) who are not as smart as we are. What about other kinds of viewers, however, viewers such as those the show depicts, who are more thoughtless and less interested in analyzing the show as a cultural artifact? Thornton Caldwell suggests that,

> Smart iconic references, visual embellishments, tableaus, and historical masquerades, not just dialogue, make up [an] intellectual surplus. . . . Because [such shows do] not even underline or draw attention to the flood of these references, many of them become little more than fleeting asides even to viewers who might actually know or care about their significance. By rewarding this degree of recognition and discrimination, hip and prestige primetime shows . . . also help justify the yuppie-requisite college educations that have helped produce [their] quality demographics. Such audiences feel good, that is, because they "get" the string of smart and stylistic references.[28]

Caldwell's comment suggests that the kinds of people likely not only to watch *The Simpsons* but to read (and write) critical articles about it in a collection such as this are also complicit in the kind of cultural and intellectual elitism the show depicts as dangerous.

Perhaps this is the show's ultimate rhetorical trick: anyone who spends time thinking about it will discover himself or herself a target of its satire. It is at once a lampoon of media addiction and media literacy, a call for more and also more sensitive media consumption. In Rushkoff's terms, it is clearly a "media virus," a "countercultural missile" launched from within a media stronghold at a largely complacent consuming public, but the way this message gets used may differ ultimately from Rushkoff's construction.

Who, we must ask, is responsible for this message? In general, the Fox network, on which *The Simpsons* airs, seems eager to create for itself the aura of the maverick, the upstart. By working a younger, hipper, twenty-something demographic with self-conscious, post-MTV stylizations and a rebellious attitude, Fox seems almost like a media virus all by itself. We must recall, though, that whatever the network's persona, it is still an economic entity of considerable size and sophistication. As the product of this kind of corporate entity, *The Simpsons* is part of a mainstream, high-end commercial process. However rebellious its attitude, conservative, profit-centered ideologies and agendas underlie the creation of any prime-time television cartoon. As a cartoon, it is admittedly a product we may be tempted to receive as inherently frivolous or childish. On the other hand, we probably suspect that it bears some kind of complicated or subversive message. Do we receive it as kitsch, which is implicitly hegemonic, or is it more of an avant-garde statement, an implicit critique? Do we imagine that the show's intention is to help foster a revolution?

Sideshow Bob's career raises just this question, but with a different spin, probably, than Rushkoff imagines. Bob and the social position he represents pose a serious threat to Springfield because he feels that he knows what is best for the masses, and he is ruthless and violent in imposing that judgment. Structurally, Bob stands opposed to Bart, the symbol, the poster child, for the generation brought up by the generation brought up on television. Bart is everything the mass culture theorists warned us about: insouciant cultural dissipation. In these terms, Bart presents little to admire, but when we set him next to Bob, whose hatred of Bart is one of the show's master narratives, a structural opposition develops that insists, at the bottom, that whatever Bart represents, it is a better option than bitter, frustrated, violent cultural intolerance. The Simpson family, representatives of the kind of mass-cultural evacuation Bob targets, seem immune to his attacks, well intended or not. Some inherent strength protects them from high culture, and this perdurability must be counted as the show's basic statement. *The Simpsons* co-opts and naturalizes Bob as an internal anti-television, anti-low-culture comment whose impact is undercut by his repeated failure, and also by the fact that he is a criminal and a laughable snob. His irrational hatred of Bart, however, suggests that the central structure of the show is more than a contest of the highbrow against the low. Rather, this narrative describes the forces at work within a single medium, the pull both of the conservative and the revolutionary. Bob's disruptions are the show's and the medium's recollections of their own histories. On *The Simpsons,* television is both excoriated as a subversive, culturally corrosive force and praised as a teacher, a democratizer. So various are the complaints leveled against television that its status as a cultural force can never be stable, and what *The Simpsons* provides, in its polymorphous depictions of these conflicts, is more than anything a way of reading, a way of negotiating television as text and of finding our own uses for it.

NOTES

1. Matthew Arnold, *Culture and Anarchy* (Cambridge: Cambridge University Press, 1932), 6.

2. Matthew Arnold, "Democracy." Introduction to "The Popular Education of France" in *The Complete Prose Works of Matthew Arnold,* R. H. Super, ed. 12 volumes, Vol. 2 (Ann Arbor: University of Michigan Press, 1962), 17, 18.

3. F. R. Leavis, *Education and the University* (London: Chatto and Windus, 1961), 143.

4. F. R. Leavis, *Nor Shall My Sword* (London: Chatto and Windus, 1972), 169.

5. Q. D. Leavis, *Fiction and the Reading Public* (London: Chatto and Windus, 1932), 270–271.

6. Dwight MacDonald, "A Theory of Mass Culture," in *Mass Culture: The Popular Arts in America,* ed. Bernard Rosenberg and David Manning White (Glencoe: The Free Press, 1957), 62.

7. MacDonald, "A Theory of Mass Culture," 60.

8. Theodor Adorno, *The Culture Industry* (London: Routledge, 1991), 85.

9. Adorno, *The Culture Industry,* 41.

10. Bernard Rosenberg and David Manning White, eds. *Mass Culture: The Popular Arts in America* (Glencoe: The Free Press, 1957), 5.

11. Rosenberg and White, *Mass Culture,* 9.

12. Raymond Williams, ed. *May Day Manifesto, 1968* (Harmondsworth: Penguin, 1968), 289, 301.

13. Raymond Williams, "Base and Superstructure in Marxist Cultural Theory." *New Left Review* 82 (1973): 9.

14. Raymond Williams, *The Long Revolution* (Harmondsworth: Penguin, 1971), 375.

15. Richard Hoggart, *The Uses of Literacy* (London: Chatto and Windus, 1957), 339.

16. John Hartley, *The Uses of Television* (London: Routledge, 1999), 25–26.

17. Hartley, *The Uses of Television*, 16.

18. Hartley, *The Uses of Television*, 26, 16.

19. Herbert Marcuse, "Some Social Implications of Technology," in *The Essential Frankfurt School Reader*, ed. Andrew Arato and Eike Gebhardt (New York: Continuum, 1988), 141–42.

20. Marcuse, "Some Social Implications of Technology," 142.

21. Marcuse, "Some Social Implications of Technology," 146.

22. Marcuse, "Some Social Implications of Technology," 159.

23. Ien Ang, *Desperately Seeking the Audience* (London: Routledge, 1991), 10.

24. David Bianculli, *Teleliteracy: Taking Television Seriously* (New York: Continuum, 1992), 6.

25. Douglas Rushkoff, *Media Virus! Hidden Agendas in Popular Culture* (New York: Ballantine, 1994), 5–6.

26. Rushkoff, *Media Virus!* 6–7.

27. Rushkoff, *Media Virus!* 7.

28. Thornton Caldwell, *Televisuality* (London: Routledge, 1993), 253.

Commodity Culture and Its Discontents: Mr. Bennett, Bart Simpson, and the Rhetoric of Modernism

KURT M. KOENIGSBERGER

I n the opening moments of the episode of *The Simpsons* titled "The Springfield Connection," Marge and Homer Simpson attend an outdoor performance of the Springfield Pops.[1] As the orchestra plays the theme to *Star Wars,* Marge turns to Homer and asks, "Aren't you glad we got out of the house and came downtown for a little culture?" Disgusted because he hears a bassoon come in late, Homer replies, "They're butchering the classics!" When Marge prompts him again—"Aw, come on, Homer, there's lasers. You like lasers"—the outraged Homer erupts: "Laser effects, mirrored balls—John Williams must be rolling around in his grave!" The joke in this opening scene involves a confusion of high and popular artistic production: Marge treats the Springfield Pops as "culture" and expects that the usually boorish Homer will need to be drawn in by a spectacle. Homer, however, takes *Star Wars* even more seriously than Marge does, since to him it appears to be not just "a little culture" but a "classic"— and a "classic," he implies, must have a dead composer and be treated as a highbrow cultural artifact, not be enhanced by such lowbrow theatrical effects as glitter-balls and light-shows. Homer does not seem to entertain the possibility that the composer of *Star Wars* might be alive or that the music was originally designed to accompany the flash of laser light during the disco era.

In separating *Star Wars* from its popular cinematic context by elevating the theme music into the realm of "the classics," Homer deploys a strategy characteristic of literary modernism. Throughout the first half of the twentieth century, this dominant literary mode distinguished itself through a repudiation of popular culture and of the masses, fostering what John Carey calls an "abyss" and Andreas Huyssen terms a "great divide" that separated elite culture from popular culture.[2] In our own era, Fredric Jameson asserts, this distinction between the high and low has collapsed under the weight of the "democracy of the visual and the aural," as contemporary aesthetic production has come to rely more heavily upon media other than print and upon generic forms besides the poem and the novel.[3] Postmodern texts, by contrast with their modernist predecessors, court popular audiences with the rich mélange of artistic styles they promote. As the Springfield Orchestra makes the gradual transition from *Star Wars* to "Twinkle, Twinkle, Little Star," modulating from a film score to a nursery song about stars, Dr. Julius Hibbert—*The Simpsons*'s postmodern counterpart to Homer the modernist—takes a sophisticated pleasure in the incongruity. "Deviliciously satirical!" he exclaims, "I wonder if anyone else got that?" Indeed, Homer notices the incongruity (without grasping the aural pun on stars), but experiences it as an affront to a classic, a nursery song undermining the supposed eminence of *Star Wars*. "We're out of here," Homer declares in exasperation, dragging Marge from the amphitheater. While both Dr. Hibbert and Homer Simpson see the collapse of *Star Wars* into a nursery song as somehow "satirical," for Dr. Hibbert, the satire itself becomes "a little culture" and constitutes the pleasure of the performance, while for Homer the satire suggests "they're butchering the classics" and provokes his disgust and outrage.

As a set piece, Homer's experience of the Springfield Pops seems funny precisely because his reaction runs counter to the one *The Simpsons* normally seeks from its own viewers. *The Simpsons* deliberately collapses the distance between high and low culture and attempts to solicit from its audience not Homer's disgust but rather the response of Dr. Hibbert: "Deviliciously satirical! I wonder if anyone else got that?" The *modus operandi* of *The Simpsons* replicates that of the Springfield Pops, conflating the high and the low in episodes that feature cultural references ranging from the lowbrow adolescent fictions of Judy Blume to the highbrow poetry of Pablo Neruda ("Bart Sells His Soul"). Such breadth of literary allusion often originates with the figure of Bart Simpson: he begins a prayer by parodying Blume's *Are You There God? It's Me, Margaret,* and when his sister Lisa invokes a Neruda dictum on laughter's relation to the soul, Bart responds dismissively, "I am *familiar* with the works of Neruda." While Bart may be familiar with the canon of Chilean poetry, the joke takes its force in part from the probability that *The Simpsons*'s viewers are not. Bart's deflation of Lisa's pretensions to a kind of arcane knowledge about modern literature nevertheless does not retract or undermine her allusion itself, and it is typical of *The Simpsons* to aim for a broad inclusiveness of cultural reference, even as the show ironizes the materials it incorporates, in much the same way as the set-piece at the Springfield Pops does. Such inclusiveness extends to the show's subject-matter as well: from episode to episode, *The Simpsons* seeks out new perspectives on the totality of contemporary social relations, pressing such perspectives into the elastic boundaries of the city of Springfield.

In rejecting the exclusivity typical of difficult modernist forms while indulging inclusive and totalizing aspirations, *The Simpsons* returns to something like the critical orientation of the pre-modernist British author Arnold Bennett (1867–1931) toward his audience and society. Bennett, who produced some thirty-five novels, seven collections of stories, numerous volumes of journalism and reviews, nineteen plays, a series of "how-to" and "self-help" guides, and even an opera libretto and motion-picture screenplay, resolutely refused to indulge in what might be perceived as pedantry, insisting upon the accessibility of his work as he sought to craft a critical mirror in which London high society and the provincial English middle classes alike could see themselves. The accolades sought by Bennett for promoting what he called "the democratisation of art" and for helping "the crowd . . . really to see the spectacle of the world" disappointingly evaporated, however, as what Huyssen calls "the great divide" between high art and mass culture widened in the modernist era.[4] Yet in moments such as Dr. Hibbert's implicit rejection of Homer's reverence for the Springfield Pops, John Williams, and *Star Wars* in favor of the pleasure of the "deviliciously satirical," *The Simpsons* orients itself toward the culture of the early twenty-first century in a way that closely resembles Bennett's relation to society of the early twentieth century, though as a cluster of serial productions rather than in the monumental form of the novel.

The Simpsons recuperates Bennett's position on the function of art, but with an important difference, one that results from the commodity's saturation of the entire cultural field. In fostering what Jameson calls "the democracy of the visual," *The Simpsons* exploits certain stylistic strategies alien to Bennett, strategies distilled from reified modernisms and deployed by contemporary advertising and corporate cultures. Both Bennett and Matt Groening, creator of *The Simpsons,* engage in a kind of cultural critique through their strategies of inclusivity and ironic totalization. This essay, however, concerns itself with whether a space exists after modernism in which such critique can oppose the inequities of late capitalism. The attempts of Bennett's fiction and of *The Simpsons* to engage in oppositional critique are always circumscribed by the very structures they seek to criticize, because commodity culture, across the twentieth and twenty-first centuries, represents the constraining condition of possibility for both forms of art. While a sustainable posture of oppositionality itself becomes impossible as the languages of modernism are assimilated in late capitalism, by way of compensation *The Simpsons* offers dramatizations of local, tactical possibilities of resistance.

In prosecuting this argument, I first consider the places of Bennett and *The Simpsons* in the history of twentieth-century aesthetic production, paying particular attention to Bennett's theoretical statements and to the media through which *The Simpsons* continually disseminates and constitutes itself. Such considerations lead me to Bennett's early novel, *Anna of the Five Towns,* and to the *Simpsons* episode, "Bart Sells His Soul," which reveal the way in which material and commercial realities mediate individual experience. This third section of the essay concentrates on the attitudes of the texts toward popular culture and on their engagements with the notion of social totality, a keyword for Western Marxist aesthetics in setting out a program for cultural critique. In the closing section, I read *Anna of the Five Towns* and "Bart Sells His Soul" as allegories that dramatize the dilemma faced both by Arnold Bennett's aesthetics and by *The Simpsons*'s social satire. These readings suggest that the potential for oppositionality both in the pre-high modernist fiction of Bennett and in the postmodernist *Simpsons* is partially constrained by an inclusivity designed to solve the problem of the "great divide" between high and low texts, on the one hand, and to represent a whole way of life, on the other.

MR. BENNETT AND THE PROBLEM OF THE GREAT DIVIDE

It might seem eccentric to pair a relatively neglected British novelist from the beginning of the last century with a postmodern, mass-medium production such as *The Simpsons*. After all, if one were to identify a single British author whose influence bears upon *The Simpsons*, surely that writer would be Charles Dickens. Dickens appears in "Mother Simpson" as a highbrow figure juxtaposed to popular television culture when Lisa Simpson describes the mystery of Homer's parentage as "so weird . . . like something out of Dickens or *Melrose Place*." The episode titled "Burns's Heir," a kind of *Great Expectations* parody in which Mr. Burns stands in for Miss Havisham while Bart simultaneously plays the parts of Pip and Estella, invokes "A Christmas Carol" when a boy with a mock-Cockney accent informs Mr. Burns, "Why, today is Christmas Day, sir." In "Cape Feare," Bart hopes to take on a new identity as Gus the Lovable Chimney Sweep, "best in all Westminster," and in "Whacking Day," Bart imagines that "I'll make my way as a bootblack. Shine yer shoes, guv'nor?" thus provoking Homer's censure: "No son of mine is going to be a nineteenth-century Cockney bootblack."

The fact that *The Simpsons* so frequently invokes Dickens and the Victorian London he made his own attests to Dickens's survival in the contemporary world, beyond the vicissitudes of twentieth-century critical fashion.[5] By contrast, Arnold Bennett figures in this essay not because he participates directly in *The Simpsons*, appearing alongside Magilla Gorilla, Paul McCartney, and Thomas Jefferson as half-digested fodder for satire and intertextual play—he doesn't—but rather because *The Simpsons* orients itself toward the culture of the late twentieth and early twenty-first centuries in a way that closely resembles Bennett's relation to society of the late nineteenth and early twentieth centuries. Bennett is significant to this essay precisely because he has been forgotten in the United States—because, that is, modernism's ascendance largely succeeded in erasing his influence. In the opening decades of the twentieth century when British culture was still clearly hegemonic, Bennett was viewed in the United States as the heir to "Boz": when he crossed the United States in 1911 on a lecture and reading tour, his American publisher recollected, "No other author had had such a reception since the visit of Charles Dickens."[6] Unlike the popular enterprises pioneered and promoted by Charles Dickens—*Household Words* and *All the Year Round* for example—Bennett's literary productions appeared in a context in which elite art and popular culture were rapidly parting ways, and his intervention in this widening breach between high and low culture concerns me in these pages, together with the later intervention of the postmodern *Simpsons*.

To understand any relation that Bennett's fiction might bear to *The Simpsons,* we need to consider what looms imposingly between their crowd-pleasing texts: the works of high modernism, which dominated the literary field roughly from the 'Teens into the 'Sixties. John Carey's polemical reading of literary modernism, *Intellectuals and the Masses,* locates one of the crises to which European modernism responded in what the Spanish philosopher José Ortega y Gasset calls "the revolt of the masses." As metropolitan populations swelled and certain progressivist ideals were realized through near-universal education, a burgeoning segment of the lower and middle classes in England became literate and sustained a wide array of written media of its own, from popular newspapers such as the *Daily Mirror* to illustrated weeklies such as *Woman* and magazines such as *Tit-Bits.*[7] In Carey's account, intellectuals from Ortega and Friedrich Nietzsche to Virginia Woolf and D. H. Lawrence viewed this proliferation of print-media as a threat to the cultural authority of the intellectual. Many writers responded to the apparent encroachment of popular forms upon traditionally "literary" domains by expressing a measure of pessimism about the newly literate classes, a pessimism the cost of which was exacted at the level of literary production:

> The intellectuals could not, of course, actually prevent the masses from attaining literacy. But they could prevent them reading literature by making it too difficult for them to understand—and this is what they did. The early twentieth century saw a determined effort, on the part of the European intelligentsia, to exclude the masses from culture. In England this movement has become known as modernism.[8]

Carey concludes, "the principle around which modernist literature and culture fashioned themselves was the exclusion of the masses."[9] Carey calls a chapter that discusses Bennett's fiction "Narrowing the Abyss," at once deploying Andreas Huyssen's notion of "the great divide" between modernism and mass culture and suggesting that the split between "intellectuals" and "mass culture" already preceded Bennett's entrance on the British literary scene at the end of the nineteenth century. Huyssen himself concludes that

> Modernism constituted itself through a conscious strategy of exclusion, an anxiety of contamination by its other: an increasingly consuming and

engulfing mass culture. Not surprisingly, this anxiety of contamination has appeared in the guise of an irreconcilable opposition, especially . . . in the official canonization of "high modernism" in literature and literary criticism.[10]

The culture of modernism, in part by holding mass culture at arm's length, consolidated a range of cultural production as one monolithic movement, so that the conservative forms of English literary modernism, those produced by Yeats, Eliot, and Pound for example, came to be lumped together with the revolutionary forms of the radical avant-garde.

Carey claims Arnold Bennett as "the hero" of his book because Bennett refused to reject a mass reading public.[11] Bennett felt an enormous obligation to his audience and committed himself to giving it what it wanted. In Bennett's view, any repudiation of the mass reading public masked a petty jealousy for public acclaim: "I can divide all the imaginative writers I have ever met into two classes—those who admitted and sometimes proclaimed loudly that they desired popularity; and those who expressed a noble scorn or a gentle contempt for popularity. The latter, however, always failed to conceal their envy of popular authors."[12] To fulfill what he perceived to be his obligation, Bennett kept the popular reading audience resolutely in his sights and indeed sought to be a "professional" writer. His first compensated piece of writing appeared in *Tit-Bits,* he found his first serious literary employment as editor of the women's weekly magazine *Woman* in the 1890s, and throughout his career he wrote review columns for papers such as the *Daily Express* and the *Evening Standard.* Yet he also considered himself a highly self-conscious artist, and he sought to achieve by means of the popular media, on the one hand, and the more artistically respectable form of the novel, on the other, a reconciliation between the "average reader" of what he calls the "inartistic majority" and the elite, critical reader of the "artistic minority." In the process, he hoped to promote "that democratisation of art which it is surely the duty of the minority to undertake, and to undertake in a religious spirit."[13]

In his introductory essay to the collection *Fame and Fiction* (1901), titled "The 'Average Reader' and the Recipe for Popularity," Bennett seeks not only to explain to "the more artistic minority" the mass appeal of popular fiction, but also to indicate the horizon toward which he pushed throughout his literary career:

> there is a theory that the great public can appreciate a great novel, that the highest modern expression of literary art need not appeal in vain to the average reader. And I believe this to be true—provided that such a novel is written with intent, and with a full knowledge of the peculiar conditions to be satisfied; I believe that a novel could be written which would unite in a mild ecstasy of praise the two extremes—the most inclusive majority and the most exclusive minority.[14]

"The peculiar conditions to be satisfied" include not just the consideration that "the average reader likes an imposing plot, heroical characters, and fine actions" but also the state of the book trade in general.[15] Bennett was acutely aware of the importance of marketing himself diversely as an author. Alongside his thirty-odd novels, the most important of which include *Anna of the Five Towns* (1902), *The Old Wives' Tale* (1908), *Clayhanger* (1910), and *Riceyman Steps* (1923), he produced stage-plays with West End runs exceeded at the time only by G. B. Shaw's, an operatic libretto based on the apocryphal *Book of Judith,* a motion picture screenplay called *Piccadilly,* and books such as *The Author's Craft* and *The Truth About an Author* that sought to demystify the aura surrounding creative writers. He also composed a series of "Pocket Philosophies," including *Literary Taste, and How to Form It, With Detailed Instructions for Collecting a Complete Library of English Literature* (1912), which provides chapters on "Why a Classic Is a Classic," "How to Read a Classic," and "System in Reading."[16]

Bennett recognized that "the peculiar conditions to be satisfied" in order to produce a "great novel" that promotes the "democratisation of art" were the material conditions of commodity culture in its monopoly capitalist phase: those of the market, of the readership, of the subject-matter treated, and of the producer (he described himself alternately as a "public weighing-machine," a confectioner, and a tradesman).[17] Bennett was fascinated by, if often critical of, the material conditions of everyday life in the early twentieth century and he chastened his peers for turning their backs on the material world in favor of the abstract and the idealistic. In a letter of 30 September 1905, for instance, he admonished H.G. Wells: "You are not really interested in individual humanity. . . . You will never see it, but in rejecting surface values you are wrong. As a fact they are just as important as other values."[18] Bennett's friendly jab at Wells in defense of "surface values" assumes formal definition in an essay of 1913, in which he takes to task novels that reject such values:

> Every street is a mirror, an illustration, an exposition, an explanation, of
> the human beings who live in it. Nothing in it is to be neglected. Every-
> thing in it is valuable, if the perspective is maintained. Nevertheless, in
> the narrow individualistic novels of English literature—and in some of
> the best—you will find a domestic organism described as though it
> existed in a vacuum, or in the Sahara . . . ; as though it reacted on noth-
> ing and was reacted on by nothing; and as though it could be adequately
> rendered without reference to anything exterior to itself.[19]

Bennett's formulation suggests that without strict attention to "the street,"
any representation of "a domestic organism" must appear as a free-float-
ing ego and will ultimately prove inadequate and narrow due to a loss of
perspective.

This point of view anticipates Georg Lukács's assertion in *Realism in
Our Time* that since "in any work of art, perspective is of overriding
importance," modernism's modes necessarily represent the impoverish-
ment of subjectivity when they inevitably "deprive literature of a sense
of perspective."[20] Lukács's "perspective," like Bennett's, involves setting
the individual against the totality of social relations and requires understanding that characters' "individual existence . . . cannot be distinguished from their historical environment. Their human significance,
their specific individuality cannot be separated from the context in which
they were created."[21] Such an emphasis on material context entails,
according to Raymond Williams, "valuing a whole way of life, a society
that is larger than any of the individuals composing it, and at the same
time valuing creations of human beings who, while belonging to and
affected by and helping to define this way of life, are also, in their own
terms, absolute ends in themselves."[22] Ignoring the historical situation
and material conditions for Lukács means denying "specific individuality" and for Williams produces a "damaging unbalance,"[23] just as Bennett
in his letter to Wells asserts that ignoring "surface values" implies a special lack of interest in "individual humanity."

Bennett's aesthetic arises as a response to market forces ("the peculiar
conditions to be satisfied") and with the aim to "unite in a mild ecstasy of
praise the two extremes—the most inclusive majority and the most exclusive minority." It claims to promote the "democratisation of art" by establishing a perspective on the totality of social relations, representing the
essential as that in which social and subjective relations are bound up with

material and historical conditions: "all physical phenomena are interrelated . . . there is nothing which does not bear on everything else. The whole spectacular and sensual show—what the eye sees, the ear hears, the nose scents, the tongue tastes and the skin touches—is a cause or an effect of human conduct."[24] Bennett embraces, in other words, the kind of individual humanity that enjoys lasers and mirrored balls as well as "classics" such as *Star Wars*. Bennett's most famous meditations on "physical phenomena" appear in his "Five Towns" novels, set in the Staffordshire Potteries in the era of high industrialism. These historical conditions, a representation of what Raymond Williams calls "a whole way of life," provide the necessary counterpart to and explanation of what Bennett calls "individual humanity." In this respect, Bennett seems to agree with Lukács that only through the successful achievement of perspective in relation to the totality of social processes can it be said that "in realistic literature each descriptive detail is both *individual* and *typical*," that is, that each detail helps "create . . . and judge . . . the quality of a whole way of life in terms of the qualities of persons."[25] Such a judgment need not be an affirmation, by any means: Bennett argues that "Life being imperfect, the novelist's attitude must be not merely critical, but critical, often, in an adverse sense."[26] Can this "adverse critical sense," however, produce a genuinely oppositional art and still coexist with a flourishing culture of the commodity? Moreover, what happens to the promise of a democratic art and the possibility of oppositional criticism when the growing chasm between modernism and popular culture gapes wider?

THE SIMPSONS AND COMMODITY CULTURE

If, as Andreas Huyssen maintains, what was once a "dialectic" between the avant-garde and mass culture devolved into an open opposition between modernism and popular culture, then the wave of new cultural production that began to emerge in the 1960s and was christened "postmodernism" appears as a "relief," the consequence of a sort of emetic transition from a monumental "monopoly capitalism" to more fluid "late capitalisms." For Fredric Jameson, the emergence of postmodernism as "the cultural logic of late capitalism" means the sweeping out of "modernist formal values (now considered 'elitist'), along with a range of crucial related categories such as the work or the subject," but this crumbling of monolithic modernisms in the wake of the "postmodern" also means "that the price of this new textual freedom [evinced in postmodernism] is paid for by language and the linguistic arts, which retreat before the democracy of the visual and the aural."[27] Kurt Andersen of the *New Yorker* identifies as a "key event" in this new "cleansing cultural flood tide" the moment in 1989 when *The Simpsons* hit the television airwaves.[28] Through postmodern forms such as *The Simpsons,* what Arnold Bennett calls "the democratisation of art" comes to mean the assumption to cultural hegemony of those very forms of mass media which appeal to the "spectacular and sensual," the repudiation of which crystallized the modernist moment. The "great divide" separating mass culture from modernism seems to have resolved itself.[29] In the wake of a massive "flood tide" of new cultural production, of postmodern stuff of which *The Simpsons* is such an important part, it is worth asking how this resolution or dialectical reconciliation took place. Did the "excluded" forms of mass culture return to crack open a monumental modernism as something like the return of the repressed, or did prodigal modernist forms merely return to the popular fold in a movement of modernism from the cultural periphery to the center? What does this return of the repressed or new recentering look like?

In effect, postmodernism represents both a return of the repressed and a recentering, and this double movement produces the kind of cultural production of which *The Simpsons* is typical. From one point of view, the antiestablishment politics of modernism (whether the reactionary poetry of Ezra Pound or the radical works of the socialist avant-garde) become disengaged from the stylistic strategies through which they found articulation as late capitalist advertising culture assimilates and exploits those strategies. Postmodernism recenters itself around typically modernist formal features including montage, fragmentation, and alienation-effects. Jameson posits that the stylistics of literary modernism, especially in Britain, fulfilled the new conditions of a society in imperial decline, substituting for the immanent meaning of existential experience a linguistic fragmentation and spatialized meaning.[30] When domestic English culture is made to feel the full-blown effects of monopoly capitalism, by Jameson's account, modernism necessarily becomes the emergent cultural logic, and the older mode of realism to which Bennett subscribed begins to look increasingly like the expression of a residual cultural logic. As advertising culture appropriates modernist stylistic conventions, however, modernist conventions themselves no longer seem adequate vehicles for emergent ideologies and instead become a part of the dominant cultural logic, as they move from the periphery to the center of aesthetic production.

In Jameson's formulation, modernism's "new spatial language"—its "style"—functions as the place-holder for "the unrepresentable totality" of social relations in the era of monopoly capitalism, and modernist stylistics seem only to defer the desire typical of realism for representing social relations in their entirety.[31] Postmodernism constitutes a double return of the repressed in terms of strategies of totalization and in its desire for a broad audience. The first of these returns coincides with the leveling of the "uneven moment of social development" to which "modernism must ... be seen as uniquely corresponding," according to Jameson.[32] If a whole way of life tends to appear unrepresentable for modernists, this is because the unevenness of modernity prevents there being a single apprehensible "way of life." With the incremental smoothing-out of unevenness, however, the possibility of pursuing a new representation of the whole reemerges. The balancing of this "unevenness" also promises to reconcile the intellectuals to the masses, and it signals the second of the two returns, obviating the opposition of mass culture to modernism. If in fact the lowbrow is what modernism must disavow to be fully itself, then the reintegration of mass culture with high artistic aspirations would seem to represent a kind of return of the repressed. The resolution of the "uneven moment of social development" in the period of late capitalism entails the deconstruction of the opposition of the intellectuals to the masses, modernism to mass culture, and reopens the possibility for a form of cultural production that modernist stylistics temporarily held suspended: the critical representation of a whole way of life that was part of Bennett's vision of the "democratisation of art."

To claim that postmodern forms once again engage the possibility of a totalizing aesthetic is not, however, to suggest that postmodernism has any more a privileged perspective on the social totality in the era of multinational capitalism than modernism had during the phase of monopoly capitalism. It is, rather, to argue that modernist style no longer serves its place-holding function once it encounters "the cultural logic of late capitalism" which insists, for instance, upon "the democracy of the visual and the aural" rather than upon the primacy of the literary. Indeed the modernist emphases upon individual psychology, social fragmentation, and formal novelty in literature and art rapidly became, by most accounts, inflexible, monumental, and reified. What strategy then comes to satisfy the operations of "perspective" in lieu of modernist stylistics? In aesthetic production what seems practicable as an approach to totality seems to be a "partial summing up," what Jameson after Sartre calls "totalization," an "act of imagination" that dynamically *approximates* a "whole way of life" rather than describing it as an "inert . . . synthetic unity."[33]

In such "totalizations," something akin to Bennett's aesthetic theory returns to center-stage, exemplified by the orientation of *The Simpsons* toward society; "surface values" and material context once more become crucial to representing "the essential," as the distinction between popular and high culture breaks down before "the democracy of the visual and aural." In this sense, what Herbert Marcuse had anticipated as a "post-bourgeois" conception of essence—a defining kernel of humanity, which is not located in the depths of the Cartesian ego, but rather in external material and social relations—appears not in any real sense "post-bourgeois" but rather "post-modern."[34] The steady leveling of "uneven development" characteristic of late capitalism diminishes the efficacy of the designation "bourgeois" as a meaningful descriptive term, as bourgeois values extend their province across the cultural matrix to such a degree that "post-bourgeois" simply indicates the impossibility of an oppositional position outside of "bourgeois culture." The distinction between the postmodern aesthetic of *The Simpsons* and the premodernist orientation of Bennett's theory with respect to totalization depends upon the conviction that there is no longer one satisfactory "perspective" from which to apprehend the totality; there can be no single street that can serve as "a mirror, an illustration, an exposition, an explanation" of the individual. Rather, there must be multiple mirrors, local illustrations, and a plastic play of multifarious contexts that situate and motivate the individual subject.

The contextual play of *The Simpsons* results in a broad crossover appeal suggestive of what Jameson calls "the democracy of the visual." Peter Roth, president of Fox Broadcasting, notes, "the profit potential on a show like 'The Simpsons' is astronomical. The animated form is universal in its appeal."[35] *The Simpsons* insistently presents totalizations of social relations in its representations of the fictional community of Springfield.[36] The plastic limits of Springfield circumscribe American social relations in their entirety, but partially and serially. Where Bennett's novels strive to capture a whole system of relations in one sweeping glance, *The Simpsons* presents its holistic vision of American society across time, in a series of totalizing scenes that emerge each Sunday evening. Springfield metamorphoses from episode to episode, and even within episodes *The Simpsons*'s "perspective" on "a whole way of life" can shift with great rapidity, since "you can have 40 scenes in an animated show, whereas there might be 7 or 8 in the typical sitcom. . . . That's a big difference, and a good writer can really take advantage of that. You can go anywhere, do anything."[37] Springfield, moreover, can be anything: it appears variously as a small town or metropolis, in the Midwest, the Southwest, the West Coast, or the Eastern Seaboard.[38] It is small enough for all its citizens to gather for a PTA meeting or a church service yet expansive enough to fill stadiums for football games and arenas for monster truck rallies. This elasticity distinguishes *The Simpsons*'s mode of situating character from Arnold Bennett's, which constructs individual "perspective" by faithfully reproducing in exacting detail the Five Towns and their industry. Yet Springfield and the Five Towns reflect a shared concern with "surface details." Indeed, as two-dimensional animation, *The Simpsons* functions entirely as surface—its medium resists those realistic conventions of depth conveyed through the camera.[39] Both Bennett's Five Towns and *The Simpsons*'s Springfield share industrial economic bases (the Staffordshire pottery-works and Mr. Burns's nuclear power plant), both encompass a full range of cultural institutions (the church, government, school, commerce, pub or bar, art, etc.), and both aim to describe a "whole way of life" through the case of a single family or person.

Like Bennett's novels, *The Simpsons* aspires to give a sense of the social totality, but whereas Bennett's fiction seeks to convey a single "perspective" through a dialectical project involving individual and context, "individual humanity" and concrete historical situation, *The Simpsons* produces multiple, serial totalizations, "partial summings up," that emerge within and across episodes through a play of context and layerings of cultural and historical allusion. Bennett's fiction appears in a field controlled by what Roland Barthes calls "the author function" so that the appearance of any new Bennett novel inevitably calls up *Anna of the Five Towns* and the authorial persona constructed in *The Truth About an Author*. *The Simpsons*, on the other hand, is a collective project, with a shifting corps of writers and directors and a production unit that stretches around the globe. As did Bennett's fiction, *The Simpsons* emerged from journalistic forums: while *Anna of the Five Towns* developed during Bennett's time as editor of *Woman*, *The Simpsons* gestated among such figures as Akbar and

Jeff in Matt Groening's syndicated newspaper cartoon *Life In Hell* before
its birth as "shorts" on the *Tracy Ullman Show*. Since 1989, however, the
demands of the television medium prohibit Groening from appearing as
the author of each—or any—episode; he appears, rather, as the "creator"
of the show. *The Simpsons* undermines, therefore, the vatic position of the
traditional author so that there cannot be books about *The Simpsons* such
as *The Truth About an Author* or *The Author's Craft* but rather compendia
such as *The Simpsons: A Complete Guide to Our Favorite Family* that reflect
both the collective quality of the project and its democratic aim: to give
us "*our* favorite family." Yet if *The Simpsons* is a collective creative project,
it is also corporate in another sense. A commercial enterprise, *The Simpsons* is finally beholden to Fox Broadcasting, as the president of Fox suggests in connecting the "universality of its appeal" with "astronomical
profit potential."

The Simpsons as a corporate production has controlling interests that
are acutely aware of the market-function of the television show, as was
Arnold Bennett with respect to his own value on the literary markets. *The
Simpsons* was, of course, at the forefront of the Fox network's successful
bid to break into a national television market previously the exclusive
province of the network triumvirate of ABC, NBC, and CBS. It helped build
a solid anchor night for the network and provided an audience for new
shows such as *King of the Hill, That '70s Show, Malcolm in the Middle,* and
Groening's own *Futurama*. Not only was the show used to promote the network and Fox's other shows, it also spawned an array of products ranging
from such standard promotional materials as bumper stickers, comic books,
calendars, candy dispensers, window decals, refrigerator magnets, T-Shirts,
and dolls and figurines, to more eccentric items such as chess sets, alarm
clocks, and full-length albums with titles like *The Simpsons Sing the Blues*
and *The Yellow Album*. Perhaps the most dramatic instance of self-promotion involved a collaboration among Fox, Pepsi, and a California-based
builder to construct a 2,200-square foot reproduction of the Simpsons'
house in Henderson, Nevada.[40] "Merchandising" to this extent—and especially the merchandising of sheer simulacra—is not a scheme that every
television show can sustain. "You don't see a lot of 'Home Improvement'
T-Shirts out there, but we get an enormous number of requests for 'The
Simpsons' merchandise. . . . It can be very profitable," reports the president of Twentieth Century Television.[41] In this sense, the producers of *The
Simpsons* understand that "the particular conditions to be satisfied"

include a need for marketing *The Simpsons* as a cultural commodity that exceeds its ostensible cultural function as twenty-two minutes of engaging television material per week.

The Simpsons serves, moreover, as a cultural site from which to promote other products, and so it becomes part of a larger consumer culture, selling candy bars, long-distance service, and even computer microprocessors. Yet the corporate interests for the show are also intent to preserve the conventional intellectual property and commercial rights associated with such promotion. When, for example, the South Australian Brewing Company produced a canned beer called Duff (Homer Simpson's favorite brand), Fox sued the company in order to stop production.[42] While *The Simpsons* announces itself as a democratic form (anyone can turn on the television or consume the products it licenses), its corporate ownership also makes clear an investment in maintaining the boundaries and property rights that keep *The Simpsons* from belonging to everyone. This sort of protectionism gives the lie to the promise of the "Little Land of Duff" song that plays with mind-numbing insistence at Duff Gardens:

> Duff Beer for me
> Duff Beer for you
> I'll have a Duff
> You have one too.
> ("Selma's Choice")

The writers for *The Simpsons* are certainly aware of the double sense in which *The Simpsons* is a corporate production, and the show signals such an awareness when, for example, the characters express an incredulity (or contempt) about discovering a Simpson on a T-shirt. In "Bart vs. Thanksgiving," Bart complains about the dated balloons of cartoon figures in the parade, and Homer replies, "If you start building a balloon for every flash-in-the-pan cartoon character, you'd turn the parade into a farce," just as a balloon in Bart's form slides across the Simpsons' television screen. The irony reminds us that the show as a commercial product is not timeless, but finds its place in a particular marketing period—and yet this irony does not slow the furious pace at which *The Simpsons* itself is marketed one bit.

Perhaps the most extended exploration of such a benign self-awareness appears in the episode "Bart Gets Famous," in which Bart becomes a "flash-in-the-pan" star because of one line—"I didn't do it"—on the *Krusty the Klown Show*. After losing his cachet as the "I Didn't Do It Kid," Bart comes to terms with his return to a normal life, and by the end of the program the Simpsons household appears as it did at the beginning of the episode. In other episodes, too, the characters frequently draw attention to their own static natures, pointing out that despite a new adventure each week, the Simpson family emerges unchanged the next week ("Homer Loves Flanders"). *Time Magazine* connects this static quality of the characters with *The Simpsons*'s market position, describing the show's "staying power": Bart "stay[s] in the fourth grade . . . stay[s] glued to the living-room tube to watch his idol, Krusty the Clown [sic] [and] stay[s] for years in the hearts and humors of a fickle, worldwide TV audience."[43] This "staying power" extends to the other characters as well: Homer Simpson, despite being fired repeatedly and taking on a number of different occupations (sideshow freak, clown, team mascot, pin jockey, food critic, manager for a country music star), remains employed at the Springfield Nuclear Power Plant; Marge Simpson continues on as a dutiful wife and homemaker; Lisa perpetually attends Miss Hoover's class; and the baby Maggie never says more than her first word. Nor does the Simpsons' economic situation change. However successful or unsuccessful Homer Simpson finds himself in his career, despite the fact that Marge might take a job as well, the Simpsons remain what Homer calls "us upper-lower-middle class types" ("The Springfield Connection"). The association of a distinctive voice with each animated character represents a constant that concretely realizes this static quality: Homer's anguished "D'oh" or jubilant "Woohoo"; Marge's ambivalent "mmnnh"; Bart's "Don't have a cow, man"; and Krusty the Klown's "Hey hey, kids" establish and lend stability to their personalities.

While there are distinct and "staying" pleasures to be found in this reliable fixity of character, the dynamic element in the show—what draws audiences in week after week—comes not from the characters but rather from the changing contexts within which the characters find themselves. For this reason, "surface values" in the sense Arnold Bennett marks out in his letter to Wells are extremely important to *The Simpsons*, and the mimetic and critical functions of the show are achieved through the capacity of Springfield to approximate the manifold conditions of American life. In this way, *The Simpsons* implicitly shares Bennett's conviction that "every street is a mirror, an illustration, an exposition, an explanation, of the human beings who live in it." Indeed, *The Simpsons,* if not strictly a literary form, is certainly the most literate of all situation comedies. From parodies of Poe ("The Raven" in "Treehouse of Horror," "The Telltale Heart" in "Lisa's Rival"), to disparagements of Whitman ("Damn you, Walt Whitman! . . . *Leaves of Grass* my ass!" in "Mother Simpson"), to imitations of Allen Ginsberg (Lisa's poem "Howl of the Unappreciated" in "Bart vs. Thanksgiving"), *The Simpsons* is steeped in the American literary context into which Arnold Bennett made such a splash on his tour in 1911. One educator even sees *The Simpsons* as reviving for the late twentieth century the role that Mark Twain performed for the late nineteenth century.[44] Yet, as *Time* notes, Bart "embodies a century of popular culture and is one of the richest characters in it," and the wedding of several centuries of literariness to "a century of popular culture" challenges the privileged place of literary studies in the canons of late twentieth and early twenty-first century culture.[45]

The Simpsons's literary and cultural awareness extends, finally, to the conventions of its own medium. In "Boy-Scoutz N the Hood," Bart criticizes an "Itchy & Scratchy" episode because Itchy stakes down Scratchy's appendages and props his belly to form a tent with faulty knots. With Homer looking on from the couch, Lisa reminds Bart that cartoons do not simply reproduce reality, a point hammered home as a second Homer meanders past the living-room window. This moment and the many others like it reveal a strong sense of self-awareness within the show, an awareness especially characteristic of high modernism.[46] An Associated Press columnist notes that "Fox's 'The Simpsons' . . . parodies every corner of mass media it can find—including Fox's 'The Simpsons,' " and Kurt Andersen calls the show "smarter, sharper, and more allusive than any other show on television."[47] *Time* describes Bart as a "jagged, modernist silhouette," and indeed *The Simpsons* displays many of the stylistic features Eugene Lunn describes as typical of modernism: aesthetic self-consciousness and self-reflexiveness; simultaneity and juxtaposition; paradox, ambiguity, and uncertainty; and explorations of the fragmented and alienated individual experience of modern urban and industrial society.[48] In this sense, *The Simpsons* participates in the "recentering" of the unconventional modernist forms that accompanied the marginal, oppositional politics of the early modernists.

As did Arnold Bennett, *The Simpsons* aims for a double inclusiveness both for marketing and for aesthetic reasons. The show seeks to incorporate broad and representative sections of contemporary social and economic life, and it targets a wide audience without discriminating among its viewers. It is literary, but not insistently so. If viewers fail to "get" the allusions and the ironies, they can enjoy the spectacular and the sensual features of the visual humor and the attractively nonrealistic contours of the cartoon—in other words, the lasers and mirror-balls, if not the aural puns of the Springfield Pops. One can see the program as "deviliciously satirical" or innocuously goofy. "We're out of here," that sense of outrage or exclusion fostered by modernism's difficulty, is a reaction rarely encouraged by *The Simpsons*. The show criticizes the slices of society it captures, its popular peers and rivals,[49] and the material culture in which it takes part to an extent that Arnold Bennett could not have fathomed. It remains to be seen, however, whether *The Simpsons*'s strategies of inclusivity and totalization sustain the possibility of a genuinely oppositional culture in the era of late capitalism better than Bennett's strategies did during the era of monopoly capitalism.

THE EDWARDIAN MONEY-TRAIN
AND A BART SALES EVENT

Bennett emphasizes "materiality" and "surface values" in his fiction, and in his early novel *Anna of the Five Towns* (1902) he stages a dialectical encounter between subjectivity and objectivity, an encounter in which social relations are informed by "surface values" and the material realm. The novel opens on the eve of Anna Tellwright's twenty-first birthday and traces her initiation into the world of capital. As she comes of age, she unexpectedly inherits fifty thousand pounds. With this money comes the responsibility of managing a series of real estate investments, and the conflict in the novel emerges from the tension between sound business practices and the rhetoric of Christian morality to which Anna subscribes. Her acquiescence in her miserly father's ruthless business advice forces one of her tenants into bankruptcy and allies her in a business venture with a man who courts her for her money. At the end of the novel, Anna faces a choice between marrying her business partner, for whom she does not care, and running away to Australia with the bankrupt tenant, whom she loves. Anna's entry into the adult world of the Five Towns brings her to the understanding that her subjectivity is determined by and bound up within a network of oppressive discursive structures—those of patriarchy, Methodism, and capitalism—which exert their force through the material practices of the Five Towns society.

The novel's critical exploration of this network results in several occasions for satire. Anna's father Ephraim, who methodically turns a bequest of eighteen thousand pounds into the fifty thousand that Anna inherits, is a chief target of such satire. Ephraim was once a prominent Methodist preacher, who "expounded the mystery of the Atonement in village conventicles and grew garrulous with God at prayer-meetings."[50] Yet, we discover, "he did these things as routine, without skill and without enthusiasm, because they gave him an unassailable position within the central group of the society." Ostensibly a spiritual man, in fact "his chief interest lay in those fiscal schemes of organization without whose aid no religious propaganda can possibly succeed. It was in the finance of salvation that he rose supreme." The important distinction between the commercial enterprise of "finance" and the spiritual process of "salvation" collapses for Ephraim, and the discrepancy between Ephraim's impoverished spiritual life and the position of great importance the Methodist community accords him constitutes a biting indictment both of Ephraim and of the Methodists.

When Ephraim transfers his investments to his daughter on her birthday, Anna—ignorant of all but the most routine commercial transactions—expresses bewilderment: "Anna had sensations such as a child might have who has received a traction-engine to play with in a back yard. 'What am I to do with it?' she asked plaintively."[51] The intrusion of the money into her life leaves her feeling displaced: "To Anna . . . the arrival of moneys out of space, unearned, unasked, was a disturbing experience. . . . Practically, Anna could not believe that she was rich; and in fact she was not rich—she was merely a fixed point through which moneys that she was unable to arrest passed with the rapidity of trains."[52] The vehicle of Bennett's metaphor—the train—is an image of industrialization, commerce, and expansion, appropriate to the era of modernity. The tenor of the metaphor strikes us perhaps as suitably postmodern, with Anna's "fixed point" anticipating, for example, contemporary notions of subject positions discursively constituted. Bennett intends to survey life in the Five Towns during the 1880s through the perspective of this single "fixed point," Anna Tellwright, and the novel's title—*Anna of the Five Towns*—indicates an effort to represent both "individuality" and "typicality," those categories described by Lukács and Raymond Williams as requisite for a critical realism. The novel weaves a web in which religion, industry, commerce, domestic life, gender codes, and patriarchal relations reinforce one another, and the material effect of these various institutions on Anna seems to be totalized, summed up, in the sphere of the economic. *Anna of the Five Towns* thus seems to exhibit what Bennett describes as "a definite critical attitude towards life": in seeking to represent life in the Five Towns in its totality, Bennett demonstrates that at least three dominant discourses—of Methodism, patriarchy, and commerce—derive from and express themselves through concrete materiality. The realm of the material coordinates social life in the Five Towns, and circulations of capital determine even Anna's form of inner experience.

As in *Anna of the Five Towns,* a good deal of the enjoyment to be had from the episode of *The Simpsons* titled "Bart Sells His Soul" results from the exposure of the hypocrisy behind "the finance of salvation" and the ambivalent operations of the commercial world. In this episode, Bart Simpson experiences a spiritual crisis similar to Anna's that emerges after he sells his soul to Milhouse, exchanging five dollars for a piece of First Church of Springfield letter-head inscribed with the words "Bart Simpson's Soul." *The Simpsons* explores social dynamics similar to those of *Anna of the Five Towns,* on the one hand dramatizing the exclusions upon which "high" cultural institutional forms depend and on the other hand putting those forms under erasure. Where Bennett illustrates the exclusion of popular enjoyment and romantic love from "God's work" and demonstrates that exclusion's damaging effects on the individual, *The Simpsons* poses a more pointed challenge to the distinctions sustaining religion's "seriousness." The opening shot takes in a church marquee announcing, "No Shirt, No Shoes, No Salvation," suggesting that this form of organized religion functions at once as a business and as an institution catering to a particular social class (those who understand and adhere to an implicit dress code). Inside, Bart hands out sheet music, crying, "Hymns here, hymns here, get 'em while they're holy! Fresh from God's brain to your mouth!" In fact, the sheets Bart hands out contain the music and lyrics to Iron Butterfly's "In-A-Gadda-Da-Vida," which Reverend Lovejoy willfully misreads as "In the Garden of Eden." The performance of the "hymn" provokes a destabilizing and profane confusion between the church's "high" and serious cultural function and the "low" entertainment value of mass-marketed music.[53] Only Reverend Lovejoy seems disturbed, however. When he begins to suspect the lowbrow origins of the "hymn," he says, "Wait a minute—this sounds like rock and/or roll!" On the other hand, the congregation seems not to see the incongruity of Iron Butterfly's music in the services of the First Church of Springfield: Homer turns to Marge and says, "remember when we used to make out to this hymn?" and the congregation produces candles at the end of the organist's epic solo, as die-hard devotees might present a salute of cigarette lighters at a rock concert.

We can see here the highly concentrated "play" of contexts typical of *The Simpsons*. The episode conflates the ecclesiastical setting (hymns, organs) with popular culture (rock anthems, keyboards, and guitars), the latter context compromising the privileged social function of the former. That the congregation seems not to perceive that anything untoward has happened suggests a preexisting alienation from the mystifying "high" cultural ethos of the church embodied by Reverend Lovejoy. The organ inflections of "In-A-Gadda-Da-Vida" penetrate to the heart of the church, all the more ironically if we understand this introduction of Iron Butterfly into the church service as a kind of return of the repressed; the liner notes to the LP *In-A-Gadda-Da-Vida* tell us that the father of Doug Ingle, "the Butterfly's leader and spokesman," "was a church organist and much of the classical influence of the church is evident in [Doug's] writing."[54] That this represents a powerful return, in which "In-A-Gadda-Da-Vida" deflates the sanctified function of the church and troubles the distinction between the ecclesiastical and the popular, becomes clear when, after both the seventeen-minute hymn and the church service have ended, Reverend Lovejoy forces Bart and Milhouse to "clean each and every one of these organ pipes you have befouled with your popular music!" Reverend Lovejoy here reprises Homer's outrage at the Springfield Pops as he displays an anxiety about the church's contamination by "popular music" that approximates the modernist reaction to mass culture traced by John Carey and Andreas Huyssen.

While cleaning the organ pipes, Bart trades his soul to Milhouse to prove that "there's no such thing as a soul. It's just something [adults] made up to scare kids, like the Bogeyman or Michael Jackson." As the half-hour episode progresses, however, Bart comes to feel the material effects of losing his soul: automatic doors decline to open for him; his breath will not congeal on a freezer window; the household pets become hostile; and he loses his sense of humor. Meanwhile, Bart's soul begins to circulate throughout Springfield and comes to be traded publicly. When, convinced that he was wrong about the existence of the soul, Bart goes to Milhouse to buy back the piece of paper, he discovers Milhouse in the back yard playing with it in the dirt. Milhouse has none of the problems making use of Bart's soul that Anna does in Bennett's novel in finding a use for her fifty thousand pounds legacy, the arrival of which she treats "as a child might have who has received a traction-engine to play with in a back yard." Milhouse responds to Anna's question, "What am I to do with it?" by drawing his investment into the arena of global politics. Bart's soul becomes a trophy in a staged battle between the United States and Iran, as Milhouse's plastic army men descend, accompanied by machine-gun bursts, upon an enemy encampment: "Cover me, Sarge! I'm going after Bart's soul!" Milhouse bawls. Rather than surrender Bart's soul, however, the enemy attempts to destroy it. Milhouse drives a tank over the paper, declaring, "If the Ayatollah can't have it, no one can!"

In Milhouse's mock war, Bart's soul occupies a position very much resembling the Kuwaiti oil fields burned by Saddam Hussein's troops in the Gulf War in the early 1990s (a conflict with Iraq rather than Iran, however), and like the price of oil during that crisis, the value of Bart's soul appreciates. When Bart bids to get it back, Milhouse says, "You want to buy it back, Bart? Sure, no problem. *Fifty bucks.*" As Bart's soul circulates, it takes on exchange value and accrues an interest of one thousand percent. Milhouse goes on to trade the soul to the proprietor of The Android's Dungeon and Baseball Card Shop for POGs bearing the image of ALF, before at last Lisa purchases the soul and returns it to him.[55] Bart's soul can only regain use value, rather than exchange value—that is, can only counteract the material effects of its lack—if Bart negates its material instantiation: he eats the piece of paper, thereby taking his soul out of circulation.

Before he realizes the nature of the marketplace, Bart offers to sell his conscience and sense of decency as well, announcing a "Bart sales event—everything about me must go!" Bart's self-commodification, then, shows how easily use value can convert to exchange value in the marketplace, the spiritual can manifest itself in the material, and "high culture" (Bart and Lisa discuss Neruda in this episode) can be bound up with "low culture" (ALF POGs are perhaps as transitory and faddishly lowbrow a currency imaginable). If we fail to read Bart's plot as one that deals primarily with commodity culture's control of the individual, the episode's subplot points out this determination of the individual life by economic imperatives, as Moe attempts to open a family restaurant, staking its success upon his personal charisma. While preparing for the grand opening of the restaurant, Moe consults with Homer about a name for the restaurant "that says friendly, all-American cooking"; Homer offers the absurd suggestion, "Chairman Moe's Magic Wok," which an inebriated Barney Gumble enthusiastically seconds. Homer's confusion of traditional American capitalism and Maoist China is typical of the sort of juxtaposition sustained by *The Simpsons,* but it also exemplifies what Bennett calls the "particular [market] conditions to be satisfied"—an American viewing public that, like Homer, Barney, and Andy Warhol's pop art, turns even Mao Zedong into exchange value, commodifying his image. Moe finally settles on "Uncle Moe's Family Feedbag" for his restaurant, a name that requires him to perform the role of "Uncle Moe" in order to sell his product. Moe's restaurant becomes, therefore, a project that has much in common with the self-commodification suggested by the "Bart sales event" that drives the main plot line. Both projects—the circulation of Bart's soul and the commerce that Moe stakes upon marketing himself as "Uncle Moe"—fail because Bart and Moe come to understand too late the nature of the market to which they are proffering themselves as commodities.

By contrast, this episode, replete with deliberate confusions, returns of the repressed, and erasures of exclusions, is acutely aware of that market, and its satire finds a kind of voice even against the commercial context within which "Bart Sells His Soul" appeared in its initial airing on the local Nashville Fox affiliate. The show fit comfortably into a commercial environment advertising other animated programs and hi-tech video games, with the opening sequence and the beginning of this episode framing a commercial for a Fox show titled *AlieNation: Body and Soul* (a program that neatly reflects the theme of Bart's episode) and another for an episode of *Married . . . with Children* in which Al Bundy founds his own religion based on misogynistic and boorish precepts.[56] The apparently uncritical ease with which these advertisements for other Fox shows coexisted with *The Simpsons* was, however, partially compensated by the spillover of the episode's satirical theme into the next commercial break: Bart's irreverence for the spiritual and ecclesiastical institutions in Springfield seemed to comment upon an advertisement for a Nashville luxury car dealer which flashed, "Open Sunday after church," on the screen during its pitch, a commercial strategy that resonated uncannily with The First Church of Springfield's announcement on its marquee, "No Shoes, No Shirt, No Salvation."[57]

The Simpsons, then, erases the exclusions by means of which organized religion claims moral precedence over popular cultural forms, so
that religion is exposed as a class-specific institution, the ecclesiastical and
the popular become virtually indistinguishable, body and soul entwine,
and even the boundary between the show and its advertising context
threatens to dissolve. The failures of Moe and Bart in the marketplace suggest an indictment of capitalism itself, which commodifies labor and determines the forms of subjectivity and selfhood, and the satire of Bart's
substitute hymn suggests the same possibility of "a definite critical attitude towards life" laid out by Bennett sixty-six years earlier. However, as
one of my students wondered after viewing and discussing this episode,
does *The Simpsons* extend cultural critique, the percipient laying bare of
cultural contradictions, to the point of sustaining an alternative, even a
purely negative one?[58] In other words, can the sorts of critique in which
Bennett and *The Simpsons* engage afford us a space from which to entertain the possibility of an oppositional culture?

ALLEGORIES OF RESIGNATION, POSSIBILITIES OF RESISTANCE; OR, HOW BART EARNED HIS SOUL AND ATE IT, TOO

The answers to the previous questions, as I have already hinted, are a pair
of qualified negatives, though for a different reason in each case. In Bennett's case, the "democratisation of art" and the assumption of "a definite
critical attitude toward life" come to appear as incompatible goals. Once
we understand that for Bennett "the average reader," like Homer and the
general audience for Bennett's fiction, "does not care to have the basic
ideas of his existence disturbed[,] may be emotionally aroused, but men-
tally . . . must be soothed, lulled, drugged," it becomes difficult to con-
ceive a literary product that critically opposes the dominant "basic ideas"
of modern social organization.[59] The critical realism practiced by Bennett,
through its orientation toward the complacent "average reader," necessarily gives more weight to the real as a representation of the status quo
than to sustained criticism as a possibility of a revised or alternative order.
In this respect *Anna of the Five Towns* is exemplary, serving as an allegory
of the impossibility of anything more than a local, unsustained resistance
to dominant discourses.

If for Anna the power of such discourses precludes overturning or resisting them in a comprehensive way, for Bennett the impossibility of oppositionality seems to arise from his allegiance both to the status quo, signaled by his emphasis upon existing "surface values," and to the limited possibilities those values offer in themselves. For this reason, D. H. Lawrence repudiated Bennett's brand of fiction, declaring, "I hate Bennett's resignation. Tragedy ought really to be a great kick at misery. But *Anna of the Five Towns* seems like an acceptance."[60] Virginia Woolf saw rather more critical potential in his fiction but felt that his novels failed to re-envision the whole fabric of society. Instead she felt that they "leave one with so strange a feeling of uncompleteness and dissatisfaction. In order to complete them it seems necessary to do something—to join a society, or more desperately, to write a cheque."[61] Bennett's modernist contemporaries, in other words, saw his appeal to the average reader and his allegiance to the extant real as complicit with the kinds of social forces at work in *Anna of the Five Towns*.

Likewise, in the view of Terry Eagleton, "a lot of postmodernism is politically oppositional but economically complicit," and this formula announces that political oppositionality already may be contained within the circuits of commodity culture.[62] Matt Groening, for example, positions the satire of *The Simpsons* in opposition to political power, asserting that the cartoon is about "not taking ourselves too seriously. Solemnity is always used by authority to stop critical thinking."[63] Yet when network television disseminates the show, such an oppositional stance can relax into a much more affirmative posture. Groening's conception of satire as opposing authority and promoting a critical attitude all too easily lapses into something far less challenging. "The nature of the best satire," the *Christian Science Monitor* quips in an enthusiastic review of *The Simpsons*, "is, of course, to poke fun at human foibles," a sort of critique that cannot really be described as oppositional.[64] When consumed as a product like those advertised during the commercial breaks rather than as a head-on assault on political authority, *The Simpsons* can seem more like conduct literature, a series of incitements to remedy one's personal "foibles," than significant (much less revolutionary) social criticism.[65] Kurt Andersen of the *New Yorker* especially praises *The Simpsons* for its refusal to use canned laughter, arguing, "we have the luxury of grinning or chuckling or guffawing without electronic encouragement—by ourselves, at home, in real life."[66] Yet the cherished terms of this "luxury" are hardly critical, for they emphasize social compartmentalization, if not isolation, and privatization—hallmarks of modern capitalism—binding them through the premise that these "luxuries" constitute "real life." Andersen concludes, "Thanks to cartoons, we can respond like human beings," suggesting that the critical promise offered by *The Simpsons* involves making us more humane rather than anything more pointed or politically "oppositional."

Nor is satire in itself necessarily hostile to religion. The *National Catholic Reporter* suggests that productions such as *The Simpsons* allow a new generation to "fashion an ironic, original spirituality that has a good deal to recommend it."[67] This spirituality seems to emerge less as a result of a dialectical rapprochement with an oppositional culture than as a co-optation of that culture, and the conclusion of "Bart Sells His Soul" dramatizes such a preemption. At the beginning of the episode, Bart's open hostility to organized religion results in the irreverence of the performance of "In-A-Gadda-Da-Vida" and in the unsettling conclusion that "there's no such thing as a soul," a conclusion based on the notion that the soul is a regulatory fiction in service of the "finance of salvation," to use Bennett's turn of phrase. By the end of the episode, however, Bart becomes convinced of the reality of the soul, and kneels to pray to God for its return. "Are you there, God? It's me, Bart Simpson," his prayer begins, invoking Judy Blume's adolescent novel *Are You There God? It's Me, Margaret.* The allusion, though amusing, does not diminish the earnestness with which Bart prays, and indeed his prayer is answered as his soul flutters into his hands from above. It is not God who responds to his prayer, however, but Lisa, who purchases his soul from the Android's Dungeon and Baseball Card Shop. Lisa lectures Bart as he reintegrates his soul and his body by eating the sheet of paper: "You know Bart, some philosophers believe that nobody is born with a soul—that you have to earn one through suffering and thought and prayer, like you did last night." This conclusion apparently reveals that Milhouse has been right from the very start about the nature of the soul, and right to feel guilt for jeopardizing his soul by abetting Bart in his blasphemous prank. In other words, the half-hour episode may bring us back—by the *via negativa,* through irony and satire—to the starting point we initially thought naïve. An "ironic, original spirituality," indeed.

Lisa's rhetoric and the visual framing of the scene suggest a dissident reading, however. When Bart prays, he addresses God, but he faces the iconic portrait of Krusty the Klown, and Krusty's comic image appears in

each frame, even after Bart concludes his prayer. The seemingly complacent reading of the episode, in which Bart discovers the reality of the soul
and suffers in order to gain it, is countered by this ironic reading over
which Krusty, god of commodity culture, presides. In this interpretation,
Bart's soul is equivalent to any other commodity traded openly on the market and is not granted to him by God but, as Lisa says, "earned" or pur-
chased. The culmination of such a reading sees in Bart's chewing and
swallowing of the paper soul a consummate image of modern consumption. Yet the important point to be made about this alternative reading is
that while it may seem playfully irreverent, "deviliciously satirical" to use
Dr. Hibbert's phrase, it is not really incompatible with the first interpretation. Even Bart's final act of consumption, cynical as it may seem, has
been anticipated by the religious authority he seeks to outrage at the outset. The prophet Ezekiel records that

> when I looked, behold, an hand was sent unto me; and, lo, a roll of a
> book was therein; And he spread it before me; and it was written within
> and without: and there was written therein lamentations, and mourn-
> ing, and woe. Moreover he said unto me, Son of man, eat that thou find-
> est; eat this roll, and go speak unto the house of Israel. So I opened my
> mouth, and he caused me to eat the roll.[68]

St. John in Revelation rehearses Ezekiel's prophecy: "I went unto the
angel, and said unto him, Give me the little book. And he said unto me,
Take it, and eat it up."[69] Like the limited options Bennett poses Anna Tellwright—submitting herself and her fortune to her "respectable" fiancé or
eloping to Australia with her lover—*The Simpsons* appears to offer two
possibilities, one conventional and one dissident, even oppositional, and
yet the discourses that are ostensibly subject to critique already circumscribe those possibilities.[70] Consumer culture enables both readings available to us at the conclusion to "Bart Sells His Soul," and the religious
establishment Bart opposes from the beginning of the episode anticipates
both as well. The very commodity culture that sustains *The Simpsons* as a
mass-medium form (the "democracy of the visual") anticipates and contains the possibilities for a clear sense of oppositionality, the power to outrage the status quo that, for example, Homer Simpson experiences at the
Springfield Pops. If *The Simpsons* resists the modernist tendency to
exclude the masses, the means of engaging its audience—commercial, net-

work television—ensures that its content will always be "economically complicit." It is not that *The Simpsons* sells out, as D. H. Lawrence accuses Bennett of doing, but that its very condition of possibility precludes a space from which to oppose the commodity culture of late capitalism.

This conclusion need not, however, return us to the conclusions of the modernists about the fiction of Bennett and his peers. Oppositionality, properly the rhetorical province of modernism,[71] formed a dialectic with the culture of monopoly capitalism, the sublation of the terms of which brings us many of the pleasures of postmodernism. To lament the impossibility of oppositional spaces in the culture of late capitalism evinces a paralyzing nostalgia for, among other things, the age of the modernist masterwork. Instead of oppositionality, we might point to *The Simpsons's* capacity for resistance in the discrete moments that Michel Foucault has taught us emerge wherever we find exhibitions of power. In *The History of Sexuality,* Foucault writes,

> Where there is power, there is resistance, and yet, or rather consequently, this resistance is never in a position of exteriority in relation to power. . . . These points of resistance are present everywhere in the power network. Hence there is no single locus of great Refusal, no soul of revolt, source of all rebellions, or pure law of the revolutionary. Instead there is a plurality of resistances, each of them a special case[, and] often one is dealing with mobile and transitory points of resistance.[72]

If oppositionality bears a direct relationship to the notion of totality, insofar as opposition implies standing outside and opposing a whole system, and the fragmentation of the notion of totality (a thing, or vestige of a process) within the cultural logic of late capitalism leaves us only with totalization (a process, in Jameson's reading of Sartre), then resistance as tactical process rather than strategic perspective may emerge from within those "partial summings up."[73] In other words, even if we can no longer really exercise Homer's option on a historical scale and say, "We're out of here!" we can join Dr. Hibbert in declaring "Deviliciously satirical!" and hope with some confidence that Bart continues to engage in signal acts of resistance that produce what Arnold Bennett in 1929 called the "adversely critical attitude toward life." Even if, like Anna, Bart feels himself to be "a fixed point through which moneys that [he is] unable to arrest pass . . . with the rapidity of trains"—or, as is more likely, a constellation of cultural sites through which information runs with the rapidity of point to point protocols—we likely will find him still befouling the complacent organs of commodity culture with the plangent and dissident strains of "In-A-Gadda-Da-Vida."

NOTES

1. I am deeply indebted to Jay Clayton and J. David Macey, Jr., for their valuable comments on an early version of this essay.

2. See John Carey, *The Intellectuals and the Masses* (London: Faber and Faber, 1992); and Andreas Huyssen, *After the Great Divide: Modernism, Mass Culture, Postmodernism* (Bloomington and Indianapolis: Indiana University Press, 1986). While authors such as James Joyce and T. S. Eliot often worked with forms of, and with references to, popular culture, texts such as *Ulysses* and *The Waste Land* embed such popular shards in new and difficult forms that tend to exclude a broad audience.

3. Fredric Jameson, *Postmodernism or, The Cultural Logic of Late Capitalism* (Durham: Duke University Press, 1991), 318.

4. Arnold Bennett, *Fame and Fiction: An Enquiry into Certain Popularities* (London: Grant Richards, 1901), 5; *The Author's Craft* (London: Hodder and Stoughton, 1914), 11.

5. Jay Clayton discusses Dickens's postmodern "afterlife" at some length in "Is Pip Postmodern? Or, Dickens at the End of the Twentieth Century," in Charles Dickens, *Great Expectations*, ed. Janice Carlisle (Boston: Bedford Books, 1996), 606–24.

6. George Doran quoted in Reginald Pound, *Arnold Bennett: A Biography* (London: Heinemann, 1952), 228.

7. John Carey, *Intellectuals and the Masses*, 8, 20. Tellingly, Leopold Bloom fashions the pages of *Tit-Bits* into a serviceable toilet tissue in the "Calypso" episode of James Joyce's *Ulysses*, in a pointed modernist gesture to dispose of a popular cultural medium.

8. Carey, *Intellectuals and the Masses*, 16–17.

9. Carey, *Intellectuals and the Masses*, 21.

10. Huyssen, *After the Great Divide*, vii.

11. Carey, *Intellectuals and the Masses*, 152.

12. Bennett, *The Author's Craft*, 103.

13. Bennett, *Fame and Fiction*, 5.

14. Bennett, *Fame and Fiction*, 16.

15. Bennett, *Fame and Fiction*, 11.

16. Many of these books anticipate the self-help genre parodied in *The Simpsons* by Troy McClure, who appears in such videos as *Smoke Yourself Thin* and *Get Confident, Stupid!* See "Bart's Inner Child."

17. *The Truth About an Author* (New York: Doran, 1911), 5.

18. Letter to Wells, 30 September 1905, reprinted in *Arnold Bennett and H. G. Wells,* ed. Harris Wilson (Urbana: University of Illinois Press, 1960), 122–25.

19. Bennett, *The Author's Craft,* 23–24

20. Georg Lukács, *Realism in Our Time: Literature and the Class Struggle,* ed. Ruth Nanda Anshen, trans. John and Necke Mander (New York: Harper, 1962), 33, author's emphasis.

21. Lukács, *Realism in Our Time,* 19.

22. Williams, *The Long Revolution* (London: Chatto and Windus, 1961), 278.

23. Williams, *The Long Revolution,* 279.

24. Bennett, *The Author's Craft,* 19.

25. Lukács, *Realism in Our Time,* 43 (author's emphasis); Williams, *The Long Revolution,* 278.

26. Arnold Bennett, "The Progress of the Novel," *The Author's Craft and Other Critical Writings of Arnold Bennett,* ed. Samuel Hynes (Lincoln: University of Nebraska Press, 1968), 90–98.

27. Jameson, *Postmodernism,* 317, 318.

28. Kurt Andersen, "Animation Nation: The Toons Take Over." *New Yorker* 16 (June 1997): 7.

29. This dialectical resolution effaces, however, both "mass culture" and "avant-garde" as meaningful terms within the postmodern by sublating those terms.

30. Fredric Jameson, "Modernism and Imperialism," *Nationalism, Colonialism, and Literature,* ed. Terry Eagleton, Fredric Jameson, and Edward W. Said (Minneapolis: University of Minnesota Press, 1990), 50–51.

31. Jameson, "Modernism and Imperialism," 58.

32. Jameson, *Postmodernism,* 307.

33. Jameson, *Postmodernism,* 332. Jean-Paul Sartre, *Critique of Dialectical Reason, Vol. I: Theory of Practical Ensembles,* ed. Jonathan Rée, trans. Alan Sheridan-Smith (London: NLB, 1976), 45.

34. See Herbert Marcuse, "The Concept of Essence," *Negations,* trans. Jeremy J. Shapiro (Boston: Beacon, 1968).

35. Quoted in James Sterngold, "*The Simpsons* and Their Progeny Colonize Television in a Golden Era for Animation." *New York Times* 16 (March 1998): D8.

36. *The Simpsons's* emphasis upon totalization distinguishes it from other cultural forms that bridge the divide between high and low culture in the twentieth century. The Warner Brothers animated short *What's Opera, Doc?* (1957), for instance, features Bugs Bunny's ironic interpretations of operatic classics. *What's Opera, Doc?*

does not pretend, however, to marry its satirical treatment of high culture to any broader vision of modern social relations. Warner Brothers cartoons are of course bound up with the social history of the American twentieth century, as Kevin S. Sandler's recent collection of essays demonstrates, and yet they rarely explore social relations directly (and never in a comprehensive way). See Kevin S. Sandler, ed., *Reading the Rabbit* (New Brunswick, NJ: Rutgers University Press, 1998).

37. Garth Ancier quoted in Sterngold, "*The Simpsons* and Their Progeny," D8.

38. For example, Kim Basinger and Alec Baldwin select Springfield as their hideaway from Hollywood because "No one knows where it is" in "When You Dish Upon a Star."

39. See John Fiske, *Television Culture* (London: Methuen, 1987), especially 1–20, for a discussion of television's visual conventions. *The Simpsons* is certainly aware of its two-dimensional medium; a portion of the 1995 Halloween episode casts Homer and Bart into the third dimension, which they find extraordinarily alien. See "Treehouse of Horror VI."

40. Patricia Dane Rogers, "At Home with *The Simpsons*." *The Washington Post* 8 (January 1998, Late Edition): T5.

41. Rick Jacobson quoted in Sterngold, "*The Simpsons* and Their Progeny," D8.

42. Jouni Paakkinen, "Duff Beer for Sale," *The Simpsons Archive,* <http://www.snpp.com/news/040398.html#duff >, 4 February 2002.

43. Richard Corliss, "The Cartoon Character: Bart Simpson." *Time* 8 (June 1998): 204.

44. See Renee Hobbs, "*The Simpsons* Meet Mark Twain: Analyzing Popular Media Texts in the Classroom." *English Journal* (January 1998, English Edition): 49–51.

45. Corliss, "The Cartoon Character: Bart Simpson," 205.

46. Warner Brothers' *Duck Amuck* (1953), in which Daffy Duck finds himself compelled to explore his medium along with his animator, foregrounds such a modernist self-awareness of medium. At the end of the twentieth century, *The Simpsons* returns *Duck Amuck*'s modernist self-reflexivity from the exotic world of Hollywood cartoon production and Daffy's star contract to the realm of television consumption in quotidian Springfield, as Bart and Lisa watch *The Itchy & Scratchy Show* in their living room.

47. Ted Anthony, "TV Critic Traces Gen Xers' Fascination With TV, Media." *The Rockford Register Star* (4 June 1997): 4B; Andersen, "Animation Nation," 7–8.

48. Corliss, "The Cartoon Character: Bart Simpson," 204; Eugene Lunn, *Marxism and Modernism* (Berkeley: University of California Press, 1982), 2.

49. See, for instance, "D'oh-in' in the Wind," which features Grampa Simpson and his friend Jasper in a parody of Mike Judge's *Beavis and Butt-head*.

50. Bennett, *Anna,* 32.

51. Bennett, *Anna,* 43.

52. Bennett, *Anna,* 109–110.

53. Bart's act echoes similar tactics of the avant-garde, and particularly recalls a similar prank of the French lettrists—the "sabotage of the Easter high mass at Notre-Dame in 1950"—described by Christopher Gray in his Situationist anthology, in which a small group of 66 lettrists. . . . caught, gagged, stripped and bound one of the priests. [One] lettrist put on the priest's vestments and, just before the service was about to begin, gravely ascended the steps to the main pulpit. A moment's respectful silence. "*Frères, Dieu est mort,*" he said; and began benignly to discuss the implications of this conclusion. (Christopher Gray, *Leaving the 20th Century: The Incomplete Work of the Situationist International.* 1974. London: Rebel Press, 1998, 3.) The Lettrists—and perhaps Bart by extension—are practicing a form of what Guy Debord calls *détournement* (or diversion), an "insurrectional style," a "device" that responds to "the necessity for *distance* to be maintained toward whatever has been turned into an official verity" (*The Society of the Spectacle,* trans. Donald Nicholson-Smith. New York: Zone Books, 1994, 144–45). See also the stunt described by Greil Marcus: "On 17 November 1918 . . . Berlin dadaist Johannes Baader entered Berlin Cathedral. . . . In the heart of the cathedral . . . on horseback . . . he announced: . . ."CHRIST IS A SAUSAGE!" (*Lipstick Traces: A Secret History of the Twentieth Century.* Cambridge, MA: Harvard University Press, 1989, 314–15).

54. Liner notes, Iron Butterfly, *In-A-Gadda-Da-Vida,* Atco Records, 1968.

55. ALF (an acronym of "Alien Life Form") was a furry puppet character in a 1980s sitcom of the same name. "Remember ALF?" Milhouse quips. "He's back in POG form!" "POG" is the brand name for playing pieces—originally caps to bottles of papaya, orange, and guava (POG) fruit juice sold in Hawaii—in a game popular for several years in the mid-1990s.

56. Al Bundy's blasphemous "Church of No Ma'am" represents a more distasteful version of Homer's hedonistic faith in "Homer the Heretic." For a study of the relation of advertising and television programming, see Robin Andersen, *Consumer Culture and TV Programming* (Boulder: Westview, 1995), in which Andersen discusses *The Simpsons* as the kind of "meta-television" whose "strategies are by definition self-referential; they do not include . . . alternative views" (270).

57. This observation derives from the perspicuity of the students in my prose fiction course at Vanderbilt University in the fall semester 1995. They felt as though the car dealer had walked into a trap laid by *The Simpsons,* a feeling that crystallized for them an awareness of cultural critique. I qualify this awareness by saying it only "partially compensates" for the complicity with, say, the misogyny of *Married . . . with Children* because another group of students did not notice the ad at all. They felt that *The Simpsons* exists chiefly in its privileged fictional space and has little to do with its advertising context.

58. Whit Miller voiced this question—really an expression of skepticism about the efficacy of satire as an oppositional mode—in my prose fiction course at Vanderbilt University in the fall semester 1998.

59. Bennett, *Fame and Fiction,* 15.

60. *The Letters of D. H. Lawrence,* ed. Aldous Huxley (New York: Viking Press, 1937), 66–67.

61. "Mr. Bennett and Mrs. Brown," *Collected Essays,* ed. Leonard Woolf, 4 vols (New York: Harcourt, Brace, & World, 1967), 1.326.

62. Terry Eagleton, *The Illusions of Postmodernism* (Oxford: Blackwell, 1996), 132.

63. Quoted in M. S. Mason, "'Simpsons' Creator on Poking Fun." *Christian Science Monitor* (17 April 1998): B7.

64. Mason, "'Simpsons' Creator," B7.

65. See David Morley, *Television Audiences and Cultural Studies* (London: Routledge, 1992), especially Chapter Ten, "The Consumption of Television as a Commodity," for a discussion of the ways in which television viewing takes on a form similar "to that of the purchase of consumer goods" (213).

66. Andersen, "Animation Nation," 8.

67. John L. Allen, Jr., "'Simpsons,' Pop Culture and Christianity." *National Catholic Reporter* (17 July 1998): 25.

68. Ezekiel 2:9–10, 3:1, *King James Version.*

69. Revelation 10:9, *KJV.*

70. Were Anna to run away to Australia, she would no more oppose those institutions she finds oppressive than she does by marrying, for such migrations (ubiquitous in Dickens's fiction) attended British colonization of the globe and ultimately extended the reach of those very institutions.

71. Woolf and Lawrence, for instance, sought rhetorical spaces outside of the dominant order from which to mount oppositional attacks upon the culture of monopoly capitalism and patriarchy, respectively. Lawrence retreated into "primitive" spaces and the isolation of Taos, New Mexico (he also entertained notions of emigrating to rural Africa), while Woolf in *Three Guineas* (1938) proposed an "Outsiders' Society" that refused to respect the boundaries of the patriarchal state.

72. Michel Foucault, *The History of Sexuality: An Introduction,* trans. Robert Hurley (New York: Vintage, 1990), 95–96.

73. This conclusion also suggests that Foucault's thought is distinctly postmodernist, when *grands récits* and "great Refusals" are denied cultural loci of their own. Foucault's reading of resistance as bound up with power relations is, then, a historically and politically *necessary* insight if, as I have argued, the breakdown of narratives of totality precludes a space for oppositionality.

The Simpsons and Hanna-Barbera's Animation Legacy

MEGAN MULLEN

There is no doubt that *The Simpsons* was a remarkable addition to U.S. prime-time television when it first appeared as a series on the Fox network in 1990. Its longevity in prime time, as well as its success in syndication, attest that its appeal has been more than mere faddishness. Not only did *The Simpsons*'s animated format breathe new life into the tired family sitcom genre, it also brought to audiences a degree of social satire seldom seen in the mainstream media. Through its clever use of pastiche, this program has called attention to the flaws and hypocrisies of such sacred institutions as government, organized religion, and the health care system. It has asked us to scrutinize our adoration of public figures by bringing animated caricatures (often with the actual celebrity providing the voice) into the program's stories. And it has unapologetically extended both its messages and its images into popular culture at large through both authorized and unauthorized marketing tie-in products.

As innovative and successful as the program has been, *The Simpsons* has not been the first of its kind. Its creators have readily (and humorously) acknowledged that they are indebted to a much earlier effort in television animation: Hanna-Barbera's "prehistoric" animated sitcom *The Flintstones,* which debuted in prime time on ABC in September 1960. In *The Simpsons* episode "Kamp Krusty," the Simpson family, as usual, is shown arriving home in chaotic fashion, only this time they find Fred and Wilma Flintstone sitting on their couch (perhaps watching themselves on television). In "Marge vs. the Monorail," the first scene after the opening credits and commercial break finds Homer leaving work in a sequence that mimics the opening credits of *The Flintstones.* The whistle blows and Homer jumps into his car singing, "Simpson, Homer Simpson. He's the

63

greatest guy in his-to-ry. From the town of Springfield, he's about to hit a chestnut tree." At the point where Homer actually does crash into the tree, the song ends and the episode—narratively unrelated to this homage sequence—begins. These tributes not only add to *The Simpsons*'s extensive repertoire of intertextual images, they remind audiences of a rich tradition in television animation.

This essay surveys and theorizes historical precedents for *The Simpsons,* specifically those set by *The Flintstones* as well as its "space age" counterpart, *The Jetsons,* by discussing the factors leading up to the creation of these programs in the early 1960s and situating them within the dominant situation comedy paradigm of their era. It then looks at how these programs tapped into animation's extraordinary capacity for pastiche as a form of ironic humor. Finally, it surveys the success of the programs in syndication and their extraordinary merchandising longevity. The ultimate goal is to show how *The Simpsons,* remarkable as it has been, had some significant animation predecessors to help guide its creation. It is hard to know how aware *The Flintstones*'s creators might initially have been of any subversive potential in their program. Viewing it in retrospect, however, we can observe embryonic forms of modern "adult cartoon" satire that would be explored more thoroughly in *The Simpsons* and its progeny.

HANNA-BARBERA'S PRIME-TIME SITCOMS

In 1960, the three-year-old Hanna-Barbera Productions noted some surprising reactions to its afternoon children's cartoon variety show, *Huckleberry Hound.*[1] Apparently adults were watching the program, too. As reported in *Newsweek,* fan mail even included a petition from seven scientists working at Los Alamos, New Mexico, to have *Huckleberry Hound* moved to a timeslot later in the day so they would not miss it.[2] Veteran cartoonists William Hanna and Joseph Barbera saw in this surprising fandom a new potential audience for television animation. So, drawing from existing conventions for domestic family sitcoms—a genre that had come to comprise a large portion of the prime-time schedule by that point—Hanna-Barbera Productions began to develop a cartoon that would address both adults and children.

As Hanna recalls, he in particular had been fond of *The Honeymooners,* the popular working-class sitcom from the early 1950s, and wanted to model an animated sitcom family on that show's main characters, Ralph and Alice Kramden. Since animation offered a potential for exotic and fantastic settings to an extent unattainable by live-action television, it was decided that the prime-time cartoon should take place in a time other than the present day. Hanna-Barbera considered several prototype characters and families, including Pilgrims and toga-clad Romans, before deciding on what they called "a big-mouthed guy wearing animal skins."[3]

As a married couple, Fred and Wilma are similar to other sitcom couples. Fred holds a less-than-fulfilling blue-collar job and frequently is in conflict with his boss, Mr. Slate. However, he occasionally also takes on fantasy jobs or mingles with celebrity "guests." Wilma manages the household, though in this case it is a household filled with talking dinosaur "appliances." Fred and Wilma's best friends are their next-door neighbors, Barney and Betty Rubble. As with typical sitcom neighbors, the Rubbles provide both camaraderie and conflict in the Flintstones's lives. However, unlike typical live-action sitcoms, the characters' interactions are often accented with the sorts of unrealistic slapstick sight gags that are familiar to children's cartoons, such as when large objects fall on top of the characters and they emerge with only minor injuries (often symbolized by stars floating around the character's head). As will be discussed in more detail below, animation allowed *The Flintstones*'s creators to develop the familiar sitcom formula into something that turned the familiar, perhaps already clichéd, conventions of the genre inside out.

At the time of *The Flintstones*'s first episode, audiences and critics were not prepared for such an innovation in prime-time entertainment. Critic Gilbert Seldes, writing for *TV Guide,* suggested that *Flintstones* viewers were "settling for second and third best" and that the series easily could be supplanted by higher quality animation if such programming were to become available.[4] *Variety*'s review of the first episode proclaimed that *The Flintstones* did not have "staying power."[5] Of course, in retrospect we can laugh at the lack of prophecy in such observations; few television programs have maintained anything close to the cultural currency of *The Flintstones*. In fact, as early as *The Flintstones*'s second season, *Variety* had revised its assessment, explaining that the show had "matured sufficiently during its first season to be worthy of an adult as well as a juve [sic] following."[6] The program remained in ABC's prime-time line-up until September 1966. In September 1962, encouraged by the success of *The Flintstones,* ABC and Hanna-Barbera introduced audiences to *The Jetsons,* a thematically similar cartoon program that is set in a fully automated (though nonetheless dysfunctional) future.

THE SITCOM GENRE
AND THE RISE OF MAGICOMS

Looking at *The Simpsons* in the context of its animated ancestors can shed light on its success. *The Simpsons* entered into a well-established sitcom paradigm in 1990; the new show certainly surprised audiences but clearly did not alienate them. By that point, audiences were becoming used to the notion of live-action sitcoms challenging the status quo. During the 1970s, *All in the Family* had exposed the heated disagreements—political as well as personal—that typify real-life families, *The Mary Tyler Moore Show* questioned the assumed gender roles upon which most earlier sitcoms had rested, and a wave of other "socially relevant" sitcoms explored risky thematic territory. By the late 1980s, audiences were prepared for the in-your-face social commentary of programs such as *Roseanne*. When *The Simpsons* entered the scene, it was able to use animation to surpass the narrative capabilities of any of these live-action programs and thus to make some radical observations about the status quo. *The Simpsons* also owes some of its success as a generic variant to Hanna-Barbera's pioneering forays into prime time three decades earlier. These pioneering programs demonstrated that animation can accomplish much more than simply reproducing stock sitcom characters and themes in colorful, two-dimensional form.

The sitcom format was already well known by the time *The Flintstones* was first aired. In fact, this popular genre had emerged with commercial network television itself in the late 1940s and early 1950s. By 1959, there were more than a dozen sitcoms in the weekly prime time schedule. However, the situations typically portrayed in these comedies changed over the course of the decade. Working-class or ethnic comedy (e.g., *The Honeymooners, Mama, The Goldbergs*), with its frequently satirical bent, gave way to middle-class prosperity (in shows such as *Father Knows Best* and *Leave It to Beaver*). In large part, this shift can be attributed to a change in the dominant format of television sponsorship: from the single-sponsor format to the multiple-sponsor or "magazine" format. When commercial sponsors controlled program production, content not only could be tailored to accommodate commercial messages, those messages actually could be integrated into the program narratives. With multiple sponsors, the networks controlled program production and thus faced the challenge of making program content a showcase for a variety of commercial messages. Various scholars have suggested that the goal was to make the idealized lifestyle pitched to consumers during commercial breaks no less apparent in the sitcoms themselves.[7] The physical centerpiece of this utopia was a modern home with a host of "labor-saving" appliances. The central storyline revolved around a blissfully contented and extraordinarily unremarkable nuclear family whose minor dilemmas could be resolved within the diegetic timeframes of individual episodes.

Yet by 1960, the idealized "normal" family already had become clichéd, and producers were seeking ways to add variety to the sitcom formula, to make it less routine and predictable. Newer sitcoms began to parody the conventions of older sitcoms. This evolution is a typical stage in the progression of a popular entertainment genre: audiences can be assumed to be thoroughly familiar with plotlines and character types and therefore may be treated as insiders in jokes that are made about the genre.[8] Throughout the early-to-mid 1960s, sitcoms such as *Bewitched, The Munsters, The Addams Family, Mister Ed, I Dream of Jeannie,* and *My Mother the Car* began to populate prime time. These shows, known as "magicoms," invested otherwise ordinary domestic sitcom characters and settings with magical powers. These programs either anthropomorphized animals and machinery or they rewrote sitcom families as monsters and ghouls. In other words, magicoms parodied earlier domestic sitcoms by introducing fantasy elements into familiar formulas. While a model mom like Margaret Anderson of *Father Knows Best* might have made household chores seem incredibly simple, Samantha Stevens of *Bewitched* could make them disappear with a twitch of her nose. While the Cleavers of *Leave It to Beaver* maintained the status quo in Mayfield, the Munsters brought a somewhat different notion of domesticity to Mockingbird Heights.

A single character's superhuman abilities were the factor that distinguished magicoms like *Bewitched* and *I Dream of Jeannie* from earlier domestic sitcoms. The magical power seemed to call attention to the ordinariness of the other characters and the mise-en-scène. *The Munsters* and *The Addams Family* featured fantastic costumes and settings, yet the humor in these monster sitcoms was premised on the contrast between the main characters, who perceived themselves as normal, and the "real" world that existed beyond the gates of their large haunted houses. Both types of magicom were based on a parodic juxtaposition between the supernatural or weird and the status quo familiar to television audiences of the early 1960s. They did not try to undermine the status quo other than to draw attention to its monotony.

I would characterize magicoms as what Linda Hutcheon calls "post-modern parodies." She explains that "it is the complicity of [this form of] parody—its inscribing as well as undermining of that which it parodies—that is crucial to its ability to be understood."[9] To some extent, a post-modern parody opens possibilities for resistant or negotiated readings, but it neither encourages them nor allows them to alter the status quo. On *Bewitched,* Samantha is frequently reprimanded by her mortal husband Darren for using witchcraft to ease the burden of household chores. Darren feels that his position as family patriarch entitles him to as "normal" a life as possible and constantly struggles against his wife and her even less cooperative relatives to keep his domicile free of supernatural influences. Samantha, by frequently resorting to witchcraft in violation of her husband's stringent guidelines for "normal" behavior, might be understood as exposing or resisting certain hegemonic and patriarchal norms. Nevertheless, the sitcom formula is a static one, and Samantha's witchcraft can never permanently disrupt the Stevens's domestic sphere, much less alter the larger social structure.

THE FLINTSTONES, THE JETSONS, AND THE SITCOM GENRE

The Flintstones and *The Jetsons* also fit this pattern. Indeed, compared to live-action magicoms, these shows prove to be doubly parodic, both by having imaginary elements and by being animated. Animation allowed the programs' narratives to break away from verisimilitude in unprecedented ways. The magicom formula in general breathed new life into the predictable domestic family sitcom. *The Flintstones* and *The Jetsons* went beyond this by completely overturning "adult" verisimilitude, using narrative tools and conventions that had been the exclusive domain of children's fantasy. We can see that, like the live-action magicoms, these programs were able both to question and to reinforce the dominant social values typically represented in sitcoms.

The Flintstones

From the "stone-age" setting to the exaggerated physical features of the characters to the slapstick humor, nothing about *The Flintstones* looks real. Like many other sitcom households, the Flintstones's ranch-style cave boasts a typical collection of modern household appliances, only here they are portrayed as animals, such as a hungry vulture garbage disposal and a mastodon vacuum cleaner, who frequently discuss their tasks with the show's characters.

While this might seem odd in view of their apparently comfortable suburban lifestyle (even if in parody form), *Flintstones* characters themselves signify a working-class lifestyle more typical of early 1950s ethnic and working-class urban sitcoms than of late 1950s middle-class suburban sitcoms. *The Flintstones*'s personalities and physical attributes clearly establish the program as a successor to *The Honeymooners*. Fred and Wilma look, speak, and quarrel like Ralph and Alice Kramden. Fred and his buddy Barney Rubble belong to a fraternal organization similar to that of Ralph and his buddy Ed Norton. Fred (a dinosaur-crane operator), like Ralph (a bus driver), feels demeaned by his job. Both work for low wages, and both are fired and grudgingly rehired frequently over the course of the respective programs' extended narratives.

Also, the Flintstones's relationship with their neighbors, the Rubbles, is drawn directly from the Kramdens and the Nortons of *The Honeymooners*. Both programs represent situations in which ad hoc extended families substitute for the nuclear family. In both, the men represent the irrational children, while their wives are the adult, parental figures. Fred and Barney, like Ralph Kramden and Ed Norton, inevitably quarrel over something trivial or find themselves mired in ill-fated get-rich-quick schemes. Fred, like Ralph, tries to gain authority by outsmarting his friend. Even though *The Flintstones* and the Rubbles do eventually have children, unlike their live-action counterparts, the parent-child dynamic is subordinated to the already-established relationships among the adult characters. Fred and Barney continue to be childlike in their behavior as well.

Yet in spite of the similarities between *The Honeymooners* and *The Flintstones,* the latter was clearly a stage ahead in the evolution of the domestic situation comedy. Among sitcoms of its time, *The Flintstones* was an anomaly with regard to its class signifiers. As discussed above, the working-class sitcom formula had faded out several years before *The Flintstones* went into production. Low-income urban settings had become less popular with advertisers because the middle-class furnishings advertisers wanted to pitch during the shows seemed out of place there. *Honeymooners* narratives of social struggle and frustration would be completely unconvincing if set in a *Father Knows Best* home. As George Lipsitz has argued, even though financially strapped characters could make very compelling pitches about consumer products they longed to buy, this strategy also had the effect of calling attention to the expense and extravagance of the idealized middle-class lifestyle.[10] Among other things, *Honeymooners* episodes frequently remind viewers of the imprudence of relying on consumer credit for household luxuries.

In contrast, since everything about *The Flintstones*'s mise-en-scène is completely implausible to begin with, it makes no sense to question its compatibility with the program's narratives or characters. *Flintstones* episodes use fantasy to promote consumerism in a way remarkably similar to the contrived middle-class prosperity of its live-action counterparts: by making a host of consumer products seem essential to a comfortable home and by obscuring the means by which these products have been acquired. While both Ralph Kramden and Fred Flintstone transfer their job insecurities onto their domestic lives, Fred seems to have solved (or had solved for him through fantasy) many of the consumer difficulties Ralph was never able to surmount. *The Flintstones*'s fantasy element (clearly part of its children's programming heritage) makes it seem possible for this working-class couple to consume well beyond their means. On this program, consumer power does not seem directly tied to monetary wealth; a profusion of consumer gadgets and their ranch-style cave seem as natural to their lifestyle as the Kramdens' cramped apartment and outmoded appliances seemed to theirs.

The Flintstones thus uses the production and narrative conventions of children's cartoon programming to teach the values of consumerism in an innocuous way to viewers of all ages. On this program, fiscal impunity serves the interests of slapstick comedy as much as resistance to physical injury does. We do not expect Fred and Wilma to pay a price for their apparent extravagance any more than we expect Barney to be rushed to the hospital when Fred drops a bowling ball on his head. Financial capital seems to have been replaced by what might be called fantasy capital. The appliances are a given; we seldom witness their purchase, and we do not see Fred and Wilma debating about what they can afford. As farfetched as the individual stories might be, each episode of *The Flintstones* culminates in a restoration of domestic order.

Clearly, *The Flintstones*'s use of animated fantasy techniques to add novelty to a prime-time sitcom was years ahead of its time. Not only did this place it ahead of the curve in terms of production innovation, it gave the show an edge in its ability to promote consumerism.

The Jetsons

As did *The Flintstones, The Jetsons* exploited the capabilities of animation to overturn the generic conventions and expectations set by its live-action predecessors. On *The Jetsons,* the "latest" home appliances are a host of push-button gadgets that simplify the most complex jobs, clearly an exaggeration of the claims made by advertisers. Fixing meals is no more complicated than selecting which series of buttons to push (Jane Jetson often complains of her weary fingers), and parking the car is a matter of pushing a button to collapse it and pack it into a briefcase. Not unlike *The Flintstones*'s use of animation and slapstick both to challenge and to reinforce the status quo, *The Jetsons* uses animation to obliquely address some of the cultural tensions of the mid-twentieth century.

In exaggerating the supposedly simplified lifestyle brought about by appliances, the program seems to have drawn from an atmosphere of ambivalence and unease over the growing technologization of modern society. Some of this anxiety seems to have derived from a fear that patriarchal authority in the domestic sphere was being undermined by women's control over the new household technology. This "gray flannel rebel" theme, as described by Barbara Ehrenreich, and its manifestations as technological angst are dominant themes of *The Jetsons*.[11] To give an example: one of the plots in the series' first episode concerns appliances gone wrong.[12] The automatic food-preparer has short-circuited, so bacon is undercooked and eggs come out fried but cold. The state-of-the-art home has failed, and, unable to "cook" to her husband George's satisfaction, Jane, too, has failed. She pleads with George to buy a new machine, but he responds in effect that she is too demanding.

Yet this assertion of patriarchal authority is gradually undermined as the episode progresses. Forgetting about the defunct food preparer, George allows his boss, Mr. Spacely, to coerce him into a dinner invitation. George does nothing to prepare his wife for this. Fortuitously, however, and unbeknownst to George, Jane has hired a maid, Rosie, an antiquated robot with a personality reminiscent of television's Hazel. Rosie not only prepares a perfect dinner but also gives Spacely a piece of her mind, something that George has always wanted to do but has lacked the nerve. Spacely ultimately responds well, offering George a raise so that the family will be able to keep Rosie.

By the end of the episode, virtually all of the family's problems have been solved. George appears satisfied that both his work and domestic lives have been restored to order. The audience nonetheless realizes that the nature of his agency in this episode really comes down to his failure to have acted decisively and in accordance with the norm in two separate instances: by not providing the requisite consumer gadget for his wife and by allowing himself to be manipulated by his boss. George thereby has done more to create the dilemma than to solve it.

The job pressures always return for George Jetson; in fact, these are a major theme of nearly every *Jetsons* episode. He frequently falls victim to the ejector chair in Spacely's office or has to test potentially dangerous new inventions, and he perpetually submits to these abuses. At home, as a nuclear family patriarch, George's role might be compared to that of Jim Anderson of *Father Knows Best*. However, all the patriarchal authority vested in the congenial and competent Jim Anderson seems to have been inverted in George. Unlike Jim Anderson, who always has simple and instructive solutions to his family's dilemmas, George is well-intentioned but a perpetual failure who most often finds his wife, children, and even his dog extricating him from difficult situations.

The animated social critique of *The Jetsons* no doubt surpassed what was taking place in live-action sitcoms (even other magicoms) at the time. *The Jetsons*'s run in prime time lasted only one season. Much as its individual episode narratives were ahead of their time, the series as an extended narrative did not have nearly as much time for development and experimentation as *The Flintstones* did, particularly in the area of caricature and pastiche.

THE FLINTSTONES, THE SIMPSONS, AND PASTICHE

As do *The Simpsons* and other recent animated series, *The Flintstones* features rampantly intertextual narratives, a strategy that, as Mimi White has theorized, rewards regular television viewing (and therefore absorption of commercial messages) and helps the medium maintain a desirable balance of familiarity and novelty.[13] *Flintstones* narratives exploit animation's unique potential for caricature to "bring" animated versions of live-action television characters "to Bedrock." Such a commingling of celebrities with the prototypical "common man" is yet another way in which *The Flintstones* comically elides class divisions, making anything possible for its characters. Caricatured celebrities from throughout the entertainment world, including "Ann-Margrock," "Stoney Curtis," and "Roger Marble," frequently enter the day-to-day life of this extraordinary animated family.

Here the combination of "insider" appeal and attention-grabbing disjuncture seem ideally suited to network cross-promotion. In "Samantha," Betty and Wilma, having been left behind from their husbands' camping expedition, decide to introduce themselves to their new neighbors.[14] The neighbors turn out to be animated versions of Samantha and Darren Stevens from the concurrently airing ABC series *Bewitched* (voices provided by *Bewitched* actors Elizabeth Montgomery and Dick Sargent). As on any live-action *Bewitched* episode, Darren is warning his wife not to use her powers of magic ("So no hocus-pocus, okay? . . . It's for the best. It never really helps people, anyway").

This sort of intertextuality on *The Flintstones* was not limited to references to other sitcoms, either. In the classic February 1963 birth of Pebbles episode, the concurrently running ABC medical drama *Ben Casey* was the object of parody.[15] Fred, rushing through hospital corridors in search of his pregnant wife, encounters two doctors who bear striking resemblance to Dr. Ben Casey and his mentor, Dr. Zorba (with the older doctor addressing the younger as "Len"). Fred pauses long enough to glance up at a sign that flashes the words "on air," and says, "Hmm . . . I think I've seen those two before." In the case of *Ben Casey* especially, intertextual humor such as this would have been lost on young children. The medical drama, clearly aimed at adults, was aired during the latest hours of prime time.

Such a narrative strategy has been developed much more extensively in *The Simpsons*, making the program's intended audience very hard to determine. As with its Hanna-Barbera predecessors, *The Simpsons* never fails to please children with its bright colors, comical characters, and slapstick antics. But every *Simpsons* episode is also packed with cultural references that address a very wide audience, an audience so diverse, in fact, that it seems unlikely that any single viewer could notice all of them. In

"Marge vs. The Monorail," for example, Leonard Nimoy makes a guest appearance as himself (in animated form, of course). While various references are made to his role on *Star Trek*, there is also a brief allusion to his role as host of *In Search of . . .* , a documentary series that ran in syndication from 1976–1982. Few people under the age of 30 are likely to remember Nimoy's role in this obscure program about unexplained phenomena. The younger audience is much more likely to recognize the cartoon caricature of Luke Perry, a star of Fox's recently concluded series *Beverly Hills 90210*. In addition to the eclectic mix of celebrity "guests," this particular episode mimics everything from historical preservation efforts to the anonymous telephone voice that tells a caller that a number is out of service.

The Simpsons's extensive use of intertextuality is just one component of a much larger satiric sensibility. The program uses a different type of adult-oriented parody to poke fun at venerated, yet often flawed, social institutions. The humor in *The Simpsons*'s version of the television medical drama, the episode entitled "Homer's Triple Bypass," is clearly intended for mature sensibilities. After multiple heart attacks, Homer is told by his doctor that he needs a bypass operation. However, as Homer explains to his exasperated wife, he and his coworkers gave up health insurance so they could get a pinball machine in the employee lounge. But, Homer quips, there is no need to worry because "America's health care system is second only to Japan . . . Canada . . . Sweden . . . Great Britain . . . Well, all of Europe. But you can thank your lucky stars we don't live in Paraguay!" With no other options, they finally resort to the services of Dr. Nick Riviera, whose television advertisement promises that he will perform any operation for "only $129.95." Unfortunately, when Dr. Riviera arrives in the operating theater, his only recollections from medical school appear to be of fraternity parties. So brainy young Lisa Simpson, sitting in the gallery, calls out instructions to the inept surgeon, thus, presumably, saving her father's life. This *Simpsons* episode not only mocks the failings of the U.S. health care system, it uses familiar images from throughout popular culture to do so. For instance, Dr. Riviera's television pitch imitates the myriad commercials for litigation attorneys seen on late-night TV. Though narratively unrelated to the surgery plot, this episode also begins with a spoof to the popular "reality" program, *Cops*.

While it is clear that *The Simpsons* has built upon techniques used much earlier in *The Flintstones,* it is also clear that these techniques are much more developed in the later series. Part of *The Simpsons*'s success with parody and intertextuality must be attributed to a greater audience familiarity with these postmodern narrative devices. In the three decades between the debut of *The Flintstones* and that of *The Simpsons,* audiences have witnessed multiple spin-off programs, guest appearances in which a character from one program "visited" the characters of another, and public figures from "real life" visiting fictional television characters. One might even say that by 1990, animation was one of very few fresh vehicles for television comedy. Of course, the 1990 television audience was very different in this regard from the audience *The Flintstones* faced in the early 1960s. To begin with, it could be argued that *The Simpsons* owes some of its initial success to the fact that its television audience has had three decades of exposure to Hanna-Barbera cartoons.

THE FLINTSTONES AND *THE JETSONS*: RECONTEXTUALIZED AND REWRITTEN

As of the early-to-mid 1960s, subtle adult-oriented jokes apparently were not enough to alter the popular perception of cartoons as children's entertainment. The unusual look of *The Flintstones* undoubtedly helped shape the program's syndication afterlife, one very different from those of its live-action contemporaries. Innovative as it was, *The Flintstones* did not mark the beginning of a new prime-time programming trend. Instead, when its original prime-time episodes were discontinued in 1966, *The Flintstones* moved effortlessly into the children's programming market. Both *The Flintstones* and *The Jetsons* have remained extremely popular as children's entertainment.

Almost immediately following the 1966 discontinuation of the original episodes, *Flintstones* reruns began on NBC and ran on that network on Saturday mornings from January 1967 through September 1970. Since then, some 100 original *Flintstones* episodes have been widely available on independent broadcast stations, cable networks, and home video. The program is shown around the world and has been translated into approximately two dozen languages. Every context in which it has appeared on television has been one intended primarily for children. Unlike other off-network sitcoms, *The Flintstones* virtually never is scheduled for late evening or nighttime viewing. The position of *Flintstones* episodes on today's television is paralleled to a large extent by the location of *Flintstones* videos in the "children's" or "family" sections of video stores.

The Flintstones's irreverent intertextual humor made it ideally suited for its new target market since most successful children's programs also have appeal for adults, often in the form of pastiche-packed insider jokes (one only has to think of *Sesame Street* in this regard). Marsha Kinder has discussed how intertextuality in children's cartoons such as *Garfield, The Muppet Babies,* and *Teenage Mutant Ninja Turtles* appeals to viewers of different ages. She argues that the intertextual references potentially encourage consumption of the programs and their tie-in products beyond childhood.[16] *The Flintstones* seems even more lucrative in this respect since the original prime-time series blended humor appropriate to adults and children. The program does not bore adults because it was *produced* for adults. Rather than alienating child viewers, as many adult-themed shows do, however, *The Flintstones* allows children to observe adult behavior through the lens of a familiar entertainment format, the cartoon. This technique gives children a chance to laugh at adults while also subtly teaching them about expected social roles and consumer behavior.

This entertainment strategy eventually was extended into new *Flintstones*-based productions. In addition to the adoption of the original episodes for use as children's entertainment, *Flintstones* characters began to be recycled into new children's narratives in the early 1970s, further fixing their new role in the public mind.[17] Among a lengthy list of remakes and reissues, *Flintstones* characters have been featured in the Hanna-Barbera children's program, *Pebbles and Bamm-Bamm* (which ran Saturday mornings in 1971–72 and 1975–76), and the related *Flintstones Comedy Hour* (which ran in 1972–73). The comic intertextuality and generic mixing that characterized the original *Flintstones* resurfaced in these programs, although this time around the parody was aimed at juvenile sensibilities. For example, a running theme of *The Flintstones Comedy Hour* finds Wilma and Betty as erstwhile newspaper reporters who often encounter a misguided superhero called Captain Caveman, clearly a parody of the popular Saturday morning superhero programs. In Hanna-Barbera's more recent animated children's series, *The Flintstones Kids* (1986–88), Fred, Wilma, Barney, and Betty appear in "miniature"—child versions of the original characters—a popular Saturday morning format also used in such programs as *The Brady Kids* and *The Muppet Babies*.

These examples are evidence of Hanna-Barbera's satisfaction (as well as that of the general television audience) with the success of *The Flintstones* as children's programming along with the wealth of other *Flintstones* media products targeted toward children. Nevertheless, the impulse to draw adult viewers as well has not disappeared. The most radical remake of the original *Flintstones* series so far, and no doubt an attempt at restoring *The Flintstones*'s combined adult-child following, was the star-studded 1994 live-action theatrical film, *The Flintstones: The Movie.*[18] While most of the movie, particularly the special effects that included large mechanized puppets from Jim Henson's Creature Shop, was designed to appeal to children, there was no shortage of gratuitous sexual innuendo and other "adult" content.

As a heavily promoted $45 million summer blockbuster, the movie drew a fairly large audience, and it was mildly entertaining. Any true *Flintstones* aficionado, however, probably would contend that the live-action movie is much less of a genuine *Flintstones* narrative than are any of the animated children's remakes. The persistent centrality of the *Flintstones* cartoon images in our culture and the ability of animation, as a narrative strategy, to extend fantasy beyond the limits of even the most sophisticated special effects undercut the overall impact of the film. The theatrical version is a rather clever parody of the original *Flintstones*—an insider joke for people who grew up with *The Flintstones*—since it is packed with references not only to the original series but also to its creation (e.g., Fred is mistakenly referred to as "Mr. Flagstone," the name Hanna and Barbera originally gave the animated character), but the all-too-familiar Hollywood face of John Goodman seems an unconvincing imitation of the even more familiar cartoon face of Fred Flintstone. While remaking *The Flintstones* as a live-action movie confirmed the original characters' cultural currency, it does not seem to have changed significantly the ways in which we understand or relate to them. We still think of the original *Flintstones* series, not the more recent movie, when these fictional characters are mentioned.

Like its "prehistoric" cartoon counterpart, *The Jetsons* has enjoyed considerable longevity as children's entertainment. Indeed, syndication made *Jetsons* reruns so popular that Hanna-Barbera produced enough new episodes specifically for the syndication market to bring the total package up to 75: 41 new episodes in 1985 and 10 more in 1987. *The Jetsons: The Movie,* an animated feature, played in theaters in summer 1990, and *The Jetsons* characters have "met" the Flintstone characters in an animated made-for-television/video feature, *The Jetsons Meet The Flintstones.* Characters from the two series have also appeared in animated television specials alongside other Hanna-Barbera favorites such as Yogi Bear and Scooby-Doo.

The longevity of *The Flintstones* and *The Jetsons* is unique for sitcoms. Of course, many live-action sitcoms have remained popular in syndication, and like them original episodes of *The Flintstones* and *The Jetsons* continue to entertain audiences today at least as much as they did during their original runs in the early 1960s. Nearly four decades after the shows' initial conception, audiences remain extraordinarily familiar with their characters, and most people can recite a few plotlines from original episodes. However, these programs are not at all appropriate to the nostalgia-evoking programming strategies used by cable networks like Nick at Nite and TV Land to showcase live-action reruns. *The Flintstones* and *The Jetsons* lack any verisimilitude and therefore refer only obliquely to the era of their creation. These programs were fantasies to begin with, so it would be ridiculous to say they appear either outdated or "classic" today. It is true that these cartoon programs carried on a tradition of social parody familiar to early 1960s prime-time sitcom audiences, including both adults and children, but it should not be surprising that when *The Flintstones* and *The Jetsons* entered syndication in the late 1960s, they were immediately enlisted as children's entertainment, an identity reinforced by subsequent remakes that featured versions of the original characters in narratives clearly aimed at young sensibilities.

There are already indications that *The Simpsons* will increase its juvenile following in syndication as well. This development might seem surprising. Ever since the series' first season, when Bart Simpson uttered the phrase, "I'm Bart Simpson. Who the hell are you?" some parents and educators have lamented the poor example set by the program. Children watching this cartoon program are exposed to at least as many dirty words, adult themes, and danger-provoking antics as they would see on most live-action sitcoms. Yet the show's prime-time slot continues to be Sunday at 8:00 P.M. EDT, and reruns tend to appear during the dinner hour. *Simpsons*-licensed merchandise continues to be aimed at children, and there has been relatively little recent outcry about the program's influence. As a cartoon, *The Simpsons,* like its Hanna-Barbera predecessors, is naturally suited to a cultural role that appeals to many and alienates few.

CARTOON CHARACTERS
AS ADVERTISING ICONS

Cartoon figures in general are colorful, defy verisimilitude, and have distinctive features that are easily reproduced. Add to this their established popularity among the population at large, and it is easy to see why cartoon characters serve as excellent advertising "spokespersons" who also can be used as product logos. These characters are eternally familiar, since their looks are fixed (e.g., they do not cut their hair or change their clothes without some sort of narrative motivation). Cartoons do not visibly feature live actors who could have aged or moved on to new roles, so there is no potentially jarring disjuncture between their original and later appearances.

Moreover, cartoon characters have no off-screen lives that might make them seem irrelevant to younger generations or interfere with the intended meanings of commercial messages. With human performers, there always is a risk that off-screen behavior will shed an unfavorable light on on-screen performances (in this context, consider the negative publicity for Hertz Rent-a-Car following the murder trial of its spokesperson, OJ Simpson). Fred Flintstone and Barney Rubble have been pitching Flintstones vitamins and Pebbles cereal successfully for years, in addition to being featured in bold colors on the packages.

In fact, the original *Flintstones* characters have appeared in various non-narrative or quasi-narrative commercial contexts. These have included:

> advertising for Winston cigarettes, One-a-Day vitamins, Pebbles cereal, and Welch's grape juice; a Busch beer promotional film; Viewmaster reels adventures; the 1966 TV special *Alice in Wonderland (Or What's a Nice Kid Like You Doing In a Place Like This?)*; trading cards; comic books; campaigns for Operation Baby Buckle, the American Humane Society, the American Automobile Association's safety program, and Easter Seals; the prevention special "Strong Kids, Safe Kids"; television retrospectives on the show; a theme ride at Universal Studios; and the hundreds of licensed and unlicensed products that form a highly lucrative collectors' market.[19]

Commercial use of *Flintstones* characters has become so commonplace we barely notice new instances.

Adults find the characters appealing, and the use of *Flintstones* characters can add flair to otherwise drab product pitches and public service announcements. But the children's market has been where *The Flintstones* has proven most profitable and instructive to its creators. Perhaps *The*

Flintstones's enduring appeal to children came as a surprise to its producers, Hanna and Barbera, but the lesson has hardly been lost on the prolific animation company they founded. Hanna-Barbera has remained at the forefront of linking children's television programs to consumer products. They have successfully produced cartoon programs whose narratives easily accommodate tie-in products, and they have aggressively pursued the strategic partnerships that make those tie-ins work. Along with the various *Flintstones* sequels and remakes, Hanna-Barbera has produced such children's favorites as *The Adventures of Jonny Quest; Scooby-Doo, Where Are You?; Josie and the Pussycats; The Smurfs;* and *Pound Puppies,* all of which have led to various licensed products such as lunch boxes, coloring books, action figures, and games.[20]

The innovative production style of *The Flintstones* expanded the number of situations in which we encounter this particular sitcom family and the possible life-stages at which we might become familiar with them. The authorized remakes and authorized licensing of *The Flintstones* discussed so far in this essay, however, have given us a finite set of behaviors to expect from characters all controlled by the commercial interests of Hanna-Barbera. So perhaps a more telling indicator of the program's cultural endurance, particularly regarding adults' continued relationships with the program, is the amount of *unlicensed* appearances it has generated. In the case of *The Flintstones,* these range from cheap imitations of popular *Flintstones*-licensed merchandise to the characters' incorporation in political cartoons to risqué reconfigurations of their images. *Flintstones* pornography and other unauthorized uses actually are fairly common, available widely on the Internet, and sometimes featured in alternative music venues.

One particularly notable departure from authorized uses of *Flintstones* characters is an illustration (captioned "Betty Gets It!") that appeared in a 1992 issue of *QW*, a publication for gays and lesbians.[21] The drawing features Wilma and Betty (with anatomies we never knew they had) in an intense sexual encounter. Portraying *Flintstones* characters as homosexual lovers (a practice known as "slashing") could be seen as an attempt to subvert some of mainstream culture's most popular and "safe" commercial icons.[22] Surely it is a radical break from the narratives of the original *Flintstones* series and even more of a radical break from subsequent *Flintstones* narratives produced especially for children. It also speaks fairly directly to the heterosexual, patriarchal norms reinforced by most of commercial television, including the various *Flintstones* series. If the Wilma and Betty illustration seems more shocking than other pornographic images, it is because the narrative universe of the domestic sitcom is so static, so predictable, and so indelibly inscribed within cultural memory. It is also because *The Flintstones* has been absorbed by the supposedly innocent world of children's programming.

Not surprisingly, this "Trojan horse" capacity of *The Flintstones* is even more fully developed in *The Simpsons*. In the case of *The Flintstones*, it is more an effect of the program's long-term familiarity, but it is built into the narrative of virtually every *Simpsons* episode. As a cartoon, *The Simpsons* has virtually guaranteed appeal to children. With its bright colors, comical characters, and slapstick comedy, the show resembles not only *The Flintstones* and *The Jetsons* but also a large portion of the Saturday morning and after-school programming menu. Yet, as indicated throughout this essay, *The Simpsons* offers a very sophisticated second level of entertainment that is obviously meant for adults. *Simpsons* episodes are rich with pastiche, quotation, cultural critique, and insider jokes, so much so that no viewer is likely to absorb every one without multiple viewings. As Douglas Rushkoff suggests in *Media Virus!* the childlike innocence of *The Simpsons*'s narrative form and its widespread popularity allow its creators to release some radical ideas into the cultural mainstream.[23] The fact that the program's producers, through extensive licensing, embrace the commercialism that surrounds *The Simpsons* only reinforces this effect. Could *The Simpsons* be slashed (or used in some similar unauthorized fashion) as *The Flintstones* has been? The question hardly seems relevant. The subversive content deliberately inscribed in every *Simpsons* episode would make any unauthorized use of the show seem trite. Unlike *The Flintstones*, *The Simpsons* has embodied inventive rebelliousness from the start; if any jokes *were* to be played using *Simpsons* characters, the show's creators would no doubt be among those laughing the loudest.

CONCLUSIONS

The Simpsons, with its very successful variety of animated humor, has had imitators since its 1990 debut. A wave of cartoon family (or quasi-family) sitcoms has followed *The Simpsons* on the various new television networks, including Fox's *King of the Hill,* MTV's *Daria,* and Comedy Central's *South*

Park. Indeed, animation in general made a brief comeback in prime-time schedules. While not family sitcoms specifically, such programs as MTV's *Beavis and Butt-head* and *Liquid Television,* Comedy Central's *Dr. Katz,* ABC's *The Critic,* and The Cartoon Network's *Spaceghost* have all enjoyed some popularity. Of course, the success of any new generic variant introduced on contemporary television owes some credit to the proliferation of new television networks—both broadcast and cable—that began in the 1980s. Certainly the fledgling Fox network's drive to pull in young audiences had a lot to do with its cultivation of *The Simpsons* after the cartoon had been spun off *The Tracey Ullman Show. The Simpsons* unquestionably established a popular prime-time programming trend for the 1990s.

All of these programs, in turn, owe a different sort of debt to Hanna-Barbera's two early cartoon sitcoms. As has been discussed, the narrative devices that make *The Simpsons* (and its successors) so appealing were not entirely new in 1990. Rather, the new series picked up the threads left hanging by animated prime-time series that had debuted decades earlier. The creators of *The Flintstones* and *The Jetsons* had exploited the unique potential of animation as a device to convey irony in an innocuous way, a strategy inherited and further developed by *The Simpsons*'s creators decades later. While the sitcom genre itself offers a way to pack stories about common human experiences into less than thirty minutes, animation eliminates any need to meet expectations of verisimilitude. As with children's cartoons, viewers approach these "adult" cartoon sitcoms with suspended disbelief, and in the process absorb significant social commentary. How many of us would have laughed at Dr. Riviera's careless heart surgery if Homer Simpson's character had been played by a human actor? Probably not many. But we can laugh at an unrealistic looking *caricature* of a human being who, in any other episode, probably would have inflicted even more harm on himself, whether by crashing his car into a tree or by behaving negligently at his nuclear power plant job. And in the process of watching Homer's unbelievable antics, we are reminded of important truths about our society.

The Flintstones and *The Jetsons* may have poked fun at the institution of marriage or the hypocrisies employees face in the workplace, but the critical insights on these programs were never as pointed or expository as those regularly incorporated into *Simpsons* narratives. In this sense, *The Simpsons* has indeed carved out new territory in television comedy. Yet this does not contradict the claim that *The Flintstones* and *The Jetsons* were also breakthroughs in television entertainment. These early Hanna-Barbera efforts were as novel as prime-time sitcoms reasonably could be at the time. Their syndication and marketing after lives attest to an appeal not fully understood by audiences (or, perhaps, even by Hanna and Barbera themselves) during their ABC prime-time runs: the capacity to entertain not by segmenting the audience into adults and children, but rather by offering narratives rich enough to bridge gaps among different generations of viewers.

What will the future hold for *The Simpsons*? *The Flintstones* and *The Jetsons* give us some clues about the long-term fortunes of *The Simpsons*. The longevity and popularity of the earlier programs has been comprised of many of the same factors that have made *The Simpsons* such a smash hit: broad-based appeal, unchanging characters, amenability to the tie-in market, to name a few. Perhaps if we can still turn on our televisions in 2025 and find Homer, Marge, Bart, Lisa, and Maggie grinning back at us—as we surely do today with *Flintstones* and *Jetsons* characters—then we will know that the pioneering Hanna-Barbera programs have found their legitimate heir.

NOTES

1. Along with the title character, this program introduced audiences to such characters as Yogi Bear, Mr. Jinx, Pixie and Dixie, and Snagglepuss.

2. "Too Good for the Brats?" *Newsweek* (18 July 1960): 84.

3. William Hanna and Joseph Barbera, Introduction. *Flintstones Personal Favorites* [videocassette], Vestron: 1988.

4. Review of *The Flintstones. TV Guide* (18 March 1961): 15.

5. "Chan," review of *The Flintstones. Variety* (5 October 1960).

6. "Herm," review of *The Jetsons. Variety* (26 September 1962).

7. See especially Mary Beth Haralovich, "Sit-coms and Suburbs: Positioning the 1950s Homemaker," in *Private Screenings: Television and the Female Consumer* (Minneapolis: University of Minnesota Press, 1992), 110–41; Lynn Spigel, *Make Room for TV: Television and the Family Ideal in Postwar America* (Chicago: University of Chicago Press, 1992); and George Lipsitz, *Time Passages: Collective Memory and American Popular Culture* (Minneapolis: University of Minnesota Press, 1992).

8. See, for example, Thomas Schatz's theory of genre in *Hollywood Genres* (New York: Random House, 1981).

9. Linda Hutcheon, *The Politics of Postmodernism* (New York: Routledge, 1989), 105.

10. George Lipsitz, *Time Passages: Collective Memory and American Popular Culture* (Minneapolis: University of Minnesota Press, 1990).

11. Barbara Ehrenreich, *The Hearts of Men: American Dreams and the Flight from Commitment* (New York: Anchor, 1983), 39.

12. "Rosie the Robot," ABC, September 23, 1962.

13. "Crossing Wavelengths: The Diegetic and Referential Imaginary of American Commercial Television." *Cinema Journal* 25 (Winter 1986): 51–64.

14. "Samantha," ABC, November 22, 1965.

15. "The Blessed Event," ABC, February 22, 1963.

16. *Playing With Power in Movies, Television, and Video Games: From Muppet Babies to Teenage Mutant Ninja Turtles* (Berkeley: University of California Press, 1991), 43–44.

17. It should be pointed out that several live-action sitcoms have been remade as children's cartoons (Hanna-Barbera alone has produced *The Addams Family, The Partridge Family: 2200 A.D., Fonz and the Happy Days Gang, Mork and Mindy,* and *Laverne and Shirley*), but this has not caused the original programs to be understood exclusively as children's entertainment.

18. *The Flintstones,* prod. Steven Spielberg, dir. Brian Levant, MCA/Universal, 1994. John Goodman (Fred), Rick Moranis (Barney), Elizabeth Perkins (Wilma), Rosie O'Donnell (Betty), and Elizabeth Taylor (Wilma's mother, Pearl Slaghoople) appear in costumed versions of the original animated characters. Kyle MacLachlan (Cliff Vandercave) and Halle Berry (Sharon Stone) play the villains in the movie's embezzlement plot.

19. This list was found on the WWW site, "*The Flintstones* and Hanna-Barbera" <http://www.topthat.net/webrock/faq/faq27.htm>, maintained by John Paul Murphy.

20. For example, in the 1961 Little Golden Book, *The Flintstones,* Fred and Wilma have a son named Junior Flintstone and a pet dinosaur named Harvey. The characters' physical features also differ slightly from those in the television series.

21. "Betty Gets It!" [illustration]. *QW* (26 July 1992): 33.

22. The term "slashing" is derived from the punctuation used to denote the newly defined relationship (for example, "K/S" fan culture suggests a homoerotic relationship between Star Trek's Kirk and Spock). As Henry Jenkins and others have discussed, subcultural groups have been known to "rewrite" media texts, ascribing romantic relationships to familiar pairs of television characters, so as to give the narratives new, less complicitous, meanings. See his *Textual Poachers: Television Fans and Participatory Culture* (New York: Routledge, 1992).

23. Douglas Rushkoff, *Media Virus! Hidden Agendas in Popular Culture* (NY: Ballantine Books, 1996).

Countercultural Literacy:
Learning Irony with *The Simpsons*

KEVIN J. H. DETTMAR

A s American culture has in the past two or three decades adopted an increasingly ironic mode of expression, a number of commentators have become troubled at the prospect of a public rhetorical field in which nothing is—indeed, nothing can be—affirmed. Instead, an all-purpose irony is used primarily to reinforce and reinscribe an "ingroup" (wink-wink, nudge-nudge): yes, of course, The Cardigans's "Lovefool" is a bad song, but those of us in the know understand that it's bad on purpose. If you didn't get it, looks like you're the fool.

Irony, this argument runs, has become reactionary rather than revolutionary; instead of critique, irony is used to reassure the hip kids that they are still hip, and the status quo is in the process smirkingly reaffirmed. The most prominent recent spokesperson for this viewpoint—though it now looks like his fifteen minutes of fame may have run out—is Jedediah Purdy, whose 1999 manifesto, *For Common Things: Irony, Trust, and Commitment in America Today,* suggests that

> We practice a form of irony insistently doubtful of the qualities that would make us take another person seriously: the integrity of personality, sincere motivation, the idea that opinions are more than symptoms of fear or desire. We are wary of hope, because we see little that can support it. Believing in nothing much, especially not in people, is a point of vague pride, and conviction can seem embarrassingly naive.[1]

To commentators with a long cultural memory, the style of irony Purdy and others condemn looks suspiciously like the modernist irony of writers like T. S. Eliot and Ezra Pound, deployed in an attempt to shore up something like an elite cultural Tradition in the face of contemporary anarchy. And yet postmodern irony, and postmodernism more generally, were supposed to be different: more democratic, more inclusive, more open and fluid.

Thus a genuinely postmodern irony, some would say, must not be content simply to wield the considerable rhetorical power of a sophisticated irony—as fun as that exercise is—but must at the same time make the discourse of irony accessible to all honest seekers: irony, in other words, ought to be democratic, rather than smugly hermetic. And here, of course, we run into a significant obstacle. For according to the unwritten rules of contemporary artistic discourse, irony that tips its hand is not really irony; indeed, the trajectory of ironic discourse since the beginning of the twentieth century (Joseph Conrad's *Heart of Darkness* [1898] makes a convenient marker) has been toward a less clearly inflected, more carefully disguised, irony.[2] Although profoundly distasteful in many respects, Bret Easton Ellis's 1991 novel *American Psycho* makes a brilliant case study in postmodern irony; it is, for all intents and purposes, completely unmarked in its irony (which, of course, then begs the question of whether it is in fact ironic).

There is nothing new about putting irony on prime-time television: *M*A*S*H* (1972–83) did a masterful job of combining verbal and situational ironies to underscore the absurdity of war, and *All in the Family* (1971–79) was the first sitcom to feature a dysfunctional American family whose patriarch was satirically castigated by nearly everyone who walked in the Bunker's front door. The progenitor of the form, *The Honeymooners,* was ironic to the core—or at least centered on a character sarcastic to his very core: "You're a real gem, Alice. A real gem." These programs, however, trafficked in what Wayne Booth would call "stable irony": their irony was *intended* ("deliberately created by some human beings to be heard or read and understood with some precision by other human beings"), *covert* ("intended to be reconstructed with meanings different from those on the surface"), *stable* ("once a reconstruction of meaning has been made, the reader is not then invited to undermine it with further demolitions and reconstructions"), and *finite* ("the reconstructed meanings are in some sense local, limited").[3]

All in the Family is often invoked in discussion of *The Simpsons,* and for good reason: of all *The Simpsons*'s television forebears (*The Honeymooners* and its cartoon stepchild *The Flintstones,* satiric targets such as

Ozzie and Harriet and *Father Knows Best*), it owes the most to *All in the Family*. This debt is acknowledged quite openly by the program itself. In "Make Room for Lisa," for instance, Homer takes Lisa and Bart to see a traveling exhibition from the Smithsonian Institute. Homer unwittingly pulls the Bill of Rights out of an unguarded display case—the guards and visitors are much more interested in seeing Fonzie's jacket—and he sits down in Archie Bunker's wing chair to read it.[4] Immediately he is accosted by two security guards, who ironically assault him using the kind of language we have learned to expect from the erstwhile occupant of that chair:

SECURITY OFFICER #1: Get out of Archie Bunker's chair. Now!

HOMER: Relax! I'm just boning up on the old Constitution.

SECURITY OFFICER #2: Oh! You're going to regret that, Pinko! [Raises his billy club to strike Homer]

[Homer cowers, holding the Bill of Rights in front of his face]

SECURITY OFFICER #1: I'm so sick of people hiding behind the Bill of Rights!

SECURITY OFFICE #2: Look! He got chocolate on it!

HOMER: I didn't mean to! Look! [Homer licks the chocolate off; unfortunately, some of the ink comes off as well]

SECURITY OFFICER #1: Mn-hn. You just licked off the part that forbids cruel and unusual punishment.

SECURITY OFFICER #2 [pounding brass knuckles into his palm]: Heh heh heh. Beautiful.

A number of ironies are put into play in this thirty-second scene. To begin with, Homer Simpson is visually likened to Archie Bunker as he sits in his chair; Groening and his writers, rather than erasing the television genealogy of *The Simpsons*, here mockingly embrace it. That an adult, literate American should be unfamiliar with the Bill of Rights is probably not ironic, since surveys have shown that when Americans are read sections of the Bill of Rights without the source being identified, they often object to it. That one of the officers would call Homer a "Pinko"—and surely that is an Archie Bunker word—for reading the Bill of Rights is ironic; the Bill of Rights is one thing even Archie Bunker would acknowledge separates us from the "Pinkos." The other officer's complaint about citizens "hiding behind the Bill of Rights" is made quite literal as Homer attempts to shield himself from the blows of the officers with the actual manuscript (and in an ironic sight gag, the Bill of Rights is made to look quite flimsy when faced with night sticks). One of the rights outlined there, of course, is intended to protect citizens from abuse at the hands of the police. Finally, it is ironic in some cosmic sense—some Alanis Morrisette sense, really—that in defacing the Bill of Rights Homer effaces the section that protects him from cruel and unusual punishment. Such surely awaits him; hard blows are a-gonna fall.

The Simpsons is the most consistently, intelligently ironic show on television. Running against the implicit logic of the sitcom, it relentlessly works to explore and exploit the gap between the American Dream and contemporary American reality. Douglas Rushkoff observes that "the Simpson family is meant as a nineties answer to the media reality presented to us in the fifties and sixties. This is the American media family turned on its head, told from the point of view of not the smartest member of the family, but the most ironic."[5] The Simpsons does not resolve the large structural problems of American culture in twenty-three minutes, as The Cosby Show, for example, typically did; instead, the show suggests that the culture's flaws are too deep and longstanding to admit of simple answers, but that one can remain happy and sane living at a somewhat oblique angle to that culture. Thus, The Simpsons doesn't always eschew the traditional sitcom "happy ending," but that happy ending is likely to be the commitment to continue living on the margins of the American Dream rather than being magically reconciled to it.

In a program that seeks to expose the foibles of our culture without flinching, irony is the obvious analytical tool of choice. On one level, The Simpsons's pervasive irony is just a manifestation of an even more rampant self-consciousness. The critique of television generally, and the gentle and not-so-gentle barbs directed at the Fox network specifically, are extremely important elements of the program, of course, though I will not explore them in detail here. I do want to pause, however, to consider the way The Simpsons focuses on "scenes of viewing" and attempts to situate us as viewers. Rushkoff quotes one of the show's writers, Al Jean, as saying "Some of the most creative stuff we write comes from just having the Simpsons watch TV." Rushkoff continues: "Many episodes are *about* what happens on their TV set, allowing the characters to feed off television, which itself is feeding off other television."[6] The show frequently opens with the family gathered around the tube, reflecting the posture of many of its suburban viewers as they sit to watch the week's new episode. Indeed, the famous opening credit sequence always ends with some variation of the family jockeying for position on the sofa in front of the set. In "And Maggie Makes Three," for instance, the opening credits fade down as the Simpsons are watching an episode of *Knight Boat,* a parody of the pre-*Baywatch* David Hasselhoff vehicle *Knight Rider.* The plot is completely outlandish, but Homer is taken in:

> MICHAEL: Come on, Knight Boat! We've gotta catch those starfish poachers.
>
> KNIGHT BOAT: You don't have to yell, Michael. I'm all around you.
>
> MICHAEL: Oh no, they're headed for land. We'll never catch them now.
>
> KNIGHT BOAT: Incorrect. Look. A canal.
>
> HOMER: Go, Knight Boat, go!

Bart and Lisa, however, find the contrived plot an insult to their televisual literacy:

> BART: Oh, every week there's a canal.
>
> LISA: Or an inlet.
>
> BART: Or a fjord.
>
> HOMER: Quiet! I will not hear another word against the boat.

The model of television viewing that Homer embodies is the passive consumption of the "boob tube" so frequently (and unreflectively) derided by both the cultural right and left; television, as it is used by Homer Simpson, certainly fits the "vast wasteland" characterization. As Rushkoff observes, "Homer . . . represents an earlier generation and can easily be manipulated by TV commercials and publicity stunts.[7]

Television is something different for Bart and Lisa, and this generational dynamic mirrors a split between viewers of Homer's age, born before the complete cultural ascendancy of television, and Gen X viewers such as Bart and Lisa, who have never known a world without television. Homer is completely taken in by the preposterous plot and "suspense" of *Knight Boat* and both refuses a more critical consumption and forbids it his family members. The kids, on the other hand, in stark contrast to the stereotypes of remote-controlled televisual youth, refuse to be reduced to the status of passive consumers of such pap. The scene is further complicated

by the fact that the terms the kids trot out—"canal," "inlet," "fjord"—
sound like the geography terms that their teachers at Springfield Elementary would be trying to get them to learn. Even though they criticize the
show as mindless, Bart and Lisa watch it, and perhaps even learn something from it.

The scene closes on an appropriately ironic—and ambiguous—note:

MARGE: O.K., TV off. It's family time.

HOMER: Oh, but Marge. Knight Boat! The *crime-solving* boat!

MARGE: Homer, you promised! One night of family time a week. Besides,
that back-talking boat sets a bad example.

BART: Says you, woman!

[Marge snaps the television off with the remote.]

The in-joke here, of course, is that parents across the country have pro-
hibited their children from watching *The Simpsons* precisely because the
back-talking Bart ("Eat my shorts!") "sets a bad example." As if to prove
his mother's point—and the warnings of mothers and fathers across the
country—Bart immediately responds as predicted, back-talking his
mother. The question that goes unasked, however, is whether Bart's
unthinking retort is evidence of his conditioning by the tube (Marge's
angry response certainly seems to assume this reading) or is instead a clev-
erly reflexive and ironic response—" 'Says you, woman!' as a back-talking kid might say." Bart's response, one might argue, may actually be a
parody of the conservative stereotype of "Bart Simpson." In fact, it is hard
to think of another example of Bart treating his mother with such naked
disrespect in any other episode. His father gets this kind of treatment all
the time, but not Marge. This realization makes the ironic reading of Bart's
retort a bit more plausible. If that is what Bart is doing—and I am aware
of the problems associated with attributing both agency and intention to
a cartoon character—it suggests that he has developed some pretty sophisticated rhetorical skills for a ten-year-old.

But sophisticated to what end? What good is a kid's irony if his parents do not get it? Bart may have won a rhetorical victory, but the fact is
the television is shut off for the night, and the kids are forced to look
through the family photo album with their parents. This is irony's inescapable gamble. As Wayne Booth describes it, irony "risks disaster more

aggressively than any other device. But if it succeeds, it will succeed more strongly than any literal statement can do."[8] I would suggest, tentatively, though this is a question to which we shall have to return, that the irony in this scene, and in *The Simpsons* more generally, succeeds in so far as the program encourages its viewers to watch television, and more generally to read our mediated culture, as Bart does. Marge does not "get" Bart's irony and snaps the Simpsons' television off, but we leave ours on.

One final moral might be drawn from this small allegory of watching television and reading culture. Recent writing about irony has insisted that irony is not merely a quality of texts or of intending producers: irony is equally a property of readers. As Stanley Fish puts it, "Irony . . . is neither the property of works, nor the creation of an unfettered imagination, but a way of reading, an interpretive strategy that produces the object of its attention, an object that will be perspicuous to those who share or have been persuaded to share the same strategy."[9] Watching Bart and Lisa and Homer watching television, we are not only presented with two models of spectatorship and televisual consumption, we are also presented with two quite distinct forms of irony. For it is surely ironic that Marge forbids her family to watch *Knight Boat* because of the bad example the back-talking boat sets (a back-talking boat?!); the recognition of this irony requires only that the viewer have some familiarity with the controversies that have surrounded *The Simpsons* since its premiere, and recognition of this irony assures viewers that the writers of the program are also aware of the criticism. Bart's smart answer might then be taken as the show's declaration that it does not give a damn about such criticisms. On the other hand, Bart's answer might represent another level, and a very different style, of irony: the show giving the lie to the "bad role model" criticisms leveled at it by conservative groups, showing that because kids are more cunning consumers of television than adults are, they are in a better position to use it intelligently. The beauty of this gesture is that the grown-ups do not even get it. As Groening has said in an interview, "It's always fun—kids know this—to tell a joke that makes all the kids laugh but which confuses and annoys the teacher. And that's what I try to do as a grown-up—entertain part of the audience and annoy another part."[10]

Some episodes clearly take the stakes of ironic politics to another level. In these episodes, the irony is directed scattershot against all targets; nothing is safe, nothing is sacred, and nothing, seemingly, is left to believe in when the shooting is over. This shooting metaphor is especially appropriate to a discussion of what is perhaps the most disturbing episode of *The Simpsons* yet produced. Originally aired in the U.S. by Fox on November 2, 1997, "The Cartridge Family" takes on one of the most important and controversial elements in contemporary American politics—gun violence and gun control—and rather than using the occasion simply to satirize gun rights advocates such as the National Rifle Association, it creates an ambiguous moral scene in which any kind of othering is impossible. The episode was so controversial, in fact, that *The Simpsons*'s British home network, SkyTV, refused to air the episode, calling it "too strong, even for a late slot." In a rich irony that Lionel Hutz would appreciate, however, they have released the episode on a commercial video called *Too Hot for TV*.

The episode begins, of course, with the family watching television. The episode actually begins, though, with the frame so tight on the Simpsons's television set that the commercial they are watching is all we see: a soccer match coming to Springfield Stadium which "will determine once and for all which nation is the greatest on earth: Mexico or Portugal." Homer initially is not drawn in—he complains that he has never heard of any of the players (all of whose names sound strangely similar: "Arriaga! Arriaga II! Barriaga!"). When the voice-over announcer promises that "they'll all be signing autographs!," however, Homer blurts out his signature "Woo-hoo!" and the decision to go is made. Thus, if the opening of "And Maggie Makes Three" suggests a couple of different modes of consuming television, the opening of "The Cartridge Family" presents only one: complete and utter surrender. It may be worth remembering, in this context, that it is a commercial and not programming that they are watching.

To this point, "The Cartridge Family" presents no insuperable problems for interpretation. The commercial announcing the upcoming match is somewhat racist—the fact that all the players' names sound alike suggests the inability of the American public to tell them apart—but Homer and his kids are "on the same page" and all desperately want to attend the match, though in all likelihood none has ever considered attending a soccer match before. Marge, perhaps strategically, is cropped out of the frame as the kids ask Homer if they can go. In the face of the fast-paced, quick-cut commercial, Homer can only answer them, "Yes, yes, oh God, yes!" One might argue, in fact, that this is a parodic version of how advertising works, making us believe we cannot live without something we never knew we wanted, and since *The Simpsons* is wise enough not to believe in any hard-and-fast distinctions between "advertising" and "programming," there is a caution here about the persuasive powers of television more generally. These kinds of questions aside, the opening minutes do not provoke any thorny interpretive questions. The soccer commercial is an illogical, glitzy piece of hype (which opens, for instance, with a man in western wear taking a soccer ball off the barbeque and thrusting it toward the camera while shouting, "Open wide for some soccer!") and Homer and the kids are fools for taking the bait. It is just that simple.

All of Springfield turns out for the match, but the crowd grows bored when the players seem only to pass the ball to one another; before long, a riot breaks out among the spectators. The rioting and looting spread throughout Springfield, and in their wake, Homer decides that he must buy a weapon to defend his family. The five minutes of program before the first commercial break end with a dark and troubling irony. Homer goes to "Bloodbath & Beyond" to buy a handgun. When he tells the man at the counter, "I'd like to buy your deadliest gun, please," he is told that they are on "Aisle 6. Next to the sympathy cards." The screen goes dark and, mutatis mutandis, we watch another commercial.

If a viewer were to take stock at this point, s/he would probably expect that the show has just turned from a rather playful, farcical opening into a more serious critique of private gun ownership. We have little to go on so far, to be sure: there has been no suggestion, until Homer walks into the gun shop right before the commercial, that he is thinking of buying a firearm. What contextual clues we are given, though, are menacing. First, in response to Marge's plea, "Homer, we need something to protect this family," Homer replies only, "I couldn't agree more, Marjorie. You deserve peace of mind, and peace of mind is what you shall have." Homer has just escorted a home security expert—albeit an unscrupulous one—out of their house, and in response to the salesman's suggestion, "But surely you can't put a price on your family's lives?" Homer replies, "I wouldn't have thought so either. But here we are." What this all adds up to, based on our knowledge of Homer's behavior in similar situations, is that he is going to do this on the cheap, and he does not want to let Marge in on his plan (his calling her "Marjorie" is part of a larger strategy of keeping her at arm's length). The handgun will be his surprise, presumably because he knows she would object to his buying it. This is the same man, after all, who once bought Marge (who does not bowl) a bowling ball with the name "HOMER" inscribed on it for her birthday. So we are primed, on some level, to suspect that whatever Homer has in mind, it is a bad idea. When Homer gets to the gun shop, a few visual clues reinforce this impression: Homer's eyes are preternaturally wide as he asks the clerk for his "deadliest gun," and the store itself is drab and depressing. It is drawn so as to invoke the menacing gun shop in *Pulp Fiction* (which also makes an appearance in "22 Short Films about Springfield"). The clerk looks vaguely disreputable and does not flinch at Homer's strange—even sinister—request.

So we viewers come back from the commercial ready for an episode focusing on Homer's foolishness in having bought a gun for his home. Many extra-textual clues might strengthen this impression: Matt Groening, for instance, is a man of notably liberal political leanings, and *The Simpsons* has taken passing swipes at America's gun culture in a number of episodes. Perhaps the most salient in this context—though it was not broadcast until the season following "The Cartridge Family"—is "Bart the Mother." That episode opens with Bart falling under the spell of Nelson's BB gun, with which he accidentally kills a mother bird sitting on her nest. What is especially poignant about the episode and its critique of private gun ownership, however, is not the plot but the closing credits. This was the last episode produced featuring the voice talents of the late Phil Hartman; the episode is dedicated "In loving memory of our friend, Phil Hartman." Hartman, it will be remembered, was murdered in his sleep by his wife with their handgun.

For the next several minutes, "The Cartridge Family" does little if anything to complicate the sense that we're watching a critique of private gun ownership and the fanaticism of gun owners. When we return from the commercial break, the gun shop clerk is trying to interest Homer in an accessory kit: holster, bandolier, silencer, "loudener," and speed-cocker (Homer: "I like the sound of that!"). When the clerk shows Homer an attachment "for shooting down police helicopters," Homer's reply is the ambivalent and unsettling "I don't need anything like that . . . [narrowing his eyes] . . . yet." Homer then attempts to close the sale:

HOMER: Just give me my gun.

CLERK: Sorry. The law requires a five-day waiting period. We've got to run a background check.

HOMER: Five days! But I'm mad now! [Tussles with clerk.] I'd kill you if I had my gun!

CLERK: Yeah, well, you don't.

HOMER [muttering]: Lousy big shot. Thinks he's so big because he's got a lot of guns. But if he didn't have those guns I'd show him a thing or two.

Besides being deliciously funny, this is just what the logic of the episode has led us to expect. Homer is something of a poster boy for the Brady Law; the clerk, on the other hand, adheres closely to what the law requires of him. Thus the only real nuance that has been introduced into traditional anti-gun rhetoric to this point is that the gun store clerk is conscientious in carrying out what the law requires (though his advocacy of a speed-cocker and a device "for shooting down police helicopters" is perhaps beyond the pale). The logic of the scene suggests a slight variation on what is received wisdom among handgun advocates: "Guns (and speed-cockers) don't kill people; Homers kill people."

After a period of anguished waiting with Tom Petty's "The Waiting" playing in the background—"Awwh, how am I supposed to last five days without shooting something?"—Homer returns to Bloodbath & Beyond to pick up his handgun.

> HOMER: Now, I believe you have some sort of firearm for me?
>
> CLERK: Well, let's see here. According to your background check, you've been in a mental institution.
>
> HOMER: Yeah.
>
> CLERK: Frequent problems with alcohol.
>
> HOMER: Ho-ho-ho yeah.
>
> CLERK: You beat up President Bush.
>
> HOMER: *Former* President.
>
> [Clerk rubber stamps the application.]
>
> HOMER [reading]: "Potentially dangerous"?
>
> CLERK: Relax. That just limits you to three handguns or less.

Homer returns home with the gun. While Bart is alarmingly enthusiastic about the gun, condemnation—both from Marge and from the hypothesized viewer—is quick. To be certain, Homer picks an unfortunate strategy for introducing the weapon into his home:

> HOMER: Close your eyes, Marge. I've got a surprise for you!
>
> MARGE: Hmmm! [Closes her eyes.]
>
> [The "camera" shifts to Marge's point of view and the screen goes black.]
>
> HOMER: O.K., open your eyes.

[As Marge's eyes open we join her in staring down the barrel of a pistol.
Marge screams]

HOMER: Hee-hee! It's a handgun!

Homer goes on to demonstrate his knowledge of small arms, which does
nothing to instill confidence: "This is the trigger, and this is the thing you
point at whatever you want to die." Homer makes it plain from the start
that there will be some strict rules regarding the weapon:

BART: Hey, Dad, can I borrow the gun tomorrow? I want to scare that
old security guard at the bank.

HOMER: Only if you clean your room.

Marge, however, makes clear her feeling that her home is not safer
with a handgun but is in fact demonstrably less safe. Knowing well how
to get through to her husband, Marge tells Homer, "The TV said you're
58% more likely to shoot a family member than an intruder." Homer does
not really want to deal with this data, but he knows he cannot deny the
authority of Marge's source: "The TV said that?" Statistics notwithstanding, however, Homer suggests that he is somehow *required* by the Constitution to keep a gun: "But I have to have a gun! It's in the Constitution!"
At this point Lisa, typically the program's mouthpiece for liberal ortho-
doxy, presents a gun-control interpretation of "the right to bear arms":

LISA: Dad, the Second Amendment is just a remnant from Revolutionary days. It has no meaning today!

HOMER: You couldn't be more wrong, Lisa. If I didn't have this gun, the
King of England could just walk in here any time he wants and just
start shoving you around. [Shoves her shoulder.] Do you want that?
Huh? Do you?

LISA [mutters]: No.

HOMER: All right, then.

While he is able to bully Lisa into capitulation, Marge will not budge.
Having reached a stalemate, Homer explains to Marge that she is laboring
under a misunderstanding: "A gun is not a weapon, Marge! It's a tool, like
a butcher knife or a harpoon or uh- uh- an alligator." Deciding that she
"just need[s] more education on the subject," Homer devises a "compro-

mise": "Tell you what. You come with me to an NRA meeting, and if you still don't think guns are great, we'll argue some more."

There is probably no way to go much further with this analysis without declaring my own allegiances, for clearly my own feelings as a viewer on the question of private gun ownership will affect profoundly the way I experience the show. So in the interest of full disclosure, I would describe myself as a strong advocate of rather strict gun control measures, and those beliefs have doubtless colored my analysis of "The Cartridge Family" to this point, and you may have been able to discern my beliefs in various turns of phrase over the preceding pages. But from this point in "The Cartridge Family," I suspect that a viewer's presuppositions not only influence, but probably even dictate, the program s/he sees. As Fish argues in the passage cited earlier, irony has the tendency to confirm whatever angle of vision a reader or viewer brings with him/her to the text, and this raises troubling questions about the efficacy of irony as a political strategy.

Homer drags Marge to an NRA meeting. The seriousness of the gathering is comically undercut from the very start: a sign at the door invites members to "Come In and Shoot Your Mouth Off," and attendees are required to walk though a metal detector; those found to be without a weapon are sent back (where a weapon is provided for them). As we enter the meeting, Lenny, Homer's colleague from the power plant, is making an apologia for assault weapons: "Assault weapons have gotten a lot of bad press lately, but they're manufactured for a reason: to take out today's modern super-animals, such as the flying squirrel and the electric eel." To my mistrustful eyes, the meeting begins to take on some salient similarities to a twelve-step meeting—with the obvious difference that the attendees are here not to break with but rather to celebrate their particular abuse problem. So when the bartender Moe Szyslak steps up to the podium, he introduces himself and is greeted in the familiar Alcoholics Anonymous fashion—"Uh hi. I'm Moe S." "Hi, Moe!"—with the significant difference that the alcoholic at an AA meeting would follow his name with the admission, "I am an alcoholic." These gun aficionados see no need to tender any such confession.

The testimony Moe gives is anything but an admission of his powerlessness:

> MOE: Yeah, so last night I was closin' up the bar, when some young punk
> comes in and tries to stick me up.
> ALL: Oh!

SIDESHOW MEL: Whatever did you do, Moe?

MOE: Well, it could have been a real ugly situation. But, I managed to
   . . . shoot him in the spine.

ALL: [Cheers]

The ellipses in Moe's tale are quite significant; we are never told, for instance if or how the assailant was armed, and the fact that Moe shot this young punk "in the spine" suggests, of course, that he shot him in the back and was, at that point in the hold-up, no longer in any real danger. Moe feels comfortable enough with what he has done—and the loud applause he gets from the audience certainly bolsters his confidence—to close his talk with a stunningly tasteless joke: "I guess the next place he robs better have a ramp!" This remark comes after Moe has been egged on by the accolades of the crowd; in one pithy sentence he manages to celebrate gun violence, take a cheap shot at the disabled, and flaunt his violation of the Americans with Disabilities Act (since Moe's Tavern certainly does not "have a ramp").

This scene is likely to draw different responses from different audiences. Some portion of the television audience will have roughly the reaction I think intended by Groening and his writers: while embarrassed to find ourselves cheering Moe's exploits along with the meeting audience and laughing at Moe's very un-PC joke, we position ourselves in opposition to the kind of vigilante solution that Moe has adopted. Other viewers, however, will side with Moe and the meeting audience, celebrating the triumph of the honest small businessman over this young punk. While subsequent events in the episode make the point not worth arguing about here, I believe that while the show allows at least two very different responses to Moe's actions (and his narration of them), the available context points to the moral superiority of one: we are meant to side with Marge. This is something of an enduring structural feature of *The Simpsons*, familiar to anyone who has watched the show: when Homer and Marge disagree, the smart money is on Marge (though, as here, Marge often chooses the right side as the outcome of an unsatisfactorily reductive analytical process). We should not forget, however, that some people watched *All in the Family* and thought Archie Bunker the moral center.

To this point, while we might consciously or unconsciously reject the position toward which the program's inexorable logic is leading us, there has been little if any moral ambiguity presented. Nor is the moral significantly complicated in the scenes that immediately follow. Homer joins the NRA and generally makes himself a lethal nuisance around the house with his gun. When the gun goes off at the dinner table—while Homer is trying to put the safety on—Marge finally delivers an ultimatum: "I'm asking you: If you really care about me and the children, please, *please* get rid of the gun!" Homer pretends to capitulate, but instead of getting rid of the gun, he simply "hides" it in the vegetable crisper. When Marge walks in from the grocery store to find Bart and Milhouse playing William Tell in the dining room—with Milhouse holding the apple in his mouth rather than balancing it on his head—Marge decides to leave home and Homer. "Until you decide what's more important—our gun or your family—we can't live in the same house."

It might be useful, before describing how all the conventional gun control pieties are systematically unraveled in the show's final two minutes, to tot up the various rhetorical and semiotic elements of the program to this point tending either to support or condemn private gun ownership—at least in Homer's case. Such a list might look something like this:

Supporting:
1. The self-protection alternatives—the Springfield police, home security system—are shown to be inadequate.
2. Gun ownership is a Constitutionally protected right.

Condemning
1. Homer's secrecy in purchasing the gun.
2. The tawdry quality of the Bloodbath & Beyond Gun Shop and its clerk (including echoes of *Pulp Fiction*).
3. Homer's interest in "accessories" clearly having nothing to do with his ability to defend his home.
4. Homer's violent rage at being made to wait five days for his gun.
5. The background check is made to look like a hollow exercise.
6. The gun owner is not required to learn anything about his handgun or about handgun safety.
7. Homer's bad judgment about keeping the gun away from the children.
8. The gun is driving a wedge between Homer and Marge.
9. Family members are significantly more likely than intruders to be shot by the homeowner's gun.

10. The right to bear arms is criticized by Lisa as an anachronism, and Homer's lame defense does not do anything to restore its luster.
11. Lenny's defense of assault weapons is preposterous.
12. Gun possession is likened to substance abuse.
13. A gun (in Moe's case) is made to seem the weapon of a coward.
14. Members of the local NRA chapter shoot at disturbing targets at the gun range: a man with his hands up, a mother and child.
15. When Homer inadvertently walks into the Kwik-E-Mart, he is tempted to hold up Apu.
16. Homer's recklessness destroys much of the Simpsons' household property and seriously jeopardizes their safety.
17. Homer's gun use is shown to bring out latent violent tendencies ("See you in hell, dinner plate!").
18. Homer's desire to keep his gun leads him to lie to Marge.
19. In a number of subtle and not-so-subtle ways, gun use is shown to be a means to bolster a man's masculinity.

This list is hardly exhaustive, of course, and one might dispute (or at least complicate) the placement of many of the show's elements. I have categorized Lisa's critique of the Second Amendment as condemning private gun ownership, but one might easily argue that her words themselves are a parody of the critique of the Second Amendment proffered by gun control advocates and are thus an ironic support for gun ownership (or at least a criticism of the rhetorical strategies used to oppose the right to bear arms). About some elements there can be little doubt, however. When Homer defends his right to own a gun on the grounds that it will keep the King of England out, it would seem to affirm rather than correct Lisa's views that the right to bear arms is an anachronism.

Back to our story. Marge takes the children to stay at the Sleep-Eazy Motel ("Hourly Rates. Adult Movies"). With a few of the letters burned out, however, it's now the Sleazy Motel, and pretty clearly it always has been. Meanwhile, Homer holds a fête for the gun club at his home, and the gathering quickly turns sour. When Homer pulls out his handgun and shoots the top off his beer, the NRA members are outraged.

DR. HIBBERT: Homer! You use your gun as a can opener?
HOMER: I use it for everything! Watch me turn on the TV. [Puts three bullets in the television, the last of which turns it on.]

MRS. SKINNER: I've never seen such recklessness!

NRA MEMBER: You might have hurt someone!

CLETUS: Are you some kind of moron?

HOMER: Yeah but.

KRUSTY: Hey, yutz. Guns aren't toys. They're for family protection, hunting dangerous or delicious animals, keeping the King of England out of your face.

MOE: Your membership card please, Homer.

Because he is no longer an NRA member, Dr. Hibbert asks Homer to wait outside until the meeting is over.

Homer's ostracism by "the gun club" is a surprising turn of events. To this point in the episode, the NRA has been depicted as a dangerous group of what Marge calls "gun nuts." Homer's "recklessness," however, embarrasses even them. Suddenly, the members of the Springfield NRA chapter become not the advocates of unchecked handgun proliferation but instead spokespersons for responsible gun ownership.[11] The actions of the gun club are in accord with the NRA's official public position: as their home page states emphatically, "At the NRA, we're dedicated to the lawful, effective, responsible and above all safe use of firearms. And today, we do more to ensure Americans are safe around firearms—whether or not they choose to own them—than any other public or private group."[12] The program's unexpected decision to take the NRA seriously is somewhat undercut, of course, by Krusty the Klown's lecture to Homer, invoking again the murderous specter of King George III. Moe's opening demonstration at the gun club of how to "turn a regular gun into five guns" is also rather suspect. But the group is unanimous in condemning Homer's irresponsible gunplay.

Until this moment—until the moment when the NRA is briefly freed from caricature—"The Cartridge Family" has bordered on satire on the order of *All in the Family*. In the final few minutes, however, and especially the last two minutes, the program either deteriorates (cultural conservatives) or evolves (cultural liberals) from a modernist irony, at many points indistinguishable from satire, into full-blown, vertiginous, groundless postmodern irony. Despondent that his fetishization of guns is rejected even by his NRA chapter, Homer finally realizes that he has been wrong—or rather, realizes not that he was wrong but that he is lonely and that asking for Marge's forgiveness might serve to remedy that situation. Homer heads to the Sleep-Eazy Motel to ask Marge to come home. Marge by this point is more than ready; she and the kids have had a pretty miserable night. As a consequence, she is perhaps a bit too eager to forgive and forget and lets Homer skate by with an apology that does not involve much true repentance.

The Simpsons go down to the front desk to settle their bill. This closing of accounts in the program's final segment might be read allegorically, for the final few minutes of a sitcom is when we expect the payoff: accounts must be settled. Except in extraordinary circumstances ("TO BE CONTINUED," as in "Who Killed Mr. Burns?"), the sitcom is a series composed of discrete units. No balance, either positive or negative, can be carried into the next week or the next season. And if the Simpsons' settling of accounts at the Sleep-Eazy Motel does in some ways dramatize the narrative structure of the sitcom as a genre, then we are in for a surprise, for the Simpsons do not actually pay. They are presented with a bill—as well as their continental breakfast in an envelope—but before any money is exchanged, Snake, Springfield's favorite small-time hood, bursts in, grabs Mayor Quimby at the ice machine and holds a knife to his neck, demanding the contents of the cash drawer. His ascendancy is short-lived, however, for Homer pulls out his concealed handgun—the one that he has twice sworn to Marge that he has disposed of—and orders Snake to "Freeze, bad guy!" Homer's packin' heat, and as a result he appears poised to save the day. This reversal marks the first time—twenty-one minutes into a twenty-three-minute program—that a gun has been shown as hero rather than villain.

But it is no unproblematic heroism. To begin with, the fact that Homer has the gun at all is owing to the fact that he has lied to his wife not once, but twice (and this does not include the deception involved in buying the gun against her wishes in the first place). Second, if we hit the pause button and think for a minute, we will realize how similar this scene is—"bad guy" breaks in on an innocent small businessman and holds the place up, but a gun saves the day—to the story Moe told at the NRA/"Twelve Step" meeting. Our hypothetical viewer had tentatively concluded at this point in the program that Moe's actions in defending the bar were more reckless—and perhaps more cowardly—than heroic. If we (consciously or unconsciously) recognize a homology between these scenes, we would be inclined to expect a "happy" resolution to this standoff.

But Marge's anti-gun moralism, and more importantly her outrage at having been lied to, sets the scene for another turning of the tables. While

Homer has his gun trained on Snake, Marge begins to upbraid him for his deception. When Homer turns to defend himself—against Marge now, not against Snake—Snake seizes the opportunity and seizes Homer's gun ("Yoink!"). Advantage Snake. But again, not for long, as Homer taunts him: "The joke's on you, buddy. There's no bullets in that thing!" (Perhaps his humiliation by the gun club has taught Homer something about gun safety.) Advantage Homer. Homer teases Snake by shaking the box of bullets he pulls out of his pocket; in a Bugs Bunny-like move, Snake brandishes the gun in Homer's face and demands, "Yo. Give me the bullets." Homer, terrified by his own unloaded gun, hands them over ("O.K.! Don't shoot!"). Advantage Snake.

At that moment, however, a crack squad of four from the Springfield Chapter of the NRA, having been summoned by silent alarm, bursts into the office behind Snake and in unison orders him to "Drop it!" Advantage NRA. Thinking for a minute, Snake does drop his knife; he then rushes the counter, grabs the cash, and runs unmolested out the door. Game, set, and match to Snake.

The immediate crisis having passed, Marge takes Homer to task for continuing to put his gun before his family. Homer again apologizes to her, and for the first time we believe his repentance is sincere: "I'm sorry I lied to you, Marge, but this gun had a hold on me. I felt this incredible surge of power, like God must feel when He's holding a gun. So please, get rid of it, because I know I'll just lie to you again and again." Homer hands the gun to Marge and walks the kids out to the car. Marge has won. Guns have been proven to be dangerous, even if sometimes quite useful.

Homer heading out to the car is not the episode's last word, however, but its penultimate. Marge takes the gun to a waste can to dispose of it. Rather improbably, in the lobby of the Sleazy Motel, is an antiseptic waste can with a pedal-operated high-polish stainless-steel lid, like those found in doctor's offices. Marge depresses the pedal, anticipating dropping the firearm in the trash, but the underside of the lid forms a reflective surface almost like the mirror in an oversized cosmetic compact, and Marge is arrested by the image of herself holding a gun. If we listen carefully, we will hear the strains of the theme from television's *The Avengers* coming up, as Marge poses with the gun, invoking Emma Peel, Charlie's Angels, and even Robert De Niro's psychopathic Taxi Driver. Marge then drops the gun—not into the waste can, but into her purse. She saunters out to the parking lot to join her family with a decided swagger in her stride.

These last two minutes—from the time the Simpsons go down to the motel lobby to pay their bill until the closing credits—should be profoundly disturbing for anyone who wants to believe in the political efficacy of postmodern irony. Where would the sympathies of a careful, open-minded viewer logically reside at the conclusion of an episode as ambiguous as this one (assuming that both careful and open-minded viewers can be found)? From a producer's point of view, satire is much easier. For most of the episode, Homer is essentially a figure of satire, and clearly what is being satirized is the kind of mindless infatuation with firepower that Homer so comically embodies. In fact, however, the satire is so broad, and Homer's recklessness with his gun is so overdrawn, that no one in the viewing audience would recognize himself in Homer's behavior. No one, in other words, would be tempted, even for a moment, to defend Homer's stewardship of his gun, even if one were in favor of private gun ownership generally. If irony can sometimes harden into satire, satire is only a step from farce, and while satire might have some political potential, farce primarily reinforces prejudices rather than challenges them.

"The Cartridge Family," far from being the only episode of *The Simpsons* with this kind of ironic plot structure, is perhaps just the best example from among a number of episodes, including "Itchy & Scratchy & Marge" (where Marge goes through a metamorphosis of sorts in her thinking about television violence) and "Marge Simpson In: Screaming Yellow Honkers" (in which Marge is made to re-examine her politically correct distaste for sports utility vehicles), where the political charge of the episode seems to diffuse in a cloud of ironic turnings and returnings. Upon such an unstable moral foundation, it is difficult to build a solid political platform. Thus, while Rushkoff betrays some skepticism, writers Mike Reiss and Al Jean may in fact be telling the truth when they claim that the show "promotes no point of view on any issue."[13]

But is not that finally the point? Moralistic television is pretty easy, and pretty well played out. The platitudinous verities of *Father Knows Best* and *The Cosby Show* do not map very well onto the lived experience of many contemporary television viewers and millennial citizens. *The Simpsons,* with an episode such as "The Cartridge Family," does not necessarily try to inspire its viewers to go out to work for gun control or for the NRA. What it does do, however, and at a profound level that only irony can plumb, is heighten our awareness of the radically contingent nature of every choice we make, leaving us more tolerant of those who approach problems with very different presuppositions from our own. *The Simpsons* will not presume to teach us, in twenty-three minutes, how we should feel about private gun ownership; it can, however, begin to suggest just how complex an issue gun control really is.

Rushkoff holds the show up as a prime example of what he calls a "media virus" and explains that "a virus will always make the system it is attacking appear as confusing and unresolvable as it really is."[14] Thus, the show does not preach but instead tries to motivate us to do our own analysis of complicated social, cultural, and political issues. *The Simpsons,* at its very best, equips us to be better citizens in our postmodern, ironic democracy. It helps us to wrest irony from the producers and to transform it from a tool of oppression and exclusion into a tool for democracy and liberation. In place of a static irony of production, *The Simpsons* helps us to imagine and to deploy an irony of consumption. And that strikes me as a profoundly important—and potentially a politically efficacious—accomplishment for a cartoon.

NOTES

1. Jedediah Purdy, *For Common Things: Irony, Trust, and Commitment in America Today* (New York: Knopf, 1999), 6.

2. The distrust within Modernism of "didacticism" has been amply documented. See, for instance, Maud Ellmann, *The Poetics of Impersonality: T. S. Eliot and Ezra Pound* (Cambridge: Harvard University Press, 1987).

3. Wayne Booth, *A Rhetoric of Irony* (Chicago: University of Chicago Press, 1974), 5–6. Booth's careful distinction of "stable" from "unstable" irony, while convenient, is fraught with problems; one of the goals of the larger project from which this essay is adapted is to interrogate and refine these categories. For a brief and cogent critique of Booth's work on irony, see Stanley Fish, "Short People Got No Reason to Live: Reading Irony," *Dædalus* 112 (Winter 1998): 175–91.

4. Archie Bunker's chair from the *All in the Family* set is in fact displayed at the Smithsonian Museum in Washington.

5. Douglas Rushkoff, *Media Virus! Hidden Agendas in Popular Culture* (New York: Balantine Books, 1996), 110.

6. Rushkoff, *Media Virus!* 111.

7. Rushkoff, *Media Virus!* 111.

8. Booth, *A Rhetoric of Irony,* 41–42.

9. Stanley Fish, "Short People," 189. For another recent study that accounts for the irony of consumption (as a corrective to Booth's nearly exclusive irony of

production), see Linda Hutcheon, *Irony's Edge: The Theory and Politics of Irony* (London and New York: Routledge, 1994).

10. Jamie Angell, "Explaining Groening: One on One with the Sultan of Fun." *Simpsons Illustrated*, vol. 1, no. 9 (Summer 1993): 22–30. Posted at <http://www.labyrinth.net.au/~kwyjibo/matt.html>.

11. As Charlton Heston protested in his closing remarks to the fraught NRA Annual Meeting of Members on May 1, 1999 in Littleton, Colorado: "We're not the rustic, reckless radicals they wish for. No, the NRA spans the broadest range of American demography imaginable. We defy stereotype, except for love of country. Look in your mirror, your shopping mall, your church or grocery store. That's us. Millions of ordinary people and extraordinary people—war heroes, sports idols, several U.S. presidents and yes, movie stars" <http://www.nrahq.org/transcripts/denver_close.asp>.

12. <http://www.nrahq.org/safety/>

13. Rushkoff, *Media Virus!* 113.

14. Rushkoff, *Media Virus!* 36.

Homer Erectus: Homer Simpson
As Everyman . . . and Every Woman

VALERIE WEILUNN CHOW

Scavenging through the Springfield City Dump, Homer, Lisa, and Bart Simpson discover a box of Mr. Sparkle, a Japanese dishwashing detergent displaying what looks like Homer's face as the company logo.[1] Holding up the box, Homer whimpers, "What's going on? Why am I on a Japanese box?" His voice trails off, high-pitched and incoherent as he peers at the likeness of his own grinning head. Later at the dinner table, Homer sits mesmerized with the box propped in front of his dinner plate. When Marge asks him to remove the box from the table, Homer replies emphatically, "But I am obsessed with it! Where did it come from? What is it a box of? How did my face get on it?" The ever savvy Bart Simpson interrupts his father. "Hey, if they've got a picture of you, that means that they can see you," he declares hysterically. "They're probably watching us right now!" "That's ridiculous," Marge replies, "no one is watching us right now!" As they lapse into silence, the Simpson family begins to look paranoid; their eyes dart from side to side scanning fearfully for signs of voyeurs ("In Marge We Trust").

Bart is right. The equivocality of his statement "They're probably watching us right now" reveals an ironic hyperconsciousness about the televisual process that has produced *The Simpsons*. In "Postmodernism and Television," Jim Collins characterizes hyperconsciousness as "a hyperawareness on the part of the text itself of its cultural status, function, and history, as well as of the conditions of its circulation and reception."[2] When Bart says, "They're probably watching us right now," he is pointing to the fact that *Simpsons* viewers are watching the Simpson family going about daily activities such as sitting at the dinner table and even

107

watching television. On another level, just as *Simpsons* viewers may watch *The Simpsons* watch television, they themselves are also being watched.

In her discussion of the televisual, Mimi White states that "because commercial television is first and foremost an advertising medium, viewers are positioned as potential consumers."[3] Television audiences watch programming that has been paid for by commercial advertisers. Therefore, viewers are monitored as consumers of not only the television show themselves but also as the target market for the products advertised in the program's commercials. In other words, television audiences are themselves consumed: "Because they [viewers] are 'sold' to advertisers, viewers themselves become commodities in the act of watching television."[4] Ratings such as the infamous Nielsen system determine the advertising rates for television programs. In turn, television sponsors "buy" the viewers in audience shares. Thus, "the viewer-as-consumer is abstracted into an object of exchange value that the network or station offers to a commercial sponsor."[5] Within this circuit of televisual commodification, the viewer is ultimately like the Simpson family—both the consumer and the consumed. Thus, when Bart frets, "They're probably watching us right now," the difference between who Bart's *us* signifies and who *they are* is not so distinct.

Structuring this play of consumer-as-commodity is the television programming, which is itself predicated upon a process of recycling that both consumes and recommodifies its own narrative, genre, and character conventions. Like the box of Mr. Sparkle with Homer's face as its logo, television also recycles its images into "new" products. Indeed, the political economy of television production and programming relies on repetition and intertextual citation. Rather than taking the financial (and career) risks of developing innovative programming, television producers will return again and again to formulaic plots and stock characters that have been successful in the past.[6] Television programming reuses old plotlines, characterizations, and series premises that viewers will instantly recognize.

Indeed, within the televisual space, narrative and visual conventions are repeated in genre/generic forms such as crime dramas, soap operas, and situation comedies. *The Simpsons* is itself modeled upon the domestic sitcom form. The program centers around the wild and wacky misadventures of the Simpson nuclear family: Homer and Marge as husband and (house)wife, Lisa, Bart, and baby Maggie as what episode guest star John Waters refers to as "2.3 kids" ("Homer's Phobia"). *The Simpsons*'s storylines have also cited the images and narratives of other television commodities such as *The X-Files, Married . . . With Children, All in the Family, The Wonder Years, Hollywood Squares, Home Improvement, Nightline,* and even *The Flintstones.*[7]

If we click back to the site/sight of Homer Simpson pulling his likeness out of the city dump, we can see that the televisual conventions of repetition, citationality, and by extension, the workings of consumer culture itself are contextualized within *The Simpsons* as postmodern parody.[8] *The Simpsons* mocks the very processes of commodity capitalism from which it has been produced.

In her analysis of the televisual, Patricia Mellencamp states that "in contrast to the Marxist analysis of the commodity fetish which depends on a covert operation which severs the worker from the product . . . postmodern capital brazenly announces what was formerly concealed, like Linda Evans and Cybill Shepherd proclaiming rather than denying their use of haircolor products."[9] Like aging actresses touting the wonders of coloring their hair in commercials for hair dye, *The Simpsons* just as shamelessly reveals its own roots as a cultural commodity. The show recycles the trash, the most degraded aspects of televisual culture, into a new and improved commodity product. The self-reflexivity of the series simultaneously reproduces televisual conventions while demystifying televisual commodification by breaking down the processes of its own production, pointing to its own status as a commodity, and (re)packaging the resulting contradiction into yet another product for viewer consumption.

In the Mr. Sparkle episode, the commodification of Homer's head as a dish soap logo exposes the spectacular depths of *The Simpsons*'s metaknowledge of itself as a commodity form. When Homer sees his own image on the Japanese box, he comes face to face with the political economy of his own series. Just as Homer has been sold as a dishwashing detergent logo, so are *Simpsons* audience members monitored and sold to television advertisers. Furthermore, the reproduction of Homer's image as Mr. Sparkle points to how television produces for its viewers multiple sites of consumption. In other words, shows such as *The Simpsons* act as advertisements for products that bear the name and images of the series.

As with Homer's mass-produced face on Mr. Sparkle boxes, images of *Simpsons* characters have been sold on trading cards, as action figures, Pez dispensers, magnets, calendars, interactive CD-ROMs, and watches from Subway Sandwiches. In the past thirteen years, *The Simpsons* has endorsed

Butterfinger candy bars and Pentium processors, recorded its own CD's, offered a contest in which the lucky winner received a life-size replica of the Simpson family home, and even sparked controversy over its Bart Simpson *Under-Achiever* T-shirts.

The way in which Homer's head signifies televisual commodification in the Mr. Sparkle episode is emblematic of how the show encodes its hyperconsciousness onto the particularities of Homer's body. Indeed, the encoding of Homer's head within the episode is no exception to *Simpsons* convention. Throughout the series, the image of Homer's body is recycled again and again, revealing further levels of meta-commentary about *The Simpsons* as a commodity form. From his brainless and balding head, through his jiggling beer gut, to his exposed butt crack, Homer's corporeality reveals the very processes of commodity capitalism.

Patricia Mellencamp goes on to suggest that "U.S. television—in its commercials and in its programs and its overriding enunciation—appeals to an ideology of familialism (and happy cleanliness), to a myth of the middle-class, happy family reproduced in sitcoms."[10] However, American televisual culture is fraught with contradictions in spite of its familialism. Television is not only dependent upon the familial but also upon a cultural economy in which "all consumers are figured as feminized"[11]—a condition, Lynne Joyrich suggests, that "yields tension in a culture desperately trying to shore up traditional distinctions even as its simulations destabilize such attempts."[12]

Within the context of *The Simpsons,* Homer embodies *both* the white male head of household *and* the feminized consumer. He is a stock characterization of the "white, male, working-class buffoon" that can be recognized in other television programs such as *The Honeymooners, The Flintstones, All in the Family,* and, unsurprisingly, in Fox's other animated domestic sitcoms such as *King of the Hill* and *The Family Guy.*[13] Homer, however, is also an indiscriminate consumer, voracious to the point that he will risk his life by eating (among a variety of other toxic and/or nonfood items) sushi cut from a poisonous blowfish ("One Fish, Two Fish, Blowfish, Blue Fish").

For the purposes of this essay, I am interested in how Homer's body acts as a vehicle for postmodern parody—how the repetitive displays of Homer's body point to the (de)formation of *identities,* particularly the (dis)identification of gender within televisual culture. As Judith Butler has suggested, identities are "*fabrications* manufactured and sustained through corporeal signs and other discursive means."[14] In other words, the distinguishing characteristics that categorize gender difference are social constructions that get "instituted and inscribed on the surface of bodies"[15] In *The Simpsons,* Homer's body blurs the boundaries of difference, revealing the hazy contradictions upon which the icons of the televisual have been constructed.

As evinced by the citationality of television characters, the stability of this mode of identity formation is dependent upon repetition; consuming subjects must be able to recognize these identities as such within any given context.[16] In one episode of *The Simpsons,* the original authorship of Bart and Lisa's beloved *Itchy & Scratchy* cartoon show comes into question. In response to the allegation of fraud, *Itchy & Scratchy*'s producer casually admits that "animation is built on plagiarism. If it weren't for someone plagiarizing *The Honeymooners,* we wouldn't have *The Flintstones*" ("The Day the Violence Ended"). Here, the show itself suggests that in order to function as an icon, characters like the "white, male patriarch" must be comprehensible within the context of both *The Flintstones* and *The Simpsons.*

It is precisely this repetition of "intelligible identity" that participates in the construction of gender hierarchies.[17] Thus, the repeated representation of the archetypal male as white, a father, and the primary breadwinner and authority within the nuclear family reifies a social formation that privileges heterosexual white men at the center and all others at the margins. However, embedded within this process of citationality is the production of new modes of contradiction, of "*dis*continuity . . . the possibility of a failure to repeat, a de-formity, or a parodic repetition of abiding identity as a politically tenuous construction."[18]

Homer Simpson embodies that contradiction in that he is figured as both the hegemonic characterization of a white male patriarch as "the professional/managerial husband . . . the sensible, mature partner" and (de)formed as the simpering cartoon caricature, Homer J. Simpson, moaning over a box.[19] Additionally, as part of a *Simpsons* storyline, Homer's signifying characteristics are again recopied into a signifier of a Japanese dish soap. Homer's head as Mr. Sparkle is emblematic of the way that *The Simpsons* text as a whole constructs the dynamics between the visuality of Homer's body and the series storyline. The relationship between the two enacts a meta-commentary about gender iconicity within the televisual system of representation. Resistance to the modes of patriarchy can be located in this possibility of variation and contradiction within normative representations. Indeed, Butler asserts that "it is only *within* the practices of repetitive signifying that a subversion of identity becomes possible."[20]

If the visual impetus of *The Simpsons* is ultimately about recycling what goes in and out of consumer culture, then this essay will follow the flow of consumption and commodification as it cycles through the recurring appearances of Homer's body within *The Simpsons* as a series. What is at stake in Homer's figuration is the possibility of oppositional readings enabled by the hyperconsciousness of the text itself.[21] If "broadcast TV," as Andrew Ross suggests, " is permeated by a discourse of self-criticism," then by taking pleasure in the degraded image of Homer's body, *Simpsons* viewers are encouraged to believe that they are decoding the text in a way that challenges commodity capitalism.[22]

However, within a postmodern society, the difference between an oppositional and a negotiated reading is an ambivalent one. By chuckling at his hairless head, his beer belly, his bare butt, we *buy* into being a savvier consumer than the Homer Simpsons of the world. However, what *Simpsons* audiences are really buying into is a more sophisticated version of consumer mystification. Any opposition to dominant ideology is always already tainted by the economics of late capitalism; participation in consumerism is virtually unavoidable.

In her influential 1990 essay, "Banality In Cultural Studies," Meaghan Morris described two tendencies endemic to the field of cultural studies that can apply to pop culture criticism in general: celebratory (albeit apologetic) analyses of all things banal versus elitist lamentations about the contamination of the culture by mass commodification. Often, there is an elision within these two modes of criticism of the politics of hierarchy and difference within popular culture. The selling point of this essay is that my discursive reproduction of Homer's body will indicate a change in programming—a resistance to both the celebratory and the nay-saying wasteland, the *more of the same* banality that Morris warned against.[23]

Within academia, popular culture bears the burden of legitimating itself as an object of study. Taking my cue from Lauren Berlant, I would like to acknowledge *The Simpsons* as, indeed, a "silly object" of study. However, it is precisely that banality, the sense of an animated sitcom as the trash of American sociocultural life, which makes it a worthwhile subject of critique.[24] Indeed, popular culture both reflects and shapes American consciousness. In his discussion of the MTV animated series, *Beavis and Butt-head,* Douglas Kellner states that "media culture provides resources to make meanings, pleasure, and identity but also shape and form specific identities."[25] In other words, American popular culture is at once guilty of reinforcing traditional hegemonic representations as well as providing widely accessible sites of resistance, thus providing the valuable potential for representation to individuals such as women and people of color that have been historically shut out of the cultural arena.

Ironically, in my critique of *The Simpsons* I am striving not to be banal about banality. The resistant or even *oppositional* value that *The Simpsons* offers is that it provides a cross-sectional view into the consistently recycled tropes of mass culture precisely because it is a kind of cultural waste material. It is these processes of recycling that reveal how the banal is formed. With the expansion of capitalism to a global level, consumer culture will become an increasingly equal opportunity sales representative, ever willing to represent the voices of not only the hegemony but also its detractors—as long, of course, as the commodified voice *sells*. What is at stake then is the possibility for change from within the televisual system of representation. The commodification of self-reflexivity within *The Simpsons* is a tool with which we can unpack what constitutes the normative: the exclusionary boundaries of what is considered "normal" or even "natural" within culture. What the series parodies, and *partially* challenges, is the norm: where white, patriarchal families litter the landscape of the televisual world.

TV AS HOMER'S HEAD: (RE)COGNIZING TELEVISUAL KNOWLEDGE

At the core of *The Simpsons*'s postmodern parody is the way that the series constantly points to itself and knows its own status as a televisual product even if its characters do not. Thus, *Simpsons* viewers are placed in the self-affirming position of knowing more, if not knowing better, than the Simpson family. Andrew Ross has characterized this *knowing better* as "pop irony," a postmodern cultural literacy that encourages viewers to critique the workings of commodity culture; by consuming satiric shows such as *The Simpsons,* viewers have "a way of reconciling [their] dissident youthful past with [their] professional managerial present."[26] In one episode, Homer recounts Bart's first year in school. He anchors his account with an ironic citation of *The Simpsons*'s own history as a television show. "The year was 1990," Homer begins, "and Tracey Ullman was entertaining America with songs, sketches, and crudely drawn filler material" ("Lisa's Sax"). In this case, the "crudely drawn filler material" to which Homer refers is *The Simpsons*'s own beginnings on *The Tracey Ullman Show*.

However, when Homer situates Bart's first year of school within television history, he does so incorrectly. *The Simpsons* premiered in 1987 as a series of satirical animation shorts wedged in between live-action sketches on *The Tracey Ullman Show*. Eventually, *The Simpsons* spun off into its own highly rated domestic sitcom, ultimately outlasting the cancellation of its parent show. The disparity of Homer's reference is that by 1990, Lisa and Bart had already been attending school in the animation shorts for three years. Regardless of these inconsistencies, in the world-according-to-Homer the televisual is privileged as the primary source of information. Indeed, Homer's memory is completely constructed by the televisual as such.

One of the pleasures of the series derives precisely from this construction of Homer as an iconic televisual subject: a misquoting, unknowing fool who is easily duped by commodity consumption.[27] However, if Homer is an icon of televisual consumption, he is an ironic one. The hyperconsciousness of *The Simpsons* reproduces Homer as the stereotypical consumer within commodity capitalism. What is ironic is that the idealized nature of iconicity as a concept makes it impossible by definition for the sign (Homer Simpson) to accurately resemble both of its referents (head-of-household *and* feminized consumer).

What is revealed by *The Simpsons* is the very failure of the televisual to represent the norm as such. Thus, the viewer's pleasure in *The Simpsons* is derived from the appraisal of Homer as a social deviant, in spite of his trappings of normativity. The audience can assume that they know better than to be suckered like Homer. Homer does not know that he is really citing himself when he refers to the "crudely drawn filler material" on *The Tracey Ullman Show* because, unlike *The Simpsons* viewer, he cannot situate himself within the processes of televisual consumption. When Homer refers to *The Tracey Ullman Show*, televisual "knowledge" is juxtaposed over and against Homer's lack of knowledge of himself as both commodity and consumer.

If we click back to the Mr. Sparkle episode once again, we find Homer placed in a position of unknowing vis à vis television as a source of information. When Homer pulls the box out of the Springfield city dump, he finds that his head has been recycled and recommodified in the form of a dish soap icon. Desperate to sight how his face ended up on the box, Homer turns to television for information. After calling the Japanese manufacturer, he receives a videotape in the mail. Homer and the children end up watching what is really a promotional video for potential Mr. Sparkle investors. Frustrated, Homer still cannot cite where the logo comes from. On all fours in front of the television set, he complains, "That doesn't explain anything! All I know is that they stole my face and used it for their stupid logo. There is no other explanation."

However, by the end of the video, Homer is led to believe that Mr. Sparkle did not *steal his face* but simply recycled the image from the logos of the two companies that co-produce the dish detergent: the fish logo of Matsumara Fishworks and the light bulb from Tamaribuchi Heavy Manufacturing Concern. On the video, Mr. Sparkle's eyes are shown to be from the fish; the shape of the head is from the light bulb logo. At the conclusion of his viewing, Homer walks away satisfied with the televisual explanation, even though it has not given him the complete picture. He is satisfied because he can now make reference to the sign's "origin." Like a television hero after he has saved the day, Homer says sentimentally, "Let's go home." "But we *are* home," the more commercially savvy Bart and Lisa reply.

Here, *The Simpsons* as a series is satirizing the paradigmatic consumer. As a kind of blue-collar Everyman, Homer is encoded as the subject formation characterized by Stuart Hall as the "cultural dupe."[28] As such, Homer readily buys into whatever "knowledge" is fed to him, up to and including the origin narrative of why he looks like Mr. Sparkle. Unlike *The Simpsons* viewer, Homer is duped into believing that the televisual images that he sees are iconic, that they unequivocally "mean" what they claim to signify. Furthermore, he trusts that he is not like Mr. Sparkle—that he is not a "stupid logo." If Homer, the "cultural dupe," believes (and makes reference to) everything that he sees on television, then he has television for a brain. In other words, Homer does not actually know anything about Mr. Sparkle or even his own son's first year in school; he can only cite what he has seen on television.

Homer's inability reveals the constant deferral of "true" knowledge or meaning within postmodern television allusions. What is ultimately being commodified in *The Simpsons* as a text is a more complex reproduction of televisual banality. Within the recycling logic of consumption, sighting the televisual is not about *knowing* but about being able to identify an allusion's *iterability* within a system of representation.[29] Rather than recognizing the relationship between televisual signifiers and signifieds as arbitrary, televisual representations are encoded as having a direct resemblance to their referents. In order to decode television with any sense of coherence, the viewer must be able to read the signifiers, the television characters, as iconic. What is ultimately reproduced is not access to some version of the "real" or even an understanding of what is being signified, but the expectation that the social and cultural hierarchies within the televisual remain consistent.

Within this context, Homer's declaration to his children, "Let's go home," only furthers the point. Homer's suggestion, "Let's go home," while standing in his own living room is a *non sequitur* outside of the realm of televisual convention. In order to make sense of Homer's statement, the viewer must consume enough television to be able to cite the cliché as a statement of dramatic closure—one traditionally attributed to the white male hero after he has saved the day. The irony, of course is that Homer has not saved the day—far from it. His bumbling ineffectualness extends, once again, to an inappropriate and decontextualized citation. The declaration reveals that Homer as an avid television watcher can only cite information that he has gleaned from television; he cannot determine what the statement actually means. As a "cultural dupe," Homer does not think because television is doing the thinking for him.

Therefore, Homer is able to process the Mr. Sparkle logo without really knowing where his resemblance to Mr. Sparkle comes from per se. Like his citation, "Let's go home," Homer does not really know what his likeness to the dish detergent is supposed to mean because within the realm of the televisual, every product is a copy; there is no original since everything bears the cites/sights of others. Inscribed within the Mr. Sparkle logo are the traces of two other company logos that, in turn, cite the signifying characteristics of Homer's face; Homer's face is itself troping the "working-class buffoon" of *The Honeymooners*, *The Flintstones* or *All in the Family* fame. There is no determinable origin for either Mr. Sparkle or Homer J. Simpson, only an endless (tele)play of the televisual recycling itself over and over again. In pointing to the difficulty of tracing the origin of an image, *The Simpsons* produces this obstacle only to surmount it through its own hyperconsciousness.

Juxtaposed against Homer's figuration as the "cultural dupe" is the knowing *Simpsons* viewer who derives pleasure precisely from the irony of knowing what Homer does not. Unlike Homer, *The Simpsons* audience is supposed to know that Mr. Sparkle is more than just the recycled image of two company logos. Whether the Japanese dish soap is "real" or not, the *Simpsons* viewer is hailed as an oppositional reader precisely through the hyperconsciousness of the text. The audience is supposed to know that Mr. Sparkle looks like Homer just as it recognizes Homer as an iconic "cultural dupe." Thus, the viewer can deny that Homer Simpson is an accurate representation of her own consuming habits; she can reject the kind of behavior solicited by a consumer culture. However, upon closer examination, Homer's ignorance contaminates the realm of the supposedly cynical *Simpsons* viewer. It is the television sponsors, not the viewer, who have the last laugh.

After all, what does *The Simpsons* audience really know? They know that Homer is the average or iconic televisual subject; they also know that they are not like Homer Simpson. But what does this all mean? If Homer is not a representation of the average *Simpsons* viewer, then the knowing *Simpsons* audiences are not normative televisual subjects. However, if *The Simpsons* viewers are not the norm, then who are? Who is Homer a copy of? If the show is predicated upon the viewer's ability to recognize Homer as Everyman, the ideal televisual subject, yet the audience is not hailed as such, then the norm that Homer is supposed to signify is rendered unstable, unintelligible, even unknowable. The viewer may be able to recognize the "cultural dupe" archetype, yet that identification is itself dependent on reference or citation; all the audience can really do is cite Homer's similarity to other characters they have seen on TV.

In an interesting plot twist, this makes *The Simpsons* viewer just like Homer. Within the logic of televisual consumption, what *The Simpsons* audience really knows is the *unknowability* or inability to find meaning within icons like Mr. Sparkle and Homer J. Simpson. Thus, what is being consumed within *The Simpsons* is not a mimetic representation—an image that reflects some kind of "real" world, external to the televisual. What is being consumed is the commodification of the very processes of television as a medium, the inability of television to point to anything other than itself.

What is at stake is the way that Homer as the iconic television viewer is (dis)continuous with his identity as the patriarch of a nuclear family. In *Make Room for TV: Television and the Family Ideal in Postwar America,* television historian Lynn Spigel discusses the relationship between television and the nuclear family within American consumer culture.[30] From its inception, television was introduced to baby boomers as a window on the world, reconnecting suburban families to the urban happenings of the "outside world" while keeping them nestled within the safety of their subdivisions. As the new organizational center of the nuclear family activity, "Television was supposed to bring the family together but still allow for social and sexual divisions at home."[31] Mothers, fathers, and children shared "quality time" together in front of the television. However, "making room for TV" meant that Daddy had to move aside. Television became the new, improved patriarch within post 1950's American culture, demoting dear old Dad to second-in-command.

If we rewind to Homer, Bart, and Lisa watching the Mr. Sparkle video, we see that Homer is on his hands and knees inches away from the television set. He gapes at the television deferentially while his children watch their father's degradation from the family couch. The visuality of the Simpson family patriarch in a position of subordination can be read as self-reflexive, referencing precisely the nuclear family dynamics that Spigel discusses. Vis-à-vis television, Homer's status as an icon of heterosexual white masculinity is jeopardized. The repeated visuality of the Simpson family patriarch bowing down to the authority of the television set, allowing, even insisting, that television think for him, can be read as a resignification of the role of Father within the nuclear family.

Again and again within *The Simpsons* as a series, television displaces Homer as the head of the family. Since "the rules that govern intelligible identity . . . partially structured along the matrices of gender and compulsory heterosexuality, operate through repetition," the Homer Simpson copy of both White Male Patriarch and "Cultural Dupe" challenges the iconicity of white masculinity within the domestic sphere.[32] Ward Cleaver, Homer is not. With his swollen body and vacuous brain, Homer is a parody of white masculinity, what Judith Butler might call a "failed copy."[33] Through his repetition of the identifying characteristics of white masculinity (father, breadwinner, head of the household), Homer's inconsistencies reveals that the primacy of white masculinity is purely performative—something that is not instinctual or biological but can be impersonated or even, in Homer's case, (mis)impersonated.[34] In the case of *The Simpsons*, television is really the Head of the Household; Homer just plays one on TV. Thus, Homer Simpson's subservience to the television set reveals the contradictions within consumer culture. He is left on his hands and knees, suggesting to his children, "Let's go home," back to those tele-visual moments when Father, not television, knew best.

HOMER'S GUT:
THE CONTRADICTION IN-DIGESTION

If television is the intellectual head of the Simpson household, then the sight of Homer's beer belly provides ample additional testimony to the contradiction between the role of the patriarch and the role of the con-sumer within commodity culture. His gut signifies how consumption gets processed by the two conflicting identities. In *The Simpsons,* the modes of Homer's consumption amass like a stone in the bowels of the Simpson nuclear family—his uncontrollable desire to consume gets in the way of the performance of his fatherly duties.

Susan Bordo theorizes the consumer subject as a "bulimic personality." On one side of the scale, the consumer must maintain control over her body; she must "repress desire for immediate gratification . . . [in favor of] the work ethic." She must bear the responsibility of producing goods and services for the consumption of others. On the other side of the scales, she must also be an insatiable consumer, tipping the scales with her gluttony. The two com-peting directives result in the "unstable double bind of consumer capital-ism."[35] The ideal worker/consumer cannot balance the two sides of the scales; what results is a kind of bulimia—a binge and purge mentality in which so-called leisure time is spent in manic consumption—a habit that must be expunged before the alarm goes off on Monday morning.

What must be noted in Bordo's characterizations is that the ideal con-sumer subject is gendered female. In advertisements and other mass media from World War II to the present, the representation of consumption has been encoded as a deliberately feminine one. Within the confines of the nuclear family, the sexual division of labor is constructed around a binary in which the husband is the sole breadwinner while the duties of the (house)wife include both the maintenance of the domestic sphere and the labor of buying the products that would ensure a sparkling clean and com-fortable home.

The gendering of the consumer subject is reified by the televisual. Patricia Mellencamp suggests that "television's version of 'the family'—

and its gendered address to women and men—are key areas of contradiction."[36] Thus, Homer Simpson's encoding as not only the head of the household but also as the most avaricious consumer in the family disrupts the division between *woman's work* and *man's work* within the Simpson nuclear family. Homer's consumption emasculates him, rendering him an impotent head of the family. He is a feminized consumer who can only binge—to the point that his belly bulges, pregnant with his uncontrollable cravings.

In one episode of *The Simpsons,* Homer's excesses nearly cost him his life. After suffering a heart attack, Homer lies prone on the floor of the office of his boss, Montgomery Burns. After Homer's spirit drifts out of his body, Burns says to his assistant, "Oh, dear. Send a ham to his widow." Contemplating the ham, Homer moans, "Mmm . . . ham." Instantly, his spirit jumps back into his body and his eyes fly open, eager to eat ("Homer's Triple By-Pass"). Homer's ability to will himself back to life for the love of ham demonstrates the profundity of his consumerism. In turn, his signification as the consummate consumer is linked to femininity. In spite of his miraculous recovery, Homer still has to undergo triple by-pass surgery. Standing at his hospital bed, Homer's friend and fellow drunk Barney declares sincerely, "When I first heard about the operation, I was against it. But then I thought, 'If Homer wants to be a woman, so be it.' "

Homer's uncontrollable desire to consume is what causes his heart attack. However, the central conflict in the episode is not Homer's unhealthy eating habits, but his inability as a breadwinner *to pay for it.* The very catalyst for his heart attack is a sound tongue lashing from his boss. When he is diagnosed as in dire need of a triple bypass, it is revealed that Homer as lazy worker cannot afford the $40,000 surgery. The rest of the episode centers on the family scrambling to find an alternative to the costly procedure. Once again, television provides the answer for Homer. Upon hearing a commercial advertising any operation for $129.95, Homer, ever the gullible consumer, hires a third-rate surgeon to perform the job.

Indeed, Homer is not only an ineffectual breadwinner but also an unwilling one. An often-recycled trope within *The Simpsons* is Homer's desire to shirk his responsibilities as head of the household in favor of unbridled consumption. He consistently aspires not only to be away from his job but also away from his family. Within this context, consumerism is a disease of compulsion that entices the father away from his family. In one episode, Apu, the local convenience store manager, pretends to be married to Marge.[37] Freed from the duties of marriage and family, Homer's idea of ultimate indulgence is to check himself into his father's nursing home under an assumed name.[38] Once in the home, Homer splays himself out on a hospital bed wearing nothing but his tightie-whities, his rotund gut the focal center of the scene.

With Apu standing in as the head of the Simpson household, Homer is able to binge without having to produce for his family. Indeed, ultimate bliss for Homer is immobilized consumption—when he does not even need to expend energy to consume. Until Apu's marriage to Marge is exposed as a sham, Homer resides happily in the nursing home either being pushed to the dining table in a wheelchair or prone on the hospital bed, hooked up to a potato chip IV.

Flipping to another episode, we find Marge and Homer discussing the possibility of Marge working outside of the home. Homer flutters his fingers together gleefully. "Hey, then I can follow my dream," he says, "living in the woods and keeping a journal of my thoughts." The scene cuts to Homer sitting under a tree, notebook in hand. "March fifteenth," he muses, "I wish I had a TV . . . Oh, God, how I miss TV" ("Marge Gets A Job"). Again, the implication of Homer's fantasy is that with Marge (rather than Apu this time) filling in as the breadwinner, he can be not only unemployed, but also living away from his family. Isolated, what he longs for is not his wife and children but television. Here the opposition between consumption and family takes the specific form of the television set. Thus, if television acts as a kind of Head of the Household within the nuclear family, it also takes the role of Daddy's mistress, a lover that lures Daddy's attention away from his responsibility to his family.

Homer's desire to consume contradicts his role as head of household in "Homer vs. Lisa and the Eighth Commandment." The episode's conflict begins when Homer, who is unable to afford cable, is willing to beg, borrow, steal, or otherwise abase himself for the sake of television. Upon hearing that the cable installer has offered his neighbor an illegal hook-up, Homer rushes after him. Throwing himself in front of the cable worker's van, Homer is knocked flat on his back. Nonplussed, Homer begs, "I want free cable!" When the cable is connected, a home-shopping channel flashes on the screen. Homer, the "cultural dupe" *par excellence,* claps his hands blissfully. "Cable—it's more wonderful than I dared hope," he declares.[39] Thanks to his illegal transaction, Homer is now able to hyperconsume in spite of his inability to pay for the commodity.

When Lisa questions her father on the ethics of stealing cable, Homer draws his daughter lovingly on his knee and attempts to justify his theft. However, as soon as the television announces the *Bout to Knock the Other Guy Out* show, Homer jumps up, cheering. Lisa topples to the ground. While his daughter lies on the floor, Homer rushes to the television set, arms outstretched. Sinking to his knees, Homer drapes the cable around his body. Kissing the cord fervently, he muses, "How can one little insulated wire bring so much happiness?" The shot switches to a rear view of Homer. From the sofa, Lisa watches her father smooching the cable behind the television set. All that can be seen is his body from the neck down. Here again, we see that Homer's hyperconsumption has led both his literal head and his status as head of the family to be obstructed by the television set.

Within the cable episode, television takes on more than the status as Head of Household: television competes with Marge and the children for Homer's attention. When Lisa sees Homer on his knees behind the television set, it is important to note that Homer is kissing the television more fervently than he has ever kissed his wife. As the episode progresses, Homer is increasingly alienated from the women in the family. He fights with Marge over whether or not to continue stealing cable, while Lisa protests the theft through conscientious objection.[40] At the end of the episode, Homer's insistence upon cable television once again lures him away from his familial responsibilities. He is pictured in the living room watching a boxing match, surrounded by all of the other men in Springfield, from the local police to his boss. Exiled from the home, Marge, Lisa, and baby Maggie sit in protest on the front lawn.

However, when confronted with the thought that he could be jailed for his theft and barred from his family, Homer ultimately chooses family over cable. As Homer literally cuts his ties to his television mistress, the stability of the Simpson family is reinstated. However, like Homer's triple bypass, the "lesson" to be learned is not the consequences of binge consumption per se. Once again, the conflict is over Homer's abilities as the family breadwinner. What doesn't sit right about consuming cable television is that his binging occurs in opposition to his role as patriarch. Homer has problems because, like his heart surgery, he is once again unable to pay for his consumption. When Homer steals cable, he is consuming something that he as a breadwinner is unable to buy for his family. Furthermore, it is something that he wants to indulge in alone, apart particularly from the women in the family.

In the context of *The Simpsons,* Homer is cast into two contradictory identities: the hyperconsumer "cultural dupe" and the white male patriarch. However, *The Simpsons* negotiates the unstable connections between consumer and patriarch by mapping the contradiction onto a specifically marked socioeconomic class. As long as the "cultural dupe" remains within the televisual recycling of the "working-class buffoon," then the encoding of authority onto the white patriarch of the nuclear family can be recuperated. In his discussion of the "working-class buffoon," Richard Butsch argues that the lack of authority a blue-collar father may have within a sitcom is symptomatic of social class markers within the televisual as a whole.[41] The contradiction is encoded as the individual consumer's failure to earn rather than a symptom of the consumptive nature of commodity capitalism itself. What is at stake in Homer's figuration is not white masculinity as such but a particularly working class white masculinity. Homer cannot be both father and consumer because he does not make enough money. Within *The Simpsons,* there is the suggestion that Homer is emasculated not because of the size of his belly or the consequences of his excessive consumption but simply because of the size of his paycheck.

HOMER'S BUTT: CRACKING THE LIMITS OF THE NUCLEAR FAMILY

Homer has television for a head and a belly bloated by excessive consumption. As a result, his inability to perform the duties of the white male patriarch makes him the butt of the joke. Indeed, within the context of *The Simpsons,* the repeated sight of Homer's butt crack punctuates the seamy underside of consumer culture. Not only does Homer desire to consume apart from his family, but the very modes of his consumption make it impossible for him to stay within the "proper" functioning of the domestic sphere. The contradictory encodings of Homer's body as both patriarch and feminized hyperconsumer make him unable to function within the normative social realm. Within the private sphere, he cannot maintain his authority as the head of household because he has lost his head to television; within the public sphere, Homer cannot adequately provide for his family because he cannot control his compulsion to feed his gut.[42] Thus, Homer's body becomes pathologized by his socioeconomic shortcomings. His empty head, his corpulent gut, and his degraded butt crack configure Homer as a dangerous body—one whose excesses and lacks ultimately threaten the very foundation of the nuclear family.

In "Homer the Heretic," once again the white masculinity that Homer is supposed to embody loses its dignity—the revelation of Homer's butt crack emphasizes his feminized status within the household. The episode begins with the Simpson family readying themselves for church. Homer stands among the other reluctant Simpson children at the foot of the stairs, struggling to squeeze himself into his "itchy church clothes." Ripping the seat of his pants, he mutters, "One-size-fits-all, my butt." Retreating back up the stairs, Homer announces, "Forget it, I'm not going." The next shot focuses on him as he trudges off. However, the viewers cannot see the head of the household; all they can see is Homer's butt crack peeking out from his torn pants.

Here, the corporeality of Homer's buttocks is a sight gag. As he walks back up the stairs, Homer's ignorance of his exposed butt crack makes an ass out of him. In her discussion of the body, Mary Douglas states that "sometimes bodily orifices seem to represent points of entry or exit to social units."[43] Judith Butler expands on Douglas's discussion, theorizing the body as encoded with normative value judgments: "What constitutes the limit of the body is never merely material, but . . . the surface, the skin, is systematically signified by taboos and anticipated transgressions; indeed, the boundaries of the body become . . . the limits of the social *per se*."[44] If we transcribe these theories onto Homer's body, we see that the unruliness of his body ostracizes him from the realm of the socially acceptable. His body is pathologized as something that threatens to contaminate the boundaries of the social. As such, Homer's buttocks represent the consequences of breaching the confines of normative behavior.[45]

This practice of corporeal inscription is predicated upon an inside/outside binary opposition. If the body metaphorizes the strict borders of the social, then any corporeal permeability or leakage would threaten the cultural order. Embedded within this opposition is the coding of certain body "types" as outside of or excluded from the framework of social acceptability. Within this social system, excreting bodies, diseased or mucousy bodies (particularly menstruating female bodies that are vulnerable to penetration), become marked as *disorderly*. In turn, bodily excretions—blood, drool, snot, urine, feces—are rendered *dirty* in opposition to the cleanliness and order of the social body. Julia Kristeva characterizes these exclusions as the *abject,* "that which has been expelled from the body, discharged as excrement, literally rendered 'Other.' "[46] If the abject is outside the body, it is coded as a binary opposition to it. The abject is the "'not me' . . . what established the boundaries of the body which are also the first contours of the subject."[47]

Turning back to *The Simpsons,* we see Homer's abjection when his butt crack creeps out of his pants.[48] Here, Homer's buttocks are a dirty joke, dependent upon the demarcations between orderly social subjects and disorderly abjected bodies. Thus, when Homer's butt splits the seat of his pants, he is rendered unfit for public consumption; he gets to stay home. After all, as a white male, Homer's body is not supposed to leak; it is supposed to fit within the boundaries of his pants. Furthermore, as an icon of white masculinity, Homer is supposed to be the one who wears the pants in the family.

Michael Warner characterizes the public sphere as constructed around men, specifically, white men. Their bodies are inscribed with the privilege of the "norm." They are rendered iconic while bodies that are considered not-white and/or not-male become marked as Different or Other. In "The Mass Public and the Mass Subject," Warner states that within the cultural symbolic, "Self abstraction from male bodies confirms masculinity." Similarly, "Self abstraction from female bodies denies femininity."[49] Therefore, when Homer's butt crack slips out of his pants, his gross corporeality particularizes him. His buttocks mark him, preventing the self-abstraction required of masculinity. In those moments, Homer's maleness becomes a rump roasted for *The Simpsons* viewers' derisive consumption.

When Homer shows his butt, the shamefully weak foundations of the nuclear family are bared. His crack is embarrassing, revealing that the primacy of white masculinity is not an impenetrable privilege but something whose internal contradiction and disorder always threaten to expose themselves. If we turn to the way that difference between male/female, masculine/feminine is inscribed on bodies, we see that Homer's ass busts at the seams of these binary oppositions. His crack exposes the embarrassing flaws of social formation: that *wearing the pants in the family* as a signifier of masculinity is a mere *"fabrication."*[50] Thus, the private is made public—the unstable configuration of male privilege within the domestic realm threatens to contaminate masculine dominance within the public sphere. In this case, the differentiation between masculine and feminine identities, public versus private, as anything other than a construct is not so readily manifest.

In "Homer the Heretic," when Homer's unbound butt crack causes him to stay home, his body repudiates the role of white masculinity that he is expected to perform. Spending the day splashing in the shower, cooking, eating, drinking, and drooling in front of the television, Homer's body produces more dirt—leaving the house in total disorder. Within the logic of corporeal inscription, the abject filth that Homer produces makes him a polluting body, a hazard to household order. Mary Douglas defines "pollution behavior" as "the reaction which condemns any object or idea likely to confuse or contradict cherished contradictions."[51] His ignorance of white masculinity, in combination with the disorder that his body produces, endangers the borders that separate abstracted and orderly male bodies from particularized, disorderly female bodies. As a result, Homer's body becomes a liability to the structure of the nuclear family.

After a long, hard day of eating, drinking, and channel surfing, Homer falls asleep on the couch, leaving a cigar burning that sets the Simpson home on fire. The implication, of course, is that Homer does not know how to wield the phallus with any authority: he is an ineffectual patriarch. As a result, his bodily disorderliness has caused the phallic symbol to combust. In turn, the shriveling cigar endangers the household. The line of fire follows the trail of Homer's filth and disarray, all the way to the oily rags and blasting caps he has left in the basement. The house blazes while Homer dozes. At this point, Homer's abjection, the exposure of his butt crack, has become the catalyst for the potential destruction of the nuclear family right down to its literal foundations.

Homer, however, ultimately transcends his abjection. What saves him from the fire is the labor of other, marked bodies. Both Homer and the Simpson home are rescued by the Springfield volunteer fire department—an equal opportunity, coed, multicultural group composed of what Homer's minister the Reverend Lovejoy characterizes as "a Protestant, a Jew, and an Other."[52] The week following Homer's dramatic rescue, we find an unrepentant Homer back in church, snoring loudly in the front pew. Once again, Homer has managed to squeeze himself into his pants, seams intact. No matter how emasculated, stupid, or dirty Homer is, his whiteness and his maleness still somehow manage to maintain his privilege within the social.

In another episode of *The Simpsons*, the size of Homer's ass expands to the point that it becomes literally impossible for him to wear the pants in the family. The way Homer's body blurs the boundaries between feminine and masculine, the domestic sphere and the outside world, becomes uncannily apparent when Homer claims disability for his "hyperobesity" ("King Size Homer"). In the episode, Homer discovers that he can avoid going to his office altogether by getting his obesity marked as a "disability." After gleefully gaining sixty pounds, Homer attains his dream of working at home. Once again, Homer's hyperobese body is abject. Too large to fit within the norms of the public sphere, he is exiled to the private sphere—away from the masculinized bodies of the public sphere and bodies that can conform to cultural norms.

Within this episode, Homer demonstrates how his body, unlike what Michael Warner describes as "self abstracted . . . masculinity," is very much a marked and feminized body.[53] Here, however, Homer is able to juggle both his iconicity as patriarch and consumer by blurring the boundaries of gender identity: the boundaries between work and home. In this case, Homer appears to have his cake and eat it, too. He maintains his status of breadwinner without having to leave the domestic sphere—and he does so dressed as a woman. As the feminized hyperconsumer, the first thing that Homer does to celebrate his relocation to the domestic realm is to buy a new dress. Entering the "Vast Waistband" clothing store, Homer announces, "I'm looking for something loose and billowy, something comfortable for my first day of work." Too fat to fit into traditional men's trousers, Homer leaves the store wearing a flowered woman's muumuu.

For much of the rest of the episode, Homer is seen languishing in the muumuu performing the consumer duties of an iconic housewife. "Woohoo!" he declares when he discovers a free sample of fabric softener in the mail. As the obedient consumer, Homer dutifully tests the product. "Mmm . . . I can feel three kinds of softness," Homer gushes, regurgitating the fabric softener's marketing copy. Later, still in a woman's dress, Homer is glued to the television watching a soap opera. Clearly, Homer's obesity and self-imposed exile from the public sphere has feminized him.

By the end of the episode, however, the excesses of Homer's body once again become dangerous elements. But this time, Homer's gender transgressions threaten not only the safety of the domestic sphere but the public sphere as well. When Homer violates his quarantine to go to the movies, his abjected body literally and figuratively threatens to pollute the entire town of Springfield. Still wearing the muumuu, Homer abandons his post as the nuclear safety technician, leaving a toy bird in charge of watching the levels. Once he reaches the outside world, Homer's butt is seen yet again as uncontainable—a threat to public safety. "A man of your carriage couldn't possibly fit in our seats," the theater manager tells Homer. "I can sit in the aisle," Homer offers. "I'm afraid that would violate the fire code," the manager responds, offering him a garbage bag of free popcorn for consolation. As a crowd gathers staring and heckling Homer, Homer offers the public a fleeting moment of opposition. He announces,

> This may surprise you, but you can't buy me off with food. I'm sick of all of your stereotypes and cheap jokes! The overweight individuals in this country are just as smart and talented and hardworking as everybody else. And they're going to make their voices heard. . . . Hmph. . . . I'll work harder than ever before and show the world that overweight people are not undisciplined, lazy, and irresponsible.

In spite of all his activist clamoring, Homer proves all of the stereotypes true. As an overweight person, he *is* "undisciplined, lazy, and irresponsible." Upon his return home, Homer discovers that his negligence has put the town in danger. "Situation critical, explosion imminent," his computer screen flashes. Desperate to warn the plant, Homer attempts to call them. Again, the excesses of his body bar him from contact with the public sphere. The telephone recording informs him, "the fingers you have used to dial are too fat." After hijacking an ice cream truck, Homer unwittingly saves the day by falling into the exploding nuclear tank. The size of his body seals the opening.

"I think it's ironic that, for once, Dad's butt prevented the release of toxic gas," Bart later quips. Once again, Bart is right. By blocking the explosion, Homer saves the town from nuclear contamination. His body becomes the last barrier between the health of social norms and the poisonous deconstruction of gender hierarchies. In her discussion of gender, Elizabeth Grosz states that the body is always seen as "sexually specific, the body codes meaning projected onto it in sexually determinate ways."[54] Therefore, "Women's bodies [are encoded] as weaker, less controllable than men's as way of justifying patriarchal oppression."[55] When Homer is declared disabled, he becomes encoded not just as a fat person but also specifically as a fat *woman*. The implication is that his inability to keep his weight within acceptable norms has rendered him not only "disabled" but also feminized—and quarantined within the domestic sphere.

However, in spite of its corporeal transgressions, Homer's body is ultimately able to contain its own threat to cultural norms. Unlike the bodies of actual women, Homer is able to pass through his abjection with relative ease. As a reward for saving the town from contamination, Burns tells him, "If there's anything . . . I can do for you, please don't hesitate to ask." Homer responds, "Can you make me thin again?" After a brief attempt at coaching him through exercise, Burns offers him the easy way out. "Bah! I'll just pay for the blasted liposuction," he says after watching Homer struggle to do a single sit-up. "Woo hoo!" Homer declares.

"Woo hoo!" for Homer indeed. Once again, he has been able to dance beyond the borders of his own iconicity while maintaining his privileges as a white male patriarch. Just as when the excesses of his body set his house on fire, Homer is able to take the easy way out. When the Simpson home threatens to burn down, Homer sleeps while the other townspeople save the foundations of his home—and Marge sews him back into his pants. In this episode, Homer almost contaminates the entire town with his abjection. However, instead of having to work to return his body to the confines of social acceptability, Burns pays for Homer to become a "man" again—to have the fat woman literally sucked right out of him.

HOMER ERECTUS: IS HOMER THE MISSING LINK BETWEEN *US* AND *THEM*?

Within the circuit of the televisual, what is being commodified for *The Simpsons* viewers is a meta-commentary about Homer's fundamental privilege. His buttocks may expose the contradictions within white male masculinity—that it is just a recycled copy—but Homer's hierarchical positional within the commodity circuit is still fixed. He can transgress without having to pay for it. Indeed, in her discussion of gender and the postmodern, Nancy Miller cautions, "Only those who have it can play with not having it."[56] Within the context of *The Simpsons,* Homer's identity as both white male head of household and feminized hyperconsumer is a fluid one.

However, that fluidity depends upon the fixed identities of women and people of color who labor to maintain his hierarchical privilege—both the literal and metaphorical foundations of his home. Apu, the Indian convenience store manager, will stand in for Homer, giving him the freedom to consume away from the responsibilities of family. When he loses his life savings investing in pumpkin futures, Homer's butch sisters-in-law Patty and Selma loan him money—and of course, regardless of his failings, Marge his (house)wife will always be there to clean up his mess, to re-suture Homer's torn pants, sewing him back into position as the one who *wears the pants* in the family.[57]

If *The Simpsons* does little to challenge gender hierarchies, if the show is just offering us another version of the domestic sitcom, *new and improved* with the self-criticism of postmodern satire, then what, ulti-mately *is* the oppositional value of *The Simpsons*? Perhaps what is oppo-sitional about *The Simpsons is* the fact that Homer always lands on his feet week after week, episode after episode. In spite of the inefficiencies of his body—his brainless head, his corpulent gut, his uncontainable butt crack—Homer always manages to retain his position of privilege within the realm of white male masculinity. Indeed, in a typical moment of *Simp-sons* meta-commentary, even Homer's ability to *get away with* his contra-dictory roles as both head of household and avid consumer has been parodied within the show.

In "Homer's Enemy," we are introduced to Frank Grimes. Having per-severed through childhood poverty and every other imaginable disad-vantage, Frank is characterized as your typical television hero—a hard working, by-your-bootstraps kind of guy. When Frank is hired at Homer's power plant, the contradiction between Frank, the embodiment of the American dream, and Homer as his slack-jawed antithesis comes to a head. After witnessing the depths of Homer's laziness, Frank declares him his "enemy." Eager to win him over, Homer invites him to dinner. Rather than finding comfort in Homer's friendliness, Frank becomes even more incensed when he enters the Simpson home. Covetous of Homer's nuclear family, Frank leaves the dinner in a huff, vowing to humiliate Homer and expose his ineptitude.

He plots to enter Homer in a children's power plant design contest. However, rather than being humiliated by the event, Homer haplessly enters the contest and wins—to the cheers rather than jeers of his co-work-ers. Driven insane by his enemy's hapless success, Frank goes on a destruc-tive rampage around the factory. In a crazed impersonation of Homer, Frank runs through the plant shouting, "I'm peeing on the seat. Give me a raise! Now I'm returning to work without washing my hands. But it doesn't mat-

ter because I'm Homer Simpson! I don't need to do my work, 'cause someone else will do it for me. D'oh! D'oh! D'oh!" Frank's ravings come to a
tragic end when he unwittingly electrocutes himself. However, rather than
showing him respect at his funeral, the mourners laugh indulgently at
Homer who has fallen asleep and is drooling on himself.

What is so fascinating and possibly even oppositional about the Frank
Grimes episode is that Homer's abjection drives Frank crazy, ultimately
killing him. In contrast to when Homer's laziness almost burned his house
down or when his negligence almost caused the nuclear power plant to
explode, the social dangers of Homer's body are allowed to flourish within
this episode. Homer's abjection is what destroys Frank Grimes and, in turn,
the iconicity of the American Dream. Frank is driven crazy both literally
and figuratively by the fluidity of Homer's body. To Frank, Homer's body
is an excessive body, a lazy and filthy body. Frank angrily watches Homer's
dirty, leaky body pass back and forth through its own abjection while
Homer retains his social privilege. In spite of his social deviance, Homer
retains his status as the patriarch of a nuclear family—a position that Frank
has not been able to achieve in spite of his own hard work and dedication.

On the one hand, Frank Grimes is the iconic man of television past. A
hard worker and diligent pursuer of the American Dream, he plays by the
rules. He is the recycled patriarch of *Father Knows Best* and *Leave it to Beaver*
fame. The difference, the contradiction embodied by this recycled character, is that Frank Grimes *is not* the patriarch of a nuclear family. He is not a
success; he has not attained the accouterments of the American Dream: a
home, a wife, and family. In contrast, Homer's privilege within both the private and public sphere is a decisively postmodern one. He is the satire of the
iconic white male. Homer exposes the ideals of white masculinity as an
absurdity—just another useless commodity that you are suckered into buying but that never delivers on its marketing promise. Unlike Homer, Frank
Grimes has been duped by the promises of white male masculinity.

In an interesting twist, it is now Homer who becomes the savvy consumer. He stumbles through his social privilege without ever really *buying
into* the promise of white masculinity, of the attainability of the American
Dream through hard work and social restraint. Homer has a home and family; he wins contests at work even with television for a head, while wearing a woman's dress, or with his butt crack hanging out of his pants. The
contradiction of his body as both the masculinized head of household and
leaking, dirty feminized consumer *pees on the seat* of masculine power and

privilege; this abjection is what blows Frank's mind—and in turn, the mindset of the American Dream. The social logic of gender hierarchies and social norms are destroyed in the macabre moment when Frank Grimes—the proper, functioning icon of white masculinity—is electrocuted. Here the social positions become switched. Homer becomes the functional and accepted member of society—even the savvy consumer subject.

What is potentially oppositional about *The Simpsons* is precisely this moment: when the central icon of social order—the hardworking white masculine identity—is killed by the power of contradiction. What differentiates Frank as the orderly (and thus superior) social subject and Homer as the disorderly social deviant is deconstructed. Frank becomes abject, crazed, deviant, while Homer calmly looks on. Here, the Homer Simpsons of the world, abjected bodies, those that don't quite fit into social norms, win the day.

"Oh, Marge," Homer says to his wife, "cartoons don't have any meaning. They're just stupid drawings that give you a cheap laugh." Standing up, Homer reveals his butt crack seeping out of his pants. Here, the essay comes full circle. Who is Homer Simpson? Is he a cultural dupe, someone who believes that "cartoons don't have any meaning" while we, the savvier viewer, know better? Again, I would suggest that what differentiates us from Homer Simpson is not so succinct. In many ways, Homer is right. Cartoons don't have any meaning. They *do* just give us a cheap laugh. After all, when Homer is seen on his hands and knees with television for a head, when he strides out of a clothing store wearing a woman's dress, when his butt crack escapes out of his pants, the contradictory encodings of Homer's body reveal that iconic identities—the white male patriarch, the feminized consumer, their signifying hierarchies of gender—*are* nothing but a "cheap laugh."

NOTES

1. Much thanks to Robyn Wiegman for her generous guidance and support in the writing of this paper. Additional thanks to Richard House for his invaluable assistance in the revision process.
2. Jim Collins, "Postmodernism and Television," in *Channels of Discourse, Reassembled,* ed. Robert Allen (Chapel Hill: University of North Carolina Press, 1992), 335.

3. Mimi White, "Ideological Analysis and Television," in *Channels of Discourse, Reassembled,* 335.

4. White, "Ideological Analysis and Television," 335.

5. White, "Ideological Analysis and Television," 335.

6. The political economy of a televisual production "calls attention to the fact that the production and distribution of culture takes place within a specific economic and political system constituted by relations between the state and the economy" ("Part I: A Cultural Studies Approach to Gender, Race, and Class, in the Media," in *Gender, Race, and Class in Media,* ed. Gail Dines and Jean M. Humez [Thousand Oaks: Sage Publications, 1995], 16: footnote 5). Robert Allen discusses the political economy of television production when he states that "the primary purpose of American television, as it's presently constituted, is to deliver an audience to an advertiser at the lowest cost per thousand" ("Introduction," in *Channels of Discourse, Reassembled,* 21). To save money on production costs, the political economy of *The Simpsons* is a transnational one in that the animation cells are shipped to a Korean animation house where laborers are paid dramatically lower wages than their American counterparts. In yet another moment of ironic hyperconsciousness, *The Simpsons* actually point to the conditions of their own production. In "Itchy & Scratchy: The Movie," Bart and Lisa are watching news commentary on their favorite cartoon show, *Itchy & Scratchy.* The scene cuts to a reporter who is discussing "how American cartoons are really made." Behind him is a Korean animation factory where exhausted-looking workers are being prodded and coerced by a gun-toting soldier.

7. It is worth noting the show's proclivity for referencing and thus advertising other Fox shows.

8. Here I am referring to the postmodernism characterized by Fredric Jameson as "the end result of capitalism's relentless commodification of all phases of every day existence. . . . [A]ll such cultural activity is driven by a logic of 'late' capitalism, which endlessly develops new markets that it must neutralize politically by constructing a vision of success and personal happiness, expressible solely through the acquisition of commodities" (quoted in Collins, "Postmodernism and Television," 339). Within the context of *The Simpsons,* it is precisely these processes of late capitalism that are being parodied and recommodified by the series.

9. Patricia Mellencamp, *High Anxiety: Catastrophe, Scandal, Age, and Comedy* (Bloomington: Indiana University Press, 1992), 277.

10. Mellencamp, *High Anxiety,* 11.

11. Lynne Joyrich, "Critical and Textual Hypermasculinity," in *Postmodern After-Images: A Reader in Film, Television, and Video,* ed. Peter Booker and Will Booker (London: Arnold, 1997), 214.

12. Joyrich, "Critical and Textual Hypermasculinity," 214.

13. Richard Butsch, "Ralph, Fred, Archie, and Homer: Why Television Keeps Recreating the White Male Working Class Buffoon," in *Gender, Race, and Class in Media,* 409.

14. Here Butler is focusing specifically upon gender and sexual identities. For the purposes of this essay, I am extending her analysis to the formation of race and class identifications as well.

15. Judith Butler, *Gender Trouble: Feminism and the Subversion of Identity* (New York: Routledge, 1990), 137.

16. Jacques Derrida discusses the repetition or iterability of the sign as something that can and must be able to be "cited, put between quotation marks; thereby it [the sign] can break with every given context, and engender infinitely new contexts" in "Signature, Event, Context," in *Margins of Philosophy,* trans. Alan Bass (Chicago: University of Chicago Press, 1982), 320.

17. Butler, *Gender Trouble,* 145.

18. Butler, *Gender Trouble,* 141.

19. Butsch, "Ralph, Fred, Archie, and Homer," 404.

20. Butler, *Gender Trouble,* 145.

21. In his theory of "preferred reading," Stuart Hall characterizes three reading strategies (dominant, negotiated, and oppositional) that consumers may employ in response to a cultural text such as *The Simpsons.* A dominant reading unequivocally accepts or reifies governing ideological assumptions. Negotiated readings may challenge parts of the text but ultimately do not question the dominant ideology that structures the text. Subjects who recognize themselves as being fundamentally antipathetic to the cultural system that has created the text produce oppositional readings. *The Simpsons,* however, problematizes this model insofar as that which is being commodified is the very knowability of the "dominant" from a purportedly oppositional perspective. With commodities such as *The Simpsons* in development, there arises a need for a new, more complex model of response to a cultural artifact. See John Fiske, "British Cultural Studies," in *Channels of Discourse, Reassembled,* 292.

22. Andrew Ross, "Techno-Ethics and Tele-Ethics: Three Lives in the Day of Max Headroom," in *Logics of Television,* ed. Patricia Mellencamp (Bloomington: University of Indiana Press, 1990), 144.

23. Meaghan Morris, "Banality in Cultural Studies," in *Logics of Television,* 14–43.

24. In the "Introduction" to *The Queen of America Goes to Washington City: Essays of Sex and Citizenship* (Durham: Duke University Press, 1997), Lauren Berlant defends her pop culture archive (which incidentally includes *The Simpsons*), stating, "I am conducting a counterpolitics of the silly object by focusing on some instances of it and by developing a mode of criticism that reads the waste material of everyday communication in the national public sphere as pivotal doc-

uments in the construction, experience, and rhetoric of quotidian citizenship in the United States" (12).

25. Douglas Kellner, "Beavis and Butt-head: No Future for Postmodern Youth," in *Postmodern After-Images*, 214.

26. Ross, "Techno-Ethics and Tele-Ethics," 144.

27. Here I am using icon to connote a sign that resembles its referent.

28. Fiske, "British Cultural Studies and Television," 304.

29. Derrida, "Signature, Event, Context," 315.

30. Lynn Spigel, *Make Room for TV: Television and the Family Ideal in Post-war America* (Chicago: University of Chicago Press, 1992).

31. Spigel, *Make Room for TV,* 37.

32. Butler, *Gender Trouble,* 45.

33. Butler, *Gender Trouble,* 46.

34. In her definition of gender performativity, Butler states, "Words, acts, gestures, and desire produce the effect of an internal core or substance, but produce this *on the surface* of the body, through the play of signifying absences that suggest, but never reveal, the organizing principle of identity as a cause. Such acts, gestures, enactments generally construed are *performative* in the sense that the essence of identity that they purport to express are *fabrications*" (*Gender Trouble,* 136).

35. Susan Bordo, *Unbearable Weight: Feminism, Western Culture, and the Body* (Berkeley: University of California Press, 1993), 199.

36. Mellencamp, *High Anxiety,* 377.

37. "The Two Mrs. Nahasapeemapetilons." What must also be noted is the absurdly flippant way that Homer can "loan" Marge and the children to another man without meeting resistance from either her or the children.

38. The ease in which Homer is able to check into the nursing home simply by claiming to be a senior citizen again attests to the performativity of identity. Homer merely takes on a new name, a new identity, and begins acting like a convalescent.

39. Here again, the question of who is copying whom is raised. Is Homer's cable theft a copy of the Homer-the-Beef of ye olden times, or is Homer-the-Beef a copy of Homer Simpson?

40. Here I would argue that *The Simpsons* is able to play with the borders of white male patriarchy not only because it remains within the realm of the working class buffoon but also because the female characters such as Marge and Lisa remain fixed within traditional gender roles. Within this episode, Marge and Lisa provide the moral center for the Simpson family—a conscience with no apparent agency of its own. Rather than disconnecting the cable themselves, Lisa and Marge can only protest stealing the cable; they lack the power to make the final decision about whether or not to keep it. Thus, regardless of the disruptive role of television, Homer still maintains his privilege and power over Marge and Lisa.

41. Butsch, "Ralph, Fred, Archie, and Homer."

42. I am knowingly evoking a binary opposition between public and private precisely because Homer's contradictory identities ultimately show that the boundaries (and hence the gendered division) between public and private are destabilized by the processes of consumer culture—even if capitalism requires the structure of the heteronormative nuclear family in order to function.

43. Mary Douglas, *Purity and Danger: An Analysis of the Concepts of Pollution and Taboo* (New York: Routledge, 1966), 4.

44. Butler, *Gender Trouble,* 131.

45. The pants-below-the butt-crack gag is an often-recycled trope within the televisual marking the working class as degraded and disorderly.

46. Butler, *Gender Trouble,* 133.

47. Butler, *Gender Trouble,* 133.

48. On iterability, Derrida writes, "*iter,* once again, comes from *itara, other* in Sanskrit, and everything that follows may be read as an exploitation of the logic which links repetition to alterity" ("Signature, Event, Context," 315). Within this context of *iterability,* the repeated visuality of Homer with his buttocks bared reveals the *othering* or abjection inherent within the structures of citationality.

49. Michael Warner, "The Mass Public and the Mass Subject," in *Habermas and the Public Sphere,* ed. Craig Calhoun (Cambridge: MIT Press, 1992).

50. Butler, *Gender Trouble,* 136.

51. Douglas, *Purity and Danger,* 37.

52. Within this context, "Other" sardonically refers to Hinduism, the religion of Apu, the stereotypically maligned Asian Indian convenience store manager in *The Simpsons.*

53. Warner, "The Mass Public and the Mass Subject," 60.

54. Elizabeth Grosz, *Volatile Bodies: Towards a Corporeal Feminism* (Bloomington: Indiana University Press, 1994), 14.

55. Grosz, *Volatile Bodies,* 14.

56. Quoted in Lynne Joyrich, "Critical and Textual Hypermasculinity," in *Postmodern After-Images,* 212.

57. It is suggested within *The Simpsons* that Patty and Selma have the money to pay Homer's bills precisely because they are hairy-legged and butch. However, their "masculine" qualities are condemned in that they are seen as lonely spinsters, desperate for husbands.

Who Wants Candy?
Disenchantment in *The Simpsons*

ROBERT SLOANE

In the 1990s, the U.S. media landscape was marked by a subtle, if not entirely unprecedented shift: forms of "underground" media increasingly made their way above ground for the world to see. In the music industry, a genre that came to be known as "alternative" made its presence felt after the surprising success of Nirvana's 1991 album *Nevermind*. The music did not stay alternative for long, though, as major labels increasingly looked to (and bought) small independent labels to mine for new talent. A similar move happened in film: led by the critical acclaim for particular films of the late 1980s (e.g., David Lynch's *Blue Velvet*, Steven Soderbergh's *sex, lies and videotape*, the films of Spike Lee), the 1990s saw the increasing visibility and popularity of so-called "independent" films. New attention was devoted to the festival circuit (and specifically to a newcomer called Sundance), and a small company called Miramax became increasingly influential, culminating in the mid-decade successes of its films *Pulp Fiction* and *The English Patient*. Again, the major studios reacted in kind, as they started to flex their smaller, more "artsy" divisions or otherwise mined the Indies for profits, whether that meant buying up the companies outright, as Disney did Miramax, making plans to distribute the independent films, or simply signing successful independent directors to do big-studio films.

The Simpsons, I would argue, was also part of this shift. When James L. Brooks, producer of Fox's *The Tracey Ullman Show* (1987–1990), went looking for an animator who could furnish his show with cartoon "bumpers" to bridge between the show's sketches and the commercials, he called on Matt Groening, the artist of *Life in Hell*. A regular feature in many alternative newsweeklies across the United States, *Life in Hell* was known for its defiance of authority and often contained political barbs and decidedly leftist material (often embodied in the strip's gay couple, Akbar & Jeff). *The Tracey Ullman* shorts featuring *The Simpsons* did not necessarily exhibit the politics of *Life in Hell,* but they were every bit as irreverent. When Fox decided to take a chance and give *The Simpsons* a full half-hour slot, Groening had to face what every artist who has the chance to exhibit his/her work for a wide audience must face: how does one present an oppositional viewpoint and still appeal to as many people as possible? As he put it in a 1988 interview, "The secret thing I'm trying to do, behind entertainment, is to subvert. And if I can make myself and my friends laugh and can annoy the hell out of a political conservative, I feel like I've done my job."[1]

This dilemma of "going mainstream" is an important topic, because it allows us to ruminate on a hypothetical relationship between producers and audiences within texts. That is to say, when a producer is faced with this movement from a sphere of very low circulation to one of very high circulation, the texts created are worth examining to see how they negotiate this move. Do they try to maintain their oppositionality? Do they give in to a blander, more traditional tone? Or do they try to stake out a middle ground? I do not want to suggest that all art coming from underground sources is, by definition, ideologically oppositional. However, in a model of society that posits a dominant culture against many subcultures, we may say that the mainstream media maps onto the first term and alternative/underground media onto the second.[2] Thus, in its alliance with subcultures, the underground stands in "opposition" to the "mainstream," and there is accordingly much less pressure to uphold dominant cultural ideas in the former. Indeed, even these terms "mainstream," "alternative," and "underground" are becoming increasingly difficult to locate and/or define in the wake of the vast proliferation of media channels. It was a safe assumption, though, that Groening's exposure (and potential influence) would increase with his move to television.

For Stuart Hall, designations such as "dominant" or "oppositional" are potential positions held by readers, or the "decoders," of media texts.[3] I base my ideas about the circulation of texts on models elaborated by Hall and Richard Johnson, wherein the three key elements of the process consist of (1) producers ("encoders") of texts, (2) texts themselves, and (3) receivers of texts.[4] All of these elements are imbricated in and informed by various social processes and thus cannot be interpreted outside the context of those processes. When faced with texts, readers take up one of three positions: (1) the dominant-hegemonic position, which conforms to the dominant code(s) of the culture; (2) the negotiated position, which is a modified version of the hegemonic position wherein a reader adopts oppositional elements to fashion a more satisfactory situated reading; and (3) the oppositional position, which sees the dominant code at work in texts and tries to battle against it. But the problem with Hall's argument is that it assumes that the content of a television text is always already determined by the structure of television production (which is, ultimately, the capitalist mode of production). Hall states that a viewer operates within the dominant code when s/he "takes the connoted meaning from, say, a television newscast or current affairs programme full and straight, and decodes the message in terms of the reference code in which it has been encoded."[5] The encoded "reference code," therefore, is always assumed to be one that supports a capitalist mode of production; by Hall's definition, there is no text that can be encoded "oppositionally." A similar critique can be found in the work of the Frankfurt School scholars, most notably Theodor Adorno and Max Horkheimer, who maintain that texts produced by the "culture industry" always bear the marks, and support the logic, of capitalism.[6]

The Simpsons, however, may give one reason to pause in the light of this rule. Surely, the show is produced, exhibited, and received within the traditional structure of the television industry, and in that way it does support the status quo. However, once it is decided that television texts and their production are always supportive of the dominant culture, we can only study the ways in which audiences take up texts (which is the method that Hall seemingly advocates). This approach forecloses any other possibilities to analyze the logics at work in the production of television texts. Indeed, one might argue that the logic of capitalism has evolved to the point that it may support the sale of anything that proves profitable, even if the product's content explicitly defies its productive logic. Theorists often refer to this as "co-optation" or "incorporation," but this process is usually interpreted as watering down the product that moves from subcultural to dominant-culture status.[7] But again, this judgment relies on the place of the text within mainstream media, because it is assumed that this place naturally determines its content. That is, if a band makes an album on a major label, its fans will assume that the album will not retain the qualities of more independent work. To the extent that there is increased involvement by the executives who run the mainstream media, this may be true; however, I'd like to hold a place open for the possibility that a text may be *encoded* with oppositionality, and that this would not necessarily be inimical to capitalist logic.

The Simpsons has been one of the most political shows on television since its debut in 1989. It has been heralded, along with shows such as *Married . . . with Children, Roseanne,* and *Grace Under Fire,* for featuring an explicitly working class family and thereby offering a rare counterpoint to the stereotypical middle-class TV family. It also has been celebrated for featuring gay characters, and the show was rated to be the favorite among Latino/a audiences in a 1993 study.[8] The program has also devoted many shows to typically leftist concerns—the environment, labor, homosexuality, immigration, and even vegetarianism. However, the show is by no means wall-to-wall radical propaganda. At its heart, the show is about family, and no matter how much the portrayal of the Simpsons satirizes or critiques the institution of the American family, the program continually comes back to reaffirm the bond between these people.[9] Of course, the Right does not have sole dominion over family issues, as much as its adherents might think it does; but *The Simpsons* exhibits enough "family values" to satisfy right-wing operatives such as former Reagan speech writer Peggy Noonan, and that should send up a red flag for anyone concerned about finding oppositionality in the show.[10]

For the purposes of this essay, though, the exact political thrust of *The Simpsons* is not really important. I am more concerned with how the show's writers see and portray the possibility of political effectivity coming from the show. Many of the show's producers (with the exception of Groening) repeatedly claim to have no particular agenda.[11] Yet, no matter their party affiliation, the show's writers are definitely anti-authoritarian and strive to critique many institutions that shape modern life (not just politics, but work, school, religion, capitalism, etc.). Thus, the term "political" as I am using it implies a stance taken vis-à-vis the workings of the dominant culture (even from within it), not simply the advocacy of a particular political party's program.[12]

Another factor that is key to my thinking about the show is that the writers (and producers more generally) seem to enjoy a good deal of autonomy from the Fox network. In an interview, writer Mike Scully asserts:

> One of the great things about being involved with *The Simpsons* is that it's a completely unique experience as a writer, because on most shows you have to accept the input of the network and the studio, their notes on the things they want to be changed. Normally, there would be around twelve people going over your script, telling you what's wrong with it and how to fix it, and we don't have that here. We're completely autonomous. We make all our own creative decisions and so, if the show comes out great, we pat ourselves on the back; if it stinks then we have to blame ourselves.[13]

This is a significant point, if it is indeed true, because it suggests that the producers of the show can work within the "system" and yet remain relatively outside it in some ways. The hands-off approach by Fox may signal the company's willingness to accept the success of *The Simpsons* no matter how it is achieved. As long as the show is a source of profit, who cares what types of politics it promotes?

Groening has said that one of the reasons for this lack of network input, as compared to a traditional show, is that there is no set around which to congregate. Because of the disjointed and prolonged nature of each episode's production (which takes six to eight months from beginning to end), there is no central location at which network executives might focus their energies. While it is taken for granted that most media production is a collective effort—and *The Simpsons* is surely no exception, with the many people it takes to assemble animation—my readings will assume a sort of primacy in the writing staff, as far as the designation of textual content goes.[14] There is, of course, no way to confirm whether the level of autonomy claimed by the writers actually exists, but I think the explanation is not difficult to believe, given the show's content (and how that content often matches the sentiments found in interviews with members of the cast and crew). For example, jokes about the Fox network are de rigueur, and while this in itself is not enough to affirm the show's autonomy, I want to suggest that there is clearly a different model working here than that of a traditional show on one of the traditional networks.

The show's relationship to the Fox network is an interesting site for contemplation. On one hand, Fox is known for its breaking of television rules. *The Simpsons* was considered a risk when it aired as a weekly series in 1990, and yet the show contributed in a major way to Fox's success. On the other hand, many critics cannot dissociate Fox from its owner, Rupert

Murdoch, a notoriously conservative multimedia mogul whose empire continues to grow worldwide. In an interview for *E! Online,* Groening says that he met Murdoch when the latter took the writers of *The Simpsons* out to lunch: "We talked politics. My dealings with him have been extremely friendly and cordial. I speak my mind, and he speaks his."[15] Clearly, Groening's words denote a fundamental disagreement in worldviews between the two men. In the same interview, Groening describes the unique place for *The Simpsons* on Fox: "A lot of our writers, like Conan O'Brien, moved on to other things. In fact, some of them have gone on to do shows on other networks, and they've tried things they've done on *The Simpsons,* and the people at the other networks say, 'No, you can't do that.' And they say, 'We did it on *The Simpsons.*' And they're told, 'We would never have *The Simpsons* on our network.'"[16] In sum, the show seems to defy certain industry practices, at least to some extent, and for that reason should be considered in a new light.[17]

I want to proceed, then, to a textual analysis of three episodes from the eighth season (1996–1997). These three episodes, in my opinion, mark a profound shift away from some of the (relative) optimism of earlier episodes. With questions about the show's longevity and continued success placed at the fore, these shows exhibit much doubt about whether *The Simpsons* can have much of a political effect, given the conditions of its reception. In direct contrast to the playful irreverence aimed outward in earlier shows, these three episodes turn the magnifying glass toward the show itself and toward its fans, and seem to suggest, when read together, that the chance to affect people in a profound way is gone for *The Simpsons.*

Before continuing, though, I'd like to say a word about methodology. I want to state my understanding of the limits of textual analysis. As I tried to state in my discussion of Hall, I understand that texts need to be read in the context of their production and of their reception. In addition, I am aware that my own reading may be wildly different from that of many viewers, and mine is simply a single voice among many. Finally, I do not mean to overemphasize the "intent" of the show's creative team. I am not looking to discern any "true meaning"; however, I do feel that, when one considers the comments and situations of the writers (in interviews) and fans (in places such as like *The Simpsons Archive*) of *The Simpsons,* these episodes become much more understandable.[18] This approach does not, however, limit the scope of their interpretations. I hope that I can show that I have chosen these texts precisely because of the ways they implicate producers and receivers, and that they are interesting to consider for that reason. Moreover, if my own interpretation can spark an idea in a reader's head or start a conversation among fans, I will feel I have contributed to the discussion in a meaningful way.

"THE ITCHY & SCRATCHY & POOCHIE SHOW"

With its 167th episode, *The Simpsons* overtook *The Flintstones* as the longest running prime-time animation show in television history. However, instead of taking the opportunity to celebrate this landmark, *The Simpsons* presented a meditation upon the very issue of television longevity and on the pitfalls that come with keeping a show "fresh" after a number of years. The episode concerns the fallen ratings of *The Itchy & Scratchy Show,* a cat-and-mouse cartoon shown on Krusty the Klown's show. The producers of *Itchy & Scratchy* try to revive their show with a new character, Poochie the dog. Homer tries out for and wins the part of Poochie, only to see the character killed off after an abysmal reaction from fans.

The Simpsons has often used *Itchy & Scratchy* (and/or Krusty's show) as a vehicle for commenting on the production of television shows (animated or live) generally and on the state of *The Simpsons* specifically. In an episode from the second season ("Itchy & Scratchy & Marge"), Marge goes on a crusade to ban violent cartoons from television. Airing in December of 1990, when Simpsons-mania was either at or approaching its peak, the episode appeared to be a direct reference to criticisms of the show (and of Bart in particular) for providing bad role models.[19] Other episodes deal with plagiarism in animation ("The Day the Violence Died") and/or contain references to Disney iconography ("Itchy & Scratchy Land"). Others contain more overt references to *The Simpsons*. In "Itchy & Scratchy: The Movie," Lisa reports that Dustin Hoffman and Michael Jackson did cameo voices in the Itchy & Scratchy movie: "Of course, they didn't use their real names, but you could tell it was them," confirming for viewers that it truly was these two stars who contributed voices to actual episodes of *The Simpsons,* even though both used pseudonyms. In "Bart Gets Famous," Bart becomes a star on Krusty's show for a funny catchphrase ("I didn't do it"), which is clearly a reference to the ubiquity, in the early days of the show's success, of Bart-isms such as "Don't have a cow, man!" and "Ay caramba!" Thus, when we learn the troubles of the Itchy

& Scratchy production team in "The Itchy & Scratchy & Poochie Show," we may infer a similarity to production woes on *The Simpsons*.[20]

There is similar evidence of parallelism within the episode itself. As *Itchy & Scratchy* introduces their new character "Poochie," a new character mysteriously shows up in and around the Simpsons' household as well. The hip-speaking, fashionably dressed youngster "Roy" is added into the show's orbit with no introduction or explanation; he merely appears. Roy's addition to *The Simpsons* parallels Poochie's addition to *Itchy & Scratchy* and both are meant to exemplify a common tactic used in television: the injection of new personality into a show whose own characters have lost their original appeal. Throughout television history, this move is seen most prominently in shows involving children, who grow up and change too quickly for a show that is interested in longevity (the addition of "Oliver" in later episodes of *The Brady Bunch*, or the introduction of Leonardo DiCaprio's homeless street-kid "Luke" on *Growing Pains*, are two examples). However, the tactic also shows up in shows such as *Happy Days*, which needed to replace departed stars (e.g., Ron Howard) with new faces (e.g., Ted McGinley). In fact, as with nearly everything on *The Simpsons*, Roy is heavily laden with intertextuality: he calls Homer and Marge "Mr. and Mrs. S," à la Fonzie on *Happy Days* (who called the Cunninghams "Mr. and Mrs. C"), and he leaves to move in with "two sexy ladies" at the end of the episode, recalling Jack Tripper in *Three's Company*. Roy's appearance (and equally cryptic exit) act as a nexus between the main plot line of the show and a common device in television production and suggests to viewers that such gimmicks are often pathetic last-ditch efforts motivated by blatant commercial concerns. (Indeed, one would be hard pressed to think of a show that maintained its popularity after key line-up changes, although *M*A*S*H* and more recently *Law & Order* may be two examples.)

Lisa calls attention to this strategy in one crucial (and also highly self-referential) scene. When she and Bart participate in a focus group about improving *The Itchy & Scratchy Show*, producer Roger Meyers, Jr., yells at the children from behind a two-way mirror (briefly turning the light on in the observing room so that we can see him). In frustration, he tells them they do not know what they want and that is the reason the producers cannot make the show better. After he turns the light back off, restoring the mirror's full reflective capacity, Lisa walks up to it and says (to her own reflection): "Um, excuse me, sir. The thing is, there's not really anything wrong with *The Itchy & Scratchy Show*. It's as good as ever. But after so many years, the characters just can't have the same impact they once had." The fact that she says these lines to her own image in the mirror (even though she is ostensibly talking to someone "beyond" it) suggests that this is a sentiment *The Simpsons* feels about its own existence, a glimpse into the very real difficulty of producing a quality show year after year. It is a rare moment of vulnerability for the show, and stands out for the statement it seems to make about the show's continued success. When Meyers then decides to add a new character to *Itchy & Scratchy,* we know he has misinterpreted Lisa's message for the sake of his commercial concerns.

Meyers then takes his idea to a meeting of his production team, which figures prominently in the episode. Besides Meyers and Krusty, the meeting includes an unnamed "network executive" and a group of writers and illustrators who are supposedly based on actual crewmembers of *The Simpsons*.[21] Most of the interactions within this group underscore the dichotomy set up between the writers, who are highly educated, artistic/creative, and down-to-earth, and the executives, or non-creators, who approach the "improvement" of the show from the logic of business. The writers clearly come off in a more favorable light during this running joke, even when they say things such as "Itchy and Scratchy comprise a dramaturgical dyad"—it is they, not the suits, who understand the show's inner workings. Indeed, much of their credibility derives, by default, from the utter *lack* of awareness (self- or otherwise) in the suggestions of the executives. When Roger Meyers, Jr., suggests adding a dog to the show, this exchange follows:

WRITER #1: Uh, a dog? Isn't that a tad predictable?

NETWORK EXECUTIVE: In your dreams. We're talking the original dog from hell.

WRITER #2: You mean Cerberus?

NETWORK EXECUTIVE: We at the network want a dog with attitude. He's edgy, he's "in your face." You've heard the expression "Let's get busy"? Well, this is a dog who gets "biz-zay!" Consistently and thoroughly.

KRUSTY: So he's proactive, huh?

NETWORK EXECUTIVE: Oh, God, yes. We're talking about a totally outrageous paradigm.

WRITER #3: Excuse me, but "proactive" and "paradigm"? Aren't these just buzzwords that dumb people use to sound important? [backpedaling] Not that I'm accusing you of anything like that. [pause] I'm fired, aren't I?

MEYERS: Oh, yes. The rest of you writers start thinking up a name for this funky dog; I dunno, something along the line of say . . . Poochie, only more proactive.

KRUSTY: Yeah!

[Meyers, Krusty, and the network executive leave]

WRITER #2: So, Poochie okay with everybody?

ALL: [reclining in their chairs] Yeah . . .

The network executive tries to use hip language, to appear connected to the cultural zeitgeist, but she cannot keep her business-speak at bay ("Consistently and thoroughly" tells us how Poochie gets "biz-zay!"). The use of the word "proactive" nods to the trend in business to obsess on a particular (if irrelevant) concept, and it becomes a running joke throughout the episode (after making a bad first impression, Poochie later apologizes for coming across as too "proactive"). Of course, the writers can see through this, and one of them is dismissed because of it. The joke about Cerberus is a classic wiseacre put-down (delivered with the innocent sarcasm cultivated by the best class clowns) meant to expose the vapidity of the non-creators. Ultimately, though, the writers defer to the wishes of the higher-ups. When they refuse to think of a better name for Poochie, they communicate their rejection of the idea through the resignation of their creativity. At this point, they are just following the (unwise) orders of their bosses, and Poochie will live or die (and we know he will die) on the basis of the "network" involvement.

In another scene, the producers kibitz as an animator tries to come up with a sketch for Poochie. While Meyers tells him the dog needs "attitude" (conveyed through sunglasses), Krusty and the executive run through a series of subcultural identities for Poochie to inhabit:

NETWORK EXECUTIVE: Could we put him in more of a "hip-hop" context?

KRUSTY: Forget context, he's gotta be a surfer. Give me a nice shmear of surfer.

NETWORK EXECUTIVE: I feel we should Rasta-fy him by . . . 10 percent
or so.

There is still the sense that these identities are "strange" to the producer-executives, in the way the subcultures described by Dick Hebdige are to their own respective dominant cultures; but, of course, this does not stop the suits from trying to "incorporate" what they see as "rebellious" iconography.[22] We can see that the producer-executives are out of touch, that they do not really understand what they are trying to incorporate (i.e., "This is popular with the kids"), and this cultivates more identification with the writers and artistic creators of the show.

Notwithstanding the utter misunderstanding of the show's audience by its non-creative producers, the fans of *Itchy & Scratchy* are not portrayed entirely sympathetically, either. The immediate backlash against Poochie is encapsulated by the statements of the Comic Book Guy:

COMIC BOOK GUY: Last night's *Itchy & Scratchy* was, without a doubt, the worst episode ever. Rest assured that I was on the Internet within minutes, registering my disgust throughout the world.

BART: Hey, I know it wasn't great, but what right do you have to complain?

COMIC BOOK GUY: As a loyal viewer, I feel they owe me.

BART: What? They're giving you thousands of hours of entertainment for free. What could they possibly owe you? If anything, you owe them.

COMIC BOOK GUY: [pauses] Worst episode ever.

The sentiments of the Comic Book Guy seem to be a dig at the fans that inhabit electronic newsgroups such as alt.tv.simpsons, where fans discuss their favorite shows in cyberspace. Clearly, the creators of *The Simpsons* feel hurt that "loyal viewers" dismiss the product of their hard work so readily, and yet many posts on the newsgroup do just that.[23] Fans go over each episode and scene with a fine-toothed comb, rating their relative qualities with unabashed frankness. Indeed, this is an example of the "active audiences" discussed by, among others, John Fiske, who struggle to make their own meaning out of the show.[24] In this context, however, the writers seem to suggest that such nit picking can lead to an under appreciation of the show's larger project. There is no room for error in the minds of these fans.

In another scene, Homer does an in-store appearance as part of the promotion for the new character Poochie. The "hard-core fans" riddle him with questions about internal consistency and peripheral concerns (i.e., a question about the "Itchy & Scratchy CD-ROM" game). Questions of internal consistency are a major topic on *The Simpsons* newsgroup: fans endlessly discuss what state Springfield is in, or what the floor plan of the Simpsons' house would look like, etc. In some ways, this is perfectly understandable, as the animators do show an amazing attention to detail and are sometimes quite consistent, referring back to past episodes in a way that is rare in cartoons (or even in most sitcoms). The fans show their encyclopedic knowledge of *The Simpsons* oeuvre by discussing which details are consistent and which are not, but, again, amidst these discussions, there is the sense that they are missing something larger. When Homer is asked a question of internal consistency, he responds, "Let me ask you a question. Why would a man whose shirt says 'Genius at Work' spend all of his time watching a children's cartoon show?" The suggestion here is that the immense knowledge bandied about on the newsgroup might be put to better effect.

Interestingly, in each of these scenes concerning the fans (Bart's encounter with the Comic Book Guy, and Homer's press conference), it is a Simpson who speaks the critical words. Just as in the earlier scene, when Lisa declares to her reflection (and to the audience) that the characters may have lost their punch, so too do Bart and Homer critique the annoying habits of the fans. That is, instead of being the brunt of the jokes or satire, the Simpsons "stand outside" this episode in a way, speaking the writers' sentiments. The move is appropriate and effective, because the assumption is that the family itself (as the namesake of the show) is under attack, and so the family responds.

Thus, "The Itchy & Scratchy & Poochie Show" works to evince sympathy for the writers of *The Simpsons*. It is they who must fight off the insipid suggestions of their bosses, the producers, but they must also address the sometimes unreasonable demands of the audience. Ultimately, though, the struggle may be for naught. At the end of the episode, after Poochie has left the *Itchy & Scratchy* show (unceremoniously sent back to his "home planet"), Bart and Lisa revel in the "classic" *Itchy & Scratchy* formula for a moment. After a beat, Bart asks, "What else is on?" and they flip the channel, revealing a screen of television snow that brings the episode to a close. Thus, even without the meddling of intruding network types and unappreciative fans, this episode itself seems to suggest a loss of steam on *The Simpsons*. On its own, the episode does not make any grand statement about the political effect of the show. However, when considered in relation to the other two I will discuss, it takes on added resonance.

"HOMER'S ENEMY"

"Homer's Enemy" is an incisive meta-consideration of *The Simpsons*'s world, delivered by the hands that created that world. Although *The Simpsons* is known for its self-reflexivity, the show had never looked at (or critiqued) itself as directly as it does in this episode. Following the "Poochie" show by just nine episodes, "Homer's Enemy" weighs in quite cynically about the worth and/or effectivity of the series.

In the opening scene, we are introduced to Frank Grimes, the subject of an extended news feature proffered by Kent Brockman. The story tells of how Grimes ultimately triumphed over a series of adversities in his life: abandoned by parents; never attended school; worked as a delivery boy to survive; blown up in an explosion on his 18th birthday. Finally, we learn that, in spite of all this, he has earned a degree in nuclear physics through correspondence courses. Grimes' story is exaggerated, to be sure, but it is decidedly not funny. In fact, the news clip stands out for its glimpse into a world where everything does not go perfectly, where things do not resolve themselves nicely. In short, the clip appears more "realistic" than *The Simpsons*'s cartoon universe. Even Grimes himself is drawn to look more like an actual person than the cartoonish-looking Simpson family. From the beginning, then, we feel that Frank Grimes is an outsider to the world of *The Simpsons* and that he carries with him an entirely different set of beliefs and ideas about the world.

Impressed (if only fleetingly) by what he saw of Grimes' resolve in the news feature, Springfield Nuclear Power Plant owner C. Montgomery Burns asks his assistant, Mr. Smithers, to find Grimes and give him a job. Of course, this leads to Grimes' encounter with Homer, his virtual antithesis, and the episode proceeds to develop the dichotomy between the two. Indeed, Homer's actions are oafish, almost exaggeratedly so, to make the point: he tries to tell Grimes how he can avoid the security cameras and sleep at work; he chews up Grimes monogrammed pencils; he eats Grimes' "special dietetic lunch"; he calls Grimes "Stretch," and then, when corrected by Grimes, proceeds to misaddress him as "Grimey." Grimes is aghast when he realizes Homer is a safety inspector. To top it all off, Homer grabs a beaker of acid by mistake, and just before he drinks it, Grimes slaps it toward a nearby wall, which the acid instantly melts. When Burns finds the damage, he demotes Grimes, who then takes out his frustration by declaring himself Homer's "enemy." As we witness this event, another in a string of bad breaks for Grimes, we begin to conclude that Grimes' difficult life has come at the hands of (or at least, stands in opposition to) people such as Homer: careless, oblivious, and virtually unaware of the world in which they live.

This point is driven home in the episode's most crucial scene, in which Homer invites Grimes to the Simpson house in order to make reparations. Grimes can't believe the "palace" *The Simpsons* live in; he lives "in a single room above a bowling alley and below another bowling alley" (to which Homer responds, rapturously, "Wow"). When Grimes asks Homer how he can afford the house, Homer replies, "I dunno. Don't ask me how the economy works." Grimes then stares incredulously at pictures on the wall, all of which reference past episodes (Homer with Gerald Ford, Homer with the Smashing Pumpkins, Homer in outer space). When Homer asks Grimes if he would like to see Homer's Grammy award, Grimes loses his cool:

> GRIMES: No! I wouldn't! God, I've had to work hard every day of my life, and what do I have to show for it? This briefcase and this haircut! And what do you have to show for your lifetime of sloth and ignorance?
>
> HOMER: What?
>
> GRIMES: Everything! A dream house! Two cars! A beautiful wife! A son who owns a factory! Fancy clothes and [sniffs air] lobsters for dinner. And do you deserve any of it? No!
>
> HOMER: [gasps] What are you saying?
>
> GRIMES: I'm saying you're what's wrong with America, Simpson. You coast through life, you do as little as possible, and you leech off of decent, hardworking people like me. Heh, if you lived in any other country in the world, you'd have starved to death long ago.

BART: He's got you there, Dad.

GRIMES: You're a fraud. A total fraud. [leaves]

Two aspects of this scene stand out for comment. The first is the emphasis on the work ethic to which Grimes adheres. I do not think it could be said that *The Simpsons* regularly advocates the kind of allegiance to hard work that Grimes expresses. In fact, many episodes, if not addressing the work ethic specifically, skewer the logics and mechanisms of capitalism, which depends in part on a healthy work ethic for its survival. A subplot in "Homer's Enemy" involves Bart buying an abandoned factory for one dollar at a government auction. Upon arriving at his new property, filled with toxic waste and crumbling down around him, he immediately names himself president of his "company" and hires an "employee," his friend Milhouse. Bart's subplot is an interesting counterpoint to the main plot because it seems to suggest that the workings of capitalism are so ingrained in the American people that, even as children, we enact the corporate structure, even if there is no product to be made or no profit to be earned.

Grimes definitely believes in hard work, but for him it is a necessity, not a moral imperative. Unlike Homer, he has never been handed anything; he has fought for everything he has gotten. Grimes' language does come dangerously close to the kind of criticisms leveled at welfare recipients and the underclass by reactionary, upwardly mobile people ("You're what's wrong with America. . . . You leech off of decent, hardworking people like me"). But here, Grimes comes off as a sympathetic character, because we know he is right about Homer, and that he is not simply making unfounded class- or race-based generalizations. That is, we do not begrudge Grimes for his allegiance to work; there is a ring of truth to his statements. Clearly, the world of *The Simpsons* is fantasy, and our attention is explicitly called to that fact in this moment. Indeed, this sentiment may resonate with the criticism of those fans consumed with internal consistency in *The Simpsons*'s world. Here, *The Simpsons* seem to stand for "fiction," Grimes for "reality."

But the second and perhaps more important aspect that stands out in this scene is Homer's utter lack of awareness of his surroundings. He does not realize (nor appreciate) how charmed his life is, nor does he seem competent enough to explain it. This is one of the rare moments when *The Simpsons* do not seem aware that they live in a television show. Of course, all of the fantastic plot lines represented in the pictures on the wall developed from the fact that *The Simpsons* is an animated television program, which allows for a wide range of creativity. But here, the suspension of disbelief is distinctly and intentionally broken, in an effort to highlight a more "real" world "out there." Ironically, the episode provides a heightened sense of awareness of its own conditions and assumptions by portraying the ignorance of the characters (although Bart does offer a moment of critical reflection when he seconds Grimes' assertion that Homer would not survive in another country). Unlike the "Poochie" episode, it is an outsider, not one of the Simpsons (and definitely not Homer) supplying the critical lines.

Grimes may cross the line, though, when he hatches a plot to show everyone how stupid Homer really is, and that their esteem of him is profoundly misplaced. Doctoring a flyer announcing a "design your own power plant" contest for children, Grimes leaves it for Homer and Homer takes the bait. When Homer submits his power plant (a near-replica of the existing plant, with elbow macaroni and a racing stripe added), Grimes tries to shame Homer in front of the town and his co-workers, but nobody joins Grimes in his derision. No one can see why Grimes is so upset about Homer, and thus the whole community, the whole world of *The Simpsons*, joins together in the unawareness of their situation that we saw previously in Homer. This perceived mass ignorance helps to further drive a wedge between Grimes and Springfield, to the point where he seems to have gone mad by the end of the episode. In a fit of frustration, Grimes flails about the power plant, saying, "Look at me, I am a worthless employee, just like Homer Simpson! Give me a promotion! . . . I don't need to do my work, 'cause someone else will do it for me. D'oh! D'oh! D'oh!" But as he runs up to a wall panel marked "Extremely High Voltage," and begins to exclaim, "Well, I don't need safety gloves, because I'm Homer Simp-," Frank Grimes meets his untimely end.

Ultimately, Grimes' obsession with Homer kills him and thus may suggest that becoming overly concerned with the way other people live may be more destructive than constructive. However, the death of the tragic figure Frank Grimes is truly unsettling and points to a more serious conclusion. Indeed, the final scene of the episode is one of the most disturbing ever shown on *The Simpsons*. As members of the town are gathered to watch Grimes' interment, we see Homer, asleep. And yet he is talking in his sleep—he interrupts Reverend Lovejoy's eulogy to tell Marge to "change the channel." As Lenny exclaims, "That's our Homer!" the congregation (including Lovejoy) bursts into laughter as Grimes' casket is lowered into the ground. The effect is chilling.

While it is tempting to write this image off as simply dark humor, there seems to be very little about it that is funny. From beginning to end, Grimes is at odds with the people of Springfield, and if one accepts his alignment with a more "real" world than the one in which the Simpsons live, one might conclude that *The Simpsons* has become utterly divorced from reality. If this is the case, one might wonder what kind of effect the show could have on "real world" viewers. Indeed, the writers appear highly suspicious of any claims they might have to affect the world. In the context of some of the earlier episodes on political matters, "Homer's Enemy" seems to denote a loss of faith by the writing staff, a severe self-criticism (self-loathing?) that might suggest that they feel the show has lost sight of what it was once trying to do.

One could put a different spin on this reading that makes sense in the context of the producer-receiver relationship of *The Simpsons*. The contrast between the fictional world of *The Simpsons* and the "real" world of Grimes echoes a much-discussed topic on alt.tv.simpsons: whether the show has forsaken "reality" for episodes of wacky plots and situations.[25] There is a general idea among some fans that, between seasons four and five (1993), the show became less interested in the characters and real situations (and internal consistency) and more interested in the sorts of outlandish ideas that animation might allow. The episodes to which Homer refers in showing Grimes the pictures are emblematic of this latter type: Homer becomes an astronaut, wins a Grammy, tours with a rock and roll show, and meets Gerald Ford. There is a similar reference to this debate in "The Itchy & Scratchy & Poochie Show" when a focus group made up of some of Springfield's children say they want *The Itchy & Scratchy Show* to feature "real-life problems" *and* "far-out situations"—or, in the words of the focus group leader, "a realistic, down-to-earth show . . . that's completely off-the-wall and swarming with magic robots." With these details in mind, it is possible that "Homer's Enemy" is meant as a kiss-off to the fans who think *The Simpsons* lost something when it began to incorporate more fantastic situations.[26] Grimes, obsessed with exposing the idiocy of Springfield and its valorization of Homer, is consumed by his own hatred. This interpretation does not make the ending of the episode any less disturbing, but it may help to explain Grimes' obsession with exposing Homer as a fool or with convincing everyone else in Springfield that their beloved hero is a dumb lout. Grimes, in a sense, pays a price for his meddling.

In fact, I think the episode strikes a profound balance between the two readings. Much of the criticism dispensed by the writers in these shows is double-edged, as if they allow that the criticisms have merit, and yet they are stung by them as well. This continues to be true for the next episode.

"*THE SIMPSONS* SPIN-OFF SHOWCASE"

Airing just one week after "Homer's Enemy," "*The Simpsons* Spin-off Showcase" was the penultimate episode of the eighth season. "Hosted" by Troy McClure, the show purported to describe three new television series in the works, all of which would incorporate characters from *The Simpsons*. Although not as overtly self-referential as the other two episodes, "*The Simpsons* Spin-off Showcase" takes on an interesting tenor when read in the light of these other two programs. Indeed, where the "Poochie" show may exhibit hurt or defensiveness and "Homer's Enemy" a certain cynicism or self-loathing, the "Spin-off" episode seems to intone a resignation of sorts for the writers of *The Simpsons*.

First and foremost, though, the episode is a critique of the general banality of television. Like "The Itchy & Scratchy & Poochie Show," this episode takes many shots at the industry and its desperate but sometimes pathetic efforts to keep its programming fresh and entertaining. Walking the halls of the "Museum of TV and Television," the consummate hack actor McClure passes large posters for various television spin-offs of the past (*Rhoda, The Jeffersons, Fish*). McClure recounts that "not long ago, the Fox network approached the producers of *The Simpsons* with a simple request: thirty-five new shows to fill a few holes in their programming line-up. That's a pretty daunting task and the producers weren't up to it. Instead, they churned out three *Simpsons* spin-offs, transplanting already popular characters into new locales and situations." The joke about Fox is punctuated by a very funny visual of a mock weekly schedule, with the time slots for *The Simpsons* (Sunday, 8:00 P.M. Eastern), *The X-Files* (Sunday, 9:00 P.M. Eastern), and *Melrose Place* (Monday, 9:00 P.M. Eastern) filled in; all of the other slots have question marks in them.

While a knock on Fox, the joke also underscored the relative importance of *The Simpsons* to the network, even after eight seasons. Notwithstanding the self-doubt expressed in the "Poochie" show, *The Simpsons* continues to be one of Fox's most highly rated shows. The joke is a way of stating the type of creative clout the show retains, even if its staff feels like it is slipping.[27] Moreover, there is an underlying suggestion here that it takes a lot of work to produce a show as good as *The Simpsons*. Thus, when McClure says the producers "weren't up to" creating thirty-five new shows, but instead "churned out" three spin-offs, his language implies that this type of effort is lackadaisical and uninspired. The suggestion here is that, by "transplanting already popular characters into new locales and situations," spin-offs do little in the way of crossing boundaries of creativity. (Ironically, *The Simpsons* itself is a spin-off of sorts—the family was originally featured in short segments on Fox's *The Tracey Ullman Show*.)

The episode does not simply reserve its derision for spin-offs, however. The show features three seven-minute segments that spoof well-worn television program genres. In the first segment, "Chief Wiggum, P.I.," Chief Wiggum, his son Ralph, and Principal Skinner (known in his new series as "Skinny Boy") move to New Orleans to find themselves in the center of a police action drama. A number of television shows are referenced here—*Magnum, P.I.*, *Miami Vice*, even *Starsky & Hutch*—with the irony coming in the form of the ridiculousness of the characters in their new setting. Wiggum is a notably bad police officer, and the normally straight-laced Skinner is supposed to be his "man-on-the-street" (and in an attempt to look scruffier, Skinner emulates Don Johnson's trademark stubble). As a whole, the parody is not remarkably funny, filled with predictable lines from the blundering Wiggum. It derives its power from the way it underlines the silliness of its premise. When the Simpson family turns up on the streets of New Orleans for Mardi Gras, in the obligatory guest appearance made by the spin-off's "host" characters, Lisa says: "Chief Wiggum, I can't wait to hear about all the exciting, sexy adventures you're sure to have against this colorful backdrop." Even as Wiggum brushes her off, we hear the marketing-speak in Lisa's words, perfectly emulating any hypothetical promotional material for the show. The line is awkward and forced, particularly coming from the rather self-aware Lisa, and thus stands out and tells us something about this situation. In addition, at the end of the segment, when Wiggum lets his new nemesis "Big Daddy" escape, he assures Skinner, "Ah, let him go. I have the feeling we'll meet again, each and every week. Always in more sexy and exciting ways." The acknowledgment of the weekly episodic format of television shows is not new for *The Simpsons*, but here it directly references the suspension of disbelief required to believe that the same detective could meet the same criminal week after week without closure—the suspension of disbelief upon which many shows rely. As well, Wiggum's words here parallel Lisa's earlier statement ("sexy," "exciting"), and thus further cement the forced (and uninspired) nature of the sentiment. That is, it becomes painfully evident that this is simply built-in self-promotion and that it is being used to buttress an already highly unbelievable concept. The resulting feeling leaves us with a distaste for these machinations.

The second segment, entitled "The Love-matic Grandpa," spoofs the sitcom form. The premise here is that Grandpa Abe Simpson has died, but his soul now inhabits a love-testing machine in Moe's Tavern. This admittedly farfetched setup directly references 1960s' sitcoms such as *I Dream of Jeannie* and *My Mother the Car,* which featured similar fantastical situations, but the segment as a whole lampoons the sitcom genre more broadly. Again, there is the obligatory visit from the "host" (this time it is only Homer), and again, the segment is notable for its utter lack of humor. The difference is more glaring here because, unlike the police drama spoofed by "Chief Wiggum, P.I.," we expect the sitcom (situation comedy) form to be funny, or at least make overtures toward being funny. "The Love-matic Grandpa" does make such overtures, but they are pathetic, and their failure tells us something implicitly about the quality of *The Simpsons* itself.

Even as an animated show, *The Simpsons* comes closest to the sitcom form and thus offers a natural benchmark for the humor of "The Love-matic Grandpa." The first glaring difference between the segment and *The Simpsons* is noticed when "The Love-matic Grandpa" utilizes an audience reaction ("laugh") track. A standard device for sitcoms—even if taped before a live audience, as most are—the laugh track is a hidden cue to let the viewers at home know when and how it is appropriate to react during a show. As an animated show, *The Simpsons* has never used a laugh track, and thus it is absolutely startling to hear it on the show.[28] It sounds so out of place that one immediately focuses on it and realizes it is not normally there. The implication to draw here is that *The Simpsons* makes us laugh without telling us *when* to laugh. We do not need prompting. Moreover, "The Love-matic Grandpa" underscores the poor and often inappropriate use of the reaction track: in one scene, Barney tells Moe that he's going on a date with "the lady in front of the drug store who's always yelling things." Looking lovelorn, Moe responds: "She told me she was washing her hair tonight. (He sighs.) I'm so desperately lonely." In addition to the utterly clichéd comment about "washing her hair," a shot of canned laughter follows Moe's statement of loneliness, wholly inappropriate and almost mocking.

Canned reactions continue throughout the segment. When Moe tells Grandpa he "wrote the book on love," Grandpa responds, "Yeah, *All Quiet on the Western Front*," to which the supposed audience reacts with a series of "ooohs," denoting a put-down. When Homer enters, there is a barrage of applause from the pseudo-audience, as sometimes greets a favorite character (*Seinfeld*'s Kramer often got such an ovation). But again, the power of the reaction track as it is used here is to show us how reactions are often predetermined for us by a show's creators. Here, that is meant to signify a short-circuiting of the creativity of genuine humor, and thus we realize that *The Simpsons* delivers quality without pandering to such manipulations.

The segment concludes without incident, and includes the type of last-minute wrap-up of a sticky situation often seen in sitcom episodes. (Here, Moe explains to a date why he has brought the love tester with him to the fancy restaurant in which they are dining: "I ain't too good at talking to women and I really wanted to do you, so I brought along the love tester to help me. As you may have guessed, it's inhabited by the ghost of my friend's dead father.") The ending comes complete with an abrupt 180-degree turn from Moe's date, who originally appears upset with him but then confesses how flattered she is by Moe's actions. The overall banality of the non-romance, peppered with terrible jokes, is a bad enough indictment of the sitcom, but when mixed with the use of the laugh track, the difference between this segment and *The Simpsons* becomes clear, indeed.

Finally, we come to the episode's third, and I think most salient, segment. "The Simpson Family Smile-Time Variety Hour" parodies the live variety shows of the 1960s and 70s, shows such as *Laugh-In* and *The Smothers Brothers Comedy Hour* that themselves, in many ways, took their cues from the vaudeville shows of the early twentieth century. This spin-off, though, stars the actual Simpson family itself, with one exception: Lisa has chosen not to participate (for reasons unspecified), and so has been replaced with "Lisa," a blonde bimbo-ish teenager. (This device recalls a similar situation when the cast of *The Brady Bunch* moved into doing a variety show, wherein the character of Jan was replaced.) Of course, it is significant that it is Lisa who has withdrawn from the project, as she is the most politically and ethically minded Simpson. She would not go for the blatant commercialism involved in such a venture. (Indeed, in this light, her line in "Chief Wiggum, P.I." seems out of character as well, but that situation is less self-serving than the present one.) As we will see, the "Smile-Time Variety Hour" represents an utter disregard for any sort of political concern.

The signifiers for various variety shows are all in place here, making for a funny parody on its surface. At the beginning of the segment, we see Kent Brockman introducing the show from inside a broadcast booth (similar to the shots of *Laugh-In*'s announcer, Gary Owens). A clock on the wall reads 8:20, which corresponds to the actual time (on the east and west coasts) that this segment is airing, lending to the illusion that it is "live." The show features a dance troupe, the "Springfield Baggy-Pants Players" (an ensemble comedy troupe of the sort that populates *Saturday Night Live*), an orchestra, and even moving, rotating sets and props. The family is dressed in 1970s-style jumpsuits (complete with flared legs), and they perform really bad musical numbers with awkward, expository lyrics. There is even the obligatory "special guest": Tim Conway, a comic veteran from the era (most notable, perhaps, for his work on the similarly formatted *The Carol Burnett Show*). The segment proceeds through one skit, in which *The Simpsons* are dressed up like beavers. Again, there are a number of bad puns and jokes, and a reaction track is used. After the skit, there is a *Laugh-In*-like montage wherein other cast members comment on the skit itself; the sea captain McAllister does so as he opens a large porthole-like door in front of a colorful background, much like *Laugh-In*'s "Joke Wall." All of these devices highlight a form in which bad jokes were performed in the name of "zany" entertainment, and again we note that this overwrought variety-hour format stands in contradistinction to *The Simpsons* in terms of quality. Thus, it is not merely pastiche we see here, in Fredric Jameson's notion of the term, but genuine parody.[29]

The real effect of the segment, though—and of the episode in general—comes in the next skit. *The Simpsons* sit in a 1950s-style soda shop, and this interaction takes place:

MARGE: Inflation, trade deficits, horrible war atrocities . . . how are we supposed to do our big musical number with so many problems in the world?

HOMER: Well, I know one thing in this world that's still pure and good.

MARGE: Christian love?

HOMER: No. Candy! [climbs on table] Sweet, sweet, candy!

[The orchestra starts playing "I Want Candy," by the Strangeloves.]

HOMER: [singing] I want candy!

MARGE: But don't you want to end world famine?

BART: [hops out of the booth] I want candy!

MARGE: Or save the endangered Alaskan salmon?

"Lisa": I want candy!

MARGE: Well if you won't think of society's ills . . .

HOMER/BART/"LISA": [singing] I want candy!

MARGE: At least, think of our dentist bills.

The segment then goes into a medley, which includes "Peppermint Twist," "Lollipop," and "Whip It" by Devo (with a parody of the video performed by Smithers in western-style chaps, cracking licorice whips). Each song is performed in a different location, the medley created with cuts from one to the other, until we return to the Simpsons who finish "I Want Candy" as the big finale. Clearly, what is of most interest here is not the parodying of the song medley at all: it is the deliberate focus on the topic of "candy" in response to Marge's concerns about "society's ills." Not only is candy not "pure and good," it is the metaphorical antidote to any type of political awareness. When the family sings "I want candy" in a call-and-response pattern to Marge's comments, they assert that they do not want to think about such matters at all. They would rather have information that is sweet and goes down easy, not something that is troubling and ethically difficult. I read this as a statement of defiant resignation from the writers, who posit that the political aims of *The Simpsons* are generally answered with similar claims (cf., the fans obsessed with continuity referenced in "The Itchy & Scratchy & Poochie Show"). It may be that this version of the family (that is, *sans* Lisa) simply represents the politically inactive wing already; Marge is sometimes concerned with such topics and voices a concern here, but readily gives in to the overriding sentiment. However, I think that, in the context of statements made in the "Poochie" and "Homer's Enemy" shows, this "I Want Candy" sketch is a clear message about the writers' hopes for any political effectivity in *The Simpsons*.

The episode ends with a wrap-up by McClure:

That's it for our spin-off showcase. But what about the show that started it all? How do you keep *The Simpsons* fresh and funny after eight long years? Well, here's what's on tap for season nine. [Pushes a button on a remote control, and we see a still shot of Homer turning Lisa into a frog] Magic powers! [Cycles through three pictures of Selma marrying Apu, the Bee Guy, and Itchy] Wedding after wedding after wedding. [Pushes the button again, and we see Bart confronting two thinly disguised variations of himself] And did someone say, "long-lost triplets?" [Cut to a shot of *The Simpsons*] So join America's favorite TV family, [an alien appears, floating above the family] and a tiny green space alien named Ozmodiar that only Homer can see, on Fox this fall. It'll be out of this world! Right, Ozmodiar?

Here is another string of references to lame television devices—weddings, long-lost family members—that are used to try to reinvigorate failing shows, including one that directly cites *The Flintstones*. "Ozmodiar" is a replica (in both drawing and voice) to "The Great Gazoo," a green space alien (who was only visible to Fred) that was added to the show late in the game. Here again, as well, is the question of how you keep *The Simpsons* "fresh and funny after eight long years"—almost the same language that was used in "The Itchy & Scratchy & Poochie Show." Thus we come full circle: The "Spin-off" show provides a continuation of the themes explored in the "Poochie" show (including the returning reference to *The Flintstones*) and, along with "Homer's Enemy," constructs a nexus of episodes that, in the triangulations of meaning, clearly indicts the producer-audience relationship as it exists for *The Simpsons*.

At the beginning of "*The Simpsons* Spin-off Showcase," Troy McClure announces that the show is sure to be a real treat "for Simpsons fans, if any." The offhanded remark is a sign of a resignation that has set in since the show first interrogated its fans in "The Itchy & Scratchy & Poochie Show," and that the "Spin-off" episode contains the sort of double-edged criticism—of the writers and fans—that is seen in the other episodes as well. Whereas the tone of the "Poochie" episode suggested a certain questioning of the fans, and perhaps a mild defensiveness on the part of the writers, the tone in the "Spin-off" show is much more caustic and nihilistic. The fans, as McClure suggests, have given up on *The Simpsons*. While "Homer's Enemy" does not mention the fans as such, it is easy to see that episode as the sort of mirror image of the "Spin-off" show. Through the character of Frank Grimes, the writers of *The Simpsons* implicate themselves in the downfall of the show, exposing their disconnection from a "real" world with real problems. Again, this kind of theme comes back at the end of the "Spin-off" show, during the "I Want Candy" number. The cast's willful ignorance of "society's ills" echoes the utter misunderstanding between Grimes and the town of Springfield.

AFTER SEASON EIGHT

In the seasons following this crucial moment in the eighth season, *The Simpsons* continued to poke fun at the Internet fans, as well as at its own (perceived) loss of quality; however, these instances tended to be much more limited examples (i.e., not the topics of entire episodes). The tenth season (1998–99), in particular, included three episodes in a row that featured comments about the fans. In "Wild Barts Can't Be Broken," the children of Springfield try to thwart a curfew by exposing the secrets of the town's adults. In his excitement to disseminate the information, Milhouse exclaims, "We gotta spread this stuff around. Let's put it on the Internet!" to which Bart responds, "No! We have to reach people whose opinions actually matter! And I think I know how." In the next episode, "Sunday, Cruddy Sunday," Bart and Homer go to Florida to attend the Super Bowl, while Marge and Lisa stay at home painting eggs with a craft set. At the end of the show, noted football commentators Pat Summerall and John Madden, who appear as themselves in animated form, have this exchange:

> SUMMERALL: Well, John, what did you think of tonight's episode?
>
> MADDEN: I loved it! The last-minute addition of Wally Kogen to the line-up was a bit of a gamble, but it really paid off.
>
> SUMMERALL: Marge and Lisa painting eggs? Did that work for you?
>
> MADDEN: Ho, ho, big time! They came off the bench with a huge effort that allowed Homer and Bart to make some significant gains.
>
> SUMMERALL: Did it strike you as odd that in a Super Bowl show with Dolly Parton we didn't see any football or singing?
>
> MADDEN: I hadn't thought about it, Pat, but in retrospect, it was kind of a rip-off! What a way to treat the loyal fans, who put up with so much nonsense from this franchise.
>
> SUMMERALL: Any final thoughts?
>
> MADDEN: Nah, I'm too mad, let's get the heck out of here!

This conversation begins with conventional football game patter used to comment on the episode, but then takes an abrupt turn when Madden realizes, in spite of the humor, that the episode did not live up to expectations (which he has not originally noticed). Finally, in "Homer to the Max," Homer becomes a Springfield celebrity when it is discovered he shares his name with a television character. When the Comic Book Guy asks Homer to recite his "catchphrase" clearly into a tape recorder for the fan's answering machine tape, Homer lackadaisically says, "Uh, oh, Spaghetti-O's." Right on cue, of course, the Comic Book Guy offers: "Worst reading ever."

In fact, the Comic Book Guy and his "worst episode ever" line have become recurring jokes themselves, and he has become a sort of shorthand for criticism of the producer-receiver relationship. For example, in "Saddlesore Galactica," the Comic Book Guy makes an appearance to remind *The Simpsons* that they are repeating plot lines. When, during a family outing to the fairgrounds, Bart wants to save a performing horse from being put out to pasture, this exchange takes place:

MARGE (rhetorically): Should the Simpsons get a horse?

COMIC BOOK GUY (with mannered indignation): Excuse me, but I believe this family already had a horse, and the expense forced Homer to work at the Quik-E-Mart, with hilarious consequences.

HOMER: Does anybody care what this guy thinks?

ASSEMBLED CROWD: No!

This response is a clear rebuke to the obsessive fans, but it is mixed with a tacit acknowledgment that the show is retreading familiar material (in this case, "Lisa's Pony"). Later in the episode, Comic Book Guy makes another appearance. As Lisa and Marge sit at the race track to watch the horse ("Furious D") that Bart and Homer trained, Marge says, "Okay, Lisa, I've got Furious D across the board, boxed with the three and the eight, and wheeled up and down!" When Lisa responds, "Mom, I think you might be developing a gambling problem," Comic Book Guy enters the screen—wearing a T-shirt that says "Worst Episode Ever"—to warn, "Hey, I'm watching you," in response to yet another former plot line referenced here ("$pringfield [Or, How I Learned to Stop Worrying and Love Legalized Gambling]"). Finally, over the Gracie Films logo that ends the show's credits, we hear the Comic Book Guy exclaim, "Worst episode ever!" Clearly, the writers are having some fun with this character.

Another episode, "Missionary: Impossible," features a direct rebuke of the Fox network. When Homer cannot pay the $10,000 he pledges to PBS during its telethon, he seeks sanctuary in Reverend Lovejoy, who promptly sends him on a mission to a faraway island. As this farfetched plot continues, Homer builds a casino for the islanders, only to replace it with a church once they have all become addicted to gambling. Near the episode's end, Homer clings to one of the girls on the island in the church steeple as they plummet toward a river of molten lava. Suddenly, the scene is abruptly interrupted by Betty White (one of the hosts of the PBS telethon from the beginning of the show), who makes a plea to viewers: "Oh, that Homer. Always getting into trouble. And if you're one of the millions who enjoys his adventures—or should I say misadventures?—it's time to show your support." As the view pans to the phone bank, it is populated by Fox personnel: the animated characters Bender Unit 22 (from *Futurama*), Thurgood Stubbs (from *The PJs*), and Hank Hill (from *King of the Hill*); and "human" actors (although animated here, of course): Luke Perry (aka Dylan from *Beverly Hills, 90210*); the owner of Fox, Rupert Murdoch; and Gillian Anderson and David Duchovny (aka Dana Scully and Fox Mulder from *The X-Files*). White's telethon co-host states, "Sure, Fox makes a fortune from advertising, but it's still not enough," to which Murdoch bellows, "Not nearly enough!" As White walks back to the television (which features the *Family Guy* title logo) on the "telethon" set, she says, "So if you don't want to see crude, lowbrow programming disappear from the airwaves [clicks off television], please call now." Just then a phone rings, and Murdoch answers: "Hello, Murdoch here. Ten thousand dollars? You've saved my network!" The scene cuts to one of Bart at home, on the phone, and he turns to the viewer and says, "Wouldn't be the first time."

As stated earlier, it is not particularly remarkable that *The Simpsons* openly razzes its home network, even though much critical theory does not allow for such an occurrence. But this episode's finale seems to trumpet the consistent quality of *The Simpsons*, even while featuring the kind of "unrealistic" plot that fans carped about (i.e., the subject of "Homer's Enemy"). Here, they manage to get in a dig at a rival Fox cartoon show (*Family Guy*), and in so doing remind viewers that *The Simpsons* is not "crude, lowbrow programming," and that it has, in fact, been crucial to the success of the Fox network.[30]

Perhaps the most interesting episode in this vein came at the end of season eleven, with "Behind the Laughter." On its face a satire of VH1's program *Behind the Music* (as well as other popular sensationalized biography shows such as E!'s *True Hollywood Story*), the episode purports to tell the "behind the scenes truth" of the Simpson family, and it treats them as if they are real people "playing" a family (e.g., the Nelson family in *The Adventures of Ozzie and Harriet*). The episode has the look and feel of the VH1 original, using similar graphics, sounds, and even the same narrator (Jim Forbes). While it does not necessarily break new ground conceptually, "Behind the Laughter" has a strong sense of self-referentiality, and many of the criticisms and anxieties I have associated with the writers are present here. Again, there are the obligatory jokes about the Fox network: when Homer and Rupert sign a contract, they both have the same childlike chicken-scratch print. But there is also a strong thread of self-criticism in the episode. In one scene, Bart and Homer reflect on the evolution of an often-used comic bit. During a "rehearsal," we see Bart and Homer sitting on the family couch, in front of a "set" including a cameraman and a director. When the director says, "Cut," Bart objects to his father about his line: "Dad, I've never said 'Cowabunga' in my life. Your script sucks!" When Homer begins to choke Bart (leading into it with his trademark "Why, you little . . ."), the director says that the choking is funny, and so Bart and Homer break out of the "real" situation and continue to ham it up for the cameras. When the narration returns to Homer's "interview," he waxes, "And that horrible act of child abuse became one of our most beloved running gags."

Thus, this scene transcends self-referentiality and moves into self-criticism. In addition to referencing Bart's early catchphrase "Cowabunga, dude!" this scene admits that the series has often attempted to draw humor from violence. Another scene later in the episode recalls Homer's famous skateboard jump over Springfield Gorge from "Bart the Daredevil." Narrator Forbes tells us that Homer's fall down the gorge became an "instant comedy classic," but that the audience did not see the "unfunny aftermath" of the accident. The accompanying visual is Homer, falling during physical therapy, and then swallowing hundreds of painkillers. Forbes then states, "Somehow Homer became addicted to painkillers. It was the only way he could perform the bone-cracking physical comedy that made him a star." While this joke parodies the penchant to portray "hard times" (such as drug abuse) in *Behind the Music*, it also acknowledges that *The*

Simpsons is, indeed, not always "real," thus recalling the same issues raised in "Homer's Enemy" and seeming to be similarly equivocal: yes, the show often depicts preposterous situations, and this can be good and bad.

This peculiar type of have-it-both-ways self-criticism appears again later in the show, when the narrator describes the beginning of *The Simpsons*'s fall from grace: "With the family in disarray, episodes increasingly resorted to gimmicky premises and nonsensical plots." With this comment, we see a clip from "The Principal and the Pauper," wherein it is discovered that Principal Skinner is an impostor. Next, the narrator tells us that "trendy guest stars were shamelessly trotted out to grab ratings," and we see some of these "trendy" stars: Butch Patrick (aka Eddie Munster from *The Munsters*), astronaut Buzz Aldrin, golfer Tom Kite, physicist Stephen Hawking, and former child actor Gary Coleman (listed on-screen as "Sir Gary Coleman"). "The Principal and the Pauper" was reviled by many of the fans posting to the episode capsules listed in *The Simpsons Archive* (<http://www.snpp.com>) for its dispensing with series continuity, and the writers here seem to acknowledge that the episode had a weak premise. However, the use of the word "trendy" to describe the guest stars mentioned in the next line is obviously ironic, as these figures are largely obscure cultural references, not today's most sought-after personalities. It seems, then, that there is a simultaneous criticism and exaltation of the show, an equivocal tone that was set in those three episodes from season eight.

There are swipes at the fans in this episode as well, although they are not as caustic as earlier comments. Following the scene just described in "Behind the Laughter," narrator Forbes tells us that "fans reacted to these slapdash episodes with yawns . . . angry yawns." Again, here is the suggestion, echoing "The Itchy & Scratchy & Poochie Show," that fans are not merely losing interest in *The Simpsons,* but they are still watching and actively complaining about it. Also, near the end of the episode, Forbes identifies *The Simpsons* as a "northern Kentucky" family, thus putting the question "What state is Springfield in?" to rest for good. There could hardly be a more significant rebuff of the obsessive fans than this.[31]

Finally, the episode ends with the type of resignation seen in "*The Simpsons* Spin-off Showcase." As Homer begins to choke Bart again, reactivating the joke from earlier in the episode, the narrator says, "So, whether choking their son or poking some fun, *The Simpsons* will keep on gagging for years to come." We then see a shot of an editing room, with *The Simpsons* standing around a non-cartoonishly drawn editor (probably based on a crew member). As we look in on the show he is editing on the monitor, we see the family, sitting in their living room:

> MARGE: I can't believe it! We won another contest!
>
> HOMER: *The Simpsons* are going to Delaware!
>
> LISA: I wanna see Wilmington!
>
> BART: I wanna visit a screen-door factory!

Just then, the shot pulls back out to the editing room, and Homer leans over to the editor and says: "This'll be the last season," to which the editor nods. The message is clear: the show is running out of ideas.

CONCLUSIONS

So what are we to conclude from this string of episodes and the topics presented in them, and what can they tell us about the producer-receiver relation and the chance for oppositionality? Clearly, the Internet has had and will continue to have an impact on the ways producers of television learn from their fans. Whereas in the past television makers would have to hold focus groups or rely on letters from fans to gauge public opinion, Internet newsgroups and the like now offer a much more rapid feedback mechanism. In Johnson's model of the "circuit" of a media text, this corresponds to the portion called "lived cultures," which, although it cannot be reduced to Internet interaction, has been drastically affected by these Internet channels.[32]

This is not to say, however, that focus groups and letters have no effect, or are not used anymore, nor that everyone has access to the Internet. Indeed, perhaps one of the biggest mistakes made in these episodes by the writers is the assumption that the fans corresponding on the Internet represent the fans of the show as a whole. The fact that *The Simpsons* incorporated discussions from Internet fan circles into the program shows that the medium can affect television content. However, if the Internet becomes *too* influential in gauging fan opinion (and perhaps determining content), then we may see strange decisions being made at the whim of a vast minority of fans. I do not fear, though, that this will occur; ratings will always be the vote that matters most to a show's life, at least in the network's eyes.

Still, it seems clear that the writers of the show (and Groening himself) have become despondent about the reaction to the show. Groening's decision to start a new show may signal the beginning of the end for *The Simpsons*—if only because, as Lisa said, a show and its characters cannot maintain their effect on people after so many years. This question is different from, but related to, the question I started this essay with: specifically, is it possible to make the jump from less- to more-visible media channels and still retain some sense of oppositionality? Implicit in Lisa's sentiment is that *The Simpsons* could (and did) at one time have an impact, but that such an impact cannot be maintained, and any attempt to do so will necessarily devolve into hackneyed and overtly manipulative gimmicks. The show's writers seem to suggest that, whereas *The Simpsons* once offered (and may continue to offer, but perhaps less frequently) a high-quality show with political value in the otherwise mostly vacuous landscape of U. S. television, the show's effectivity has expired, and both the fans and the writers know it.

The most ironic aspect of this conclusion, I think, is that it is false. *The Simpsons* indeed continues to offer smart, politically charged television. Its 200th episode, "Trash of the Titans," won an Emmy; the show followed Homer's campaign to become Springfield's sanitation commissioner and along the way offered some pointed barbs at issues concerning municipal funding, the electorate's ignorance of such matters, and society's waste in general. The episode ends with the entire town picking up and moving itself five miles away to escape a huge pile of garbage that has accumulated under Homer's watch. The effect is humorous, but there's a critical edge lying just beneath the surface. *The Simpsons* has not, in fact, given up on trying to make a difference.

Indeed, the three episodes I have chosen to focus on represent a moment in the series when self-reflexivity and self-criticism was at a peak. Clearly, the show has continued on, and these three shows merely mark a particular sentiment that appeared in the latter half of the eighth season. The sentiment is important, though, because it can tell us something about how the writers imagine their relationship to the fans. I have tried to expose this imagined relationship within the three texts—"The Itchy & Scratchy & Poochie Show," "Homer's Enemy," and "*The Simpsons* Spin-off Showcase"—in order to suggest some limits of the political effectivity of a television show. *The Simpsons* has shown a certain political engagement during its history, but this engagement seemed to operate much less problematically when the creators had less contact with the fans. As this contact increased, through the Internet, so did the questioning of the show's political project. It remains to be seen how this more direct relationship between fans and producers will play out in the future, in other programs. But when the fans' sentiments seem at odds with the political hopes of a show's creators—as in the case with *The Simpsons*—there is a good chance the result will be the kind of disenchantment we see in these episodes.

NOTES

1. Trish Hamilton, "Rabbit Punch." *Rolling Stone,* September 1988: 81–82, 113.

2. See, for example, Dick Hebdige, *Subculture: The Meaning of Style* (London: Routledge, 1988).

3. Stuart Hall, "Encoding/Decoding," in *The Cultural Studies Reader,* ed. S. During (London: Routledge, 1993), 90–103.

4. Richard Johnson, "What Is Cultural Studies Anyway?" in *What Is Cultural Studies?: A Reader,* ed. J. Storey (London: Arnold, 1996), 75–114.

5. Hall, "Encoding/Decoding," 101.

6. See David Held, *Introduction to Critical Theory: Horkheimer to Habermas* (Berkeley: University of California Press, 1980).

7. Hebdige, *Subculture,* 92ff.

8. Mark Hudis, "Gays Back in Primetime," *Mediaweek,* December 1993: 14; Jeff Jensen, "Hispanics: 'Simpsons' no. 1," *Advertising Age,* September 1993: 34.

9. Jeremy Butler, *Television: Critical Methods and Applications* (Belmont, CA: Wadsworth, 1994).

10. Peggy Noonan, "The Realest Show on TV." *Good Housekeeping* June 1997: 216. Also note that the right-wing journal *National Review* ran a pro-*Simpsons* editorial in its May 1, 2000 issue, calling the show "possibly the most intelligent, funny, and even politically satisfying TV show ever."

11. Douglas Rushkoff, *MediaVirus!: Hidden Agendas in Popular Culture* (New York: Ballantine, 1994); Karen Levell, "The Springfield Files," in *The Simpsons Archives* [World Wide Web site] 1998, available at <http://www.snpp.com/other/interviews/scully98.html>. Groening claims that the writing staff includes "Democrats and Republicans" alike, although that statement comes from an interview in the *Christian Science Monitor* and might be aimed more at mollifying potential enemies than at capturing the essence of the writing team. See M. S. Mason, "'Simpsons' Creator on Poking Fun," *Christian Science Monitor,* April 17, 1998: B7.

12. One of the most often-remarked facts about the writers is their connection to Harvard, and specifically to that school's satirical publication, the *Harvard Lampoon*. Al Jean and Mike Reiss, two longtime writers and producers of the show, estimate that about two-thirds of the writers are Harvard alums. Again, the Harvard connection does not guarantee a liberal bent, but it does translate into very smart writing, replete with a diverse array of references to everything from Greek mythology to Cheap Trick. See Rushkoff, *MediaVirus!*, 110ff.

13. Levell, "The Springfield Files."

14. See, for example, Liesbet van Zoonen, *Feminist Media Studies* (London: Sage, 1994), 46–49.

15. Ivor Davis, "Q & A with Matt Groening: Meet the Man Behind *The Simpsons,* and See What the *Futurama* Holds," in *E! Online* [World Wide Web site] 1998, available at <http://www.eonline.com/Hot/Qa/Groening/index.html>.

16. Davis, "Q & A with Matt Groening."

17. It is possible that Fox, or any corporate media entity, treats entertainment content differently than it does information (although one might never guess this is so, considering the network's penchant for new hybrids of "infotainment"). One corrective to the type of monolithic theory I mentioned earlier—whereby a faceless mainstream media company stamps all of the opposition out of its programming, to bring it "in line" with a capitalist objective—is to suggest that information (such as "news") is produced and received differently than entertainment is. Thus, there may be a compelling reason to manipulate the news—the source of "information"—but not one for doing the same to entertainment, particularly in these days of niche marketing. Moreover, there is precedent for Murdoch "changing course" politically when it will suit him financially, as he did when his papers backed Labour's Tony Blair for British prime minister. On this topic, see Brian McNair, *The Sociology of Journalism* (London: Arnold, 1998).

18. *The Simpsons Archive* (<http://www.snpp.com>) is perhaps the most comprehensive fan site for the show on the World Wide Web. It features a dizzying array of trivia about the show, as well as episode scripts, reviews, observations, etc. The contributors are fans who participate in a Simpsons newsgroup (alt.tv.simpsons, or a.t.s.) and/or a newer listserv (Simpsons-L), which boasts over 1,000 members. Much of the information about the episodes I analyze and nearly all of the information about the fans and their thoughts come from this site.

19. In "'So Television's Responsible!': Oppositionality and the Interpretive Logic of Satire and Censorship in *The Simpsons* and *South Park*" in this collection, William Savage discusses censorship issues in "Itchy & Scratchy & Marge" in more detail.

20. Presumably, the show was not in danger of cancellation, although I do recall an interview with Yeardley Smith, the voice of Lisa, on a Washington, D.C.-area radio station some time between July 1994 and July 1995. She seemed to

think the show would just go another year or so, or that it was at least progressing on a year-to-year basis—implying that the show's creators felt like the show was losing steam. See also note 25.

21. *The Simpsons Archive* identifies the writers depicted as Bill Oakley, Josh Weinstein, George Meyer, and David S. Cohen, the credited "writer" of the episode. The illustrator is David Silverman. See <http://www.snpp.com/ episodes/4F12. html>.

22. See note 7.

23. Groening makes a similar complaint in a *Denver Post* interview. See Joanne Ostrow, "Mind Behind 'Simpsons' the Toughest Critic of All." *Denver Post,* January 14, 1998: G1.

24. John Fiske, *Television Culture* (London: Methuen, 1987).

25. This debate can be seen in several of the comments in the episode capsules in *The Simpsons Archive*. One fan, however, gives an excellent and lucid description of the topics discussed in this paper and how they are addressed in "The Itchy & Scratchy & Poochie Show." See "Musings from a veteran" at <http://www.snpp.com/episodes/4F12.html>.

26. Incidentally, it is not just fans who believe this change was detrimental to the show. In a 1994 interview, Yeardley Smith admitted: "Over the years, the sensibility of the show has changed somewhat. We've become a little bit more cartoony. Doing things that real people can't do is, of course, an advantage of a cartoon. But I think that makes it less interesting. The great thing about the Simpsons is that they were more like real people than most of the people on television. Everything about the story line and the humor were character-driven. Now we often have a joke for the sake of a joke. I take exception to that, whether it's live-action or animation. But the show, I think, is still one of the best on TV." See Paul Freeman, "Actress Gives a Voice to Young Lisa of 'The Simpsons.' " *Minneapolis Star-Tribune,* November 28, 1994, Metro Edition: 10E.

27. An interesting sidebar to this discussion is the fact that Matt Groening created a new animated show, called *Futurama,* as a mid-season replacement show on Fox in the spring of 1999. While not a spin-off of *The Simpsons,* the show features Groening's trademark animation style. See Kevin Kelly, "One-Eyed Aliens! Suicide Booths! Mom's Old Fashioned Robot Oil!" *Wired,* February 1999: 115–121, 158.

28. Although, as Jeremy Butler points out, *The Flintstones* did use a laugh track to make it seem like a "real" sitcom (*Television*).

29. Fredric Jameson, "Postmodernism, or the Cultural Logic of Late Capitalism," *New Left Review,* 146 (July/August 1984): 53–92. I tend to think that Jameson's term gets used rather carelessly by cultural critics, applied generally to refer to any so-called postmodern text. Whereas *The Simpsons* does contain elements

Jameson identifies as postmodern, there is still a clearly parodic element in the show as well.

30. The quality of *The Simpsons* is implicitly compared to PBS programming in this episode, and the writers shrewdly choose to depict public television with a wacky sitcom that Homer loves called *Do Shut Up,* about a family of "soccer hooligans." Although exaggerated, this is a parody of the sort of older British shows that air on PBS, such as *Are You Being Served?,* which do not necessarily—except in their "Britishness," a signifier of elite culture in the United States—convey the type of quality or eliteness associated with public broadcasting.

31. When this episode was aired a second time, on July 12, 2000, this line was changed to "southern Missouri family."

32. Johnson, "What Is Cultural Studies Anyway?" 84.

Myth or Consequences: Ideological Fault Lines in *The Simpsons*

VINCENT BROOK

I s a challenge to the hegemonic order possible in American commercial television, much less a network owned by a notoriously conservative global-media baron (Rupert Murdoch) and operated during its formative years by a Hollywood studio mogul (Barry Diller) who eventually left to head a home shopping network (QVC)? This essay will argue that *The Simpsons,* the hugely popular, record-breaking prime-time animated sitcom on Fox TV, has indeed managed to accomplish this Herculean feat.[1] Working within and against the class-inflected constraints of what Jane Feuer calls "quality television," *The Simpsons* both exposes and cuts through such constraints to create a consistently satirical and occasionally subversive commentary on contemporary American society.

My assessment of the ideological fault lines manifested in *The Simpsons* is grounded in an auteurist analysis of the show's "creative producers" and is supported most forcefully by an ethnographic reception study of a non-fan, non-target audience's responses to a particular program. The auteurist approach will not be uncritical; one cannot deny the constructed nature and institutional limitations of the production entity. Television ultimately functions, much as Gramsci views hegemony and ideology in general, as a dynamic process in which individuals, groups, and social forces vie for legitimation, power, and control.[2]

As for ethnography, one must be equally cautious of the recent tendency in television studies to privilege the decoding aspect of Stuart Hall's encoding/decoding binary.[3] The consequent valorizing of the power and "cultural democracy" of audiences is not only, as Ien Ang puts it, "an optimistic and self-congratulatory liberal mirage of consumer freedom and sovereignty."[4] In its more extreme expression, it is also a form of reverse elitism that both appropriates auteurism for naively populist purposes and replaces Hall's notion of a complex encoding process with a variation of the culture-industry model of a conspiratorial media empire.

This essay attempts to steer a course that acknowledges the existence of active producers as well as readers, thereby adding my voice to those of Ang, John Caldwell, Ellen Seiter, and others who have attempted to redress the encoding/decoding imbalance, granting at least a measure of progressive potential to the producers as well as the consumers of television images.[5]

CREATIVE PRODUCERS/QUALITY TV

"Not *The Jetsons!*" proclaimed the *New York Post* regarding *The Simpsons* in July 1989, six months before the show's debut in January 1990. The article went on to preview a provocative cartoon series that its producers promised would "patronize neither their audience nor their middle-American no-brow animated family of five."[6]

While the article must be taken as somewhat of a puff piece (the *Post* was owned by Murdoch's News Corp., parent company of Fox TV), it does make clear that *The Simpsons* from the outset was positioning itself as "alternative" television, as something counter to past and prevailing currents of mainstream television. Such a strategy was hardly surprising given that Fox from its inception in 1987 had relied on "counterprogramming"—scheduling against the norm of the competition—and "niche-programming"—targeting a demographically distinct segment of the mass audience—to secure its own niche in the network oligopoly.[7] The aim of both strategies was to attract not just any audience, but specifically young, urban viewers (18–34 years of age, especially females) who—so the theory goes—make up for lower overall ratings in terms of their greater purchasing power, thereby justifying higher advertising rates.[8]

If there was any hope that the progressive potential of *The Simpsons* might be more than just a marketing ploy, it rested largely with the show's trio of producers. Matt Groening, the show's creator, was a cartoonist of noted irreverence whose strip featuring alienated misfits, *Life in Hell,* melded the political satire of Jules Feiffer with the Kafkaesque angst of the painter George Tooker. One of Groening's co-producers on *The Simpsons* was Sam Simon, whose pedigree included development and production work on the acclaimed series *Taxi* (1978–83) and *Cheers* (1982–93). The third member of the triumvirate was the estimable James L. Brooks. Brooks, along with Norman Lear (and Brooks's then-partner Allan Burns), was credited with inventing the "socially relevant" sitcom of the 1970s through such groundbreaking series as *The Mary Tyler Moore Show* (1970–77), *Rhoda* (1974–79), and the aforementioned *Taxi*.[9] Brooks had also co-produced the Emmy-winning, issue-oriented dramatic series *Lou Grant* (1977–82). Indeed, Brooks's work had come to epitomize what Horace Newcomb and Robert S. Alley somewhat rhapsodically refer to as that of the "creative producer," and Jane Feuer, more ambivalently, has termed "quality television."

Newcomb and Alley posit the notion of the "creative producer" in reaction against the tendency in television studies to deny human agency or to assign it to anonymous entities such as "the networks" or "the industry."[10] This denial of agency not only obfuscates responsibility for the effects of the medium, it neglects a rich source for study. Television has been called the "producer's medium" with good reason, Newcomb and Alley insist, especially regarding the series form. It is the producer who initiates and develops the concept of a series and, opposed to the nomadic directors and writers, maintains its continuity from start to finish. However, diligence and shepherding skill are not enough; the true or "self-conscious" creative producer also supplies a "creative vision" and a "recognizable style."[11] Similar to the Hollywood film director in classical auteur theory who transcends the constraints of studio and genre through the sheer force of his or her personality, Newcomb and Alley's auteur producer expresses his or her distinctiveness and becomes a "true innovator . . . even when working deeply within one of television's strong traditional forms such as the situation comedy or crime adventure show."[12] Newcomb and Alley are aware of the problems with the auteurist model: its tendency to isolate and overestimate individual elements in a highly collaborative medium and its privileging of artist intention over social and political forces.[13] While they acknowledge that television's industrial apparatus generally serves to legitimate the social order and maintain the status quo, they decry analyses that "focus exclusively on the negative aspects of social maintenance." Such critiques become "a thinly veiled diatribe on American society and politics rather than a careful examination of how television functions in relation to them."[14] In spite of the system, Newcomb and Alley assert, "good" values do get expressed. There are individuals within the television industry who "take responsibility for their actions" and have a "demonstrated artistic talent"—a prime exponent being James L. Brooks.[15]

Brooks is also Feuer's Exhibit A on behalf of "quality television." Her brief for Brooks's "quality" reputation is inextricably linked to his affiliation with Grant Tinker's MTM Enterprises, which actively promoted a "quality" image by providing its creative staff an unusual degree of freedom and by fighting for that freedom vis à vis the networks. Allan Burns quotes Tinker as telling a pushy network executive, "The boys (Brooks and Burns) want to do it, and creatively it's up to them, not you. Our deal says you've got to put it on unless it's offensive. You can't tell them themes that they can or cannot do."[16] While such interference running appears to clear the path for potential subversion, a significant stumbling block remains, in Feuer's view. An unprecedented commitment to social relevance, artistic integrity and creative control may have set independents such as MTM and Norman Lear and Bud Yorkin's Tandem Productions (*All in the Family, Maude, Good Times, The Jeffersons*) apart, but they still had to operate "under the same economic constraints as everybody else. The kitten [the MTM logo] still had to serve the devil Nielsen [high ratings]."[17] The textual production of even the "best" television, in other words, exists in relation to commodity production. No matter how high-minded the principles or lofty the artistic aims, MTM—and therefore also Brooks and Burns—were ultimately "in the business of exchanging 'quality TV' for 'quality demographics.' "[18]

More specifically, as Feuer demonstrates, the networks in the late 1960s began reconceptualizing the television audience from "an aggregate mass" into "a differentiated mass possessing identifiable demographic characteristics."[19] With this reconstruction of the audience came a corresponding redefinition of the notion of "popularity," which increasingly tilted toward the viewing habits of the youthful, urban, consumerist segment of the population. The cable and VCR revolutions of the 1980s further reinforced the "quality" turn, causing network audience share to shrink from 90 percent in 1980 to 53 percent by 1990.[20] Clearly, then, when Fox Broadcasting chose James L. Brooks to co-produce first *The Tracey Ullman Show* and then *The Simpsons,* the fledgling fourth TV network's counter- and niche-programming strategies were nothing new. They were firmly rooted in the traditions of "quality demographics" and "quality television" which, ironically, Brooks himself had helped usher in two decades before.

What had changed by the time of *The Simpsons,* I would suggest, is a heightened awareness on the part of the "creative producer" of the "quality TV" dynamic. This hyperawareness, when injected into the television text, can be likened to what Douglas Rushkoff calls a "media virus": a deceptively potent cultural agent of "societal mutation and evolution."[21] Shows such as *The Simpsons* that camouflage their "media viruses" through an innocuous cartoon package are especially strong candidates for such progressive social change.[22] While Rushkoff focuses on content as the primary textual element in the media viral process, I believe that the subversive potential of *The Simpsons* is determined even more by its unconventional narrative structure. More specifically, I see the problematic closure—what I call "open-ended disruption"—of many *Simpsons* episodes as producing the show's broadest ideological fault lines. How such "open-ended disruption" operates, and to what effect, will be established through textual analysis of individual episodes and the delimited ethnographic survey of a non-"quality" audience. To lay the groundwork for these analyses, however, it is necessary to further contextualize the show culturally and institutionally.

THE SECOND WAVE

Alex McNeil credits *The Simpsons* with ushering in "the "second wave of adult cartoon projects (the first wave was led by *The Flintstones* in the 1960s)."[23] The *Simpsons/Flintstones* comparison is useful, not only in situating the two animated series historically, but also in pointing to the thematic and stylistic changes of the intervening twenty years. *The Flintstones,* again according to McNeil, "was little more than an animated version of *The Honeymooners.*"[24] The mock-Neolithic rendering of a working-class family headed by a bumbling, boorish patriarch took no active position in regard to its televisual antecedent; it was neither parody nor homage, simply a tamer, blandly colorized variation. *The Simpsons,* on the other hand, is all about positioning; it is both parody and homage. It preserves the blue-collar setting of *The Flintstones,* and the family constellations are similar, but the "warmedy" *Flintstone* world is turned on its ear.[25]

"I wanted to invade the mainstream," Groening stated in advance of his show's launching. *"The Simpsons* are the American family at its wildest."* Added Brooks: "[They're] a normal American family in all its beauty and all its horror."[26] The popular press (including non-Murdoch-owned papers) affirmed the intentions of the co-creators from the outset: "A feuding family with nuclear warts . . . entertaining, controversial and occasionally infuriating" (*New York Post*); "a loopy . . . sitcom cartoon about a fractious quintet of hair-don't mutants" (*New York Daily News*); "subversively witty . . . a family roundly dysfunctional . . . already [in 1990] the most clever and original cartoon ever" (*Los Angeles Times*). More surprising than the show's popularity with media critics was its astonishing mass appeal. It was Fox's top-rated show for the 1989–90 season, broke into the Top 10 ratings on several occasions, and was rated 30th overall— amazing accomplishments for an animated series.[27] As with most mega- hits, the success of *The Simpsons* would not be limited to the tube. As Mimi White observed, *Simpsons* characters "exploded beyond the confines of their own show into the larger text of American culture, appearing . . . on T-shirts, lunch boxes and balloons, in toy stores as dolls and on board games, and even on MTV as stars of music videos."[28] By the beginning of the second season, *The Chicago Sun Times* would proclaim that the show had become "as much a part of America as golden arches."[29]

The Simpsons, in short, had become a national phenomenon—not all of which was music to Matt Groening's ears. "I was completely thrown off balance," he remarked in 1994 about the show's super-celebrity. "When you see something like Simpsons' Air Freshener, you know you'd better watch out."[30] *The Simpsons* had indeed invaded the mainstream, as Rushkoff's "media virus" theory would have it, but it had also become the mainstream. The irony was not lost on academics, especially those concerned with the postmodern condition. Postmodern theorists such as Fredric Jameson regarded the relentless commodification of everyday existence by the culture industry of late capitalism as one of the defining characteristics of postmodernism.[31] John Caldwell bemoaned the tendency of postmodern television "to assimilate even oppositional or antagonistic forces and recast them within a dynamic of consumerism."[32] White drew on an episode of *The Simpsons* to savage the postmodern tendency toward programs "fully in fee to patriarchal consumer culture."[33]

Yet even within the consumerist discourse, *The Simpsons* seemed to offer oppositional potential. Of the $200 million in Simpsonia sold during the show's first year, by far the biggest-selling item was the Bart Simpson T-shirts. These featured the mischievous 4th grader's spiky-haired face along with notorious Bartisms, such as, "I'm Bart Simpson. Who the hell are you?" and "'Underachiever' . . . and proud of it!"[34] A huge hit with children, the shirts were denounced by some parents and educators and banned in schools across the country.[35] Certainly, the T-shirt to-do can be taken as another example of postmodern television's, and late capitalism's, genius for merging marketing and mayhem. However, when a high school principal avers that Bart Simpson represents a "kind of anti-establishment squirreliness that kids identify with," something a little more ideologically challenging might also be at work.[36] Groening suggested as much in his defense of the "'Underachiever'" T-shirt in 1990, pointing out that the word "Underachiever" was in quotes. In other words, Bart "has been *labeled* an underachiever. He does not aspire to be an underachiever."[37]

Although it could be argued that the semiotics of quotation marks is above the ken of the average youngster, the "Black Bart" incident indicated that at least some of them were getting the message. In summer 1990, unlicensed T-shirts with black images of Bart Simpson popped up in Five Points, Colorado, where they became a hot seller at an African American Juneteenth celebration. Among the most popular T-shirt decorations were "Air Bart"—a black Bart in a Michael Jordan-Nike takeoff; Bart as a "Young, Gifted and Black Dude"; and a dreadlock-sporting "Rasta Bart."[38] Laurie Schulze, an instructor of mass communication at the University of Denver, put a Groening-like spin on the sub-cultural display:

> [Bart] is in a relatively powerless social position. But at the same time he
> has managed to turn the tables on the system that's devalued him and
> say, "In your face. I'm not worthless, insignificant or stupid. If you want
> to label me an underachiever, I'll turn that into a badge of courage and
> say I'm proud of it." That kind of oppression is something that . . . black
> kids feel.[39]

Evelyn Hu-DeHart, director of the Center of Studies of Ethnicity and Race in America at the University of Colorado, suggested a further oppositional function for the "Black Bart" images: "[Making Bart black] is the reverse of how black and other minority cultures are co-opted by being drawn into the mainstream. . . . Blacks can appropriate Bart as one of theirs by painting him black. Once they color him black they can identify with him more."[40] Folding such interpretations into a chastened auteurist model, I would argue that the *Simpsons* characters themselves actually *encourage* such creative colorization. Although coded as white folk, the Simpson family's skin pigmentation (and those of other "whites") is not, in that most racist of descriptions, "skin tone"; it is rather a bright and quite unearthly *yellow*. In one episode, Bart even refers to himself as "yellow trash." The Simpsons are already, in other words, quite literally "people of color." A subtle form of subversion, if you will, is encoded in their animated DNA. Chalk one up for the "creative producer"—or so it would seem.

For it is precisely such multi-layered codings that pose another problem for critics of postmodernism. Their cautionary position is summarized most famously in Jean Baudrillard's notion of the simulacrum, a world of "proliferating information and shrinking sense" in which all reality is ultimately reduced to artifice. Television, moreover, is seen as both prime cause and symptom in the construction of "a seamless realm of simulations that hinder our acquisition of the *really real*."[41] Within this televisual dynamic, nothing is more regressive for the anti-postmodernists than the "radical eclecticism" of television, in which "the massive appropriation and rearticulation of previously existing signs leads to a kind of semiotic excess"—an excess which supports rather than subverts the commercial interests of global capitalism.[42]

A question not fully addressed by critics of postmodernist television is how "semiotically excessive" shows like *The Simpsons* achieve their broad appeal. Granted, points are awarded to the "privileged" reader most adept at playing Name-That-Intertext, and additional strokes go to "postmodern subjects" prone to reveling in "hyperconsciousness"—Jim Collins's term for the "hyperawareness on the part of the text itself of its cultural status, function, and history, as well as of the condition of its circulation and reception."[43] But to attract an audience beyond the young, media-savvy, "quality demographic" niche requires a more pluralistic approach. As Caldwell points out, "While prestige televisuality cultivates distinction, it also survives only if it doesn't alienate other viewers. Televisual excess, then, exploits not just stylistic embellishment, but also involves loading up different audience appeals within the same program."[44]

A-MASSING APPEAL

The Simpsons thrives not just because it is creatively strong but because its appeal is, or at least has become, so broad-based. Though it is quite successfully marketed to the "tween" demographic (12-to-17-year-olds), *The*

Simpsons is also a show for adults, baby boomers in particular.[45] As Matthew Henry points out, the boomer appeal derives partly from the animated nature of the show, which taps into "a desire for lost youth" and plays on nostalgia for "the childlike enjoyment of watching cartoons."[46]

The *New Yorker* columnist David Owen and current *Simpsons*'s executive producer Mike Scully provide personal anecdotal evidence for the ability of the show to cut across gender and generations. Owen: "My wife and I watch *The Simpsons* as avidly as the children do, and we have for years. It's the only show . . . we plan meals around, and the only one during which we don't read, fold laundry, or talk."[47] Scully: "There's something in it for everyone. . . . My wife and I tend to laugh more at some of the verbal jokes, while the kids will be laughing at Homer falling down the stairs."[48] The show's broad appeal through a mix of high- and lowbrow humor is extended analogously into the socio-political realm. As Paul Cantor summarizes, "*The Simpsons* goes *The Critique of Pure Reason* one better: it defends the common man against the intellectual but in a way that both the common man and the intellectual can understand and enjoy."[49]

Another form of cross-class appeal accrues from *The Simpsons*'s blue-collar milieu. For working-class viewers not exactly showered with televisual self-recognition (at least on prime time), such "direct" address offers a rare opportunity for identification and, one would suppose, also a measure of flattery. Moreover, given the American tendency to deny class distinctions or to subsume them within an all-encompassing "middle class," the blue collar audience gets it both ways: being able to simultaneously identify with and feel superior to itself. As for "privileged" readers, such textual "slumming" is no cause for consternation, for any lack in subject identification is compensated partly by their own unequivocally "superior" positioning, partly by their (and television's) charitable bestowal of the televisual gaze upon the "less fortunate." The centering of comedy on the "little man" has a long and honorable tradition in American popular culture. From movie slapstick (Chaplin, Keaton, Laurel and Hardy) through early television's ethnic working-class sitcoms (*The Honeymooners, The Goldbergs, Mama*) and onto more recent working-class fare (*All in the Family, Taxi, Roseanne*), the proletarian pedigree further recommends *The Simpsons* both to the legitimacy-seeking working class and the cachet-conscious "quality demographic."[50]

The Simpsons's treatment of social issues, on the other hand, appears to work in the opposite direction—toward expanding ideological fault lines rather than audience appeal. Some of the controversial topics the show has examined include nuclear power safety, environmentalism, vegetarianism, immigration, violence in children's entertainment, pervasive media influence, campaign finance reform, sexism, racism, and homophobia. For Feuer, however, such politicizing is still squarely within the "quality TV" tradition. "'Quality TV' is liberal TV," she states in regard to Brooks's MTM fare of the 70s. The "relevant" show's overall thrust must be "double-edged. It must appeal both to the 'quality' audience, a liberal, sophisticated group of upwardly mobile professionals; and it must capture a large segment of the mass audience as well." This doesn't mean that "quality television" lacks progressive elements, "only that, as with all forms of artistic production under capitalism, the progressive elements may be recuperable to an ideology of 'quality.' "[51]

Jeremy Butler reinforces the notion of "relevant" television in general, and *The Simpsons* in particular, as generally recuperative of the hegemonic order. Butler regards *The Simpsons* as existing "somewhere in the middle of the spectrum that places *The Cosby Show* on one end [high recuperation] and *Roseanne* on the other [low recuperation]. *The Simpsons* does appear to chop away at the foundations of the conventional family, but in the end it comes to reaffirm those foundations."[52] Cantor agrees, seeing the show as essentially a celebratory, if not unproblematic, return to the nuclear family after its wholesale abandonment by network television in the 1970s. For Cantor, the show's ultimate message is: "Take the worst-case scenario—the Simpsons—and even that family is better than no family."[53]

A closer look at some representative *Simpsons* episodes, I would submit, challenges Butler's and Cantor's assessments. In "Scenes from the Class Struggle in Springfield," for instance, mother Marge dreams of climbing the social ladder. After investing much energy and more money than she possesses on realizing her upscale fantasy, she retreats to her former "lowly" status, yet with renewed awareness of its deeper value: family love, in other words, is worth more than the country-club set. Yet this facile homily is undermined in various ways. First, the episode does not end with Marge's epiphany. As the family celebrates Mom's "return" at the Krusty Burger restaurant, a worker mopping the floor spoils their reunion (at least for us) by muttering, "What a dump" (about the place). Second, and even more disruptive of narrative closure, are the episode's internal contradictions. Marge's physical, emotional, and monetary investment in achieving her goal is woefully inadequate to the "pay-off." To be back where she started after all that she has expended, for something that was of such paramount importance to her, cannot help but leave a foul taste in her and an "engaged" viewer's mouth.

The inability of the narrative to contain its contradictions, due to such disruptive fillips or "kickers," is typical of *The Simpsons*. Three other examples. In the first, ("Bart the Fink"), Krusty the Klown is persuaded by Bart and Lisa to end his fugitive hiding under an assumed name and return to the friends who love him. As the three go off arm in arm, Krusty turns to blow up his houseboat by remote control in order to claim the life insurance. In the second ("Bart's Girlfriend"), Bart meets his match in the Reverend Lovejoy's daughter, Jessica, a virulent femme fatale. When, at the end, Bart asks an apparently chastened Jessica if she has learned her lesson, she replies with a smile, "Yes, I know I can make men do whatever I want." In the third ("Homer's Phobia"), Homer's episode-ending cure of his homophobia appears an all-too-neat, politically correct conclusion—until Lisa whispers in a still sexually paranoid Bart's ear, "He thinks you're gay."

As for the trope of the "pay-off" not measuring up to the effort, Lisa spends an entire episode ("Lisa the Vegetarian") desperately trying to convert not just her family but all of Springfield to vegetarianism, only to accept "others as they are" in the end. In another ("Lisa's Pony"), Lisa trades in her dream pony for Homer's markedly ephemeral affection. A flipside of the disappointing "pay-off" theme—the punishment not fitting the crime—is exemplified by another episode ("Bart Gets Hit By a Car"). Here Bart, Homer, and Homer's evil boss, Mr. Burns, all ruthlessly try to cheat the system for personal gain, only to be let off in the end with a slap of the wrist.

Such strained narrative resolution engenders a nagging textual dissatisfaction, at least for the "motivated" viewer, which leads to a corresponding discomfort with the episodes' putatively recuperative "messages." Thus, while ostensibly "happy" endings may superficially serve to broaden audience appeal, on a deep-structural level they also may widen existing ideological fault lines emanating from *The Simpsons*'s irreverent tone, exploration of social issues, and critique of the American nuclear family and other institutions. Moreover, I believe this increased fissuring is far greater than if the episodes ended more "progressively." The subversive benefits of politically correct closure tend to dissipate, folding back into the fictive world of the narrative. They also leave the viewers with a sense that the problem has been solved, freeing them both of guilt and of the necessity for political engagement. Open-ended disruption, on the other hand, reverberates with a carry-over effect that provides at least an opportunity for penetration into the social sphere.

How much of this oppositionality is consciously generated by the show's "creative producers" is difficult to ascertain. Yet an indication of at least a modicum of intentionality can be gleaned from Groening's notion of "rubber-band reality." As Groening describes it, "rubber-band reality" results from his attempt to "push characters in peculiar directions, for as far as they can go; then we have them snap back."[54] On the one hand, of course, this notion can be regarded as just another formula for containing and recuperating, Cecil B. De Mille-style, an episode's worth of transgression through a last-minute moral rescue. If we stretch Groening's metaphor to its elastic limit, however, it yields to less cynical interpretations. For example, a rubber band's snapping back produces a sting. The greater the pull, the more painful the sting; if the rubber band is pulled too far, it breaks. It is in the tension between the "sting" and the "break," particularly as signified in the show's "open-ended disruption," that *The Simpsons*'s true subversive potential lies. But to further test this proposition, we must turn to my ethnographic survey.

DEMOGRAPHICS AND TASTE CULTURES

The audience enlisted for my survey on *The Simpsons* consisted of students in two writing classes at Watterson College, a private business college in Pasadena, California, where I was employed as an instructor in 1996. Watterson's prime function was to prepare students for office support jobs in the accounting, legal, and medical fields. One of the writing classes, constituting the Primary Survey Group of 16 students, was taught by me. The second class, constituting the Follow-up Survey Group of 11 students, was taught by a colleague. I have divided the groups into Primary and Follow-up because, although the demographic make-up and survey results are similar for the two groups, I was able to gain more detailed information from the Primary Group. I will therefore focus mainly on the Primary Group, relying on the Follow-up Group only when its results deviate from or reinforce the Primary Group's in revealing ways.

I chose the above group(s) because I sought a non-fan, non-"quality" demographic for my study and believed that the Watterson students tended to fall outside either category. The non-fan status of these students was indicated by an exploratory discussion held prior to the actual survey. When I asked how many students had *ever* watched *The Simpsons,* almost all raised their hands. When I asked how many had ever or still watched *regularly,* a majority raised their hands. When I asked how many *liked* the show, no one raised his or her hand. Whether the students were being totally forthright or were perhaps too embarrassed to admit liking the show—especially a cartoon—in front of me or the rest of the class, I could not determine. However, such a dissemblance was doubtful on at least two counts: 1) the culturally iconic status the show had by then attained; and 2) the fact that *The Simpsons* from the start has had a large following among Latinos, the dominant ethnic group among my survey students (see below).[55] In any event, the likelihood that I was harboring a secret cadre of hard-core *Simpsons* fans seems slight.

My assumption (not a value judgment) that the students fell outside the "quality" demographic was based on the students' oral and written class work, as well as on sociologist Herbert Gans's taxonomy of "taste cultures." While Gans's classifications, proposed in 1974, fail to factor in postmodernity, I believe they can be adjusted for this phenomenon. Within such an adjusted schema, the "quality" demographic would encompass portions of what Gans terms "high" and "upper-middle" taste cultures. These groups are characterized by affluence, major-college education and cultural "sophistication," which—adjusted for postmodernity—would include at least a qualified embrace of popular culture[56]

My students, while upwardly striving in a class and educational sense, fit more readily into Gans's next category, "lower-middle culture." This group "is America's dominant taste culture. . . . It attracts middle- and lower-middle-class people in the lower-status professions, such as accountancy and public school teaching, and all the lowest-level white-collar jobs." This public "is not particularly interested in what it calls 'culture'"; its tastes in art tend toward the "romantic and representational," and it "provides the major audience for the mass media."[57]

The demographic questionnaire portion of my survey tended to confirm both Gans's and my assumptions. The results for the Primary Group were as follows:

Gender: 15 women, 1 man; *Ethnicity:* 12 Latinos, 4 Whites (Follow-up Group: 8 women, 3 men: all Latino); *Average Age:* 22; *Family Status:* 10

single, 3 single mothers, 2 married (1 with children), 1 separated; *Occupation:* 3 Clerical, 3 mothers, 3 salespersons, 3 unemployed, 1 cashier, 1 dockworker, 1 managerial; *Educational Level:* high school diploma, Watterson being their first college experience; *Interests, Favorite Movies/ Television Shows/Books, Other Cultural Activities:* Main Interests: movies and television, with the most popular genres and shows prevailing (*Movies:* action-adventure, comedy, romance, horror; *Television Shows: ER, Friends,* talk shows, sports). Four students listed reading as an activity: celebrity bios, romance novels, mysteries, and Dean Koontz. Other interests: exercising and sports; one student's hobby was collecting Barbie dolls. No other cultural activities were mentioned. *Frequency of viewing* The Simpsons (*past or present*): 7 "frequent" viewers; 9 "infrequent." Of the frequent viewers, all watched less than before (which may help explain why, in the exploratory oral discussion mentioned above, no students said they "liked" the show).

Judging by the exploratory discussion and the results of the demographic questionnaire, I certainly appeared to have the non-fan, non-"target" group of readers I wanted.

I am well aware that the small number of survey participants hardly qualifies as a "representative sample." On the other hand, Ien Ang's seminal study of *Dallas* was based on only 42 letters. Following Ang, I choose to regard my subjects' oral and written responses "as texts, as discourses people produce when they want to express or have to account for their own preference for, or aversion to, a highly controversial piece of popular culture."[58] While *The Simpsons* may no longer have been controversial at the time of the survey, I believe Ang's approach still affords a useful precedent for the delimited ethnographic study. Further encouragement is offered by Clifford Geertz's notion of "thick" description, which posits a trade-off between the necessarily subjective component of ethnography and its compensatory potential for broad, dense, complex analysis.[59] All that remained, then, was for my study to live up to such potential.

"LISA THE ICONOCLAST"

The particular *Simpsons* episode I chose for viewing by the survey students is called "Lisa the Iconoclast." A detailed synopsis follows:

In honor of the Simpsons' hometown of Springfield's Bicentennial, Lisa is shown a film glorifying coonskin-capped Jebediah Springfield, the town's heroic founder.[60] Wishing to learn more about the great frontiersman, Lisa visits the local historical museum, curated by Hollis Hurlbut (Donald Sutherland's voice). Examining some of Jebediah's artifacts in Hurlbut's absence, Lisa blows into Jebediah's fife and a rolled up parchment pops out, containing a confession from Jebediah that dispels his foundational myth: instead of a courageous pioneer, he was really a lying, murderous pirate who tried to kill George Washington! Stunned, Lisa tells her parents. Marge doesn't want to hear about it, but Homer, surprisingly, believes Lisa. She writes a school expose on Jebediah, but her teacher, Miss Hoover, gives it an F, fulminating: "This is nothing but dead-white-male bashing from a PC thug who wants to keep the rest of us from landing a husband!" Lisa takes her case to Mr. Hurlbut, who claims that the confession is a fraud and bans Lisa from the museum— at least for three months. Undeterred, Lisa and Homer persuade the town fathers to open Jebediah's grave to see if he still has the silver prosthetic tongue to replace the original that his "confession" alleges was lost in a knife fight. They dig up the body . . . but no silver tongue. Lisa despairs, until she finds the missing piece to the puzzle: the parchment Jebediah's confession was written on matches the missing piece of canvas in George Washington's famous portrait! Confronted with this irrefutable evidence, Hurlbut confesses to having removed the silver tongue from Jebediah's corpse. He and Lisa rush to the Bicentennial celebration and stop the parade. As Lisa mounts the podium to inform the townspeople, a sniper, with Mayor Quimby beside him, takes aim (Quimby had mentioned earlier that corporate sponsors were backing the event). As the whole town looks on, Lisa starts to divulge the truth, then stops. "Jebediah Springfield was . . . great," she finally stammers. When Hurlbut asks why she didn't tell the truth, Lisa replies, "Jebediah's myth has value too. It's brought out the best in everyone in this town." She concludes by reciting Jebediah's immortal words: "A noble spirit embiggens [sic] even the smallest man." As Lisa descends the stage, a shot (unnoticed by her or the cheering crowd) zings past. The parade resumes. Homer, who had been replaced as town crier after the grave-digging incident, bumps neighbor Ned Flanders out of the way and assumes his position at the head of the parade. Miss Hoover complains, but police chief Wiggum lets the parade roll on.

I did not choose this episode at random. It struck me as an especially cogent example of the narrative fissuring and disruptive closure described above. Lisa spends the entire episode uncovering the truth about Jebediah and courageously defending her findings against a phalanx of authority figures—Marge, Miss Hoover, Mr. Hurlbut, and the town fathers. Nor is it just any truth that she has uncovered, but one that goes to the heart of Springfield's most potent patriotic symbol. It is surely no accident that Jebediah is opposed, quite literally, to George Washington, America's paradigmatic symbol of honesty, integrity, and courage. The fact that this episode originally aired over a President's Day weekend clearly indicates the intent of the show's producers that the episode be taken allegorically within a broader political context. Jebediah, as Springfield's founding father, thus becomes a metaphor for America's founding fathers, and the show, by extension, becomes not merely a deconstruction of the myth of small-town America but a megatext on the myth of the United States as a whole. Lisa's actions, therefore, and our reaction to them, become a kind of litmus test for the democratic principles on which our nation was founded.

So what does Lisa—the best and the brightest of the Simpsons—do? Contrary to the title (and therein lies the irony), she opts in the end not to be an icono*clast* but an icono*phile,* not a breaker but a reinforcer of images. Lisa is ultimately an upholder of Myth over Truth, and it is not just any myth that she champions, but a myth based on treachery, deceit, and attempted murder, a myth which for one media-hyped, spectacle-drenched day a year (perhaps only once every hundred years!) purportedly "brings out the best in people" (e.g., Homer bumping Ned Flanders out of the parade). Lisa claims her decision was made in the common good. Yet logic and the look on her face tell us it was made more out of fear of the truth's consequences—consequences that super-smart Lisa surely perceives go deeper than raining on the town's parade (remember that sniper?).

But the narrative fissuring goes further. For not only will Lisa and Mr. Hurlbut be cursed forever with the knowledge that their home town is founded on fraud, so must we, the "attentive" audience, somehow come to grips with this disturbing "reality" as well. The sacrosanct "redundancy" factor in an episodic television series has been violated; the chain of comfortable, reassuring sameness has been broken. We are henceforth forced to view the town, Lisa, the founding fathers, the very notion of myth itself, in a hypercritical light. The illusory reconciliation of contradictions that lies at the heart of all primal myths, in Claude Levi-Strauss's famous formulation, has been shattered.[61] Springfield, and *The Simpsons,* will never be the same. If the upshot of all this, as Cantor would have it, is that the Simpsons family and their hometown of Springfield—as bad as they are—are still deemed to be better than none at all, so be it. But one can hardly—or perhaps only—accept such a dire interpretation lying down.

SURVEY RESULTS

Following a taped presentation of the episode (fast-forwarded past the commercial spots), I posed these questions:

1. What is the episode's theme?
2. What did you like/dislike about the episode?
3. What characters did you like or dislike, and why?
4. Did the characters live up to your expectations? How so/How not?
5. What do you make of the ending? Explain.
6. Do you like or dislike *The Simpsons* in general, and why?

My main interest was in the students' reaction to Question 5 (regarding the ending). I did not want to "telegraph" my intent, however, or put undue pressure on the students to come up with a "right" or "wrong" answer. The surrounding questions were thus used to camouflage my target question, as well as to provide additional context from which to interpret the responses to this question.

Responses to Question 5 can be summarized generally as follows: 8 students "agreed" with the ending; 5 "disagreed"; 3 both "agreed" and "disagreed." (In the Follow-up Group, 4 "agreed," 4 "disagreed," 3 "agreed/disagreed.") By "agree," I mean that respondents felt that Lisa did the right thing not to expose the myth of Jebediah to the inhabitants of Springfield; by "disagree," I mean that respondents felt that Lisa did the wrong thing and should have told the truth; by "agree/disagree," I mean that respondents were unable to reconcile the two positions.[62]

The thrust of the "agreer" argument was essentially that Lisa was thoughtful and considerate to put the feelings of the townspeople above her own principles. A few examples: 1) "Lisa could have ruined a special occasion to prove her discoveries, but the kindness she has for everybody kept her quiet"; 2) "The town came together in happiness and celebration.

Why destroy it with the truth if it is not hurting anything or anyone?" One "agreer" in the Follow-up Group went even further, calling Lisa "noble" (quoting Jebediah) because "she didn't disappoint all the people."

The "disagreer" argument was essentially that it is important to tell the truth no matter what the consequences. One student's response summarizes this position: "The whole show was about Lisa Simpson and her fight for the truth about her town of Springfield. When she found out that the town's history was a farce, she tried to prove it to everyone. Then after having undeniable facts, when she could have told the whole town the truth, she backed down and allowed the myth to continue. I was angry at the ending because, in my mind, it was saying that it's OK to lie, or cover up the truth."

Of particular interest in the above "disagreer's" response is the level of affect expressed: "I was *angry* at the ending." This appears to exemplify the "nagging dissatisfaction" I had hypothesized as accompanying problematic as opposed to neatly resolved closure. Whether such dissatisfaction is more likely than a quiescent response to be translated into heightened consciousness or corrective action would obviously require more extensive and long-term study, though if the history of personal transformation and social movements is any guide, such an assumption is certainly plausible. It also follows that such ideological "movement" is easiest to engender and to gauge when it comes from the already "moved" or converted, as is apparently the case here. But what of the less "proactive/committed" viewer/respondent? How do we measure the "ideological effect" on these viewers?

Other aspects of the survey offer a clue, for not all "agreers" and "disagreers" were so forthright in their opinions as the angry "disagreer"; considerable cognitive dissonance reigned. This ambiguity becomes evident in the discrepancies between some respondents' assessment of the ending versus the theme of the episode. One "agreer" liked the ending ("if one small person can bring happiness to so many, then it is best to leave it as it was"), yet maintained that the theme was critical of Lisa "because the [Jebediah Springfield] celebration was in denial of the truth." Another "agreer," while sensing the immense stakes involved in the ending ("she knew that if she said it . . . nothing would be the same anymore in Springfield"), denied there was any theme at all: "I saw it more as entertainment." Additional contradictions arose among some "agreers" in relation to Question 3 (What characters do you like/dislike, and why?). While approving of Lisa's ultimate decision to forego her commitment to the truth, two "agreers" nonetheless applauded her "tenacity"; one, her "honesty."

As for contradictory responses from "disagreers," one "disagreer" ("I didn't like the ending because Lisa didn't say the truth after all the trouble she went through") perhaps gained a measure of revenge by regarding the moral of the tale: "to stand up for what you believe, no matter what other people say." Another "disagreer" ("I didn't like that Lisa didn't say anything in front of the people") similarly rationalized the theme in the respondent's favor: "to keep your ideas and work hard to reach what you plan to do."

Most ambivalent in their reactions to the ending, of course, were the "agreers/disagreers." One of these believed that Lisa "should have said the truth," yet added that "it was kind of nice she didn't say anything to disappoint the people." Another opined, "The ending was just OK because she did not tell the truth, but she did say it brought people together no matter what type of person Jebediah was." A third said she didn't "think Lisa should have stayed quiet," but "I still liked Lisa; I think she did the correct thing." This last comment seems a poignant commentary on the moral/ethical divergence between notions of "right" and "correct."

Two of the Follow-up Group's "agreer/disagreers" also hedged their bets intriguingly: 1) "I liked the ending because it fit the adult humor. I hope kids don't take it too seriously, though"; 2) "I guess I didn't exactly dislike the ending. Things don't always turn out the way we wish they did." Without wishing to minimize—or romanticize—the subtlety of these responses, I would say that the first comment casts considerable doubt on the efficacy of *The Simpsons*'s lauded family appeal, while the second betrays an uncanny awareness of the existentialist nature of the show's "unhappy" ending.

The written survey was enhanced though oral discussion.[63] The "disagreers" tended to be more steadfast in defense of their position; "agreers" tended toward defensiveness. Some "agreers" rationalized their stance through comments such as "It's only *The Simpsons*" or "It's only a cartoon." The staunchest voice among the "agreers" emerged in the Follow-up Group, from the student who had called Lisa's actions "noble." Playing devil's advocate, I asked this student whether the "founder" of Los Angeles, Father Junipero Serra, should still be sainted if it were confirmed that he had raped, tortured, and murdered the native Gabrieleno Indians of the area. The student replied no, not in that case. But Springfield is different, she explained: "The way the town is portrayed, as a bunch of losers, they couldn't handle the truth; they'd just fall apart. Los Angeles, on the other hand, could handle it."

This last comment is illuminating in several respects: first, putting aside whether Los Angeles deserves to be considered superior to Springfield, the inverse relation drawn by the viewer between dysfunctionality and the ability to "handle the truth" poses disturbing questions about the possibility of social change. To regard "a bunch of losers" as incapable of benefiting from the truth is a "rich get richer" formula for widening economic disparity and increased prison populations. Second, while the comment implies that certain viewers might indeed read *The Simpsons*'s cartoon world as plausibly realistic, it does not necessarily follow that these same viewers regard this world as a microcosm of American society, as I myself had presumed and which would seem to be a prerequisite for the show's ideological effect. Such distancing from the show's political thrust appears to function in a similar manner to treating *The Simpsons* "more as entertainment" or as "only a cartoon." While at least partially a rationalization, such an attitude can also be read as a healthy suspicion of expecting commercial television to serve purely "useful" purposes. As John Alberti reminds us, "As academic fans of the show, and as students of popular culture, we tend to watch TV as a political document and potential source of cultural and political critique. We tend to forget that this is not a universal nor even necessarily a prudent expectation."[64]

My point here, however, is that *The Simpsons,* more than most commercial television, actively *solicits* political engagement. This solicitation occurs partially through content and style, but perhaps even more significantly through narrative structure—particularly the "open-ended disruption" of many episodes' endings.[65] Moreover, the latter effect tends to operate on a politically unconscious level that is less easily dismissed, insulated against, or rationalized away. The profound discomfort that such endings produce is evidenced, most potently, I believe, in the highly contradictory responses to "Lisa the Iconoclast," both from "agreers" and "disagreers." Even more than the affect produced in the "already converted" reader, such contradictions reveal the capacity of "open-ended disruption" to open up viewers' minds to new possibilities, new ways of thinking about the world. By radically "reframing reality," in *Simpsons* writer George Meyer's phrase, the "happy/unhappy" ending posits a narrative "solution" as ambivalent as it is never-ending.[66]

CONCLUSION

The results of my survey indicate that at least one highly charged episode of *The Simpsons,* presented to a non-fan, non-"target" audience (albeit in a highly "engaged" and "motivated" setting), has undeniably resulted in resistant or oppositional readings. I have interpreted these counter-hegemonic responses as resulting from specific ideological positions injected into the text by the "creative producer," as well as from decoding strategies utilized by individual survey students. I have also argued for a latent and even more efficacious oppositionality embedded in the problematic closure of the survey episode and other *Simpsons* episodes.

As David Morley reminds us, however, we must always look beyond mere resistance or opposition to ask *what* is being resisted or opposed: "It is only against a backdrop of some conception of a dominant ideology or set of meanings, however conceived, that any notion of 'resistance' or 'opposition' makes sense."[67] To aid in arriving at such a baseline, Morley proposes Celeste Condit's notion of "polyvalence" as preferable to the more widely used concept of "polysemy." Condit defines polyvalence as occurring "when audience members share understandings of the denotation of a text, but disagree about the value of these denotations to such a degree that they produce notably different interpretations."[68] It is a "difference in audience evaluations" rather than a "multiplicity or instability of textual meanings," Condit suggests, "that best accounts for . . . discrepant interpretations."[69]

It would appear that my survey groups' variable decodings of *The Simpsons* provide a striking example of such polyvalence. My respondents were in agreement about *what* happened in "Lisa the Iconoclast"; disagreement raged about *why* it happened and what should *be made* of it. The question remains whether other episodes, under more "normal" viewing conditions, would elicit similar results. At the very least, it is apparent that the show's "creative producers," however broadly constituted or defined, working within the commercial parameters of "quality television" and "loading up" strategies, have produced an episode, if not a series, rich in ideological fault lines. Groening's "rubber-band reality," at least in the "Lisa the Iconoclast" episode, has been pulled beyond the breaking point. Of course, the notion that such a break (cushioned by all the commercial breaks) can make any lasting impression on the hegemonic order may itself be a utopian myth. If so, we can perhaps find solace in the fact that, at least for a half-hour a week, American television viewers are not only being asked whether they want to be a millionaire but are also being forced, at least on some level, to weigh the consequences of supporting the myth of family, community and country—right or wrong.

NOTES

I would like to thank John Caldwell and John Alberti for their invaluable contributions to this essay.

1. The old record for a prime-time cartoon series was six consecutive years, established by *The Flintstones* in the 1960s.

2. See the section on "Hegemony, Relations of Force, Historical Bloc" in *An Antonio Gramosi Reader,* ed. David Forgacs (New York: Schocken Books, 1988), 189–221.

3. Stuart Hall, "Encoding/Decoding," in *Culture, Media, Language,* ed. S. Hall, D. Hobson, A Lowe, and Willis (London: Hutchinson, 1980), 128–139.

4. Ian Eng, *Watching* Dallas: *Soap Opera and the Melodramatic Imagination* (New York: Routledge, 1982), 9.

5. John Thornton Caldwell, *Televisuality: Style, Crisis and Authority in American Television* (New Brunswick: Rutgers University Press, 1995); Ellen Seiter, *Television and New Media Audiences* (New York: Clarendon Press, 1998).

6. Michelle Greppi, "Not *The Jetsons.*" *New York Post* (12 July 1989): F9.

7. Alex Ben Block, *Outfoxed: Marvin Davis, Barry Diller, Rupert Murdoch, Joan Rivers, and the Inside Story of America's Fourth Television Network* (New York: St. Martin's, 1990), 159.

8. Jane Feuer, *MTM: "Quality Television"* (London: BFI, 1984), 3.

9. Feuer, *MTM: "Quality Television,"* 5.

10. Horace Newcomb and Robert C. Alley, *The Producer's Medium: Conversations with Creators of American TV* (New York: Oxford University Press, 1983), xi–xii.

11. Newcomb and Alley, *The Producer's Medium,* xii.

12. Newcomb and Alley, *The Producer's Medium,* xiii.

13. Newcomb and Alley, *The Producer's Medium,* xii, 20.

14. Newcomb and Alley, *The Producer's Medium,* 22.

15. Newcomb and Alley, *The Producer's Medium,* 17. In terms of creative input on *The Simpsons,* considerable attention has also been paid to the gifted cadre of Harvard-educated writers who have helped make the animated series arguably the most literate show on television. See, for example, Douglas Rushkoff, in *Media Virus! Hidden Agendas in Popular Culture* (New York: Ballantine Books,

1994), 110–125, who heaps considerable praise on two of *The Simpsons* longtime writers, Mike Reiss and Al Jean; and David Owen, in "Taking Humor Seriously: George Meyer, the Funniest Man Behind the Funniest Show on TV," *New Yorker* (13 March 2000), 64–75, who grants privileged status to writer George Meyer.

16. Newcomb and Alley, *The Producer's Medium*, 216.

17. Feuer, *MTM: "Quality Television,"* 33.

18. Feuer, *MTM: "Quality Television,"* 34.

19. Feuer, "Genre Study and Television," in *Channels of Discourse, Reassembled*, ed. Robert C. Allen (Chapel Hill: University of North Carolina Press: 1987), 152.

20. Laurie Thomas and Barry R. Litman, "Fox Broadcasting Company, Why Now? An Economic Study of the Rise of the Fourth Broadcasting Network." *Journal of Broadcasting and Electronic Media* (Spring 1991): 146.

21. Rushkoff, *Media Virus!* 11, 15.

22. Rushkoff, *Media Virus!* 15.

23. Alex McNeil, *Total Television: A Comprehensive Guide to Programming from 1948 to the Present*, 4th ed. (New York: Penguin, 1996), 689. See also Megan Mullen's essay in this collection, *"The Simpsons* and Hanna-Barbera's Animation Legacy," for a further discussion of the influence of *The Flintstones* on *The Simpsons*.

24. McNeil, *Total Television*, 266.

25. Matthew McAllister ("The Simpsons," *Encyclopedia of Television* Volume 3, ed. Horace Newcomb [Chicago: Fitzroy Dearborn Publishers, 1997], 1493–95) sees the inspiration for *The Simpsons* deriving more from *The Bullwinkle Show* (1961–64) than from *The Flintstones,* specifically in its reliance on social criticism and its references to other cultural forms (1494).

26. Greppi, "Not *The Jetsons*," F9.

27. David Bianculli, "Tinsel 'Toons," *New York Post* (15 Dec. 1989): G13; McNeil, *Total Television*, 689.

28. Mimi White, *Tele-Advising: Therapeutic Discourse in American Television* (Chapel Hill: University of North Carolina Press, 1992), 173.

29. Ernest Tucker, "New 'Simpsons' Episodes Return—As Smart As Ever," *Chicago Sun Times* (10 Oct. 1990): p C11. Then-incumbent President Bush even referred to the cartoon family during the 1992 presidential campaign—disparagingly, of course—as did Secretary of Education William Bennett (McAllister, "The Simpsons," 1494). The show reciprocated soon thereafter, in typical self-reflexive fashion, by lampooning the governmental critique.

30. Ray Richmond, "'Simpsons' Keeps Getting Better," *Los Angeles Daily News* (3 Jan. 1994): A13.

31. Fredric Jameson, "The Politics of Theory: Ideological Positions in the Postmodern Debate," *New German Critique* 33 (Fall 1984): 125.

32. Caldwell, *Televisuality* 206.

33. White, *Tele-Advising*, 180.

34. David S. Wilson, "Tooned On! America Flips for Cartoons," *TV Guide* (9 June 1990): 24.

35. Bianculli, "Tinsel 'Toons," A11.

36. David Rhein, "Bart's Philosophy Concerns Some Teachers," *Des Moines Register* (26 Aug. 1990): A13. Paul Cantor sees Bart's rebelliousness as following an American tradition: "This country was founded on disrespect for authority and acts of rebellion. Bart is an American icon, an updated version of Tom Sawyer and Huckleberry Finn rolled into one. For all his troublemaking—precisely because of his troublemaking—Bart behaves just the way a young boy is supposed to in American mythology, from *Dennis the Menace* comics to *Our Gang* comedies" ("*The Simpsons*: Atomistic Politics and the Nuclear Family," *Political Theory* 27 [December 1999]: 5).

37. Rhein, "Bart's Philosophy," A13. Groening has since "recanted." In a wire-service report in early 1999, he was quoted as saying in regards to Bart's function as a role model: "I now have a 7-year-old boy and a 9-year-old boy so all I can say is I apologize. Now I know what you were talking about" (Cantor, "*The Simpsons*," 15).

38. Mark Wolf, "Rude Dude Bart Crosses Cultural Line," *Rocky Mountain News* (21 June 1990): F1.

39. Wolf, "Rude Dude Bart," F1.

40. Wolf, "Rude Dude Bart," F1.

41. Jim Collins, "Postmodernism and Television" *Channels of Discourse, Reassembled*, ed. Robert C. Allen, 331–32, emphasis his.

42. Collins, "Postmodernism," 330–31.

43. Collins, "Postmodernism," 335.

44. Caldwell, *Televisuality,* 255.

45. McAllister, "The Simpsons," 1495; Matthew Henry, "The Triumph of Popular Culture: Situation Comedy, Postmodernism and *The Simpsons*," *Studies in Popular Culture* (October 1994): 87.

46. Henry, "Triumph," 97.

47. Owen, "Taking Humor Seriously," 64.

48. Diane Werts, "10 Years? D'Oh!" *Los Angeles Times* (18 December 1999): F22.

49. Cantor, "*The Simpsons*," 14.

50. George Meyer, one of the show's chief writers, offers yet another cross-class attraction of *The Simpsons,* one that is literally built into the series: "They live in the standard middle-class house—even though it would seem that they probably couldn't afford that house. Their finances are kind of glossed over (Owen, "Taking Humor Seriously," 74).

51. Feuer, *MTM: "Quality Television,"* 56.

52. Jeremy G. Butler, *Television: Critical Methods and Applications* (Belmont: Wadsworth, 1994), 7.

53. Cantor, "*The Simpsons*," 5.

54. Mike Hughes, "'Simpsons' Creator Finds Mainstream Acceptance Mildly Amusing," *Boston Herald* (28 April 1994): F9.

55. Owen, "Taking Humor Seriously," 64. According to Owen, the loyalty of the Latino audience has been the cause for "a semi-cryptic message superimposed on the screen at the beginning of every episode: 'SAP Transmitidio en Espanol' " (64).

56. Herbert Gans, *Popular Culture and High Culture: An Analysis and Evaluation of Taste* (New York: Basic Books, 1974), 75–84.

57. Gans, *Popular Culture*, 84–86.

58. Ang, *Watching* Dallas, 11.

59. David Morley, *Television Audiences and Cultural Studies* (New York: Routledge, 1992), 192–4.

60. Springfield, not coincidentally, was also the name of the hometown of the Andersons of *Father Knows Best* fame.

61. Claude Lévi-Strauss, "The Structural Study of Myth," in *The Structuralists: From Marx to Lévi-Strauss,* ed. Richard and Fernande De George (Garden City: Anchor Books, 1972), 193. See also Bill Nichols, *Ideology and the Image: Social Representation in the Cinema and Other Media* (Bloomington: Indiana University Press, 1981), 98.

62. It should be noted that there was little correlation between whether students "agreed" or "disagreed" with the episode's ending and either their frequency in viewing *The Simpsons* or their feelings for or against the show in general (Question 8). In other words, those who watched frequently or infrequently, or those who liked or disliked the show in general, were about as likely to "agree" or "disagree" with this particular episode's ending. Such weak "party loyalty" is perhaps to be expected, given the relatively small affect expressed by the overall survey group toward *The Simpsons*.

63. I received similarly mixed responses to this episode from students I surveyed, orally and more informally, in a television history class I taught at California State University Los Angeles in fall 1999.

64. John Alberti, "Simpsons Essay," email message to Vincent Brook, Highland Heights, Kentucky/Los Angeles, California: 12 Jan. 2000.

65. Tucker quoted in Owen, "Taking Humor Seriously," 64.

66. Owen, "Taking Humor Seriously," 70.

67. Morley, *Television Audiences,* 38.

68. Celeste Michelle Condit, "The Rhetorical Limits of Polysemy," *Television: The Critical View,* ed. Horace Newcomb (New York: Oxford University Press, 1994), 430.

69. Condit, "Rhetorical Limits," 430.

"So Television's Responsible!": Oppositionality and the Interpretive Logic of Satire and Censorship in *The Simpsons* and *South Park*

WILLIAM J. SAVAGE, JR.

I

Generally, as Peter Rabinowitz has demonstrated, when readers interpret a popular text, whether a novel, film, or animated television program such as *The Simpsons* or *South Park,* they expect and attend to certain aspects of it, especially the workings-out of plot. When reading texts regarded as "serious," however, readers expect more, or, to be more accurate, *different* sorts of interpretive rewards.[1] Primarily, expectation of textual seriousness lead readers to seek thematic engagement with important cultural issues, such as the dynamic of high and low culture in relation to censorship and animation. When readers/viewers approach any serious text, they assume that there is more to it than the obvious surface significance; serious reading is always about multiple levels of meaning and interpretation, so-called hidden or latent meanings. So, as scholars and critics of animation and politics, asking whether cartoons such as *The Simpsons* and *South Park* are oppositional can imply that we are reading them as merely popular, not "serious," texts. Instead, we should ask what sorts of interpretive strategies can enable our students and us to discover whether these shows have any substantial oppositional content to offer. (Whether that content is any good or not, whether its cultural critique will suffice, is another question.) First, scholars interested in the political content of mass media have to move cartoons and other popular forms out of the category of not-worth-arguing-about and into the arena of serious discussion. While scholars in media studies have been working towards this goal for years, creative artists in animation have been giving us direction as well.

One hint Matt Groening and the team of Trey Parker and Matt Stone, the creators of *The Simpsons* and *South Park,* respectively, give that indicates their audience should attempt to read their texts seriously is the satiric ways in which the two shows depict cartoons within their fictive worlds. When novelists or playwrights include novels-within-novels or plays-within-plays in their works, sophisticated readers usually take that as an authorial hint regarding what (or how) to think about their medium. The cartoons-within-cartoons, and their audiences, on both *The Simpsons* and *South Park,* serve the same purpose: they give both general audiences and scholars a fairly reliable indication of how the show's writers and producers want viewers to think about the cultural status of the medium, especially regarding its ideological content. This technique enables the shows to make political points not in spite of their status as children's programming but because of it.

In the case of both *The Simpsons* and *South Park,* the cartoons-within-cartoons are clearly satires, not just of the media in general but of the content and culture of animation in particular. On *The Simpsons, The Itchy & Scratchy Show* mocks the violent and nonsensical generic conventions of cat-and-mouse cartoons such as *Tom and Jerry,* but it also touches on other issues as well. Most interestingly, perhaps, is how the cartoonists have consistently referred to the history of American animation, from Disney to Warner Brothers, Hanna-Barbera, and John Kricfalusi's *Ren and Stimpy.*[2] This self-conscious referentiality places *The Simpsons*'s take on animation firmly within what might be called the high-art tradition of American animation. Yet the show goes further, thematizing corporate capitalism as, in various episodes, the portrayal of Itchy & Scratchy International satirizes the combination of corporate life and artistic endeavor out of which *The Simpsons* emerges. In *South Park,* the title characters of the cartoon-within-a-cartoon "Terrence and Philip" are as single-mindedly scatological as Beavis and Butt-head were purported to be. "Terrence and Philip" (even more crudely put together than the purposefully rough computerized construction paper cut-outs used to animate the rest of *South Park*) really is just a series of fart jokes, nothing more.

A certain self-effacing humor is one of the reasons why animation studies have lagged behind film and other media as an area of scholarly inquiry. Terrance R. Lindvall and J. Matthew Melton write that, "The casual way in which animation and the cartoon are treated by film theorists is due in part to the self-deprecating humour of the cartoon itself. Like the post-modernism of Jean-François Lyotard, the cartoon is a playful art. Without pretensions, it teases both those who neglect it and those who take it too seriously."[3] The connection that Lindval and Melton draw between this style of humor and postmodern sensibility suggests that a long view of the medium's self-referentiality should remind us that we also have a historical reason for taking cartoons, and how they portray their own art form, seriously. Many aspects of postmodernism are nothing new. If part of postmodernist self referentiality combines an exploration of the relations between aesthetics and the business of art, the ways in which an aesthetic object is produced and consumed, cartoonists have been thematizing their own artifice and commerce, as well as exploiting the distinction between high and low culture, for decades. Vintage Warner Brothers cartoons such as *Duck Amuck*, which shows Daffy Duck arguing with the artist drawing him (who turns out to be Bugs Bunny) as scenes and costumes and plots shift with dizzying speed and hilarious effect, or numerous cartoons depicting silhouettes of patrons in the theater getting in the way of other viewers, much to the consternation of the animated characters "onscreen," should remind scholars of the ways in which cartoons can take, and have taken, a sophisticated position in relation to their own commodity status.[4] The question now becomes how to read this self-referentiality in relation to the politics of oppositionality in American culture today: does this aesthetic sophistication lead to an ideological payoff? Dana Polan, for example, suggests that *Duck Amuck* rejects politics because of the way it thematizes "the nature of animation technique itself," or, as Lindvall and Melton claim, *Duck Amuck* "embodies a consciously apolitical self-reflexivity."[5]

I would argue instead that, given the fact that such art is produced within a corporate culture that is often the subject of attack, this self-referentiality need not lead to a retreat from political engagement into pure aesthetics. Lindvall and Melton themselves argue that in cartoons, "Postmodern sensibilities are stylistically realized . . . with the fusion of high and low art, the tinkering with hybrid forms, the tones of irony and parody, the incredulity toward meta-narratives and the principle of double coding, all of which frolic merrily in the realm of the intertextual."[6] Self-referentiality in animation "reflects upon its own construction and its relationship to the context out of which it has been created."[7] Such attention

to its own sources, its "means and motives of production," can make consumers of the text *more* rather than less conscious of the cartoon as an
object of commerce and therefore of the whole corporate system, the dominant culture.

Understood in this context, *The Simpsons* and *South Park* are very
much a part of their medium's mainstream, not postmodern extremes.
Claims that *South Park,* in particular, has gone farther than earlier cartoons
as regards violence inspired this reaction in a syndicated daily comic strip,
Arlo and Janis: a father asks his son, "You mean there's this little kid . . .
And he gets *killed* in every cartoon?!" Watching television, the son replies,
"Yeah, Dad, that's *so* different from a coyote falling off a cliff!"[8] This generational divide, one which is replicated in the episodes to be discussed
below, where the parents of cartoon viewers are shocked and appalled to
see what their children find funny, brings the issue of the audience—as
depicted by satirists, assumed by censors, and analyzed by scholars seeking oppositional texts—into the argument.

The issue of censorship pertains to the argument over whether cartoons can be oppositional because the interpretive logic of censorship and
satire are mirror images. Censors assume a norm against which certain
things represented in art are opposed, and so consumption of those aesthetic objects must be controlled or prevented in order to preserve that
norm. (And while, strictly speaking, the matter at hand is *censure,* or an
expression of political disapproval without the direct power of government regulation, the practical effect sought is the suppression of the text
being attacked, as though by a government censor.) Satire assumes a norm
that must be opposed and so artistically exaggerates things as they are in
order to have a political effect. Satire, like any serious genre, depends upon
the existence of multiple levels of signification and the reader's willingness to participate in serious interpretive behavior, to read deeply. The
interpretive logic of censorship, on the other hand, is typically singular.
When encountering a text, censors read at one level or another: they tend
to focus either entirely on the obvious, seeing anything which offends a
narrowly defined set of surface criteria as the total interpretive package a
text has to offer, or they read at an absurdly deep level to ferret out practically invisible nefarious influences. In the interpretive logic of censorship, either the scatological and pyromaniacal surface of *Beavis and
Butt-head* is all there is to the text (and it should be banned because of the
bad influence it will have on its putative audience of impressionable

youth), or a close examination of the background in the latest Disney animated movie with a large-screen television, a VCR, and a finger on the pause button reveals subliminal sexual messages invisible to the naked eye.[9] At whichever level they work, censors generally make two assumptions about audience: first, because the viewers of cartoons are morally and intellectually unable to handle objectionable material, they will be influenced to behave in unacceptable ways by it, and so they must be protected. Second, censors assume that audiences are monoliths and will read in one way and one way only.

In satire, on the other hand, artists expect savvy readers or viewers to read beyond the obvious surface level in order to understand the writer's true point, to interpret on at least two levels at once. To take a (perhaps *the*) canonical example, Swift's *A Modest Proposal*, most readers understand that, no, Swift really doesn't advocate eating the children of the Irish poor; he favors reform of Irish and English economic policies and individual behavior in order to improve everyone's situation, although the image of the rich literally eating the poor aptly sums up the actual situation.[10] In effective satire, the surface image hits its target, but that meaning is not the real significance of the text; to understand the point, an audience must simultaneously read more deeply in relation to some thematic context and keep the surface image and its subversive richness in focus. Successful interpretation of satire—"getting it"—requires reading on more than one level at once. Here is where a postmodern mass or popular oppositional culture might exist: in being willing to read (and teaching students to read) popular texts at the deeper level of meaning which in-on-the-joke readers get, and texts will often signal the existence of such a level by representing their own commodification within their fictive worlds.

One episode of each series particularly addresses these issues: "Itchy & Scratchy & Marge," written by John Swartzwelder, in which Marge Simpson leads a temporarily successful campaign to eliminate cartoon violence from "Itchy & Scratchy"; and "Death," written by Stone and Parker, in which the parents of South Park protest the "immature toilet humor" of "Terrence and Philip." Each episode satirizes the methods and motives of would-be censors and their assumptions about the audience that they are trying to protect and each addresses such serious (and supposedly beyond the medium) issues as assisted suicide and the corporate production of art. These two episodes, read together with the significance-hunting methods we bring to any serious text, demonstrate that the issue at hand is not so much whether *The Simpsons* and *South Park* simply *are* oppositional, but instead how an audience can move beyond false dichotomies between mass and elite culture to use the interpretive strategies of satire to read for oppositional content, and then to evaluate its effectiveness.

II

The first hint that viewers are supposed to understand *The Simpsons* as more than another cartoon nuclear family in the evolutionary road of television animation leading from *The Flintstones* to *The Jetsons* is the show's logo: "The Simpsons" does not just appear on our screen—it appears on our screen on the screen of an animated television. In one sense, this image indicates that the show is a cartoon of a cartoon, self-reflexively aware of itself existing in its own fictive world, but this image also suggests that we should consider what the show has to say about its medium and its own status as a television show. "Itchy & Scratchy & Marge" begins with Marge making her famous pork chops. Homer is inspired by Marge's cooking to try to build her a spice rack, and while Homer is working in the garage, Maggie appears and brains him with a hammer, imitating what she had just seen on "Itchy & Scratchy" (and letting the show make one of its numerous postmodern parody/pastiches, in this case visual and musical reference to Alfred Hitchcock's *Psycho*). Marge asks, "Where would an innocent child get the idea to attack her father with a mallet?" as she puts Maggie down in front of the television, on which appears another "Itchy & Scratchy" short, "Kitchen Kut-ups." After both characters answer Marge's question by pounding each other with mallets, Itchy attacks Scratchy with a butcher knife, and, as the *Psycho* theme music swells, Maggie picks up a sharp pencil and heads for Homer. Marge grabs her, saying, "No, Maggie! Bad baby!" and then utters perhaps the key words in the whole argument: "So, television's responsible!"

Marge turns the television off and tells Bart and Lisa, "You won't be watching these cartoons again, ever!" After cataloguing the violence on the cartoon, Marge writes a letter to Roger Myers, the sleazy, cigar-chomping CEO of Itchy & Scratchy International, and receives a rude response (Myers: "Our research indicates that one person cannot make a difference no matter how big a screwball she is, so let me close by saying . . ." [cut to Marge] " . . . and the horse I rode in on!"). Marge protests outside I & S

Studios, and gradually her movement, SNUH (Springfieldians for Nonviolence, Understanding, and Helping) gains so much momentum that she is invited to appear on the local news talk show *Smartline* to debate the issue. The question is framed by the host, Kent Brockman, to ensure her defeat: "Are cartoons too violent for children? Most people would say, 'No, of course not, what kind of stupid question is that?' " Her request that everyone who objects to violence in children's programming write letters to I & S International succeeds, and she becomes the leader of a mass movement, or as she puts it, a "crusade," albeit one that results in the family living on (ironic drum roll, please) TV dinners because she has no time to cook. (Homer grumbles, "20 million women in the world and I had to marry Jane Fonda.") The censure expressed in the letters succeeds in making the creators of the show censor themselves, as Myers surrenders with the words, "The screwballs have spoken!" The "Itchy & Scratchy" creative team turns to Marge (who is once again cooking pork chops for dinner) to get some nonviolent plot options. Bart and Lisa get to watch their favorite cartoon again, but things have changed. In "Porch Pals," Itchy and Scratchy sit on rocking chairs, share a pitcher of lemonade, and talk about how much they love each other. Lisa opines that, "Itchy and Scratchy seem to have lost their edge," while Marge says, "I think it conveys a very nice message of sharing," and Bart, predictably, retorts with, "I think it sucks!" Maggie (accompanied once again by *Psycho* theme music) brings Homer a glass of lemonade.

At this point, Bart turns the television off, saying, "Maybe there's something else to do on this planet," and all over Springfield children step onto their front steps and rub their eyes, to the opening bars of Beethoven's Sixth Symphony, the *Pastoral*. The show then depicts a satiric vision of what Homer later characterizes as "a Golden Age," where the children, once mindless drones in front of the boob tube, skip rope, skateboard, swing, play marbles, slide, toss a Frisbee, stop their scooters to let an old man cross the street, fly a kite, dance around a maypole, play sandlot baseball, ride bikes, build a tree house, swing on a tire, roll a hoop, and—triumphantly invoking one of America's canonical icons of mischievous-but-essentially-innocent childhood, Tom Sawyer—whitewash a fence. No one shows up for Krusty's studio audience. The censor's fantasies have come true: without television, children are once again innocent, playful, respectful, and obedient. The pernicious effects of popular culture have been annihilated—accompanied, of course, by canonical classical music.

After Lisa and the newly well-behaved Bart ask to be excused from dinner to work on their soapbox racers, we cut to Florence, Italy, where workers in the background crate up Michelangelo's *David* as a museum director announces a tour of the United States. The next morning, SNUH arrives on the Simpsons' doorstep, with their anti-"Itchy & Scratchy" placards modified to oppose *David*. When asked to lead a new crusade "against this abomination" Marge replies, "But that's Michelangelo's *David*, it's a masterpiece!" Her former ally replies that, "It's filth! It graphically portrays parts of the human body, which, practical as they may be, are evil." Disappointed with the fact that Marge is "soft on full frontal nudity," the mob leaves. Cut to Marge appearing on *Smartline*, where this time the question is put, "Is it a masterpiece, or [as a blue-jeaned *David* appears on a monitor] just some guy with his pants down?" Everyone assumes Marge will speak against the statue, and when she says, "I think everyone in Springfield should see it," Marvin Monroe calls her on the fact that it is logically inconsistent to "be for one form of freedom of expression like our big naked friend over there, and be against another form like 'Itchy & Scratchy.'" When asked, "What do you say to all those Marge Simpson wannabes out there who wish to suppress *David*'s doodle?" Marge responds, "Hmmmm. I don't know, I guess one person can make a difference, but most of the time they probably shouldn't."

With "Itchy & Scratchy" free to be violent again, the scene shifts to abandoned playgrounds, creaking swings, tumbleweeds rolling past the only half-whitewashed fence. Children once again sit in front of their televisions and laugh at violent cartoons, while Maggie eyes sharp objects. The episode concludes with Marge and Homer in an unpopulated museum. Homer admiringly says, "Well, there he is, Michelangelo's *Dave*." When Marge seems upset, Homer asks her what's wrong, and she replies, "Oh, Homey, here the kids have a chance to see a great work of art, and instead they're home watching a cat and mouse disembowel each other." But Homer has good news: "Eh, don't worry Marge; pretty soon, every boy and girl in Springfield Elementary School is gonna come and see this thing" because "[t]hey're forcin' 'em! Hahaha!" Marge gets the last word, "Well, isn't that nice?" and the credits roll.

In terms of my argument regarding the relationship between censorship and the oppositional potential of animated television, the four key scenes in this episode are: Maggie attacking Homer; Marge's accounting of the violence and what that says about the role of the censor; the final scene, when Homer and Marge visit the museum to view "Michelangelo's *Dave*"; and the results of a nonviolent "Itchy & Scratchy." If audiences try to get beyond false dichotomies between the mass and the elite and read each of these scenes as a serious text, oppositional material stands out amidst the sight gags and situation comedy formulas.

First, when Maggie imitates what she sees on television, Swartzwelder eliminates one argument from the cultural debate over censoring cartoons: in this episode, television really does influence children, or at least one child, to behave violently. Maggie imitates whatever she sees Itchy and Scratchy doing, whether it is hitting Homer on the head with a hammer or offering him a glass of lemonade. This concession is vital because (as in any serious text) it takes its audience to the heart of the issue, both for censors and for critics interested in creating oppositional culture: can a cartoon (or any work of art) really change how anyone behaves or thinks? Despite Maggie's example, many people think not: as one child, quoted in a story about the potential negative effects on young minds of *South Park*, says, "It's just a cartoon!"[11]

But, logically speaking, if progressive critics expect to find expressions of oppositional culture in popular or mass forms, then they want viewers to act on what they glean from those popular forms and so must accept the idea that television can influence how people behave in the world. This issue has been especially prominent in the history of children's television, exemplified by shows such as *Sesame Street,* which was designed not just by television executives but also by researchers in education who set out to produce programs that would have a positive educational effect on children.[12] Any argument which claims that it does not matter what children watch because it is "just television" or "just a cartoon" and therefore will have no effect on them automatically disallows for real political change being motivated by popular art. (The fact that television as a medium is assumed to influence the behavior of people through commercials is another issue.) If *The Simpsons* or *South Park* could not make anyone act in accordance with corporate capitalism (or what they believe is their own inclinations as constructed by corporate capitalism), scholars and critics logically could not claim that it could do the opposite; to allow for the sort of positive effects one might want to attribute to art, one must allow for negative effects as well.

The most important example of such negative influence is the notorious case of the *Beavis and Butt-head* arsons. The *New York Times* headline says it all: "Cartoon on MTV Blamed for Fire: Mother Says Boy, 5, Started Blaze That Killed Sister After Viewing 'Beavis.' " An anonymous Associated Press writer continues:

> The mother of a 5-year-old boy who started a fire that killed his younger sister blames the MTV cartoon "Beavis and Butt-head" for promoting burning as fun, a fire official said Friday.
>
> "When you take a child in the formative years and you get these cartoon characters saying it's fun to play with fire," said Fire Chief Harold Sigler, "This is going to stick in that kid's mind and it's going to be with him for a long time."
>
> The "Beavis and Butt-head" feature portrays two teen-age cartoon characters who comment on music videos and spend time burning and destroying things.[13]

In the end, MTV eliminated references to fire from the show to avoid potential litigation.[14] This form of self-censorship might seem relatively benign (although it destroyed the American comic book industry's artistic credibility from the 1950s through the late 1980s). After all, no one wants children playing with matches.

But—to attack another needless dichotomy—both sides of the debate as it is generally framed ignore the undeniable fact that audiences are not monoliths, and that not all members of an audience will react to things in the same ways. Sure, maybe that kid in Ohio did burn down the family trailer because he was somehow directly inspired by Beavis's maniacal "Fire! Fire! Fire!" chant; but literally millions of people have seen the same shows and have not set fire to a thing; they have laughed or not laughed, turned the show off or taped it, learned whole scenes by heart or let it go in one ear and out the other. (And when the show satirically and self-referentially replaced "Fire! Fire! Fire!" with "Fryer! Fryer! Fryer!" as Beavis worked the deep-fryer at Burger World in later episodes, no one seemed to be afraid of an epidemic of children dropping mice in boiling oil.) But while audiences do not all react to anti-social behavior depicted in art in the same way, the real-world legal issues raised by the mere possibility of children imitating what they see on television has had an influence on even the supposedly beyond-the-pale *South Park*: "Even *South Park* gets censored. Believe it or not, this outrageous show has limits: A scene in which Shelley throws matches on Stan was cut at the request of Comedy Central for fear that kids might imitate the act."[15] Network censors act out of the fear of litigation, a fear based on the common assumption that television influences how children behave.

The idea that children, the putative audience for all cartoons, will be influenced negatively by what they watch is at the heart of this debate, and the decision by Swartzwelder to concede that point in this episode is, to say the least, interesting. On one level, it is just funny to see Maggie attack Homer (when Homer calls in his excuse for missing work, "I told you, my baby beat me up!" it is hard not to laugh); but on another level, if viewers approach the show with the same sort of interpretive tools brought to other serious art forms, it invites a deeper reading. Whenever interpreters look for latent meaning in a serious text, they seek patterns of signification, parallels and pairs of opposites to structure their take on the theme. A serious reading of this episode would not stop with the fact that Maggie imitates what she sees on television; other children provide a pattern, and here things get a little more complicated. Both Bart, contemporary American culture's archetypal bad boy, and Lisa, a straight-A student, love "Itchy & Scratchy." They represent both ends of the possible spectrum of childhood behavior, yet they do not just imitate what they see on cartoons. Why not? One answer suggests itself: because they are older than Maggie, and therefore (presumably) more sophisticated viewers, a more mature audience. Such an assumption is the basis for the entire movie rating system.

The issue of the age of the appropriate audience for cartoon violence leads to the next key scene, when Marge, blissfully unaware that Bart and Lisa are watching at friends' homes, catalogues the violence on "Itchy & Scratchy." Bart and Lisa escape their mother's ban on the show by invoking clichés about what they should be doing instead of watching television. Bart says, "I've got to get over to Milhouse's to . . . play sports" and Lisa adds, "And I'm going over to Janie's again . . . we're going to be making the most of our childhood years." This brief moment deftly satirizes censors' single-level reading: Marge misses the giggles, pauses, and other verbal hints that Bart and Lisa are up to something because the surface level of their statements fulfills her expectations. As Marge keeps score of the animated mayhem, the dialogue between Marge and Homer neatly sums up the problematic aspects of assumptions about who can and cannot safely watch violent cartoons:

HOMER: Hey, how come you can watch cartoons but the kids can't?

MARGE: Because.

HOMER: Because why?

MARGE: Because I said so.

HOMER: Because you said so why?

MARGE: Homer, I'm trying to work. I'm cataloguing the violence in these cartoons. I don't think adults have ever actually sat down and watched them before. What kind of warped human being would find that funny? [As Homer laughs in the background.] This is the kind of entertainment they think is suitable for younger and more impressionable viewers?

Homer's childish dialogue, like a toddler endlessly asking "why" in response to every answer, makes age an issue. Marge can watch the cartoon violence without ill effects (or laughter) because, unlike Maggie or Homer, she is mature enough to handle the material (that is, to read it on one level, like any censor). The use of the phrase, "younger and more impressionable viewers," acts as an ironic reappropriation of the words once used on PBS to warn parents that the foreign film or BBC comedy, like *Monty Python*, about to appear might be a bit much for children. It also leads to another key aspect of the interpretive logic of censorship: why censors presumably can watch something and be unaffected by it, while the "younger and more impressionable" audience they are trying to protect is supposed to be at such risk.

Censors work this way, as Nicola Beisel has demonstrated in her book, *Imperiled Innocents: Anthony Comstock and Family Reproduction in Victorian America,* because censorship movements are linked to perceived threats to children and to the perpetuation of status and class identity that children represent for the upper and middle classes.[16] *South Park* can be seen as "a danger to the democracy," *Beavis and Butt-head* as "final proof of society's degeneration," and Bart Simpson as "the downfall of Western civilization" by critics because the three shows' depictions of children who blatantly and joyfully disregard social norms threatens middle class culture's ability to reproduce itself.[17] (And, I would ask, what could be more oppositional?) Out-of-control children such as Bart Simpson and the *South Park* quartet of "little bastards" attract so much attention because, as Beisel argues in relation to the Victorian controversy over censoring "obscene" reproductions of fine art, "family reproduction involves, in part, controlling children. Preserving the social position of children is in part a policing process, an attempt to keep children from learning practices that will undermine [their] future success."[18] With this idea about censorship in mind, it is no surprise that critics and would-be censors of these shows have fixated on portrayals of bad boys (each of whom has an anti-education mantra that has appeared on T-shirts banned on school grounds), while MTV's *Daria* and *Celebrity Deathmatch* and Fox's *King of the Hill*—all animated television shows with some (in the case of *Daria*, a great deal of) countercultural content—have been ignored. It is Bart Simpson ("Underachiever and proud of it!"), the seemingly parentless Beavis and Butt-head ("Videos with words suck. If I wanted to read, I'd go to school!") and the "little bastards" of South Park ("School sucks ass!") who threaten the reproduction of a certain sort of middle-class respectability built upon conventional academic achievement. Similarly, positive depictions of children go unnoticed. Even though Lisa Simpson might be described as a mainstream counter-cultural figure—espousing, as she does, such once-radical ideas as feminism, vegetarianism, and arts education in public schools—the critics do not focus on her and praise the show for providing good role models to little girls because the positive elicits no fear and therefore merits no response. Critics of the show also do not attack the very thinly veiled homoerotic attraction of Waylon Smithers for Mr. Burns because it does not threaten an extant family unit, and, I suspect, because they do not get it. The MPAA did not get it either when they required Stone and Parker to change the title of the *South Park* movie. These censors objected to *South Park: All Hell Breaks Loose* on religious grounds but had no problem with *South Park: Bigger, Longer and Uncut,* even though, as Stephen Schaefer points out, this "sounds suspiciously like a gay porn title."[19]

The SNUH response to *David*'s nudity also precisely parallels the nineteenth-century reactions to nudity in art that Beisel describes, right down to the all-American fear of its foreign source (one SNUH protester tells the curator accompanying *David*, "We want you to get your big Italian butt outta here!"). Censors attack threats to the maintenance of family status, class identity, and the continuation of the *status quo,* and that is why these particular animated shows have drawn the wrath of the critics and censors, and one reason why they should be taken seriously as a form of oppositional culture.

The third key scene in the episode, the denouement with Marge and Homer in the Springfield Arts Museum, engages the dynamic of high and low culture with materiality and questions of audience. When Comstock argued that "reproductions of art sold to the masses were obscene but works viewed in museums were not," the division between high and low is somehow transformed from an essential property of the artwork to a matter of what it is made of and where and how it is consumed.[20] This scene provides a subtle satiric depiction of the rarely discussed flipside of censorship: instead of keeping a particular art form or object away from people who want it, the audience sees the imposition of high culture on an unwilling audience. All the children in Springfield Elementary will see Michelangelo's *David* because authority figures will be "forcin' 'em to!" The silent partner of the censor keeping children away from bad art is the schoolteacher foisting good art on children.

Traditional ideas about what sort of interpretive strategies are appropriate to what sort of texts grow out of the complex dynamic of material culture and commercial culture. In short, many intellectuals in American culture tend to distrust anything which has commercial success based on the logic that if it sells, it must be bad. Why? Because the whole culture of buying and selling is the problem. This was not always true for oppositional art; in the case of modernism, Frederic Jameson reminds us that

> The older or classical modernism was an oppositional art: it emerged within the business society of the gilded age as scandalous and offensive to the middle-class public—ugly, dissonant, bohemian, sexually shocking. . . . This is to say that whatever the explicit political content of the great high modernisms, the latter were always in some mostly implicit ways dangerous and explosive, subversive within the established order.[21]

Yet this subversive status is complicated by the commodity status of the objects being argued about. Modernism, like most avant-gardes, did not pay very well. Many postmodern mass or popular forms, on the other hand, are gold mines, including cartoons such as *The Simpsons, Beavis and Butt-head,* and *South Park,* each of which was once the highest rated show on its respective network.[22] Such popular success seems to differentiate postmodernist oppositional texts from the modernist. As Jameson puts it, "The most offensive forms of this [postmodern] art—punk rock, say, or what is called sexually explicit material—are all taken in stride by society, and they are commercially successful, unlike the productions of the older high modernisms."[23]

Modernism has, to a large degree, become a museum piece, the dominant to be opposed or problematized by the postmodern, but in its day it was truly oppositional. The scene with Homer and Marge in the museum reminds viewers that most people will assume *David* is safe for consumption. Once something is safe, canonical, a masterpiece, high culture, then it can be forced on children, where it is assumed to have a positive, elevating effect. This rarely discussed companion to censorship shows the complicated positions these supposedly simple-minded shows, mere cartoons, can take on serious issues.

Whether viewing high art will have the same sort of positive effect that not viewing low art did is another question, one that leads to the fourth key scene, the Golden Age of childhood without television. This scene shows and satirizes what the censors hope for: by eliminating cartoon violence, they hope, America will return to an idyllic nineteenth-century vision of innocent childhood, one very like the sort of thing that Comstock led his moral crusades to protect. But as the scene develops—if viewers attend to the multiple levels of the content of the images (and the music) just as in the interpretation of any serious text—it swiftly becomes absurd. The play the children perform becomes more and more archaic (has anyone rolled a hoop with a stick in decades?) and unrealistic (why are Nelson and the other kid who are whitewashing the fence barefoot and wearing overalls?). But note one subtext of this scene: it does not depict the positive effect of consuming some art form, like being taken to see *David* on a school field trip. The children here do not turn to another television show for their afternoon's entertainment; they abandon the medium altogether, and this scene satirizes what the censors hope the positive effect of abandoning the vast wasteland of American entertainment culture will result in. The incongruous and unrealistic images in the scene visually embody the cultural conservative's desire to eliminate television altogether. As in much effective satire, Swartzwelder's idea here takes its target at its word and then goes one step further to demonstrate the absurdity or impossibility of the target's desires. The censor's logic runs like this: If children watch bad television shows, they will be inspired to imitate them (as is conceded when Maggie attacks Homer); if only they were not sitting in front of the television, they would participate in wholesome, old-fashioned, good, clean, outdoor fun and games.

Yet perhaps the most telling thing about this scene and its satiric point regarding censorship and the cartoon as a medium is, once again, the presumption of a monolithic audience. Through exaggeration, this scene acts out the censor's implicit assumption that everyone reads things the same way, and if deprived of that bad influence, everyone will respond the same way. This is sheer nonsense. Audiences are not monoliths (every argument about what some particular text means demonstrates as much), but censors, reading as they usually do at one level and one level only, presume everyone is stuck at the same level. Here all the children of Springfield act as one, returning to a pre-television Golden Age. Their swift return to the tube when Itchy and Scratchy start disemboweling each other again is only what the censors should expect from the sort of monolithic audience they presuppose.

III

Stone and Parker have a much darker vision of what children deprived of their cartoons might turn to. When their favorite cartoon is cancelled, the children of South Park try to figure out what else they else might be doing. When confronting a life without "Terrence and Philip," they do not go outside to play baseball, roll hoops, or whitewash fences. Instead, they say,

> KYLE: Hey Stan, now that *Terrence and Philip* has been taken off the air, what are we gonna do for entertainment?
> STAN: I dunno. We could we could start breathing gas fumes.
> ERIC: My uncle says that smoking crack is kinda cool.
> KYLE: Hey why don't we go watch some of them porno-movie thingees?
> STAN: Cool!

In this image of children deprived of their cartoons turning to drugs and pornography, Stone and Parker use a satirical strategy opposite Swartzwelder's. Instead of showing and mocking as unrealistic the censor's assumptions about audience and the end result the censors claim they want, Stone and Parker show the censors' worst nightmares coming true. While *The Simpsons* takes the censors at their word about what would happen without television, *South Park* instead invokes the Law of Unintended

Consequences, arguing that people ought to be glad children are just watching cartoons instead of doing something worse. This fits with the generally darker tone of the series, and this episode in particular, which addresses not just cartoons and their influence on children. One of the two plots revolves around the request of Stan's 102-year-old grandfather that Stan help him commit suicide.

But first, the opening credits of the show require some attention. Like *The Simpsons, South Park* has its distinctive opening sequence. To the guitar music of the alternative rock band Primus, the town of South Park and the major and minor characters are assembled, one piece at a time: mountains, buildings, vehicles, characters' heads and bodies, background visuals. This sequence (which has become more layered and complex as the show has added more characters) overtly thematizes its own artifice, the specifics of Parker and Stone's animation style, which uses digitized construction paper cutouts to create the look of the show. Then we get the warnings. Even before it became the first show not on premium cable to carry the TV-MA rating (indicating that it is intended for adult audiences only), the show led with the following stark black-and-white warning: "All characters and events in this show—even those based on real people—are entirely fictional. All celebrity voices are impersonated . . . poorly. The following program contains coarse language and due to its content should not be viewed by anyone." On one level, the combination of these two announcements should eliminate any potential trouble from censors, because they explicitly state that children should not watch the show. This interdiction, of course, makes the show forbidden fruit and more attractive to children, and Comedy Central, which produces and distributes *South Park,* revels in its on-the-edge status. One of its earliest ads for the program read, "Alien Abductions, Anal Probes and Flaming Farts. *South Park*. Why They Created the V-Chip."[24] Yet, if an audience moves beyond false dichotomies that impede thematic reading and interprets the show in general and this episode in particular with the attention to detail and patterns of signification appropriate to the serious texts of high culture, it is patently clear that Stone and Parker consistently take on issues thought to be beyond the medium. Euthanasia is just such an issue.

The episode "Death" opens with Stan's family celebrating their grandfather's 102nd birthday. When asked what his wish is upon his breathless failure to blow out a single candle, he says, "I wish I were dead!" Stan takes Grandpa into the living room with cake to watch his favorite show,

Terrence and Philip, which his sister dismisses as immature: "That show's for babies, it's so stupid" (again, spotting an age divide among children, like that between Maggie and Bart and Lisa). And so the viewers meet Terrence and Philip, whose show consists entirely of fart jokes. After Stan's grandfather misses trying to blow his own head off with a shotgun and offers Stan a dollar to kill him (Stan refuses, not because he thinks it is wrong, but because "I'll get in trouble,"), we cut to Kyle Broslofski's house, where his mother sees the show and is shocked and appalled. When Terrence and Philip start using profanity, Mrs. Broslofski turns off the television and tells Kyle, "Young man you're not to watch that show any more, it's immature toilet humor." She calls other parents to warn them, and Mrs. Cartman tells Eric, "this show is naughty and might make you a potty-mouth." Eric's reply—"That's a bunch of crap. Kyle's mom is a dirty Jew!"—would seem to confirm the prediction. So the next day at school, where Kenny shows up with a severe case of "explosive diarrhea," their teacher Mr. Garrison explains (to the blank stares of the class) why they should not watch *Terrence and Philip*: "Shows like *Terrence and Philip* are what we call 'toilet humor.' They don't expand your minds. These kind of shows are senseless vile trash. You should be spending your time enlightening your mind with more intelligent entertainment." When he asks for questions, Stan asks if it is "OK to kill someone if they want you to." Here, the serious moral issue of the show is raised, but Mr. Garrison dodges it: "I'm not touching that one with a twenty-foot pole." Later, Chef—the only adult the kids trust and like—says he will not touch the issue of "assisted suicide" "with a forty-foot pole," and when they later call Jesus Christ's call-in local cable television show (yes, *that* Jesus Christ), he refuses to touch it "with a sixty-foot pole."

Meanwhile, back at the South Park version of SNUH, Mrs. Broslofski is speaking. "I myself was not aware of this horrible show until recently. I have a clip to demonstrate exactly what I mean," and she shows a single fart joke, which Stan's father laughs at (before being stared down by the crowd). She continues: "Not allowing our kids to watch this show is not enough; we need to boycott the entire network! All those in favor!" As all hands shoot up, Mr. Garrison comes out of the men's room (preceded by loud flatulence) and says, "I think I caught a touch of the flu from little Kenny this morning. I've got the green apple splatters." The crowd chuckles. Cut to Stan's grandpa trying to stick a fork in an outlet, while the kids arrive to watch *Terrence and Philip*. Stan again refuses to help him kill himself, but while *Terrence and Philip* distracts the boys, grandpa almost gets Stan to inadvertently help him hang himself before Shelley interrupts. They are busted, and the television news media takes over. A newscaster tells us, "Four third graders from South Park, Colorado were found trying to viciously murder an innocent grandfather," and we cut to an oily talk show host:

> HOST: Boys, how did you get driven so far to the edge, what changed you into such demonic little bastards?
> STAN: We didn't know what we were doing, we were just sitting there watching *Terrence and Philip* and—
> HOST: *Terrence and Philip*? Aha, so it is that show that is to blame!

The parents agree, and Mrs. Broslofski says, "These boys' minds have been tainted by the garbage on television that they see, and we are fed up! We have to stop this smut from going on the air. We will march to the network and protest until our demands are met. New York, here we come!" (This statement makes clear that while "to censor" and "to censure" might mean two different things, the goal of most people expressing censure is to censor.) Throughout their trip to New York, the parents make a series of jokes about the intestinal disorder plaguing them.

Back in South Park, the four boys are having the time of their lives. As Kyle puts it, "This is sweet, not having parents around!" Stan agrees: "Yeah, I hope they protest TV shows forever!" Grandpa appears and forces Stan to listen to what it feels like to be old. In a darkened room, he plays some New Age music—and turns it up. This music, which Stan describes as, "cheesy but lame and eerily soothing at the same time," makes Stan realize that he "had no idea how bad it was" for his grandfather, and so he agrees to help him kill himself. Back in New York, the network responds to the PTA's complaint with a just-barely-bleeped "Fuck you!" (a step further than the sharp cut and implied ellipses that hide the same words in Roger Myers's letter to Marge on *The Simpsons*). Deciding, "The network is not taking us seriously," the parents of South Park begin to use a giant slingshot to hurl themselves to their deaths against the Cartoon Central building. (Here again is the much more surreal attitude that *South Park* brings to the interpretive table, which goes far beyond Kenny's weekly demise.)

The boys prepare to kill Stan's grandfather by dropping a cow on him when Death—the canonical image, skeletal figure with hooded cloak and

scythe—appears, amid lightning bolts and smoke. Grandpa is delighted—
"It's about time you lazy ass son of a whore! Come on, let's go!"—but Death
instead chases the kids back to Stan's, where they call Stan's parents for help
as Death pounds on the door. Stan's parents never let him finish a sentence
and so never discover what is going on; as Death scythes through the door,
the kids make a direct-to-the-camera—that is, to the audience—speech:

> STAN: You know, [happy, uplifting-moral-of-the-story theme music
> begins] I think that if parents would spend less time worrying about
> what their kids watch on TV and more time worrying about what's
> going on in their kids' lives, this world would be a much better place.
>
> KYLE: Yeah. I think that parents only get so offended by television
> because they rely on it as a babysitter and the sole educator of their
> kids.

Kenny then speaks, his words as always unintelligible through his snow-
suit. Stan and Kyle respond, "Totally, dude," and "Good point, man," just
as Death breaks in and the chase continues. Death pursues them (perhaps
a less than Bergmanesque figure, as he's riding a tricycle), and Stan's
grandpa in his wheelchair pursues Death, until Death stops at TV World
and watches *Terrence and Philip* in the window of the store. Amused,
Death laughs and slaps his thigh, and the kids join him laughing at the
show. Meanwhile, back in New York, the network finally caves in—not
because of the dead parents on the facade, but because of the portapotties
overflowing with the results of the bug everyone caught from Kenny.

In South Park, Death, grandpa, and the boys watch as Cartoon Central
takes the show off the air with the words, "We interrupt this program to
bring you loud static." Death immediately kills Kenny. When Stan's
grandpa protests, the ghost of his own grandfather appears and tells him
that making Stan kill him would be wrong because of the effect it would
have on Stan's life and that he must wait to die of natural causes. The town's
parents return, and Mrs. Broslofski says, "Well, we did it son, we fought
a battle for your well-being and won. We got 'Terrence and Philip' taken
off the air"(Eric's reaction to Kyle: "You sonofabitch, your mom sucks!").
They tune in the replacement show, reruns of *She's the Sheriff* (Eric's reaction: "No, God, nooooo!"). Unfortunately for the censorious PTA, this
show features dialogue almost as rude as that on *Terrence and Philip*. The
parents, again outraged, head back to New York to get this show cancelled.
The three remaining kids are left to contemplate what to do without their

favorite cartoon, and we finish on a parodic take-off on pat sitcom endings, where Stan's grandfather appears dressed for travel because he has
booked a flight to Africa where hundreds of people are "naturally eaten
by lions" every year. Amid giggles, Stan says, "My silly grandpa," as Kyle
delicately farts.

The key scenes are Death watching *Terrence and Philip*, the kids' lecture to the camera, the behavior of the parents throughout, and the concurrent plot regarding Stan's grandfather. An analysis of each of these
aspects of the text—with the interpretive strategies appropriate for
satire—reveals a fine-edged attack on censors and a thoughtful and subtle consideration of issues regarding assisted suicide.

First, the scene where Death watches *Terrence and Philip* provides an
excuse for more fart jokes, and the *South Park* team rarely misses a chance
to be disgusting and juvenile. (Hence, much of the show's appeal.
Although, to the charge that the entire show is just fart jokes, Parker
replies, "I wish. It wouldn't be so hard to find writers.")[25] On the other
hand, this scene neatly ties into serious ways of thinking about why people make jokes about bodily functions at all. In the dualistic Western tradition, the fact of the human body serves one overriding purpose: to
remind everyone—for good and ill—that people are animals and will die.
Sex, eating, urination, defecation—all are animal processes and all can
evoke outrage, disgust, embarrassment, and heartfelt or nervous laughter
as a way of—at least temporarily—ignoring or laughing in the face of
death. So here in South Park, while the parents are off protesting "toilet
humor," Death stops and laughs heartily at Terrence and Philip's fart jokes.
This is a brief moment in a busy show, but it demonstrates that if readers
get beyond traditional intellectual dichotomies and interpret these texts
with an eye for the serious, it is there to be found.

Similarly, the lecture to the camera quoted in full above reveals that
the writers are aware of some of the unspoken subtexts in parental protests
over television shows and the logic of censorship: this debate revolves
around the power over who consumes what, who decides what sort of
humor is acceptable for whom, and the desire for some parents to impose
their own standards on everyone. Mrs. Broslofski claims, "Not allowing
our kids to watch this show is not enough; we need to boycott the entire
network!" (much as Marge says, "I can protect my own children, but there
are many others whose minds are being warped every afternoon at four").
This scene (as well as the almost precisely parallel lines, "So television's
responsible" and "So it is that show that is to blame"), clearly argues that

when parents put the onus for their children's behavior on the content of television, it is a dodge, a way of evading responsibility for problems which might very well have roots elsewhere. (To the claim that the shows teach children profanity, "an 8-year-old boy from Larchmont, New York says they weren't new to him: 'My daddy says them every single day.'")[26] If parents really do "rely on [television] as a babysitter and the sole educator of their kids," then the problem is with the parents, not the content of the shows. And I suspect few people would deny that "the world would be a better place [. . .] if parents would spend less time worrying about what their kids watch on TV and more time worrying about what's going on in their kids' lives." Although, treating this claim as rigorously as we would any other serious argument, we must admit that it too is a bit of a dodge, because the content of television shows *is* something going on in children's lives. Nonetheless, by placing these lines at a moment when there is an awful lot happening in the lives of these kids, what with Death chasing them around, the show surrealistically and satirically emphasizes what parents ought to attend to.

The behavior of the parents is a key issue throughout the show, as they make the same sort of jokes amongst themselves that they do not want their children to see on television. Adults who are outraged over *Terrence and Philip*'s "toilet humor" laugh when Mr. Garrison says, "I've got the green apple splatters," and when the mayor says, "I just had a brown baby boy" or asks if the next person in the portapotty line needs "to drop some friends off at the pool." The message is once again clear: some forms of humor are OK for parents but will ruin children forever. Parker and Stone do not explicitly state this; it is left, as so many of the more serious moments in both of these shows are, for the whatever part of the audience that uses serious interpretive strategies to discover. The issue of audience age returns as well. When Mrs. Broslofski describes the show as "immature," she is exactly right, as is Shelley when she says, "That show's for babies." But the audience should remember that the portrayed audience for "Terrence and Philip" on the show *is* immature, a bunch of third-graders. What would the censors expect them to do, read Rabelais for "mature" humor about bodily functions?

The most important issue throughout the episode, however, is Stan's moral dilemma. Should he help his grandfather kill himself? Stan's grandfather frames the question in a way that satirically echoes the language of cultural conservatives decrying the decline of American morals when he asks, "What is America's youth come to? Kids won't even kill their own grandparents!" but the plot is a serious one. (And it is a toss-up as to whether censorship or suicide is the main plot; the title of the episode, after all, is "Death," not "Censorship"). Assisted suicide is one of the most controversial moral and legal issues in contemporary American culture, and their parents leave the four boys of *South Park* to handle it without adult guidance because of the threat they see posed to their children (or, to return to Beisel, to the reproduction of middle class culture) by some fart jokes. This one theme ties together all of the key moments and issues in the episode—Death laughing at *Terrence and Philip,* the uplifting-moral speeches by Kyle and Stan, and the hypocrisy of the parents—and it does so subtly, without the sort of simplistic obviousness for which critics usually dismiss cartoons. Stan's grandfather helped his own grandfather kill himself, and this man's spirit (now stuck in limbo) appears and tells him that he should not ask Stan to kill him not because of any of the usual religious or legal arguments against assisted suicide, but because of the negative effect it will have on Stan's life. This is one of the less often heard positions in the debate on euthanasia, but the claim that no one should have to make such a momentous decision is one which has been put forth, and here it is subtly advanced in the midst of all the fart jokes and sight gags.

Interpretation ties all of the aspects of each episode together. If viewers read with the serious dual-level methods inherent in the interpretive logic of satire, each show thematizes several serious, and potentially oppositional, issues: the shallow one-level reading style of the interpretive logic of censorship; the hypocritical attitudes of censors towards audience; the fact that audiences are not monoliths; what is at stake in arguments over violence and profanity in relation to high and low art; and the dynamic of material culture, accessibility, and status in which these arguments take place.

IV

In the end, the issue is not whether *The Simpsons* or *South Park* simply are cultural critiques of corporate America, forms of oppositional culture, but whether sophisticated readers are prepared to interpret them as such. As with any satire, by definition oppositional, interpretation depends on the presuppositions readers bring to the text. When scholars and critics approach cartoons with the assumption that the medium is not capable of cultural critique due to its popular appeal or corporate origins, they set out on the wrong interpretive course from the beginning and so are less likely to get it. Much of the coverage of *South Park* has addressed the very issue of whether readers get it. *South Park* definitely pushes the envelope farther than *The Simpsons,* especially regarding racial, ethnic, and sexual humor. Writing in *The New York Times Magazine,* Jonathan Van Meter puts the question:

> Does everyone get it? Are some of the "South Park" fans simply laughing at Jew jokes or goofy Chinese accents or gay stereotypes, without the layers of irony that exist at the point of creation? Probably. As with all comedy that dares to articulate the things that people don't for fear of sounding mean or hateful, there's always a chance that it might be dangerously misinterpreted—or misused.[27]

To which I respond: So what? The same could be said of any work of art in any medium: do some people not get Michelangelo's *David* and just drool at the naked perfection? Do some people think Swift really advocates eating the children of the poor? The danger of misinterpretation inheres in any utterance complicated enough to be worth discussing and should not in any way disqualify *The Simpsons* or *South Park* as potential sources of cultural critique.

Neither should their popular culture appeal. In reference to another popular form that was once thought beneath serious consideration, M. M. Bakhtin recalls the value of humor and provides a way of thinking about both the postmodern condition and the potential place for oppositional culture in the products of corporate culture:

> All these diverse parodic-travestying forms constituted, as it were, a special extra-generic or inter-generic world. But this world was unified, first of all, by a common purpose: to provide the corrective of laughter and criticism to all existing straightforward genres, languages, styles, voices; to force men to experience beneath these categories a different and contradictory reality that is otherwise not captured in them.[28]

The low form thought beneath serious consideration that Bakhtin refers to here is the novel, now our literary culture's dominant genre.

Finally, I would argue that instead of disputing whether a particular text or kind of text is qualified for being considered oppositional, critics and teachers interested in texts that might oppose our dominant culture should concentrate on teaching people to use the logic of satire to discover whatever oppositional content any text might have. While I would not claim, as some interpretive theorists have, that you can find anything you go looking for in any text (I've done my best, but *Terrence and Philip* really seems to be just fart jokes), sophisticated reading strategies can make visible things which might otherwise be missed, but using those reading strategies requires a conscious decision to do so, because of the traditional low cultural status of the medium of animation. Progressively minded scholars and critics should be teaching students and readers to get it, to see the levels of satire which exist in the most otherwise beneath-consideration texts. Such readings need not, by the way, be in praise of such texts. In this essay, I have primarily been reading for oppositional attitudes within these shows in accordance with what I think the creators want us to get, but anyone could also read the shows against the counter-cultural grain, for how they actually reinscribe certain dominant cultural values. For instance, the construction of gender roles in the shows is troubling: why are both of the small-minded censors in these episodes housewives? Why are men portrayed as immature and childish? Such questions await answers, and the serious analysis of *South Park, The Simpsons* and other popular forms is just beginning; I suspect that scholars first have to demonstrate that they are worth reading seriously like elite texts in the first place before subjecting them to analysis from all angles.

When he describes the postmodern conflation of popular and elite categories, Jameson argues that,

> This [conflation] is perhaps the most distressing development of all from an academic standpoint, which has traditionally had a vested interest in preserving a realm of high or elite culture against the surrounding environment of philistinism, of schlock and kitsch, of TV series and *Reader's Digest* culture, and in transmitting difficult and complex skills of reading, listening and seeing to its initiates.[29]

I would suggest that the solution to the question of whether texts such as *The Simpsons* or *South Park* can have oppositional status in our culture is based on maintaining the old-fashioned modernist-academic claim to power; that is, the consciously postmodern academic ought to be engaged in transmitting difficult and complex skills of reading to his or her students, the skills of making use of the interpretive logic of satire in order to read for subversion in texts high, low, and middle. At the very least, scholars should never dismiss out of hand entire media or genres as inherently complicit in their own commodification and therefore beyond the pale, or as *a priori* too simplistic to be worth consideration. Jameson writes,

> There is some agreement that the older modernisms functioned against its society in ways which are variously described as critical, negative, contestatory, subversive, oppositional and the like. Can anything of the sort be affirmed about postmodernism and its social moment? We have seen that there is a way in which postmodernism replicates or reproduces-reinforces the logic of consumer capitalism; the more significant question is whether there is also a way in which it resists that logic. But that is a question we must leave open.[30]

Whether the sort of satire in "Itchy and Scratchy and Marge" and "Death" discussed here resists the logic of consumer capitalism by demonstrating the intellectual inconsistencies and logical errors of censors and the division between high and low culture or just goes for laughs is, to some degree, a matter of taste.

For some audience members, the effectiveness of the oppositional critique I see in these shows is probably lost (or invisible) in the midst of all the fart jokes. The presence of that level of humor is in part attributable to the fact that the shows seek, first and foremost, to entertain, but the idea that something written with entertainment in mind is incapable of seriousness is the worst sort of academic elitism. Critics should keep in mind how many writers who wrote to entertain (Shakespeare, Dickens, Twain) are now unassailably canonical. But, given the strong way each show makes the its points about serious topics such as censorship and assisted suicide—and the vital depiction of the fact that audiences do not all read texts the same way—I believe that if viewers employ the interpretive logic of satire to reading postmodern popular texts such as *The Simpsons* and *South Park,* then scholars can begin to answer Jameson's question in the affirmative.

NOTES

1. Peter J. Rabinowitz, *Before Reading: Narrative Conventions and the Politics of Interpretation* (Columbus: Ohio State University Press, 1997).

2. Ray Richmond, *The Simpsons: A Complete Guide to Our Favorite Family* (New York: HarperPerrenial, 1997), 146–47.

3. Terrance R. Lindvall and J. Matthew Melton, "Towards a Post-Modern Animated Discourse: Bakhtin, Intertextuality and the Cartoon Carnival," in *A Reader in Animation Studies,* ed. Jayne Pilling (London: J. Libbey, 1997), 204.

4. *Duck Amuck*, Warner Bros. 1953. Directed by Charles M. Jones; story by Michael Maltese. See also Jerry Beck and Will Friedwald, *Looney Tunes and Merrie Melodies: A Complete Illustrated Guide to the Warner Bros. Cartoons* (New York: Holt, 1989), 245–46.

5. Dana Polan, "A Brechtian Cinema? Towards a Politics of Self-Reflexive Film," in *Movies and Methods,* vol. II., ed. Bill Nichols (Los Angeles: University of California Press, 1985), 667; Lindvall and Melton, "Towards a Post-Modern Animated Discourse," 204.

6. Lindvall and Melton, "Towards a Post-Modern Animated Discourse," 204.

7. Lindvall and Melton, "Towards a Post-Modern Animated Discourse," 204.

8. Jimmy Johnson, *Arlo and Janis,* 24 September 1998.

9. "Disney Recalls 3.4 Million Copies of 'The Rescuers.' " *Chicago Tribune* (January 9, 1999, Sec. 1): 14.

10. Jonathan Swift, "A Modest Proposal for Preventing the Children of Ireland from Being a Burden to Their Parents or Country," in *Swift's Satires and Personal Writings,* ed. William Alfred Eddy (London: Oxford University Press, 1965), 19–33.

11. Rick Marin, "The Rude Tube." *Newsweek* (23 March 1998): 60.

12. Gerald S. Lesser, *Children and Television: Lessons from* Sesame Street (New York: Random House, 1974); Edward L. Palmer, *Television and America's Children: A Crisis of Neglect* (New York: Oxford University Press, 1988).

13. "Cartoon on MTV Blamed for Fire." *New York Times* (10 October 1993, Sec. 1): 30.

14. "Corrections." *New York Times* (17 October 1993, Sec 1): 2. "On Wednesday, after the section went to press, MTV, which carries 'Beavis and Butt-head,' announced that references to starting fires would be deleted from the show's episodes."

15. Stef McDonald, "25 Shocking Secrets You Need to Know About South Park." *TV Guide* 46 (28 March 1998): 24.

16. Nicola Beisel, *Imperiled Innocents: Anthony Comstock and Family Reproduction in Victorian America* (Princeton, NJ: Princeton University Press, 1997).

17. First quote in Marin, "The Rude Tube," 57; following quotes in Elizabeth Kolbert, "Keeping Beavis and Butt-head Just Stupid Enough." *New York Times* (17 October 1993, sec. 2): 33.

18. Beisel, *Imperiled Innocents,* 8.

19. Schaefer, Stephen. "'South Park' Breaks Even More Rules on the Big Screen." *The Boston Herald* (July 7, 1999, Arts & Life): 43.

20. Beisel, *Imperiled Innocents,* 13.

21. Frederic Jameson, "Postmodernism and Consumer Society," in *The Norton Anthology of Postmodern American Fiction,* ed. Paula Geyh, Fred G. Leebron, and Andrew Levy (New York: Norton, 1997), 661.

22. Marin, "The Rude Tube," 58; Kolbert, "Keeping Beavis and Butt-head," 33.

23. Jameson, "Postmodernism and Consumer Society," 661.

24. Marin, "The Rude Tube," 56.

25. Marin, "The Rude Tube," 57.

26. Marin, "The Rude Tube," 60.

27. Jonathan Van Meter, "Stupid, Inc." *The New York Times Magazine* (26 July 1998): 16.

28. M. M. Bakhtin, "From the Prehistory of Novelistic Discourse," from *The Dialogic Imagination: Four Essays,* ed. Michael Holquist, trans. Caryl Emerson and Michael Holquist (Austin: University of Texas Press, 1981), 59.

29. Jameson, "Postmodernism and Consumer Society," 655.

30. Jameson, "Postmodernism and Consumer Society," 662–663.

Looking for Amanda Hugginkiss: Gay Life on *The Simpsons*

MATTHEW HENRY

Deviations can only be perceived against a norm.
DAVID LODGE

Those who are not regular watchers might be inclined to raise an eyebrow at a topic such as gay life on *The Simpsons*. However, those who are among the faithful are likely to recognize that such a discussion is not inappropriate, considering both the show's cast of characters and its political aims. As is well known, *The Simpsons* very quickly established itself as a biting satire on American society and culture, and, although its satirical edge has waned somewhat in recent years, it continues to function in this capacity week after week, offering for our edification scathing critiques of America's numerous idiosyncrasies and eccentricities. Foremost, *The Simpsons* is a satire upon the idealized images of family life depicted by traditional domestic sitcoms (e.g., *Leave It to Beaver* and *Father Knows Best* and, more recently, *The Cosby Show* and *Family Ties*), and I have argued elsewhere for the value of *The Simpsons* on these grounds.[1] Moreover, *The Simpsons* most commonly offers its satire from a leftist political position, and it works from this position to lambaste, among other things, the universality and normativity of the so-called "traditional" family values. "Family values," which became the catch phrase of the 1990s, is a concept that has had increasingly strong cultural purchase ever since the 1992 presidential debates, during which George Bush made his infamous call for "a nation closer to the Waltons than the Simpsons."[2] What Bush failed to understand is that *The Simpsons*

225

is more representative of the contemporary American family than *The Waltons* and is certainly more attuned to the realities of contemporary life. Bush's comment was a lament for the loss of an idealized past and concept of the family. Not surprisingly, the conservative attitude returned full force in the 1996 presidential election, with Bush's sentiments strongly echoed by Bob Dole. The political rallying was for a return to "traditional family values"—meaning, it seems, male dominance, female submission, and compulsive heterosexuality. Concurrent with this argument was a push for the reflection of these values in mainstream popular art forms such as film and television.

I highlight the focus on family life here to contextualize an examination of the representation of gay life on *The Simpsons,* an element of the show that has not yet received due critical attention. More often than not, mainstream media represent gay life as existing outside the confines of traditional nuclear family structures. *The Simpsons* is no exception; however, due to its ideological agenda, I believe the show enacts a different kind of representation, one that does not position homosexuality as a threat to the traditional family. It is important that we keep in mind *The Simpsons*'s role as a satire and its continual critique of so-called "traditional" family values. Of especial relevance to my purposes here is the fact that the show consistently deplores America's exclusionary practices: in particular, it repeatedly provides critiques of the treatment of various "minorities" in American culture, notably those whose status is based on gender, religion, race, and age. Though done in a less strident manner, I believe the show also intends to deplore exclusionary practices based on sexuality. To do so, of course, it must offer representations of such sexuality, that is, of gay life.

Before proceeding, I must note that, like many, I use the term "gay" somewhat loosely, often as a way of identifying both homosexual men and women. I do not assume that this term is an accurate descriptor of the very diverse population of gay men and women, nor do I presume to speak for the entire gay community. In discussing gay life on *The Simpsons,* I am mostly referring to gay male life, particularly as it centers on Waylon Smithers. Moreover, my use of the term "gay" is meant to invoke the large set of styles and attitudes that make up that elusive thing known as the "gay sensibility." In short, the gay sensibility borrows largely from the irony and camp associated with gay males, female movie icons, and drag queens. It is important to emphasize, however, that the gay sensibility is not the exclusive province of gay people. As I hope to demonstrate, in keeping with its oppositional strategy, *The Simpsons* itself enacts a gay sensibility, which it maintains by numerous means—namely, by making abundant allusions to gay life and sexual orientation, toying with the fluid nature of sexuality, incorporating peripheral gay characters, and patiently charting the coming-out process of its one recurrent gay character, Waylon Smithers. In short, *The Simpsons* functions as oppositional mass media by foregrounding a gay sensibility, maintaining a gay character in a major recurring role, and overtly critiquing the oppression of sexual "minorities" in American culture.

HOMOSEXUALITY ON THE PERIPHERY

Until quite recently, gay life was not widely reflected in America's popular arts. Over time, therefore, gay men and women have had to look very hard to find representations of themselves, positive or otherwise. As Andy Medhurst eloquently puts it, "Denied even the remotest possibility of supportive images of homosexuality within the dominant heterosexual culture, gay people have had to fashion what [they] could out of the imageries of dominance, to snatch illicit meanings from the fabric of normality, to undertake a corrupt decoding for the purposes of satisfying marginalized desires."[3] In the wake of Stonewall and the organized gay political movements of the late 1960s and early 1970s, Hollywood made some concessions to the presence of homosexual men and women in American culture. Nonetheless, during this same time period, gay characters in Hollywood film by and large either committed suicide or were murdered by another character. On television, something similar was happening. As John Leo points out, during the 1970s many well-meaning and self-consciously liberal television shows tried to acknowledge gay life and offer direct representations of homosexuality.[4]

Notable among these are *All in the Family, Maude,* and *Soap,* which gave us Billy Crystal as Jody, prime-time's first recurring gay character. However, these shows often portrayed gayness as a "problem" to be solved; the incident was inevitably isolated and the story line focused upon a straight character trying to deal with and/or accept someone else's homosexuality. It is also important to note that this increased representation was taking place within the situation comedy. By making gay characters the butt of jokes, comedy keeps them safely "othered"; this, in turn, makes them more palatable to mainstream audiences. Moreover, as is standard with all problems on situation comedies, the "problem" of gayness can be quickly "resolved." During the 1980s, there was a strong shift back towards the genre's conventional family center and its hermetic, middle-class lifestyle, a movement that coincided with the conservative zeitgeist of the Reagan years. The erasure of gayness from everyday life led to the erasure of gayness within the television world. When it was there, it was increasingly equated with AIDS. Larry Gross has noted that by 1983, nearly all mass media attention to gay men was in the context of AIDS-related stories.[5] In short, the AIDS epidemic of the late 1980s largely reinvigorated the proscribed "roles" for gay people in film and television: namely, victim and villain.[6]

However, of late things seem to have changed, and "gay" appears to be back in vogue. In 1995, *Entertainment Weekly* published a special issue on "The Gay 90s," claiming that entertainment has "come out of the closet." In the cover story, Jess Cagle speculates on how the trend began. Maybe it was with Madonna teaching us to vogue; maybe it was with Tom Hanks accepting an Oscar for *Philadelphia*. It is certainly hard to pin down. But it has led to what Cagle calls "gay-friendly" entertainment, which he sees evident everywhere in contemporary pop culture—in music and in movies, on television, and on Broadway.[7] In particular, as Cagle accurately points out, the erotic male form is no longer on the periphery: male strippers appear with regularity on daytime talk shows; male models set new standards for the "buff" male look; and the most recent incarnations of Batman and Robin sport paste-on nipples and codpieces.[8] Of course, the trend is not limited to male eroticism: Calvin Klein now markets a gender-blending scent called CK1, k.d. lang gave Cindy Crawford a shave on the cover of *Vanity Fair,* and *Friends* premiered a lesbian wedding. Before ending its run, *Roseanne,* always on the cutting edge, had not one but two recurring gay characters and featured what is now an infamous lesbian kiss. One thread of the smart drama *My So Called Life* followed the life of a gay teen. One of the roommates on MTV's *The Real World* dealt with coming out to family and friends, and *Melrose Place* and *Party of Five* each had, for a time, continuing gay male characters. Atop this, Hollywood films are giving us an abundance of drag queens, men in drag, and boy-next-door gay men.

In light of all this, Cagle quite optimistically crows, "In 1995, the gay stream flows freely into the mainstream."[9] He refers to this as a "sea-change" and uses the word "revolution" several times. I think his claim is premature and perhaps even naive in its assumption of wide acceptance for this "gay stream." The media may have had a change in attitude, but I think the public at large has not. As John Leo more perceptively notes, although the media have opened up significantly in recent years, they have done so out of necessity. This is particularly true of television: faltering network ratings and a loss of revenue due to competition from cable and video have led to a state in which "what used to be censored as controversial is now welcomed as sensitive theme programming."[10] Leo's assessment is more accurate since it acknowledges the capitalist interests underlying this apparent change in attitude: gay sells and the media capitalize on this.

In some ways, yes, things have changed, and one cannot deny what both Cagle and Leo point out: gay characters abound on television. To verify this, one need only visit the web page of The Gay & Lesbian Alliance Against Defamation (GLAAD), which continually monitors the representation of gays in the media. According to the GLAAD TV Scoreboard, a web-based project that records the number of gay, lesbian, bisexual, and transgendered characters on television, as of November, 1998, there were 24 gay characters on television, a number that seems encouraging in the post-*Ellen* era.[11] However, most of these characters are still in minor and/or non-recurring roles. How, then, are we to categorize *The Simpsons*'s Waylon Smithers? As noted above, *The Simpsons* has placed a gay character into a major recurring role, and I contend that this is a significant political move. However, in doing so, I am also compelled to ask: is the representation of gay life on *The Simpsons* merely another example of well-intentioned liberal sentiment, sympathetic lip service akin to what was happening twenty years ago, or is it something more? To begin answering these questions, we need first to examine the show's origins.

GAY SIMPSONS

When looking over the entire series, one is struck by just how prominent the gay sensibility is on *The Simpsons;* there are abundant allusions to gay life and sexual orientation and numerous examples of high camp. Of course, the incorporation of a gay sensibility seems almost expected if one considers the career of the show's creator, Matt Groening. Groening first yoked the gay and cartoon worlds together in his *Life in Hell* comic in the form of Akbar and Jeff. The camaraderie of these two characters was read by many as a gay relationship. In response to being pointedly asked during an interview if Akbar and Jeff are indeed gay, Groening said that he designed them as "a comment on all relationships."[12] However, in this same interview, Groening made clear where his sympathies lay. He was raised with what he calls the "good lefty politics" of the 1960's, he has many close gay friends, some of whom he has lost to AIDS over the years, and he is "pissed off" at the lingering injustice he sees in America.[13] Although Groening concedes that there is a lack of representation for gay individuals in the popular media, he emphasizes that there is even more of a lack for gay couples; as he says, "gay men are starved for positive portrayals of lasting love."[14] Hence, the creation of Akbar and Jeff, who provided a much needed palliative for many.

It is thus no surprise that a gay sensibility is a large part of *The Simpsons*. Indeed, it has been there from the start. For example, in "Principal Charming," an episode from the second season, Homer is charged with the task of finding a mate for his lonely sister-in-law, Selma. His method of assessing men is objective and mechanical: a computer-style readout displaying the pros and cons of the various objects of his gaze is superimposed over his field of vision. The method appears desexualized; however, it takes on another meaning as Homer goes about chanting in a robotic fashion, "Must find man, must find man." His endeavors in vain, he concludes, "A good man really is hard to find." As the series develops, so too does the gay sensibility, especially among the show's male characters. Although all are strongly positioned as heterosexual, many of them frequently reference gay culture, toy with the notion of same sex unions, freely hug and kiss, and rather casually participate in drag. This is particularly true among the Simpson family males (Abe, Homer, and Bart), who have each been central to numerous moments of camp and one or more incidents of cross-dressing. For example, in "The Front" we are given a sequence in which Grandpa (Abe) Simpson dreams of himself as "a Queen of the Old West" who is torn between the love of two cowboys. More overtly, in "Lisa the Beauty Queen," Bart gives Lisa advice on how to compete in a local beauty contest. Lisa, who cannot manage the victory walk in high heels, is ready to quit. "There's nothin' to it," Bart quips, "Gimme those heels." As he proceeds to demonstrate the posture, Lisa asks, "Do you really think I can win?" With a swish of the hip, Bart replies,

"Hey, I'm starting to think I can win!" Mr. Burns, the show's most infirm yet firmly heterosexual male character, also adds to the gay sensibility of the show. In "Brush with Greatness," for example, we see Burns's great egotism and vanity merge in what amounts to an intriguing camp moment. In this episode, Marge is commissioned to paint Burns's portrait. While preparing his boss to be immortalized on canvas, Smithers affectionately says, "Now the world will see you as I always have, sir." "Yes, yes, yes." Burns replies. "Now don't be stingy with the blush, Smithers."

For the pop media savvy, this moment is a direct allusion to an episode of the original *Batman* television show in which Batman runs for Mayor of Gotham City. At the Batcave, in preparation for the necessary public debate, Batman steadies a vanity mirror while his butler Alfred delicately powders his face. It is a truly campy moment. In his essay, "Batman, Deviance, and Camp," Andy Medhurst meticulously illustrates and effectively argues for the gay content of the 60s television show, pointing out how the series portrayed Batman as an aesthete, pompous fool, and closet queen. In consequence, what has happened since the 1960s is the "painstaking reheterosexualization" of Batman, which Medhurst traces in the Batman comic books, the subsequent *Dark Knight* graphic novels, and Tim Burton's 1989 film, *Batman*.[15] Medhurst claims that by the late 1980s, in deference to the largely conservative mood of the nation, the camp connotations put in place by the 60s television series had been "fully purged."[16]

Medhurst's point regarding the erasure of the camp sensibility, and thereby any hint of Batman's homosexuality, is a valid one, particularly in reference to Burton's film. More significantly, Medhurst's analysis of Batman has direct bearing on my own claims for the camp sensibility of *The Simpsons*. An episode entitled "Mr. Plow" well illustrates the point. The subplot of this episode involves Bart's attendance at a comic book convention, where he meets the guest of honor, one Adam "Batman" West. It is both a humorous and revealing intertextual moment. Bart, of course, is unfamiliar with the 60s television show, and in response to West's attempts to remind the young crowd who he once was, Bart candidly asks: "Who the hell is Robin?" Bart is a child of the 1990s. As Medhurst has noted, by that point Batman had been remade into a lone and heterosexual crime fighter. In a later episode, *The Simpsons* more overtly acknowledges the camp quality of the original *Batman* series and its subsequent erasure in Burton's film by paralleling this pattern with their own stand-in for all "real world" comic book superheroes, Radioactive Man. In "Radioactive Man," Hollywood moguls are in Springfield to make a film version of the exploits of the comic book and television star. As the producers of the film say, they want to "stay as far away from the campy 70s version as possible." *The Simpsons* knows full well that *Batman* was saturated with a gay sensibility, and they highlight the fact in this episode with a flashback clip from *Radioactive Man,* going so far as to have their villain be that weird combination of pubescent effeminacy and adolescent masculinity, the boy scout. The effect is additionally underscored by having the villain, the Scoutmaster, voiced by Paul Lynde, who encourages his henchmen, "Don't be afraid to use your nails, boys." Of course, to create this effect, the show relies on some well worn and less than favorable stereotypes. As Larry Gross rightly notes, "media characterizations [typically] use popular stereotypes as a code which they know will be readily understood by the audience."[17] I concede the *Batman* parody utilizes such stereotypes; indeed, *The Simpsons* utilizes these for peripheral gay characters on a regular basis. The parade of gay characters in minor roles and singular appearances are inevitably shown as choreographers, play directors, etc. And they are usually identifiable as gay through their mannerisms (heavy sighs), their hand gestures (loose), their voice (effeminate or lisping), and their dress (bright colors and scarves). However, I believe that *The Simpsons* does this with an ulterior motive. By rehearsing the patterns of the original *Batman* series, *The Simpsons* is in effect rearticulating the gayness of the show for mainstream audiences, overtly enacting the same reading that gay men and women have covertly made for years.

By its fifth season, *The Simpsons* had moved beyond allusion to gay culture and into a frank acknowledgment of gay identity and an alternative lifestyle. The "Lisa vs. Malibu Stacey" episode provides a fine example of how the show allows gay life its own place and displays a refreshing tolerance for it. When Lisa wishes to launch a campaign against the recently marketed talking doll and presents the idea to her family, she is chastened for her continual activism. Bart, for example, notes that Lisa made the family march in a gay rights parade, brandishing a copy of the local newspaper to emphasize his point. What interests me here is the fact that it is the level of her activism they criticize ("You've been doing that a little too much lately," Marge reluctantly admonishes) and not the fact that they were photographed alongside gay men in the parade nor that this photo wound up on the front page of the Springfield newspaper. A similarly nonchalant attitude is evident in "Last Exit to Springfield," in which Homer takes on the role of union representative and has to negotiate with Mr. Burns for a dental plan. Homer, misreading Burns's metaphors for unscrupulous negotiations as come-on lines, says, "Sorry, Mr. Burns, but I don't go in for these backdoor shenanigans. Sure, I'm flattered, maybe even a little curious, but the answer is no."

MR. SMITHERS'S COMING OUT

As I have tried to demonstrate, a gay sensibility is strongly evident on *The Simpsons*. However, a discussion of gay life on *The Simpsons* would not be complete if it did not center on the show's signal gay character, the self-described sycophant, Waylon Smithers. As I noted above, it is essentially gay male life that is on display in *The Simpsons*. Those who have faithfully watched the show over the course of several years know that there has been a slow but steady coming out process for Smithers. They know also that the object of his affections is his boss, Mr. Burns. Smithers's concern for the well being of Burns was well established early on. The aforementioned episode "Brush with Greatness," in which Burns contracts Marge to paint his portrait, provides an example of Smithers's devotion. At the Simpson home, Marge accidentally walks into the bathroom to find Burns exiting from the shower, naked, and Smithers offering him a towel. Marge apologizes for the intrusion and quickly leaves. When Smithers asks, "Would you feel more comfortable if I left too, sir?" Burns replies: "Of course not, Smithers. You're . . . you're like a doctor." The comment positions Smithers in the role of caretaker and has the effect of both desexualizing their contact and affirming Burns's heterosexuality. But, for the viewer, it also provides an indication of both the physical and emotional closeness of the two men, which evidently fuels Smithers's desire. A similar circumstance is found in "Burns Verkaufen der Kraftwerk." After Burns sells the plant to a German consortium, Smithers is saddened by the loss of his job and, subsequently, his ties to Mr. Burns. Burns, meanwhile, occupies himself with bocce ball and beekeeping. But he too misses the camaraderie, so he invites Smithers for a drink at his estate. When Smithers arrives, Burns politely introduces him to the bees he is tending. Pointing, he says: "That's Buzz, that's Honey, and see that Queen over there? Her name is Smithers." Smithers replies: "That's very flattering, sir." Of course, this is subtle; understanding how this scene implies a homosexual proclivity requires a certain in-group knowledge of the term "queen," which some viewers might be lacking. Smithers's desire is a bit more overtly on display in "Dog of Death," in which Homer reluctantly turns to Burns for a loan to cover the cost of an operation for Santa's Little Helper, the family dog. Burns cannot understand the attachment and asks Smithers: "Why anyone would spend good money on a dog?" "People like dogs, Mr. Burns," Smithers replies. "Nonsense," says Burns. "Dogs are idiots. Think about it, Smithers. If I came into your house and started sniffing at your crotch and slobbering all over your face, what would you do?" Smithers's non-committal reply: "Mmmmm . . . if *you* did it, sir?" Presumably, he is savoring the image.

The first overt and truly audacious reference to Smithers's sexual orientation—the one that made many fans view the show in a whole new light—was in an episode from the fourth season, "Marge Gets a Job." Marge goes to work alongside Homer at the Springfield nuclear plant because the family needs money for home repair. Like an evil overlord, Burns watches his employees on the television monitors installed in his office, berating them all for their shoddy work: "Jackanapes, lollygaggers, noodleheads." When he sees Marge, however, he is captivated: "Enchantress," he exclaims. Infatuated, Burns begins to court Marge and in short order offers her both a raise and the adjacent office, which supplants Smithers. Later on, Burns, acting like a smitten schoolboy, attempts to express to Smithers his depth of feeling for Marge. When Burns asks Smithers, "You know that dream where they fly in through the window?" we see for the first time a clear acknowledgment and direct representation of Smithers's erotic desire. In Smithers's dream, it is Mr. Burns who flies in the window. This overt representation of desire is repeated in equally direct ways in subsequent episodes, such as "Rosebud," which appeared the following season. In this episode, Smithers laments not getting what he wants for his birthday: namely, Mr. Burns popping out of an oversized birthday cake, clad in nothing but a sash, and doing a bad impersonation of Marilyn Monroe's breathy rendition of "Happy Birthday."

What I find intriguing about these three sequences I also find a bit disheartening: they each relegate Smithers's homosexual desire to the realm of fantasy. The show is often guilty of such relegation. It does not regularly represent homosexuality as a livable lifestyle; instead, it positions it as unsatisfied sexual desire and/or unrequited love. As Smithers's coming out process was increasingly foregrounded, the creators of the show pushed the issue into the periphery by making it literally fantastic. Though visually and textually overt, the show seemed fearful of being politically overt with the issue of sexuality.

However, the show has since offered us images that move gayness out of the periphery and make it a more substantial aspect of Smithers's "actual" life. Perhaps the best example of this attempt to portray an actual gay lifestyle is from an episode entitled "Secrets of a Successful Marriage," in which Homer teaches a community college class on marriage. Deep into the fifth season, the producers decided to make it clear—at least to those who can understand the literary allusions—that Smithers is indeed a gay man. Homer initially gets the class to share personal secrets and reveal the failings of their marital relations. Smithers speaks up, saying, "I was married once. But I just couldn't keep it together." We are then given a flashback scene showing Smithers having an argument with his wife over Mr. Burns and Burns himself passionately calling out for Smithers. This flashback, a wonderfully rendered parody of scenes from two of Tennessee Williams's most famous plays, *Cat On a Hot Tin Roof* and *A Streetcar Named Desire,* has great resonance within the context of *The Simpsons*. To fully appreciate it, one must know something of not only the two plays cited but also of Williams himself, of his own struggles with both heterosexual and homosexual desires and the ways in which these struggles were incorporated into his art. The creators of *The Simpsons* offer what I think is a perfect parallel for the relationship between Smithers and Burns by combining Williams's two most notable male characters and their defining characteristics: the suppressed homosexual desire of Brick and desperate dependence of Stanley. This scene is also significant in that it provides viewers an allusion to a past experience rather than a fantasy. We are meant to read this scene literally, as one of Smithers's memories. It is, in effect, a moment from Smithers's "real" life.

I think it important, however, to keep in mind that these overt references to Smithers's sexuality did not appear on the show until the mid-90s. We must remember that *The Simpsons* first appeared when Ronald Reagan was still in the White House, and it became the phenomenon it is now during the Bush administration. Thus, the show premiered on the heels of a highly conservative decade, one in which much of the ground made by various political movements in the 1960s and 1970s was lost. This sociopolitical context is particularly relevant when we consider the current gay representation on television. Today, there seems to be a widespread faith in the media's liberalism, and gay characters have lately appeared on television with great frequency. Fred Fejes has argued that such visibility is due to the advancements made over the past twenty years by gay activists, whose political organization led to demands for increased and more accurate representation.[18] However, in the same essay, which was published in 1993, Fejes also avers that homosexuality remains a subtext on television, that gay characters exist only on the periphery, and that "a regular network program with a gay or lesbian main character is far in the future."[19]

QUEER TV

Have things changed so dramatically in the scant few years since Fejes made his rather pessimistic claim? In October of 1996, *Entertainment Weekly* published yet another cover story on "Gay TV," this time in direct response to the "controversy" surrounding *Ellen* and the sexuality of the main character, Ellen Morgan, played by comedian Ellen DeGeneres. As is well known, there had been much talk at the time about her character coming out as a lesbian in the 1997 season finale, talk that stemmed in part from speculation about DeGeneres herself in the tabloids. By the second week of the season, DeGeneres made herself visible on various daytime and nighttime talk shows discussing the issue. Notably, she appeared on *The Rosie O'Donnell Show,* where the two women joked at length about Ellen's character being "Lebanese." Of course, there had been similar speculation in the media about the sexual orientation of O'Donnell herself, thus adding an interesting double layer to the joke. The significant point, however, is that they made light of the issue, wanting to admit it without admitting it. This approach was funny, but it was also safe. The question thus remained: was America ready for its first gay character in a lead role on television? It was admittedly a precarious situation for a major network. Apparently, ABC wanted to test the waters, which is probably why the coming out of Ellen progressed so slowly. But it was soon evident that network executives were willing to risk the show (and by extension the career of DeGeneres) by allowing *Ellen* to become "a testcase for the nation's tolerance."[20] Initially, it seemed that the risk would pay off, and that the nation was ready for such overt representation. On the heels of a great deal of media attention, the infamous "coming out" episode of *Ellen* aired on April 30, 1997, and it garnered a healthy 36.2 million viewers.[21] However, in its subsequent season, the show was quickly criticized for being "too gay" and didactic. During that season, the show averaged only 12.4 million viewers and, amid some very public squabbling between DeGeneres and ABC executives, was soon canceled.[22]

In light of the rather rapid demise of *Ellen* once DeGeneres came out publicly, I think it important to examine why it seemed so likely at the time to finally have a gay character in a lead role on television, why the response was initially so positive, and why it ultimately failed. As noted before, prime time television is currently "awash in gay supporting roles."[23] Ellen DeGeneres was a logical choice for the transition to a gay lead role and ideal for making homosexuality acceptable to the public at large because she was seen as "non-threatening" to mainstream audiences. In part, DeGeneres was less threatening because *Ellen* was a situation comedy and DeGeneres herself is a lesbian. As A. J. Jacobs succinctly put it, Ellen Morgan would be "a lesbian instead of a gay man, which, like it or not, makes her more palatable."[24] The aforementioned gay kiss on *Roseanne,* for example, was also "palatable" both because it was both on a sitcom and it was between two women. As is well known, our culture more readily accepts close female relationships; emotional intimacy is perceived to more easily slip into physical intimacy among women. The so-called "straight" porn industry, for example, is filled with gayness in the form of lesbianism. However, the sexual interaction of women in these movies is filtered through the male gaze and perceived to be part of a straight male fantasy; this effectively erases the "taint" of homosexuality and the threat it poses to masculinity. But unrestrained female (homo)sexuality, overtly put forth and not confined by the male perspective, as was the case with *Ellen,* is seen as threatening and must be contained. Straight, white men, who still hold the majority of power and control in the media, are more often than not still unwilling to offer representations of homosexual relationships—female or male—in the mainstream.

This fact, alongside Jacobs's astute observation that gay men are less "palatable" to mainstream America than gay women, should then force us to question the overt homophobia directed at gay males in American culture. Gay males are still widely considered social and commercial anathema. It is no surprise that the greatest inroads of late have been made by straight women sympathetic to gay rights, by gay women themselves, and by men masquerading as women—witness, respectively, Roseanne,

Melissa Etheridge, and the films *Mrs. Doubtfire, The Birdcage,* and *To Wong Foo.* Mainstream images of gay men who are not drag queens or of successful gay male relationships are still rare. Most recently, the method of handling homophobia in the popular media has been to pair gay men with straight women, thus offering visibility in a "safe" manner, since pairing a gay male with a straight female effectively erases the male's homosexuality. The formula was very successfully employed in *My Best Friend's Wedding* (1997), which paired Rupert Everett with Julia Roberts, and then repeated with similar levels of success in the films *As Good As It Gets* (1997), *The Object of My Affection* (1998), and *The Opposite of Sex* (1998). More significantly, this formula was also used as the premise for the NBC sitcom *Will & Grace,* which has two gay male characters, one of them in a lead role. Considering what happened with *Ellen* only a year previous to the premiere of *Will & Grace,* it seemed a bit surprising that NBC would risk losing both advertisers and viewers by placing an openly gay character in a lead role. It also seemed surprising that *Will & Grace* did not meet with the same harsh criticisms as *Ellen* nor ignite another national debate over homosexuality. But upon closer inspection, it becomes clear why and how this is the case. Although Will and Grace have a platonic relationship and live together only as roommates, their living arrangement provides a pretense of heterosexuality. Not surprisingly, members of an NBC-sponsored focus group who watched the series pilot had no idea that Will was gay until told that he was.[25] In this sense, Will and Grace are an idealized couple, free of the pains associated with a (hetero)sexual relationship and benign enough to appeal to the largest demographic. In short, NBC has taken an approach that packages gay men in a non-threatening— and thereby still lucrative—way for middle America. Thus it is that the praise for the increased representation and apparent attitude of acceptance needs to be tempered by an acknowledgment of the still sad state of affairs for gay men and women. In response to *Entertainment Weekly*'s glowing portrayal of the gay 90s, one must stop and ask, "What was so gay about the 90s?" Indeed, the decade saw the passage of the Defense of Marriage Act, heterosexuality still dominated, and the pressure to remain closeted was still strong, as it remains today. Many gay men and women are still fearful of coming out to family, friends, and coworkers; gay bashing and hate crimes continue unabated in many U.S. cities; and negative and regressive images still abound.

OPPOSITIONAL POLITICS

Perhaps in response to such a cultural climate, *The Simpsons* has become, in recent years, more openly political regarding homosexuality. The show clearly has a leftist political vision, but it regularly presents and juxtaposes both liberal and conservative ideologies (usually as a means of critiquing the latter). An episode from the sixth season, "Sideshow Bob Roberts," well illustrates the battle of ideologies on the show and its engagement with the politics of sexuality. In this episode, conservative candidate Sideshow Bob runs for mayor of Springfield and, with the support of Mr. Burns, wins the election over the liberal candidate, Diamond Joe Quimby. It is clear, however, that Bob did not win the election legitimately. Lisa's subsequent investigation leads her to an anonymous source who provides her with information to expose the rigged election. After being inadvertently exposed as the source, Smithers confesses his guilt at betraying Mr. Burns. When Lisa observantly asks why he does so, Smithers states, "Unfortunately, Side Show Bob's ultraconservative views conflict with my choice of, um, lifestyle." There is no mistaking what Smithers means here, nor what the show is saying about the relationship between homosexuality and conservative politics: the two cannot coexist. Moreover, whereas in the past Smithers's sexual orientation was private and apolitical, it has now become public and overtly political.

The most open attempt to directly engage the politics of sexuality on *The Simpsons* appears in "Homer's Phobia," an episode from the ninth season. In this episode, the show finally confronts the specter of fear that surrounds gay identity by having the Simpson family befriend a gay man named John (featuring the voice of the film director John Waters), the proprietor of an antiques and collectibles shop at the Springfield Mall. John makes a living selling "kitsch" and items with "camp" appeal, such as old issues of *TV Guide,* 1970s-era toys, and inflatable furniture. Homer is incredulous that anyone would spend hard-earned money on such "junk," but in the hopes of turning a quick buck, he invites John over to the Simpson house because, as he says, "Our place is full of valuable worthless crap." Initially, Homer and John bond over their shared affinity for the "junk" the Simpsons have amassed, and they quickly become friends. The two then spend time talking and laughing together and, in a wonderfully ironic scene, even dancing to Alicia Bridges's disco classic, "I

Love the Nightlife." Despite such clear signals, Homer is oblivious to the fact that John is gay. However, Marge and Lisa both intuit this fact, and when they share this information with Homer, his homophobia comes to the fore. Initially, Homer is fearful that others will find out he has befriended a gay man, presumably because this would stigmatize him, so he refuses to go with John and the family on a tour of the sights of Springfield. In response, John is nonchalant—he does not react negatively to Homer's fears, nor does he make any apologies for being gay—and Marge tells Homer, "You don't even know what you're afraid of." What is clear to both John and the viewing audience is that Homer expects gays to be readily identifiable—he indicates as much to Marge when she chastises him for his narrow-mindedness; he says: "You know me, Marge. I like my beer cold, my TV loud, and my homosexuals flaming." In short, Homer is upset at having mistaken a gay person for a straight one; in other words, he is upset that gays do not conform to his preconceived stereotypes.

As Homer's phobia escalates, he begins to worry that John might have a negative "influence" on Bart. Homer is further convinced of such influence when he sees Bart begin to behave like John—that is, behave in what appears to be a "gay" manner. With a series of delightfully campy scenes, *The Simpsons* illustrates the telltale signs, which include Bart choosing a pink Snowball rather than a brown Hostess cupcake, using the phrase "You're the living end," and wearing a bright Hawaiian shirt which, as Bart innocently tells Homer, "just came out of the closet." The final straw for Homer comes when he sees Bart wearing a 1950s-style wig and dancing to a song by The Supremes. At this point, Homer decides to take action. He confronts John and very plainly tells him to stay away from Bart. In doing so, Homer displays a classic "us versus them" mentality. When Homer is at a loss for an adjective to describe "them," John prompts him with the word "queer," which launches Homer on yet another tirade. "That's another thing," he says, "I resent *you people* using that word. That's *our* word for making fun of *you*. We need it." With that, Homer proposes to take back both the word and his son. His plan for doing so is to "make a man" of Bart by conditioning him to like females and by training him to be aggressive through hunting. Of course, neither method works. The misguided hunting trip, for example, results in Homer, Bart, Moe, and Barney being attacked by a herd of angry reindeer and subsequently rescued by John. Although Moe and Barney lament being saved by "a sissy," Homer, having now confronted his own homophobia, rises to John's defense. Ultimately, then, Homer comes to see John as fellow person rather than labeling him a gay person.

Not surprisingly, "Homer's Phobia" received accolades from the Gay & Lesbian Alliance Against Defamation, which each year awards the best and brightest media representations of gay and lesbian individuals and the gay community. At the Ninth Annual Media Awards ceremony in April of 1998, "Homer's Phobia" won the award for "Outstanding TV: Individual Episode."[26] I think it a well-deserved award, for the episode offers its mainstream audience cogent critiques of a number of myths surrounding homosexual identity. Foremost, "Homer's Phobia" critiques what is perhaps the most common misconception about homosexuality: namely, that gayness is somehow contagious. Homer is thus a stand-in for all of the homophobic individuals in our culture who believe that homosexuality is a contagious "disease." I think that what the show intends to illustrate with this episode is the speciousness of believing that one can "catch" gayness or learn to be gay according to proximity, a timely message considering the "ex-gay" movement in America and the Religious Right proposition that homosexuality is a disease that can be "cured." It also fits in well with recent claims from within the gay community itself that a gay identity is not simply a choice that one makes. "Homer's Phobia" also critiques the narrow-minded belief that violence and aggressiveness are part and parcel of a (heterosexual) masculine identity. The episode shows that homosexuality is not a threat to such masculinity; indeed, it implies that heterosexual male identity would benefit from the incorporation of certain emotional qualities traditionally associated with gay men. Lastly, I think this episode illustrates that homosexuality itself is not a threat to the family but that homophobia is; in essence, homophobia is destructive to the heterosexual as well as the homosexual community.

CONCLUSION

As I stated at the onset, *The Simpsons* consistently critiques the mistreatment and exclusion of many so-called minority citizens in American culture. I thus see the representation of gay life on *The Simpsons* as a significant political move. By enacting a gay sensibility, *The Simpsons* is rearticulating "gayness" for its audience, thereby making mainstream what is still derisively referred to as an "alternative" lifestyle and contesting how this is generally (mis)understood in American culture. I concede that in the process of establishing a gay sensibility, *The Simpsons* relies upon stereotypes that have been often exploited in television. However, I believe that such representation is not at the expense of the gay community but in support of it. Notably, the most gratuitous stereotypes are never utilized for Smithers; more importantly, the wide range of images displayed on the show reflects the very real diversity of the gay community as it exists in American culture. *The Simpsons* ultimately wants to both acknowledge gay lives and support them by maintaining a gay character in a major recurring role and overtly politicizing his sexual identity. The show allows Smithers, who is an integral part of the show, to be both openly gay and the focal point for its critique of the oppression of sexual "minorities" in American culture. In short, *The Simpsons* continually contests the systems that oppose and oppress Smithers's lifestyle (e.g., traditional conceptions of the nuclear family). The show seeks to expose cultural homophobia, sharply criticize the institutional apparatuses that maintain it, and deplore the attendant exclusionary practices based on sexual orientation.

These claims are well illustrated, I think, by an incident that at first seems of minor importance and yet, within the context of my argument, has great resonance, enough to be the inspiration for my title. I refer here to one of the many prank phone calls Bart regularly makes to Moe's Tavern, in an episode entitled "New Kid on the Block." This time around, Bart calls the bar and asks for Amanda, "Last name Hugginkiss." Moe obediently calls out, "I'm looking for Amanda Hugginkiss. Why can't I find Amanda Hugginkiss?" In response to the aural joke, Barney says, "Maybe your standards are too high." There are two things that interest me about this small exchange. First, the response from the patrons of Moe's Tavern is so calm. Yes, it's played for laughs, but that is all; there are no "faggot" jokes, no condemnations, no reprisals. Second, and more significant, Moe's query has a dual meaning. His question can easily be read as asking, "What prevents me from finding a man to hug and kiss?" Metaphorically, I think this is applicable to gay men as well as gay women; that is, to people whose desires remain unfulfilled due to the barriers erected by homophobia in American culture. Thus, what we are left with in this scene is not a specific but rather a rhetorical question—What, indeed? As *The Simpsons* would have it, nothing should prevent gay men—or any of us— from looking for Amanda Hugginkiss.

NOTES

1. Matthew Henry, "The Triumph of Popular Culture: Situation Comedy, Postmodernism, and *The Simpsons*." *Studies in Popular Culture* 17 (Fall 1994): 85–99.

2. Harry Stein, "Our Times," *TV Guide*, May 23–29, 1992: 31.

3. Andy Medhurst, "Batman, Deviance, and Camp," rpt. in *Signs of Life in the USA*, eds. Sonia Maasik and Jack Solomon (Boston: Bedford, 1994), 328.

4. John Leo, "The Familialism of 'Man' in American Television Drama," *South Atlantic Quarterly* 88 (1989): 31.

5. Larry Gross, "What's Wrong with This Picture? Lesbian Women and Gay Men on Television," in *Queer Words, Queer Images: Communication and the Construction of Homosexuality*, ed. Jeffrey Ringer (New York: New York University Press, 1994), 145.

6. Larry Gross, "Out of the Mainstream: Sexual Minorities and the Mass Media." *Journal of Homosexuality* 21.1–2 (1991): 30.

7. Jess Cagle, "America Sees Shades of Gay." *Entertainment Weekly* 8 (September 1995): 20.

8. Cagle, "America Sees," 21.

9. Cagle, "America Sees," 23.

10. Leo, "The Familialism of 'Man,'" 39.

11. *The GLAAD TV Scoreboard*, <http://www.glaad.org>, Nov. 13, 1998.

12. Doug Sadownick, "Groening Against the Grain." *The Advocate* (February 26, 1991): 32.

13. Sadownick, "Groening," 32.

14. Sadownick, "Groening," 33.

15. Medhurst, "Batman, Deviance, and Camp," 335.

16. Medhurst, "Batman, Deviance, and Camp," 336.

17. Gross, "Out of the Mainstream," 27.

18. Fred Fejes, "Invisibility, Homophobia, and Heterosexism." *Critical Studies in Mass Communications* 10 (1993): 400.

19. Fejes, "Invisibility," 402.

20. Jess Cagle, "As Gay As It Gets?" *Entertainment Weekly* (May 8, 1998): 28.

21. Cagle, "As Gay As It Gets?" 28.

22. Cagle, "As Gay As It Gets?" 28.

23. A. J. Jacobs, "Out?" *Entertainment Weekly* (October 4, 1996): 21.

24. Jacobs, "Out?" 23.

25. A. J. Jacobs, "When Gay Men Happen to Straight Women." *Entertainment Weekly* (Oct. 23, 1998): 23.

26. *GLAAD Awards*, <http://www.glaad.org> Nov. 13, 1998.

Releasing the Hounds: *The Simpsons* As Anti-Nuclear Satire

MICK BRODERICK

This essay explores *The Simpsons* as a postmodern satire within the context of television history as "nuclear" history.[1] While it is beyond the scope of this present work to illustrate anything other than a representative sample of nuclear themes encountered within *The Simpsons* series, I will argue that we can view *The Simpsons* as a continual exploration of oppositional culture via its articulations and representations of various nuclear issues, familiar to a cross-generational mass television audience, where the references range from the banal to, at their most intertextual, the baroque.[2]

Many television commentators have discussed the evolution of the formulaic sitcom from cold-war family consensus to the dysfunctional scene of the 1990s, where work replaces the domestic scene as the entertainment locus.[3] As television audiences matured during the Cold War, a culture of socio-political sophistication emerged alongside the traditional avant-garde and liberal counter cultures, a phenomenon identified as early as 1968 and described as "bomb culture" by Jeff Nuttall. More recently, the historian Margot Henriksen has described this transitional epoch as "Dr. Strangelove's America."[4]

Television critic David Marc suggests the cynical-comedic sitcom emerged in the 1980s and, like Jean Baudrillard before him, Marc identifies television's intrinsic relationship with nuclear culture:[5]

> Television's growth and development as a mass medium, industry and art form have occurred more or less simultaneously with the nuclear threat against all life as we know it. The unspeakable horror that palpable Armageddon conjures for the rational mind makes comedy particularly

appealing. Under the threat of faceless end-of-the-world button push-ing, there is an honest urge, if not responsibility, to be a wiseguy, to find a use for the static energies of cynicism.[6]

As such, *The Simpsons* can be regarded as a primary manifestation of this phenomenon, where the expectation of catastrophe looms with every episode, whether nuclear and global or familial and domestic.

ACT I: ATOMIC CULTURE

Atomic energy has long been satirized in American culture, and on televi-sion, well before the advent of *The Simpsons*. The 1960s cartoons *Rocky and Bullwinkle* and *Roger Ramjet* lampooned the Cold War and atomic science as did crime and espionage comedy shows such as *Batman* and *Get Smart*.[7]

From the opening frames of every *Simpsons* episode, nuclear energy forms a ubiquitous presence. In the initial credit sequence, the domed nuclear reactor and twin cooling towers of the Springfield Nuclear Power Plant (SNPP), shown perched atop a hill, overshadow the town of Spring-field below. Similarly, in a postmodern reappropriation of the opening titles from both *The Jetsons* and *The Flintstones,* Homer is shown in a radi-ation protection suit clasping a glowing, irradiated rod with long metallic tongs. As soon as the plant's whistle blows, he immediately leaves work, accidentally dropping an isotope down his back, only to dislodge it later while in his car and absently throwing it from the moving vehicle, where the bouncing radioactive rod is swiped by son Bart's skateboard and knocked into a street drain destined for Springfield's sewer system.

While many episodes ostensibly do not touch on nuclear themes, the ever-present influence and immanence of the atomic age pervades *The Simpsons* like a thematic half-life whose motifs contaminate the multi-lay-ered, intertextual narratives of each episode, often as satire. Even the Simpson family decor and the Springfield mise-en-scène display nuclear "pop" aesthetics: in "Bachelor Apu," the Kwik-E-Mart has a video game called "Nuke" (featuring an iconic mushroom cloud), which is prominent in the background, while in several episodes the Simpsons' living room features a hanging portrait of the Springfield Nuclear Power Plant. This physical presence of the SNPP within the fictional animated world is par-alleled on a metanarrative and epistemological level.

Hence, *The Simpsons* mirrors culturally what Robert Lifton has termed as a psychopathology: "nuclearism."[8] For example, while the controversial episode "Homer's Phobia" concentrates on queer politics when Homer befriends a collectibles shop owner (voiced by John Waters) who happens to be gay, nuclear imagery is never far away. In the antique store (Cockamamie), some of the atomic ephemera includes Godzilla dolls and a Rex Mars Atomic Discombobulator. More significantly, Waters's character takes the Simpson family to a theme restaurant called the Sha-Boom-Ka-Boom Café, complete with a massive pink mushroom cloud facade advertising "Little Boy $3.95, Fat Man $12.95," an establishment which is saturated with atomic iconography, including pictures of the Enola Gay along with an A-bomb and crew photos. As with this episode's overt exploration of homophobia (with its related manifestations of denial and psychic numbing), nuclearism informs the very milieu and even the decor of the Simpson and Springfield world. Yet a close reading of the nuclear subtext suggests that even atomic holocaust is not beyond gay/camp ridicule, or so the episode creators might have it, which would significantly rupture the seemingly progressive agenda of "Homer's Phobia." Hence, the veneer of oppositional culture in this episode (exposing the hypocrisy of Homer and his cohorts regarding homosexuality) may be undermined by conflicting narratives which reinforce/endorse existing cultural stereotypes.[9]

In the world of *The Simpsons,* atomic culture is synonymous with popular culture; they are interchangeable and often indistinguishable. In "Marge Gets a Job," when Homer worries about his wife taking a position alongside him at the nuclear plant, Lisa enthuses, "You'll be just like Marie and Pierre Curie." Ignoramus Homer asks what was so special about them, to which Lisa replies, "They discovered radium!" adding matter-of-factly, "and they both died of radiation poisoning." Bart, however, can only comprehend this information by drawing on comic book and popular culture stereotypes, imagining the Curies as irradiated monsters the size of Godzilla razing a metropolis ("Cool!"). The potential industrial health hazards which Lisa's historical analogy raises dissipate into the Springfield ether.

Bart's juvenile mind is littered with the atomic detritus of pop culture. Several episodes center on his love of the comic book character Radioactive Man (and his trusty side-kick, Fallout Boy), who acquires incredible strength and agility after being caught in an A-bomb blast.[10] These parodies of Cold War comics, where radiation is shown to be a source of superhuman powers and/or giantism, demonstrate the powerful lingering association such fantasies still have on the collective American imaginary, from baby boomers and Generation Xers through to contemporary school children. In "Radioactive Man," Bart's pal Milhouse is chosen to play Fallout Boy in a remake of the Radioactive Man movie, and he is shown repeatedly being bombarded by real X-rays on the film set during the shoot. Similarly, in the "Revenge of Comic Book Man" sequence from "Treehouse of Horror X," Bart and Lisa acquire special powers (elasticity and super strength) when blasted with X-rays from a malfunctioning school metal detector/scanner ("Duck and cover!" warns Principal Skinner).

Homer is similarly shown to be a victim of pop culture as atomic fantasy. In "E-I-E-I (Annoyed Grunt)," Homer deduces (naturally!) that he can instantly grow giant crops on a failed farm by adding plutonium from the Springfield Plant:

> HOMER: Wake up, honey. It's time to harvest our radioactive supercrops.
>
> MARGE: But it's only been one night.
>
> HOMER: That's all it takes. If we learned one thing from *The Amazing Colossal Man* and *Grasshopperus,* it's that radiation makes stuff grow real big, real fast.
>
> MARGE: But didn't Grasshopperus kill Chad Everett?
>
> HOMER: Only because he tried to reason with him.

The fictional "Grasshopperus" reference actually parodies Bert I. Gordan's 1957 movie *The Beginning of the End,* in which Peter Graves halts a plague of rampaging giant locusts which, ironically, given Homer's unconscious conflation, are mutated from eating irradiated crops. Yet Homer himself also displays just such a monstrous pathology in "Homer Goes to College" after he causes a meltdown in a Nuclear Regulatory Commission simulation van (humorously, given the truck does not contain any nuclear material). Emerging from the sunken van, glowing bright green, Homer generically resembles any number of radiated fiends from Cold War science fiction cinema, marching menacingly forward while muttering, "Must . . . destroy . . . mankind." He halts abruptly, however, when his digital watch alarm reminds him that it is lunchtime. In *The Simpsons* universe, no one seems alarmed that Homer can manifest these "symptoms" without any *real* nuclear exposure.

But the broader, unconscious, and more insidious ideological influence of atomic culture is everywhere. In "Homer's Angel," Marge is
impressed by an enormous mall currently under construction, recounting
to her family that she has heard the mall's air conditioning system is more
powerful than a fifty-megaton nuclear bomb. As Patricia Mellencamp has
suggested, "Early stages of postmodernism can be glimpsed in the '50s
selling of television, coincident with and party to the rapid expansion of
consumer markets, nuclear experiments, and the development of nuclear
rhetoric. Shopping in the new centers was sold to the populace as one
patriotic way of easing fear of 'the bomb.'"[11] As Marge's bemused line
attests, in the *Simpsons*'s epistemology, with its cross-over audience appeal
to baby boomers, the extension of Mellencamp's point suggests that in the
post-Cold War world of Pax Americana, a permanent (cold) war economy
of conspicuous consumer consumption remains deeply inscribed by the
rhetoric of the nuclear age.

ACT II: ATOMIC HISTORY/TELEVISION HISTORY

The history of television and the nuclear age are inextricably linked. Over
a century ago, cinema emerged from the late-Victorian industrial era as a
technological apparatus coeval (1895) with the discovery of X-rays and
radiation. Similarly, the postwar atomic age witnessed the fusion of the
rudimentary televisual apparatus with atomic energy.

This synergistic genesis can be traced back prior to Trinity and
Hiroshima. While working with Enrico Fermi at Columbia University,
nuclear physicist Leo Szilard, who was responsible for initiating the Man-
hattan Project, described a major theoretical advance as they pondered the
feasibility of a sustainable atomic chain reaction—fundamental for the creation of atomic energy. The following passage presciently envisions what
would become in later years the paradigmatic state of television viewing,
one which Homer and his family exemplify par excellence and which is
self-reflexively mirrored at the end of every *Simpsons* introductory credit
sequence—the nuclear family postured passively (as "couch potatoes")
before the tube o' plenty:

> Everyone was ready. All we had to do was turn a switch, lean back, and
> watch the screen of a television tube. If flashes of light appeared on the

screen it would mean that large-scale liberation of atomic energy was just around the corner. We just turned the switch and saw the flashes. We watched for a little while. . . . That night there was very little doubt in my mind that the world was headed for grief.[12]

Joyce Nelson has aptly described television as "The Perfect Machine" of the atomic age and suggests that as early as 1946 "the TV receiver set was itself discovered to be a radiating device," yet this did little to undermine the desire of manufacturers to mass-produce "such a potentially lucrative invention."[13] Certainly consumers were ill-informed of the potential hazards until controversy erupted in the 1960s when more powerful color television sets were mass marketed. Even so, early vacuum tube, black-and-white sets were significant radiating devices. Investigating the problem, the U.S. Bureau of Radiological Heath had assumed, when compared with X-rays, that television radiation "would be soft and non-penetrating": "Instead, we found rays escaping from the vacuum tubes to be harder and of higher average energy than we expected. They penetrated the first few inches of the body as deeply as 100-kilovolt diagnostic X-rays. You get a uniform dose to the eye, testes and bone marrow."[14]

Here again we find *The Simpsons* creators cannily alluding to television history as one circumscribed by a similar nuclear association. "In Grampa vs. Sexual Inadequacy," Homer and his elderly father, Abe, visit their former home. Upon entering their old living room, Abe sights a vintage television set and points: "There she is, the old Radiation King. You'd park yourself right there and watch for hours on end." Eerily, the scene depicts a human shadow permanently burned onto the floor and wall, connoting the vaporized *hibakusha* (i.e., bomb-effected victims) of Hiroshima and Nagasaki, while a younger Homer is shown in flashback occupying the very same position and watching John F. Kennedy in black and white.

It is an association Lynn Spigel has suggested was evident in the early reception of television's popularization as a technology developed for "surveillance and reconnaissance" during World War II.[15] More ominous parallels began to emerge. In the postwar era, the cultural effect of television was increasingly "discussed in the context of warfare and atomic weaponry." In keeping with the image conjured by grandpa Simpson and Homer's synergistic flashback, Kennedy's FFC Chairman, Newton Minow, decried the television industry as a "vast wasteland" in 1961, drawing dire comparisons between television and nuclear oblivion: "Ours has been called the jet age, the atomic age, the space age," Minow railed. "It is also, I submit, the television age. And just as history will decide whether the leaders of today's world employed the atom to destroy the world or rebuild it for mankind's benefit, so will history decide whether today's broadcasters employed their powerful voice to enrich the people or debase them."[16]

Christopher Anderson has comprehensively traced the propaganda relationships among the U.S. government "Atoms for Peace programs," the Atomic Energy Commission, electricity utilities, and television networks. In *Hollywood TV*, Anderson suggests that concerned postwar scientists, politicians, and military leaders joined to prevent the use of atomic energy by individuals or corporations for commercial gain. Hence the Truman administration's Atomic Energy Act of 1946, forbidding the private ownership of nuclear materials. Truman himself considered nuclear power "too important a development to be made the subject of profit-seeking."[17] But with the election of President Eisenhower, the new administration's AEC Chairman soon promised the peaceful atom would bring about a nuclear millennium of abundance, abolishing disease and famine while providing "electric energy too cheap to meter."[18]

The deliberate manipulation of public opinion tapped an existing association, according to Anderson: "Since both television and atomic energy could be perceived as the epitome of 'electrical progress,' the campaign for the peaceful atom invoked an identification that already existed in the culture of the era, a figurative link between television and atomic energy—the two most prominent technological innovations to emerge since World War II."[19] Anderson's study deconstructs the first important television "event" of the postwar years—Edison Electric's *Light's Diamond Jubilee*—broadcast simultaneously in 1954 on the NBC, CBS, ABC, and DuMont networks and produced by David O. Selznick with a creative team including film industry luminaries Ben Hecht, William Wellman, King Vidor, James Wong Howe, and Joseph Cotton. Anderson asserts the electric industry discovered a way to "monopolize the airwaves" and push their atomic agenda as a result of the networks' experimenting with blockbuster programming in the mid-1950s:

> The electric industry's tribute to Edison, and to the wealth of consumer goods that it claimed as his legacy, dovetailed so completely with the AEC's Atoms for Peace campaign that it would have been difficult for most Americans to distinguish the government initiative from its coun-

terpart in private industry, or to perceive that the flurry of optimistic information about atomic energy actually emanated from specific sources. Both public relations campaigns debuted in late 1953 and aimed at a similar political goal: convincing legislators and the American public that the production of electrical power through nuclear fission could be managed most effectively by the commercial electric industry.[20]

A few months before *Light's Diamond Jubilee,* Eisenhower announced an "Atoms for Peace" campaign at the United Nations. As Joyce Nelson maintains, "In the subsequent publicity push for the development of nuclear reactors, television again played a central role."[21] Hundreds of hours of free motion pictures depicting America's atomic science and industry were provided to television producers and broadcasters as long as they submitted scripts to the AEC explaining how they were going to deploy the footage. Since the AEC controlled strict access to its atomic sites, the script approval process enabled the AEC to maintain a "sanitized TV portrait of atomic energy throughout the 1950s." In addition, General Electric, Westinghouse, and the AEC produced and distributed a significant number of free, pro-nuclear films to domestic television stations throughout the 1950s and 1960s.

Complementing this material, the AEC, in association with electric industry lobbying groups such as the Atomic Industrial Forum, produced and freely distributed scores of short films to churches, schools, and civic groups promoting the benefits of atomic energy in American society. In "Homer's Odyssey," in what has become a *Simpsons* series staple, an "educational/industrial" film is introduced to the characters (and the television viewing audience) in order to, ironically, unilaterally *close* all discourse on any subject. When Bart's elementary school class tours the SNPP, they are shown *Nuclear Energy—Our Misunderstood Friend,* a hilarious parody of the AEC/atomic utility 16mm films from years past. It is a genre brilliantly critiqued in the 1982 Rafferty-Loader compilation *The Atomic Café* and more recently satirized in the animated feature *The Iron Giant,* where late-1950s school children watch *Atomic Holocaust,* itself a parody of *Duck and Cover.*[22] In *The Simpsons,* the industry rhetoric is deftly ridiculed in a satirical, postmodern jibe, evoking baby-boomer nostalgia but not as some neutered, Jamesonian pastiche.[23] Over an A-bomb blast a narrator ominously intones, "When most people think of nuclear energy, they think of this . . . Ka-Boom! But when we mean nuclear energy, we mean this."

The class watches a futuristic family, Jetsons-like, admiring their nuclear-powered electrical gadgets (which, in retrospect, anticipate Matt Groening's recent and parallel television venture set in the thirtieth century, *Futurama*.)[24]

Like Dagwood and Disney before him, an animated atomic character, Smilin' Joe Fission, explains the process of generating electricity from a sustained chain reaction: "Uh-oh, looks like there's a little left-over nuclear waste. No problem!" he winks, pulling out a small brush, sweeping the cartoon waste under a rug, and stomping it down. "I'll just put it where nobody will find it for a million years!"[25]

This sequence skillfully lambastes the upbeat naiveté about all things nuclear that many related films from this era display. The "political unconscious" of these narratives frequently betrays their simplistic reassurances, such as the sequence (from *The Atomic Café*) showing a troubled man before a mirror, imagining his baldness (or worse, sterility) resulting from exposure to fallout.[26] Don't worry, the paternalistic narrator intones cheerily, if you receive enough radiation to cause sterility, you'll be dead anyhow![27]

ACT III: NUCLEAR POWER

> . . . and thank you most of all for nuclear power, which has yet to
> cause a single proven fatality. At least in this country. Amen.
> Homer's prayer while breaking bread with his family
> in "Oh, Brother, Where Art Thou?"

The Simpsons is a constant parade of the foibles of nuclear energy. The series seems to relish in displaying the cant and propaganda of the nuclear industry either via a hilarious juxtaposition, inappropriate rhetoric, or an ironic and faux nostalgia for Cold War nuclear boosterism.

Homer's blessing before the family repast is delivered as a po'-faced non sequitur. Even the normally environmentally conscious Lisa does not respond, which further adds to the gag's resonance. The statement, of course, is a total fallacy, analogous to the National Rifle Association spin that "guns don't kill, people do." Homer's seemingly innocuous regurgitation hilariously deconstructs itself through the absurdity of the domestic situation.

First, Homer merely repeats an industry cliché uncritically, like a kind of de facto employee PR automaton, or one seemingly under post-hypnotic suggestion.[28] The discursive emphasis on *"proven* fatality" recalls the tobacco lobby mantra (itself a constant butt of *The Simpsons* creators' scorn) that the relationship between cigarettes and lung cancer or nicotine and addiction is unproved.[29] Second, the implication is that *U.S.* nuclear energy is safe, unlike other countries. By pointing the finger elsewhere (Russia/ Chernobyl, etc.), the denial serves both to amplify the falsehood while repressing the speculated/anticipated post-Three Mile Island American domestic nuclear disaster. Third, Homer thanking/invoking God for nuclear power recalls an unconscious historical association with the atom as divine instrument, inherent in Truman's Hiroshima bombing announcement, "We thank *God* for sending us *His* weapon." In God we trust.

According to the *Simpsons Archive,* writer Sam Simon confesses to being primarily responsible for the program's nuclear jokes. However, Simon says that the series is "not on this mission against nuclear power; I just think it's funny that a boob like Homer can have a job in such a potentially dangerous situation."[30] This irony, of course, is not lost on the millions of viewers each week.

In "Homer's Enemy," the absurdity of Homer's employment is highlighted by a comic foil in the form of Frank Grimes—a working-class stiff who has triumphed over adversity, managing to complete a correspondence school diploma in nuclear physics. Grimes makes an appearance on Springfield television, where Springfield Nuclear Power Plant owner and demigod Montgomery Burns watches admiringly. Burns demands of his personal assistant Smithers that Grimes be hired as executive vice-president. By the next day, however, a fickle Burns has been more impressed by a "heroic dog" and gives the position to the canine, dismissively dumping Grimes, who ends up working with Homer in Sector 7-G, alongside colleagues Lenny and Carl, who both admire Grimes' diploma:

GRIMES: Oh, that's my degree in nuclear physics. I'm sure you all have one.

LENNY: Oh yeah, Carl and I each have a masters'. [Laughing] Of course, old Homer, he didn't need a degree. He just showed up the day they opened the plant.

HOMER: I didn't even know what a nuclear panner [sic] plant was.

GRIMES: Um, yeah. Well, listen, I'm sure, you all have a lot of work to do.

> Bemused by the comment, Lenny and Carl shrug and leave.
>
> HOMER: Hey, you seem like a great guy, so I'll give you a little tip. If you turn that security camera around you can sleep and no one will ever know.
>
> GRIMES: Ah, I don't think we're being paid to sleep.
>
> HOMER: Oh yeah, they're always trying to screw ya.

Homer departs Grimes's office, leaving him quaking in disbelief. The exchange commences a series of confrontations between Homer and Grimes, the latter becoming increasing irate at Homer's sloth, negligence, and laissez-faire attitude toward work. For example, Grimes is aghast when Homer stops a warning klaxon on his nuclear control panel by pouring a bucket of water across the system, shorting out the siren and his workstation. Later, when Grimes complains to colleagues that he found Homer sleeping inside a radiation suit, Lenny nonchalantly explains that Homer had three beers at lunch: "That would make anybody sleepy." The conspicuous culture of alcohol consumption in Springfield is a frequent barb for *The Simpsons* creative team, but the potentially lethal mix of alcohol and nuclear energy is, nevertheless, a sobering theme.

According to Hilgartner et al, a number of investigative media reports after Three Mile Island showed workers (including security guards) at Boston and Oregon nuclear utilities to be intoxicated at work ("I'm talking about legless") or who were arrested for selling "various illegal drugs," including cocaine.[31] To illustrate the point, the authors included an image of a "reactor control panel" that has been modified by its operator(s) by removing the control levers and replacing them with beer taps (Heineken and Michelob). Similarly, in "Homer Defined," SNPP employees are shown to have personalized coffee mugs shaped like cooling towers with atomic logos on the side.

When the President's Commission on the Accident at Three Mile Island (TMI) reported their findings, they significantly pinpointed "people-related problems" as fundamental to the accident, as opposed to structural or engineering faults. Accordingly, in "Homer's Odyssey," when *Simpsons* writer Sam Simon's "boob" Homer addresses a protest rally over the safety issues at the SNPP, he points the finger and is hardly complimentary to his former workplace: "Your lives are in the hands of men no smarter than you or I, many of them incompetent boobs. I know this because I've worked alongside them, gone bowling with them, watched them pass me over for promotions time and again. And I say—this stinks!"

Indeed. Whereas Homer's agenda is partly based on revenge for missed advancement, his point regarding institutional incompetence remains valid and continues to be much of the focus of the series' humor. But Homer is no anti-nuclear mouthpiece. In fact, he is openly contemptuous of the protesters, as his initial address to the crowd attests: "Unlike most of you, I am not a *nut*."[32]

> The Harrisburg Commission summarized the major problem as the industry's "nuclear mindset." The inquiry concluded that over the years, the belief that nuclear power plants were sufficiently safe grew into a conviction. . . . This attitude must be changed to one that says nuclear power is by its very nature potentially dangerous, and, therefore, one must continually question whether the safeguards already in place are sufficient to prevent major accidents.[33]

And who becomes responsible for continually questioning the safeguards of Springfield's reactor? Why, Homer J. Simpson, of course.

In "Homer's Enemy," when Grimes is apprised of Homer's job as the plant's official "Safety Inspector," he is incredulous:

GRIMES: That irresponsible oaf? A man who by all rights should have been killed dozens of times by now?

LENNY: Three hundred and sixteen times by my count.

GRIMES: That's the man who's in charge of our safety?! It . . . it boggles the mind.

CARL: It's best not to think about it.

Carl's resigned statement is more than a gesture towards what psychologist Robert Lifton and others have recognized as fundamental to our nuclear epoch—denial and disavowal—and it reflects the industry's nuclear "mindset."[34] To reinforce the absurdity of Homer's position, seconds later he is shown groping absent-mindedly for a drink but instead taking a beaker full of sulfuric acid. As he is about to drink it, Grimes knocks it away just in time, apparently saving Homer's life.

Among the lengthy items the Presidential Commission presented as failures, most were "people-related problems" which included operator error, poor operator training, poor reactor control-room design, and failure of communication.[35] The ultimate "people-related problem" in *The Simpsons* is shown apocalyptically in "Life's a Glitch, Then You Die," a sequence from "Treehouse of Horror X." Homer's negligence as the SNPP's official Y2K compliance officer initiates a core meltdown on January 1, 2000, which rapidly escalates to destroying the entire U.S. power grid and causing the end of civilization as we know it. Fleeing earth in a spaceship, Homer and Bart witness the global conflagration below, rendered as spiraling mushroom clouds igniting across the world.

The frequent laughs at the nuclear industry's expense did not go unnoticed for long, and the series writers came under pressure to modify their line. Sam Simon relates:

> When the show started, the United States Council for Energy Awareness, which is a fairly powerful nuclear power lobbying group, said, "You're having fun at our expense. Why don't you come down to a nuclear power plant and see what it's really like?" There's no way that writers on this show would turn down a chance like that. It was a really fun field trip that taught us that, in some ways, our show was unrealistic, but, in other ways, it was more realistic than we would have ever thought possible. They got angry that we weren't completely turned around by the field trip and that we didn't stop doing jokes about nuclear power so they issued a press release stating how upset they were. I was called by Associated Press and essentially said, "I'm sorry they feel bad about it." Then the anti-nuclear people got upset because they don't want to hear anything but a complete anti-nuclear agenda and they wanted equal time. I said, "You want equal time because I'm not listening to these other people?" It doesn't make sense! . . . People on both sides of that particular controversy don't have a sense of humor, and I'm glad that I do. We're going to keep having fun with nuclear power on the show.[36]

However, it seems highly disingenuous to suggest equivalence of purpose or resources here. Simon names an organized, "powerful" lobby group in contrast to unnamed anti-nuclear "people," themselves reacting to the publicized machinations of the nuclear industry's influence. It also belies *The Simpsons* team's dependence on such social and political polarization to effect a broad prime-time TV satire, and a successful one for more than a decade. By painting the players as "humorless," Simon attempts to deflect critical scrutiny away from the tropes, motifs, themes, and genres that *The Simpsons* regularly deploys in order to parody and critique Springfield as America in microcosm.

In the second season episode, "Two Cars in Every Garage, Three Eyes on Every Fish," *The Simpsons* devastatingly lampoons the nuclear industry's attempts to assuage public concerns over environmental contamination. According to *The Simpsons* Archive, the episode caused "quite a stir." When Lisa and Bart catch a mutant three-eyed fish swimming downstream from the SNPP, the print and television media are in a frenzy ("Fishin' Hole or Fission Hole?" one headline screams). To counter the bad publicity, Burns surrounds himself with publicists and spin doctors, deciding to run for governor against the liberal and environmentally conscious incumbent Mary Bailey. Buying up television airtime to present lengthy campaign infomercials, he moves to dispel popular concern about the plant's mutagenic byproducts. But his contempt for the common man and democratic process is hilariously depicted when the cameras catch him off-guard and on air: "By the time this paid political announcement is done, every Johnny Lunchpail in this whole stupid state will be eating out of my hands. . . . Oh, hello, friends." Sitting beside the mutant fish, whom Burns calls Blinky, he assures the audience that there is nothing wrong either with the fish or the nuclear plant. "But don't take *my* word for it," he advises, "Let's ask an actor portraying Charles Darwin what *he* thinks." Dutifully, a bearded actor walks on and presents his expedient theory of natural selection, Burns-style: "So you're saying this fish may have an advantage over other fish," Burns gushes. "It may be, in fact, a kind of Super-Fish . . . a miracle of nature, with a taste that can't be beat." Immediately after the broadcast, Burns moves ahead in the polls and seems destined to become the new governor, while the headlines shriek, "Burns nukes Bailey."

However, to show that he still has the "common touch," his advisors suggest that Burns stage a televised meal at the family home of one of his employees on the night before the election. Burns visits the Simpsons residence and, amid the media circus, Marge cunningly serves up the three-eyed fish, slicing off the head and handing it to Burns as an entrée. He is unable to swallow even a mouthful, and, spitting out his first bite live on television, Burns instantly buries his election hopes.

Again, writer Sam Simon disavows any political or ideological motive in the series' scripting:

> It's funny, you know. I just try to make the shows, and if people want to analyze them they can. I sat in a college classroom where a professor was telling students that ["Two Cars in Every Garage, Three Eyes on Every Fish"] was the most pointed piece of political satire that had aired on prime-time television in the last 10 years! I co-wrote that three-eyed fish episode and, honest to God, two of us sat in my office for a couple of days and strung together some jokes. There was no point to it.[37]

Whether or not the creative forces behind *The Simpsons* admit to, or continue to publicly eschew, an agenda to present such themes as oppositional culture is ultimately irrelevant, as are questions of authorship and/or individual agency. A close reading of separate episodes or the series as a collective whole demonstrates an ongoing antagonism towards American hegemony.

The relationship between television and nuclear energy is most pronounced in times of crisis, and here *The Simpsons* as parody is almost a textbook case. Both Patricia Mellencamp and Mary Anne Doane have identified the interdependence of television and catastrophe, particularly its articulation as *nuclear* disaster. For Doane, drawing from the works of catastrophe theorists, the fascination in televised peril is implicitly linked to the potential collapse of technology and the imagery of death. She defines catastrophe as "the conjuncture of the failure of technology's control over the forces it strives to contain [as] manifested most visibly in the accident."[38] Mellencamp, however, citing socio-psychoanalytic as well as catastrophe theory, regards the technological imperative of disaster as a historically determined coincidence, arguing that the central determinant of catastrophe is inextricably linked with the structural and institutional evolution of the (patriarchal) televisual apparatus, itself a prime historical proponent of "nuclear disavowal."[39]

In "Homer Defined," the nuclear sitcom assumes the theoretical mantle of postmodern catastrophe paragon. Homer accidentally initiates a reactor meltdown and, unable to recall his emergency training or read the schematic diagram in the operator's manual ("D'oh! Who'd have thought a nuclear reactor would be so complicated!"), narrowly avoids core criticality by randomly pressing control buttons (playing eenie-meenieminey-moe). As Doane suggests, "Television's ubiquity, its extensiveness, allows for a global experience of catastrophe which is always reminiscent of the potential of nuclear disaster, of mass rather than individual annihilation."[40] During the panic, as klaxons howl and sirens wail, Burns is telephoned by *Springfield Television News* anchor Kent Brockman. Meanwhile, Marge is at home, oblivious to the drama, watching a television soap opera when an unseen announcer says, "We interrupt *Search for the Sun* for this special news bulletin." A pro-forma television intertitle appears, "Meltdown Crisis: The First Couple of Minutes."

It is this spontaneous dislocation of television continuity which Doane suggests can only occur and be contained by televising crises:

> Catastrophe is crucial to television precisely because it functions as a denial [of the commodification/commercialization of time] and corroborates television's access to the momentary, the discontinuous, the real. Catastrophe produces the illusion that the spectator is in direct contact with the anchorperson, who interrupts regular programming to demonstrate that it can indeed be done when the referent is at stake."[41]

The sequence from "Homer Defined" is worth quoting at length since it brilliantly displays *The Simpsons*'s satirical acumen as postmodern critique of contemporary television news tropes:

> BROCKMAN: On the line with us now is plant owner C. Montgomery Burns. Mr. Burns?
>
> BURNS: Oh, hello, Kent. [Pulsing klaxons throb in the background] Right now, skilled nuclear energy technicians are calmly correcting a minor, piffling malfunction. [Montage of panic across the plant] But I can assure you and the public that there is absolutely no danger whatsoever. [Air raid siren wails] Things couldn't be more shipshape. [In Burns's office, he is quickly donning a radiation suit]
>
> BROCKMAN: Uh, Mr. Burns, people are calling this a *meltdown*.
>
> BURNS: [chuckling] Oh, "meltdown." It's one of those annoying buzzwords. We prefer to call it an *unrequested fission surplus*.

Burns's euphemistic double-speak recalls Dwight Eisenhower's directive to the AEC in the mid-1950s to "keep the public confused" about the technical terms of nuclear technology in order to limit concern and the potential for protest. It became standard operational PR procedure in the nuclear industry during the 1960s and 1970s to "eliminate objectionable words from the atomic lexicon" and replace the "scare words" with "palatable synonyms."[42]

As the crisis escalates, Burns confesses to Smithers that the end is nigh, lamenting, "I guess there's nothing left but to kiss my sorry ass goodbye." Back on television, familiar series nerd Professor Frink stands before a map depicting various bull's-eyes:

> FRINK: These unfortunate people here will be instantly killed. [pointing] This circle—which I am sad to say we are in—will experience a slower, considerably more painful death.
> BROCKMAN: Good Lord!

As Mary Anne Doane argues, the crucial interrelationships propelling catastrophe and crisis combine TV anchor, expert commentary, simulation, and proximity, and this *Simpsons* episode, self-reflexively, has it all:

> The inability of television to capture the precise moment of the [disaster] activates a compensatory discourse of eyewitness accounts and animated reenactment of the disaster—a simulated vision. . . . What becomes crucial for the act of reportage, the announcement of the catastrophe, is the simple gesture of being on the scene, where it happened, so that the presence in space compensates for the inevitable temporal lag. Hence, while the voice-over of the anchor ultimately organizes the event for us, the status of the image as indexical truth is not inconsequential—through it the "story" touches the ground of the real. Nevertheless, the catastrophe must be immediately subjected to analysis, speculation, and explanation.[43]

Finally, Homer manages to hit the right button and the automated computer voice reassures him the problem has been neutralized. Marge, however, remains glued to the on-going news special:

> BURNS: Yes, we've solved the problem. Wouldn't you know—false alarm.
> MARGE: [Transfixed at home before the screen] Phew!

BURNS: It seems a single wayward crow flew into our warning system.[44]

KENT: Very good. Well, sir, your point about nuclear hysteria is well-taken. This reporter promises to be more trusting and less vigilant in the future.

BURNS: [In his office, still wearing his radiation suit] Excellent. Well, ta-ta!

From the early 1960s on, the nuclear industry publicly congratulated itself on "winning over" the media, as Kent Brockman's sycophantic apology to Burns at the end of the Meltdown Crisis hilariously demonstrates. Hal Stroube, one of the industry's early PR strategists, implored fellow publicists at an American Nuclear Society conference to gain the confidence of the press: "We won the respect of the news people . . . and with it we won entree into the minds of our public through the news media. Even more impressive and encouraging, we found that newsmen paid less and less attention to the "anti's" as they found that their stories and accusations and suspicions just didn't jibe with the facts which we gave them."[45] *The Simpsons* shows scorn for what it presents to be the inherently unsafe, corrupt, and dishonest profiteering from "civilian" nuclear energy, yet the program's comic musings on atomic arsenals and the "other" possibilities of nuclear catastrophe are no less potent.

ACT IV: NUCLEAR WEAPONS

If, as we have seen, atomic energy became synonymous with the new entertainment medium, so too did the association with militaristic outcomes. The effective combination of "war machine" technologies is what Paul Virilio has termed the "logistics of military perception."[46] Within twelve months of the atomic "closure" of World War II, RCA, Westinghouse, Motorola, General Electric, and other manufacturers—many of whom were responsible for the original (and later) development of nuclear weapons and commercial reactors—began supplying domestic television sets. At the same time, Operation Crossroads saw a further two weapons detonated in the Pacific basin at Bikini Atoll. Amongst the vast array of scientific, cinematic, and press representations were a small number of television transmitters relaying distant images to the assembled spectators and defense personnel.

Just as industry and government pushed its Atoms for Peace campaign throughout the 1950s, Fred MacDonald has demonstrated that the other half of the propaganda dichotomy—atoms for war—also prominently utilized television: "This mixture of government involvement in production and distribution of misleading films, and overly simplified messages stressing nuclear survival was evident in a package of free motion pictures offered by the FCDA [Federal Civil Defense Administration] to every American TV station in late 1951."[47] As in the other atomic energy industry shorts described above, these ten-minute films promoted the ability of Americans to survive a nuclear attack, often employing respected journalists (CBS's Edward Murrow) and film/TV stars (Fred MacMurray, Glenn Ford, Jack Webb) as narrators, encouraging citizens to construct domestic bomb shelters and stockpile food and water.

Even at the most marginal, *The Simpsons* demonstrates a baby boomer affection for the post-apocalyptic. The various references to the *Planet of the Apes* series suggest that Homer fully expects a nuclear war as inevitable, with a future world populated by mutant apes or *Omega Man*-style zombies, as the French neutron bomb sketch depicts in "Homega Man" from *The Simpsons* Halloween special "Treehouse of Horror VIII." As early as 1987, Homer was readying his family for the anticipated nuclear apocalypse. Prior to its record-breaking series run on Fox, *The Simpsons* was entertaining nuclear themes in short satirical animation spots on the *Tracey Ullman Show*. The sketch "World War III" depicted Homer as an obsessive survivalist, repeatedly drilling his family at all hours in preparation for an imminent atomic holocaust.

An explicit link between civilian nuclear energy and weapons production is also hinted at in "Homer's Odyssey," where one of the comically depicted "warning" signs inside the SNPP shows nuclear waste being sent off for missile reprocessing. In reality, however, the reverse is true. In order to find an economic, as opposed to military, value for the increasing stockpile (hundreds of tons) of plutonium from decommissioned nuclear weapons, the Department of Energy is trialing MOX (a mixture of plutonium and uranium) for commercial nuclear utilities to use in powering their reactors.

In "Bart's Comet," the shelter trope is again presented comically when the uninvited Simpson family effectively takes over the shelter of neighbor Ned Flanders to avoid a cometary impact on Springfield (Moe's tavern is shown as ground zero). Soon the entire town seems squashed into the bunker (presumably a homage to Groucho's cabin room in *A Night at the Opera*), so much so that the door cannot close. Someone must leave the shelter for the common good. The ensuing debate about who should remain in the post-holocaust world recalls the final moments of *Dr. Strangelove,* where self-interest compels protagonists to expediently justify their personal inclusion. After Christian do-gooder Flanders is booted out at Homer's instigation, his pitiful self-sacrifice leads the others to emerge and join him outside. But as Homer has earlier predicted, the doomsday comet burns up in the atmosphere, buffeted by the pollution and smog above Springfield, and a piece no bigger than a chihuahua's head finally levels the now abandoned Flanders shelter. The irony of the shelter's utter destruction is a marvelous slight at fallacious civil defense rhetoric from Eisenhower to Reagan, where, in an era of multi-megaton hydrogen bombs, public fallout shelters would be no more than death-traps and suburban ones ineffective against heat and blast. As Spencer Weart points out in his analysis of atomic anxiety, *Nuclear Fear,* "Of course, it was natural for government officials and merchants to emphasize fallout, since that was the only thing that people stood any chance of protecting themselves against."[48]

As discussed earlier, the rhetoric of Kennedy's FFC Chairman attests historically to a perception at the highest levels of a militaristic, atomic-television technological binarism. Minow's 1961 industry broadside informs, perhaps unconsciously, a similar tirade thirty years later by *Simpsons*'s character (and Bart's arch-nemesis) Sideshow Bob in a brilliant episode where highbrow sentiments also align with television and the terror of nuclear weapons.[49] In "Sideshow Bob's Last Gleaming," Krusty the Clown's former sidekick, the erudite and dreadlocked Sideshow Bob, escapes from prison where he is serving a term for attempted murder, ultimately driven out from the penal institution by the incessant prattle of his fellow inmates' televisions.[50] Sideshow Bob echoes FFC Chairman Minow's discourse, his refined trans-Atlantic voice displaying an affectation of patrician sensibility as he terrorizes Springfield, demanding an end to broadcast television. Disgusted by his fellow cons' laughter at Krusty's show, Bob chastises them: "Oh, must you bray night and day at that infernal television?" But the inmates quickly recall that Bob used to appear on the very same program. "Don't remind me," Bob laments. "My foolish capering destroyed more young minds than syphilis and pinball combined. Oh, how I loathe that box; its omnidirectional sludge pump droning and burping."[51]

While working on a prison detail next to a local air force base, Bob hatches his plan to rid Springfield of television. He easily evades both the prison and base security in order to steal a nuclear device, parroting the demoralizing invective of base Commander Hapablap (as voiced brilliantly by *Full Metal Jacket*'s Lee Ermy) and thereby brow-beating his way into a secure (one guard!) nuclear weapons store: "Sweet Enola Gay, son! I'm going to come in there and corpse you up—corpse you up and mail you to mama!"[52]

At the air show, the Simpsons family impatiently awaits the thundering aviation display while the real Hapablap enthuses over the base public address system, "What a day for an air show. Not a cloud in the sky!"[53] The next shot reveals Bob, whistling nonchalantly, while pushing a wheelbarrow that contains a 10-megaton bomb (conspicuously shaped like Hiroshima's "Little Boy").[54] Upon hearing Hapablap's warm-up line, Bob smugly asides, "Except, perhaps, a mushroom cloud," and cackles away hysterically, his mirth nearly tipping over/triggering the bomb.

Shortly after, Sideshow Bob interrupts proceedings by cutting into the airship's transmission over a huge television screen. Amid gasps and screams from the audience, Bob's towering image occupies the vast screen.

> BOB: Hello, Springfield. Sorry to divert your attention from all the big noises and shiny things. But something's been troubling me lately—television! Wouldn't our lives be so much richer if television were done away with? . . . Why, we could revive the lost arts of conversation, and scrimshaw. Thus, I submit to you, we abolish television, *permanently*!
>
> HOMER: Go back to Massachusetts, pinko!
>
> BOB: Oh, and one more thing. I've . . . stolen a nuclear weapon. If you do not rid this city of television within two hours, I will detonate it. Farewell.

The television goes blank, and as the crowd panics, Bob's image again fills the screen. "By the way," he chides, "I'm aware of the irony of appearing on TV in order to decry it. So don't bother pointing that out."

Too clever for Hapablap's men, Sideshow Bob seems about to have his demands met. In a war-room bunker scene generically reminiscent of *Dr. Strangelove* and *Fail-Safe,* Mayor Quimby looks for answers with his customary Massachusetts drawl, while Herman Khan-like, he starts thinking about the unthinkable: "Gentlemen, it's time we face up to the un-face-up-to-able. We must sacrifice television in order to save the lives of our townspeople."

However, Krusty the Clown, who is present as "an esteemed representative of television," disagrees, invoking the familiar Cold War discourse of "better dead than Red": "Whoa! Whoa-ho-ho! Let's not go nuts. Would it really be worth living in a world without television? I think the survivors would envy the dead!" The somber mayor replies with abundant pathos and resignation: "I appreciate your passion on behalf of your medium. But I'm afraid we are out of options. Television must go. May God have mercy on our souls."[55]

After seeing images of television transmission towers being destroyed around Springfield, a deliriously happy Bob's victory is shown to be short-lived. Within seconds of checking the airwaves for static, he comes across the ancient Emergency Broadcast System, where Krusty is back on the air. "My utopia lies in ruins!" Bob laments. "How naive of me to think a mere atom bomb could fell the chattering Cyclops."

True to his threat, Bob detonates his weapon. A flash of over-exposed light fills the screen. In a rapid montage recalling the stylized depiction of nuclear explosion effects on populaces from *Fail-Safe* to the television movies *World War III* and *The Day After,* representative mini-scenes of Springfield in microcosm are shown.[56] But the rising mushroom cloud that appears is shown to be a mere tiny puff of smoke. The bomb is a dud. The device implodes and collapses as rats emerge and run away. Foiled, Bob reads from the metal casing: "'Best before November 1959.' Dammit, Bob, there were plenty of brand new bombs, but you had to go for that retro Fifties charm."

Retro chic, as we have seen in the nuclear mise-en-scène of "Homer's Phobia," with its camp atomic-theme restaurant, is problematic. However, as the self-conscious aesthetic element that ultimately leads to Bob's downfall, even this jest subversively reminds viewers of the enormous American nuclear arsenal and its continual post-cold war "modernization." Plenty of brand new bombs indeed. If the U.S. Air Force is given *The Simpsons*'s treatment in "Sideshow Bob's Last Gleaming," then the U.S. Navy—

and the omnipresent potential for global atomic annihilation—is similarly parodied in "Simpson Tide" when Homer commandeers a nuclear submarine and heads for Russian territorial waters, nearly causing World War III. Before boarding the sub he tells his family not to worry since he is merely playing in war games and that the crew has orders to fire only on Greenpeace.

EPILOGUE: ATOMS FOR SATIRE

As we have seen, *The Simpsons* revels in playfully foregrounding narratives of nuclearism. Homer is depicted as a smug, if stupid, company man who automatically and defensively spouts nuclear industry propaganda that even his elementary school son Bart recognizes as lame and phony ("keep those mutants comin', Homer"). Burns, the nuclear plant owner, is depicted as a ruthless capitalist, bribing officials, manipulating the media (especially television) and bankrolling election campaigns to consolidate his wealth and power or to evade prosecution for larceny, pollution and endangering public safety.[57] He is an opportunistic libertarian ready to sell out his community and country for profit and expedience. Such a persona draws upon mythic American tycoons such as William Randolph Hearst and Orson Welles's filmic simulacra Charles Foster Kane (Burns even has his own "Rosebud" episode). But the nuclear industry, personified by Burns (and other *Simpsons* "captains of industry" such as Aristotle Amadopolis, owner of the Shelbyville atomic plant), is merely symptomatic of what is rotten in the entire *Simpsons* epistemology.[58] Like some unchecked background radiation, the program's decade-long relentless depiction of pervasive corruption, greed, and hypocrisy systemically works its way into, and contaminates, virtually all the principal and peripheral characters. Local and state politicians are corrupt, the police are inept and on the take, educators are slothful and vengeful, the clergy are duplicitous, physicians are either quacks or uncaring, foreigners are jingoistically ridiculed, and the extended family shown as surly, dysfunctional, incompetent, and/or institutionalized.

Yet among this ensemble of characters, the only ones to be treated with ongoing respect by the series creators are those portrayed working for the Nuclear Regulatory Commission (NRC) or the Environment Protection Agency (EPA). In "Two Cars in Every Garage, Three Eyes on Every Fish," a snap NRC inspection has Burns alerting his staff ("faceless employees") in advance, telling them to "look busy" and warning them to "keep your mouths shut." Inside the plant, the NRC team, wearing white coats and hard-hats, switch on their Geiger counters, which immediately crackle uncontrollably. In a quick flash of vignettes, the chief inspector rattles off defects, including, "Gum used to seal crack in coolant tower; plutonium rod used as paperweight; monitoring station unmanned [Homer is caught napping at his control panel]; nuclear waste shin-deep in hallway." A single green drop of toxic waste drips onto the inspector's damning inventory and burns a hole straight through his clipboard.

This amusing list of deficiencies, however, is not that far-fetched. Hilgartner et al identify a "special internal file of problems at nuclear plants" kept by a senior NRC safety inspector, released under a Freedom of Information Act request. Among the litany of *Simpsons*-like complaints were workers using a *basketball* to plug a leak in a spent fuel pool cooling system (Homer would have surely used a bowling ball), radioactive water found in a plant drinking fountain, and various critical engineering equipment installed side-ways or using the wrong size.[59]

Seriously unimpressed, the inspector admonishes Burns: "in twenty years, I have never seen such a shoddy, deplorable. . . ." But Burns interjects with a flagrant bribe: "Oh, look! Some careless person has left thousands and thousands of dollars just lying here on my coffee table. Um, Smithers, why don't we leave the room, and hopefully, when we return, the pile of money will be gone." Burns leaves, waits outside, and then promptly returns, adding sarcastically, "Ooh. Look Smithers, the money and a very stupid man are still here."[60] "Burns," the inspector replies suspiciously, "If I didn't know better, I'd think you were trying to bribe me." To which Burns replies condescendingly, shoving bills into the man's lab coat pockets, "Is there some confusion about this? Take it! Take it! Take it, you poor schmo!" Defiantly in control, the inspector presents Burns and Smithers with his inventory of 342 violations.

Considering the Swiftian nature of the social satire, this is a curious concession by *The Simpsons*'s producers, directors, and writers. It suggests a cultural and political boundary that should not be crossed, the narrative point at which one might abandon all hope if the agency to keep the Burnses of this world in check is similarly corrupt and open to question.

The Realpolitik of avoiding a serious critique of (or even lampooning) a federal bureaucracy such as the NRC or EPA appears, for *The Simpsons*, to be the ideological barrier at which its sense of oppositional culture must retreat. Hence, the series avoids "going critical" (in both senses of the term) and potentially losing its mass audience appeal. Rather, in this instance, it embraces social commentary/comedy closer to the legacy of Preston Sturges and Frank Capra, rather than transmuting into the black, sardonic realm of what Stanley Kubrick dubbed "nightmare comedy."

NOTES

For Jonathan

1. "Releasing the hounds" refers to Springfield Nuclear Power plant owner Montgomery Burns and his penchant for unleashing a trained pack of blood-thirsty dogs on unsuspecting visitors to his private estate or nuclear facility. This usually comes as a command to his sycophantic lieutenant: "Smithers, release the hounds!" In the context of this essay, the cry connotes the capacity of *The Simpsons*'s creators to release their own form of ravaging social satire upon a national television audience. More obliquely, this catch phrase invokes mythological association with the multi-headed canine monster, Cerberus, who guarded the entrance to Hades, which resonates intertextually with Dr. Soberin's description of the mysterious and lethal atomic energy source, "the Great Whatsit," in Robert Aldrich's noir classic, *Kiss Me Deadly*.

2. Ross Gibson, "Yondering," *Art & Text* 19: 24–33.

3. See, for example, Ella Taylor, *Prime Time Families: Television Culture in Postwar America,* (Berkeley: University of California Press, 1989) and Lyn Spigel, *Make Room for TV* (Chicago: University of Chicago Press, 1992).

4. Margot A. Henriksen, *Dr. Strangelove's America: Society and Culture in the Atomic Age* (Berkeley: University of California Press, 1997).

5. In *The Evil Demon of Images* (Sydney: Power Publications, 1984), Jean Baudrillard comments:

> TV and nuclear power are of the same kind, behind the "hot" and negen-tropic concepts of energy and information, they have the same dissuasive force as cold systems. TV is also a nuclear, chain-reactive process, but implo-sive: it cools and neutralizes the meaning and energy of events. Thus, behind the presumed risk of explosion, that is, of hot catastrophe, the nuclear con-ceals a long, cold catastrophe—the universalization of a system of dissua-sion, of deterrence. . . . The homology between television and nuclear power can be read directly in the images. Nothing resembles the command and con-trol center of the reactor more than the TV studios, and the nuclear consoles share the same imaginary as the recording and broadcasting studios. Every-

thing happens between these two poles: the other core, that of the reactor, in principle the real core of the affair, remains concealed from us, like the real; buried and indecipherable, ultimately of no importance. The drama is acted out on the screens and nowhere else. (19–20)

6. David Marc, *Comic Visions: Television Comedy and American Culture,* 2nd ed. (Malden, MA: Blackwell Publishers, 1997), 148.

7. One bizarre attempt, made around the same time *The Simpsons* commenced on Fox, was the series *Whoops!* which featured a post-holocaust band of survivors eking out an existence, similar to the characters of *Gilligan's Island.*

8. See Robert. J. Lifton and Richard Falk, *Indefensible Weapons: The Political and Psychological Case Against Nuclearism* (New York: Basic Books, 1982).

9. This makes an interesting comparison with the *South Park* episode featuring Sparky the gay dog, which is far more risqué and blunter in its depiction of perceived social stereotypes.

10. Many comic characters were either created by radioactivity—Spider Man and the Hulk, for instance—or encountered atomic energy on lurid cover art (such as Captain Marvel, Jr., or Superman in *Action Comics*).

11. Patricia Mellencamp, *High Anxiety: Catastrophe, Scandal, Age, and Comedy* (Bloomington: Indiana University Press, 1992), 140.

12. Nelson, Joyce. *The Perfect Machine: Television and the Bomb* (Philadelphia: New Society, 1992), 34.

13. Joyce, *The Perfect Machine,* 130.

14. Joyce, *The Perfect Machine,* 130.

15. Spigel, *Make Room for TV,* 46.

16. Spigel, *Make Room for TV,* 82.

17. Christopher Anderson, *Hollywood TV: The Studio System in the Fifties* (Austin: University of Texas Press, 1994), 76.

18. Anderson, *Hollywood TV,* 77. The apocalyptic, millenarian, and utopian dimensions of nuclear energy have been covered by Paul Boyer in *By the Bomb's Early Light: American Thought and Culture at the Dawn of the Atomic Age* (New York: Pantheon, 1985) and *When Time Shall Be No More: Prophetic Belief In Modern American Culture* (Cambridge, MA: Belknap Press, 1992).

19. Anderson, *Hollywood TV,* 93.

20. Anderson, *Hollywood TV,* 77–78.

21. Nelson, *The Perfect Machine,* 44.

22. In "Homer Defined," as the countdown to core meltdown engulfs Springfield, Principal Skinner has Lisa's class dive under their desks: "They called me old-fashioned for teaching the duck-and-cover method, but who's laughing now!"

23. Fredric Jameson regards pastiche as a key component of conservative postmodernism, differentiated from parody and satire. See his "Postmodernism, or The Cultural Logic of Late Capitalism," *New Left Review* 146 (1984): 53–92.

24. A popular poster has *Futurama*'s central character Frye saying, "This long-time exposure to radiation is making me thirsty!"

25. But Smilin' Joe Fission isn't kidding about the duplicitous dumping of toxic nuclear waste. In Marge vs. the Monorail, Carl and Lenny are shown sealing up barrels (Toxic Waste—Do Not Eat) and discussing their ultimate destination. Carl figures they are buried in an abandoned chalk mine. Lenny thinks they are sent to a Southern state run by a crooked governor. When they leave, Burns and Smithers take the barrels away, with Smithers inquiring, "Well, sir, where should we dump *this* batch . . . playground?" Burns replies emphatically, "No. All those bald children are arousing suspicion." Later, they are caught by the EPA dumping barrels at a public park. In another episode, Homer is punished by Burns by having to eat several barrels of radioactive waste.

26. Fredric Jameson, *The Political Unconscious: Narrative as a Socially Symbolic Act* (Ithaca: Cornell University Press, 1981).

27. *The Atomic Café*, dir. Pierce Rafferty, Jayne Loader, and Kevin Rafferty, Film Archive Project, 1982.

28. For an insight into nefarious nuclear industry public relations strategies, post-Three Mile Island, see S. Hilgartner, R. C. Bell, and R. O'Connor, *Nukespeak: The Selling of Nuclear Technology in America* (Penguin Books, Harmondsworth, 1982), chapter 6, "Polls, Ads, and PR."

29. In "E-I-E-I-(Annoyed Grunt)," Homer uses plutonium from the SNPP to irradiate crops and produces a new addictive product that he dubs Tomacco, a nuclear hybrid of tobacco and tomato, which rivals cigarettes.

30. *The Simpsons Archive*, <http://www.snpp.com>, 1999.

31. Hilgartner, *Nukespeak*, 140–41.

32. Among the assembled protest signs is "People Against People for Nuclear Energy."

33. Hilgartner, *Nukespeak*, 135.

34. See Lifton and Falk, *Indefensible Weapons: The Political and Psychological Case Against Nuclearism*, and Spencer Weart, *Nuclear Fear, a History of Images* (Cambridge, MA: Harvard University Press, 1988).

35. Hilgartner, *Nukespeak*, 136. *The Simpsons* demonstrates, and Homer personifies, all of these deficiencies. In "Homer Goes to College," when the Nuclear Regulatory Commission recommends Homer be tested in a simulator outside the plant, he causes the simulator to meltdown!

36. *The Simpsons Archive*.

37. *The Simpsons Archive*.

38. Mary Anne Doane, "Information, Crisis, Catastrophe," in *Logics of Television: Essays in Cultural Criticism*, ed. Patricia Mellencamp (Bloomington: Indiana University Press, 1990), 229.

39. Mellencamp, *High Anxiety*, 139–46.

40. Doane, "Information, Crisis, Catastrophe," 230.

41. Doane, "Information, Crisis, Catastrophe," 238.

42. Hilgartner, *Nukespeak*, 78.

43. Doane, "Information, Crisis, Catastrophe," 229–30.

44. Burns's explanation is simply preposterous. Ironically, however, it is exactly the type of disclosure given for several Cold War accidents and nuclear alerts, common at strategic air force bases.

45. Hilgartner, *Nukespeak*, 77.

46. Paul Virilio, *War and Cinema: The Logistics of Perception*, trans. Patrick Vamiller (Verso: London, 1989), 1.

47. Fred MacDonald, *Television and the Red Menace: The Video Road to Vietnam* (New York: Praeger, 1985), 42.

48. Spencer, *Nuclear Fear*, 257–58.

49. As nuclear historian Paul Boyer comments in *Fallout*, the episode "exploits the familiar ephemera of America's nuclear arsenal" (Columbus: Ohio State University, 1998), 219.

50. The program's title refers to Robert Aldrich's much undervalued *Twilight's Last Gleaming* (1977), in which a former U.S. General (Burt Lancaster) blackmails the U.S. government after occupying an underground ICBM silo control center.

51. At which point another prisoner interrupts, looking suspiciously like Fox head Rupert Murdoch, and attempts to strangle Sideshow Bob for his insolence, saying in an appalling mock-Australian accent, "Look here, that's enough now! I own 60 per cent of that network."

52. Several *Simpsons* episodes show guards sleeping or completely oblivious to security incursions while ostensibly protecting nuclear facilities. Even more comic are the juxtaposed signs warning of lethal force or extreme danger while the guards slumber on.

53. Displays of militarism are normally anathema to Lisa Simpson, but even she is excited by news of the Air Show, telling Marge, "I want to meet the first female Stealth Bomber pilot. During the Gulf War, she destroyed 70 mosques, and her name is Lisa, too!"

54. The nuclear bomb is a staple icon of the series, usually present at the military surplus store owned by one-armed Herman, appearing in "Bart the General," "Homer the Vigilante," and several *Itchy and Scratchy* cartoons (e.g., "Deaf Comedy Blam").

55. As Patricia Mellencamp has amusingly suggested, post-Meaghan Morris, the *real* catastrophe on television would be the total absence of signal.

56. The sequence includes an image of Maggie picking flower petals, which evokes the Democrats' notorious anti-Goldwater TV commercial from 1964 which, according to Joe Manfre on the *Simpson Archive* website,

featured a little girl in a field counting petals as she pulled them from a daisy. As the camera zoomed in on the girl, her counting mixed with a voice on a speaker giving a countdown to liftoff, then the scene showed a nuclear explosion. Finally, there was a message to the tune of "Whom do you trust with this power?" The point of the commercial was that Goldwater was a merciless hawk who couldn't be trusted with his finger on the button, and that Johnson would consider all the little girls in the country before deciding to engage in a nuclear attack. Johnson, of course, won re-election.

Tony Hill adds, "The 'Daisy Girl' ad only ran once, but the fury it touched off resulted in much of the campaign advertising regulation that existed in the U.S. for twenty years thereafter."

57. In "Burns's Heir," he admits to having sunk a Greenpeace ship, as in the infamous Rainbow Warrior sinking in New Zealand by the French secret service in the early 1980's.

58. Yet Burns is also victim of the nuclear industry he runs. In the *X-Files* spoof episode, "The Springfield Files," an irradiated, luminescent Burns admits, "A lifetime of working at a nuclear power plant has given me a healthy green glow—and left me as impotent as a Nevada boxing commissioner."

59. Hilgartner, *Nukespeak,* 139.

60. In a related episode, "Homer Goes to College," Burns is surprised by another snap NRC inspection, caustically remarking to the inspectors, "The watchdog of public safety. Is there any lower form of life?"

Local Satire with a Global Reach: Ethnic Stereotyping and Cross-Cultural Conflicts in *The Simpsons*

DUNCAN STUART BEARD

One of the principal ways in which *The Simpsons* may be considered "oppositional" is through its ironic use of pre-existing mass media stereotypes precisely in order to destabilize them. For example, at the end of "Bart Gets Famous," when Lisa critiques the trite, two-dimensional characterization of people by hackneyed catchphrases, the major *Simpsons* characters respond with their own trademark expressions: Homer yelps "D'oh!," Bart exclaims "Ay caramba," Marge groans in her distinctive fashion, Maggie sucks on her pacifier, Mr. Burns rubs his hands and murmurs "Excellent," Barney belches, and so on. Lisa herself concludes the episode by resorting to her ironically conventional protest: "I'm going to my room." Through the repetition of such instantly recognizable media voices as Troy McClure's television-host speak: "Hi. I'm actor Troy McClure. You might remember me from such films as . . ." and Dr. Nick Riviera's infomercial catch-cry: "Hi, everybody!" (responded to automatically and in unison by the other characters with the reply dictated by infomercial conventions: "Hi, Dr. Nick!"), a reflexive form of postmodern discourse is presented, television referring to the conventions and archetypes of its own medium.

In such a manner, the show presents multiple levels of pastiche-driven self-reflexivity. Often this is purely for comedic purposes. On Bart and Lisa's visit to the *Itchy and Scratchy* "cartoon factory," for example, the producer of the cartoon explains that, rather than going to the trouble of having to draw a new background for each separate cartoon, often the same background is used over and over to reduce costs. This explanation occurs at the same time as the three walk through the blatantly repeated background of a corridor and a woman mopping the floor appearing in exactly the same pose more than five or six times ("The Front"). This mise-en-abyme of multiple levels of self-referentiality often also contains a satiric impulse. A later presentation in another episode of the cartoon production process of a group of sweating, overworked Korean laborers draped over drawing boards, who are prodded by soldiers with bayonets, in what could only be described as a "cartoon work-camp," can be interpreted as referring to the dubious ethical property of the modes of production of American cartoon shows, including *The Simpsons* itself, which is partially animated at Rough Draft Studios in Korea ("Itchy & Scratchy: The Movie").

While *The Simpsons*'s use of pastiche and self-reflexivity threatens to abolish almost completely any textual norm by which its intentions might be interpreted, this self-reflexive impetus is driven by the parodic use of character stereotypes. The members of the Simpson family themselves conform to a particular popular conception of "the American family": Homer is a willfully ignorant, lazy, beer-swilling blue-collar worker, in love with junk food and trashy television; Marge is a formalized representation of the suffocatingly over-anxious, nagging wife; Lisa is the very vision of the precocious and unpopular nerd driven by a desire for scholastic success; Bart is a prototypical "problem child," the wise-talking prankster who longs for the glamour of crime; and Maggie, being a baby, does little but suck on a pacifier. That these conventions are recognizable to an American audience as consciously intended stereotypes constitutes their very possibility to function as satirical tools. Through continued narrative focus, many characters' clichéd characteristics serve not only as a means to critique elements of American society that are seen to have become stereotypical, but also as a method of undermining the perceived validity of the bland, two-dimensional views of American national identity presented by the mainstream mass media. The juxtaposition of the overly polite Ned Flanders with the crass abrasiveness of Homer Simpson, for example, functions to provide a less than subtle critique of both the inconsiderate self-centeredness of Homer and the deceptively intolerant Christian fundamentalism represented by Ned Flanders. The character-driven conflicts that are represented as existing between such symbolically imbued figures as Homer Simpson and Ned Flanders exemplify the show's satiric interrogation of competing definitions of

American national identity. The eccentric cast of characters who constitute *The Simpsons*'s heterogeneous vision of the American public provides
a solid foundation upon which to base its critique of numerous elements
of American life. In regard to the massive success of the show in foreign
markets, however, this factor has also created interpretative problems for
international audiences, particularly concerning the show's satiric intent.

Viewed from almost any perspective, the contemporary world appears
to be shrinking rapidly. With the global spread of electronic communications, epitomized by, but not restricted to, the relatively egalitarian
medium of television, some commentators suggest that we are in the grip
of a series of cultural changes whose impact is as radical as that of the
industrial revolution or even the Renaissance. What happens to questions
of national cultural identity in the midst of the global spread of television
shows such as *The Simpsons*? While traditional realist approaches to
national identity have tended to view nation-states as relatively unitary
actors, we now realize that there is no one notion of cultural "identity"
but instead a fluid scene of plurality and heterogeneity produced by the
act of boundary-making, itself a practice that divides the idea of Self from
the idea of the Other ("us" as against "them"). In expressing ideas of Self
and Other, what is articulated is a set of relations about locating a sense of
self and a sense of belonging, a sense of place, predicated on maintaining
the distinction between those who are included (us) and those who are
excluded (them).

The identity thus invoked forms the locus for further boundary-making. Which came first historically is less important than the recognition
that these processes occur and that they appear to be based on complex
forms of conflict or friction. What becomes mapped as boundaries are
those areas where relations between identities come into conflict, collision,
or collusion with other actors at a number of levels. What, then, are we
left with when these boundaries are penetrated and traversed by the mass
media? While complex networks of communication have existed from the
Marathon runners of Pheidippides to Chappe's "optical telegraph" sema-
phore tower network in France, the unprecedented geographical span of
contemporary mass media has served to disperse these questions of cultural identity across a global arena. In doing so, the globalized mass media
have generated a new set of processes which question the notion of distinct cultural identities. Keeping in mind that with eighty percent of the
world's population having never made a telephone call and more than half

the world's population living more than one hundred miles from the nearest telephone line, then clearly the world in not yet living with a truly global information super-highway, and if English, as the ruling language of the mass media, serves to erect rather than remove barriers to access by those countries for whom English is not their main language, it behooves us to be somewhat careful in explicating the impact of global mass media upon notions of cultural identity. This said, the flow of entertainment across borders does have some important implications. For example, there are the potential dangers of cultural standardization and of the loss of linguistic diversity. These particular questions have been with us, however, since people began trading and communicating across cultural borders. Our purpose here is to examine what the reception of satire across national boundaries can tell us about the process of identity-formation and the function of irony and parody in a global media system.

I

When asked why *The Simpsons* is so valorized by its Australian audience, members of its Australian cult-following invariably provide answers somewhat akin to: "It takes the piss out of [i.e., satirizes] Americans." The satiric content of the program, read by an Australian audience as directed against the perceived deficiencies and eccentric failings of the American populace, is lapped up by a nation who regularly express a broad sense of antipathy towards the "Americanization of Australia," a denigrating phrase commonly heard in academic, cultural, and political discourses. This response also represents the Australian categorization of Americans as insipid egotists who lack a basic understanding of any form of subtlety, such as ironic content. As an Australian fan of *The Simpsons* might suggest, "It takes the piss out of Americans. *And they don't get it.*" It is this issue that provides the most noticeable point of coherence for the diverse Australian audiences of *The Simpsons*.

It is an unavoidable fact that such a popular prime-time television show as *The Simpsons* inevitably obtains a heterogeneous audience whose "readings" of the show differ enormously. During my undergraduate years at the Australian National University in Canberra, for example, I was witness to a weekly congregation of *Simpsons* fans from predominantly "educated" backgrounds. On "*Simpsons* Night," as it was fondly known, the

University bar would fill with all manner of undergraduates, postgraduates, and professors, all eager to view the latest installment of the show with a keen eye for subtle cultural, historical, and political references. Film students, in particular, would devote zealous attention to the masterful filmic allusions presented each week, notably the show's almost obsessive references to the films of Stanley Kubrick. *The Shining, A Clockwork Orange, Dr. Strangelove, 2001: A Space Odyssey, Full Metal Jacket,* and *Spartacus* have all been targets of *The Simpsons*'s parodic gaze. It was almost as if the admittance of these films into the show's pantheon of intertextual allusions finally marked their entry into the deepest subconscious levels of the global pop cultural mind. At the same time, outside the confines of the University, thousands upon thousands of television sets were tuned to the same channel. Many were scrutinized by a similar sort of audience for similar reasons, but many were also watched by children enraptured with the sheer visceral pleasure of following the foibles of animated characters or attended to by viewers who enjoyed the relaxing entertainment provided by yet another goofy sitcom about a dumb dad and his rascally kids.

This broad range of audiences that *The Simpsons* boasts problematizes any attempt at a comprehensive analysis of the efficacy of its satirical elements. For while the satiric intent of the show is, at times, less than subtle, its overall open-endedness often leaves ample space for diverse viewer interpretations. As an example of the evasion of such "wrap-up" narrative devices, the expeditious denouements unerringly provided by most conventional family based sitcoms are wryly skewered by Homer's offhand reply to the question of the "moral" of one particular episode: "There is no moral, it's just a bunch of stuff that happened" ("Blood Feud"). Through a repeated parodic refusal to conform to the sort of neat synthesis of issues provided nightly by most mainstream television shows, the ultimate significance of the "bunch of stuff" that the show presents is left open-ended.

This issue of how diverse readings of the show affect the potential efficacy of its satirical element not only encompasses such factors as the relevant differences in age, gender, education, and class among viewers of *The Simpsons* but also relates to culturally divergent interpretations of the show. This is the focal point of this essay: What happens to the readings of such a satirical show when its exposure is almost global? *The Simpsons* is broadcast to a vast array of countries, from Russia and Germany to Peru and Italy. Can the "critical edge" of the show be properly translated or "travel" in any comprehensible form to all of these diverse and divergent cultures? The reception of *The Simpsons* in Australia presents a particularly telling case. For while recognizing the inescapable sociocultural, political, and historical distinctions that do exist between the two nation-states, no one would argue that the wealthy, western nation of Australia is *radically* distinct in worldview and ethical outlook from its diplomatic, economic, and military ally, the United States of America. If the reception of *The Simpsons* in Australia can be said to present a case of cross-cultural conflict, then surely this demonstrates the extent to which such discord must be present in other nations' conceptions of the show.

Whereas an Australian audience enjoys the parodic function of stereotyping in *The Simpsons* through familiarity with the conventions of American television, this same Australian audience was greatly dismayed by the parodic content of the heavily advertised and repackaged "*The Simpsons* Down-Under" special, also known as "Bart vs. Australia." In this episode, the Simpson family, prompted by an American diplomat (the Under-secretary for International Protocol: Brat and Punk Division), travels to Australia in order for Bart to apologize to the Australian people for making a mockery of their justice system. Bart had made a collect call to Australia in order to ascertain whether the toilets in the southern hemisphere drained clockwise or counter-clockwise, a point of contention with his sister. When the recipient of his phone call, a young boy called Tobias, was asked by Bart to check the toilet in his neighbor's bathroom, his journey from one large rural property to the next (from "Squatter's Crog" to "the Koolamuggerys' place") resulted in a massive phone bill. Tobias's father, Bruno Drundridge, made a complaint that eventually traveled to the Prime Minister of Australia, who attempted to obtain a formal apology for Bart's heinous deed.

The screening of this particular episode created a media furor in Australia. Magazines and newspapers devoted an unprecedented amount of criticism to the episode, which was seen to constitute an attack on Australian national identity. Due to the prominence of such parodic scenes as a building signboard that reads: "Cultural Centre: Cart Your Arse On In," *The Simpsons* became viewed less as a paradigm of oppositional culture than as "the opposition." The unsatisfactory Australian accents presented in the show were attacked as being New Zealand accents (this perhaps demonstrating Australia's parochial disdain for its New Zealand neighbors, more often than not characterized as ignorant sheep-fetishists). That the Australian government was shown to be a mock colonial-British affair complete with black robes and wigs, that the Prime Minister was represented swilling beer while floating in a rubber ring, and that a litany of boomerangs, didgeridoos, koalas, and kangaroos was seen as constituting an exhaustive vision of Australian life, was all taken to be deeply insulting. The episode was, in fact, seen as perpetuating the sort of irrelevant stereotypical view of Australia that followed in the wake of the American success of the blockbuster movie *Crocodile Dundee* (itself alluded to in the episode).

However, it was possibly the treatment of the subject of corporal punishment in the episode that was most criticized by Australian *Simpsons* fans. In the episode, Bart is condemned to undergo "the boot" as a form of retribution for his misdeeds. Portrayed as an Australian national tradition of a "kick up the bum," the show's presentation of the fictional ritual of "the boot" becomes embroiled in a condemnation of corporal punishment. At the same time, Australian audiences saw this plot development as implying that America is humanely superior to its backward Australian cousins. It was eventually discovered that the episode was actually part of a previously aired season of *The Simpsons,* and that the Australian network involved had deliberately held back its screening, fearing the possibility of lost ratings due to the controversial representation of Australia in the episode.

Alternative interpretations of this episode differ vastly from the critical reception it was immediately granted in this Australian context. Far from implying that America is ethically superior to Australia in the area of corporal punishment, the reference to "the boot" can be seen as referring to the topical debate that was raging in America at that time over the prospect of an American teenager, Michael Fay, about to receive a public caning in Singapore for vandalizing automobiles. The Australian flag presented in the episode contains a veiled reference to Singapore: Singapore's flag has five stars above a moon, in white on a red field, with a white field underneath the red; the Australian flag shown in the episode (which is not Australia's actual flag) also had five stars above a moon, directing the attentive and culturally connected viewer towards the Michael Fay incident. The event provoked much heated discussion over whether the government of the United States should intervene and register its opposition to such "brutal" and "barbaric" actions, or whether the United States itself should re-instate corporal punishment, support for these arguments coming, broadly speaking, from left- and right-wing commentators, respectively.

As a result, Homer's speech, made against an unruly Australian mob howling for violent vengeance against Bart, may thus be seen either as foregrounding American racist provincialism and the long tradition of American brutality or as ironically revealing America as having little or no control over its children:

> When will you Australians learn? In America we stopped using corporal punishment, and things have never been better! The streets are safe. Old people strut confidently through the darkest alleys. And the weak and nerdy are admired for their computer-programming abilities. So, like us, let your children run wild and free, because, as the old saying goes, "Let your children run wild and free."

Another example of significantly divergent readings of the episode contrasts interpreting "Bart vs. Australia" as mocking Australia versus seeing the episode as a parody of America's condescending and short-lived fascination with Australia. This latter reading seems overtly reflected in the comments of the American diplomat, who explains the tentative state of American-Australian diplomatic relations to the Simpson family: "As I'm sure you remember, in the late 1980s the U.S. experienced a short-lived infatuation with Australian culture. For some bizarre reason, the Aussies thought this would be a permanent thing. Of course, it wasn't." As he speaks, a slide projector shows pictures of an abandoned cinema with the title, "Yahoo Serious Film Festival," above the doors. Numerous allusions to Australian films, such as Bart's line about a dingo eating your baby (referring to the disappearance/dingo-murder of baby Azaria Chamberlain portrayed in the movie *Evil Angels* [U.S. title *A Cry in the Dark*]), the *Crocodile Dundee* character who alludes to the infamous line "That's not a knife," and the *Mad Max* car chase that occurs when Australian characters pursue the Simpsons, may thus be interpreted as being less motivated by cultural arrogance than by an interrogation of cultural arrogance.

The distinction between the two sorts of readings of the episode outlined above articulates the estrangement between interpretations of the episode which focus upon American content, in which case the Australian setting seems to function mostly as a convenient backdrop from which to elicit satirical situations, and interpretations which focus upon the show's representation of Australia itself. This interpretative divide is symptomatic of the divergent cultural positions of its audiences. While American viewers interpret the show through their worldview, Australians view it through their own distinct set of cultural understandings.

An Australian audience's recognition of the episode's satirical allusions to the Michael Fay affair, for example, may have fed into such heated topical debates as the question, put to the Australian public by a popular and controversial book published just prior to the screening of the episode, *Is Australia an Asian Country?*[1] The association made between Australia and Singapore in the show's presentation of an "Asian" event in an Australian context, whether consciously intended by its American producers or not, highlights the ambiguity of Australia's geographic and cultural position in relation to its "Asian" neighbors. Australia is a fundamentally multicultural society, its population comprising a colorful patchwork of cultures and ethnic backgrounds, including a high percentage of "Asians." The episode's stereotypical presentation of the Australian populace as a post-colonial nation of white Anglo-Saxon Protestants is thus highly problematic. One notable element of the episode was the inclusion of aboriginal culture, albeit in the rather clichéd form of didgeridoos and boomerangs, at the same time as there was a total absence of aboriginal characters. The didgeridoo was played by Lisa Simpson, a white American, and a crowd of white Australians threw the boomerang at the Simpson family.

The problematic definition of all Australians as WASPs was particularly evident when the Australian parliament was presented as a colonial imitation of the British system of government, with politicians wearing black robes and wigs. The episode further foregrounds Australia's colonial background by the presentation of a group of Australians creeping towards Marge Simpson, intending to steal her handbag, as she recounts Australia's convict past to Lisa, and also through a statue that depicts Australia's first Prime Minister as an English convict, whereas Australia's first Prime Minister was actually named in 1901 after the country had been formed from independent colonies in much the same way as the United States, itself a similarly multicultural society with a colonial past. Consciously or otherwise, the broad base of Australian *Simpsons* fans viewed the "Bart vs. Australia" episode with an eye to its relevance to contemporary Australian identity politics, to the questions posed by Australia's confused and confusing place in a changing world, and to the face that Australia should wear in the global arena, and they found it resoundingly unsatisfactory. Yet this line of thinking might lead one to ask: Why should

The Simpsons be burdened with the responsibility of defining Australia's place in the world? Put simply, it shouldn't. Yet culturally located audiences always seem to have their own uses for things, and the show's representation of Australia was still seen as promulgating irrelevant and outdated myths about the homogeneity of Australian cultural identity.

The inherent problems of exclusion that are involved in the episode's definition of the Australian population further highlight concerns over the show's definition of what being a "foreigner" or "Other" means as opposed to being an "American." However much the parodic use of mass-media stereotypes in *The Simpsons* may function in destabilizing these conventions, the show's presentation of "Others" may also be seen as perpetuating rather than alleviating stereotypical visions of foreign national identities. While the term "Other" obviously raises issues that are not exclusively concerned with the show's presentation of "foreign" characters (a gamut of recognizably American "Others," such as "New Americans," Native Americans, African Americans, Latino Americans, and more have all been witnessed by the show in various forms), a focus on the presentation of ethnic identities in *The Simpsons* is particularly useful in that the broader issues of cultural stereotyping thus raised are transferable (though not exhaustively) to other areas of perceived alterity.

II

Perhaps the most complex presentation of an American "Other"/"foreigner" on *The Simpsons* occurs in the figure of the Indian immigrant owner of Kwik-E-Mart, Apu. At times, Apu is presented as being almost fully "American" through his deracination and incorporation into mainstream consumer culture. In his position as a convenience store owner, for example, he is shown as being involved in such stereotypical activities as shameless profiteering, placing out-of-date food items on sale, being shot by armed robbers on numerous occasions, and always having a loaded gun under the counter. At other times, Apu's background is foregrounded as being distinctly "Other" through *The Simpsons*'s somewhat less-than-critical adherence to stereotypical American mass-media representations of Indians. Such stereotypes are often deployed despite their contradictory nature: Apu is sometimes shown wearing a Sikh turban, for example, despite being more consistently presented as a Hindu, as when telling Lisa about his vegetarianism or invoking Hindu deities. The elephant-headed god Ganeesha, in particular, is referred to in numerous episodes. In "Homer the Heretic," Homer offers Apu's statue of Ganeesha a peanut. In a later episode, Homer actually dresses up as Ganeesha in order to prevent Apu's (equally stereotypical) arranged marriage, the stereotypical characteristics of the arranged marriage also being played out in this episode ("The Two Mrs. Nahasapeemapetilons"). Just as the contrived absurdity of Apu's full name, Apu Nahasapeemapetilon, is relied upon for simple amusement, the "foreign-ness" of Apu's cultural traditions serves as a perpetual object of mockery. However, it is perhaps in his position as a hybrid "American-Other" that the character of Apu eventually comes to rest, despite the representational tensions that continually pull his character towards one pole or the other in exploring questions of American identity in a multicultural society.

This notion of American hybridity is admirably presented by the episode entitled "Much Apu About Nothing," in which the inhabits of Springfield, including Marge and Homer, staunchly support "Proposition 24," a proposal to deport all illegal immigrants from Springfield, until, that is, they learn that it would adversely affect Apu. Apu buys fraudulent identification documents from Fat Tony in order to remain in the country he has come to love, parodically acting the part of a stereotypical American in order to deflect the detection of this ruse, wearing a cowboy hat and baseball jersey while asking Homer, "What do you say we take a relaxed attitude towards work and watch the baseball game? The nye [New York] Mets are my favorite squadron." Apu's response to the threat of deportation thus satirizes the perceived exclusivity of the stereotypical definition of the "ordinary American." The episode also directs satirical attention to American xenophobia, which is shown to arise from ignorance. A mob supporting Proposition 24 carries placards that become progressively more absurd: "Yes on 24"; "Buy American"; "United States for United Statesians"; "The only good Foreigner is Rod Stewart"; and "Get Eurass Back To Eurasia." At one point in the show, the young hooligan Nelson tells a German boy, "Go back to Germania!" The show also presents a biting spoof of the classic Army Recruitment Poster: "I Want You . . . Out!"

The Proposition 24 controversy mirrored the real-life California Proposition 187, one of the most divisive issues on the 1994 California ballot. The proposition essentially sought to deny government services such as education, welfare, and medical aid to people who had entered the country illegally. Supporters of the law said that it would stop foreigners (who were not even supposed to be in the country in the first place) from draining public funds. Opponents argued that Proposition 187 unfairly punished people who were trying to make a better life in America. Since most immigrants (both legal and otherwise) in California were of Hispanic or Latino descent, some Proposition 187 opponents saw the law as racially motivated. Proposition 187 passed at the polls and should have taken effect January 1st of 1995 but was eventually overturned by the courts as unconstitutional. It was argued that the law gave the police the power to deport anyone who was not either a citizen or a legal immigrant (ironically, a power already allowed under U.S. federal immigration law). Notably absent from the proposition were any sanctions against employers that hire illegal aliens. Right-wing talk-show host Rush Limbaugh argued that aliens were not getting jobs as busboys, maids, and migrant farm workers, but were risking everything so they could go on welfare, a belief satirized by *The Simpsons* in Apu's question, "Which way to the welfare office?" Then-Governor Pete Wilson attached himself to the proposition and began hyping it, turning an issue with which few people were concerned into the centerpiece of his re-election campaign. In so doing, he was accused of willfully ignoring more important issues, such as the fact that California had remained in a recession from which the rest of the country was recovering, a situation having notable similarities to *The Simpsons*'s Mayor Quimby diverting attention from "bear tax" complaints to illegal immigrants. As Election Day approached, Proposition 187 became "politically incorrect" (and few people would publicly admit to supporting it). On Election Day, however, the proposition passed with a huge majority, an outcome alluded to by the people of Springfield chanting their opposition to Proposition 24 while a disturbing 95 percent of them eventually vote "yes."

Apu eventually avoids deportation by taking a citizenship test. In so doing, he reveals a complexity of understanding concerning the history of the United States unmatched by any of the "American" characters on the show, particularly Homer, who teaches Apu that the 13 stripes on the American flag are for "good luck." After Apu passes the citizenship test, the cast of characters appears happy with the positive resolution of the issue. However, while references are made to the diverse ethnic backgrounds of a whole gamut of *Simpsons* characters, a dark undertone is provided by a shot of the Scottish grounds keeper Willy bitterly complaining whilst being shipped away from America. The episode ends with a discussion among Lisa, Homer, and Apu that not only states directly the fact that America is a multicultural society but also raises issues pertaining to the problematic ambiguities inherent in popular definitions of "American" and "Indian":

> LISA: You know, in a way, all Americans are immigrants. Except, of course, Native Americans.
>
> HOMER: Yeah, Native Americans like us.
>
> LISA: No, I mean American Indians.
>
> APU: Like me.

From these few, short lines there are a startling number of inferences that can be made concerning the complexities of the multicultural composition of the American republic. Yet, however admirably such notions of the heterogeneity of America are addressed, the issue of the representation of overtly foreign national identities is still relegated to the sidelines and is largely ignored in favor of internal inquiry. While the "Much Apu About Nothing" episode interrogates the cultural plurality of America, asserting its status as a multicultural nation, America is still one nation amongst many others that regularly watch *The Simpsons*. Are we to conclude then that, at least with regard to the global presentations of the mass media, cultural plurality is, as the end of the episode seems to allude, a source of confusion, if not a complete contradiction to the notion of a determinate definition of identity?

The key issue with regard to the representations of foreign national identities on *The Simpsons* is the ambiguity and ambivalence that exists concerning the show's endorsement or parody of stereotypes. A viewer-oriented analysis of this issue, problematized by the show's diverse audiences and its own open-endedness, would have to focus on the possibility of identifying some sort of essential difference between parody and uncritical presentation. Complicating matters further is the fact that these two terms, at least from the position of a reader-based theory, are not mutually exclusive. The noted differences of interpretations that arise from culturally distinct readings of "Bart vs. Australia" testify to this fact, with many Australians viewing the episode as uncritically endorsing stereotypical presentations of Australia, while an alternative "inter-American" reading of the show seeing a parodic use of these stereotypes precisely for the purpose of critiquing American social practices, including America's culturally bound outlook.

Within *The Simpsons,* America is often satirically presented as an insular nation that knows little or nothing about what lies beyond its own shores. At the beginning of the "Bart vs. Australia" episode, for example, Lisa actually has to show Bart on a globe that there is a southern hemisphere beyond the shores of America. Although such instances function as focal points of satiric irony, the broader symptom of this critique of American insularity often leads to the relegation of foreign nations to the status of a backdrop for major characters to dramatically enact such satirical circumstances. When Homer and Apu travel to India in order to get Apu's job back, for example, they visit "the world's first convenience store," which is (rather inconveniently) located on the top of a mountain, run by a parodic "guru" whom Apu refers to as "The benevolent and enlightened president and C.E.O. of Kwik-E-Mart—and in Ohio, Stop-O-Mart" ("Homer and Apu"). Despite a few allusions to certain clichéd aspects of Indian culture, this incident serves primarily as an extended parody of the peculiarities of the American convenience store. As the two enter the store, for example, a bell dings noticeably over the sounds of Muzak, while behind them is a sign announcing: "The Master Knows All (except combination to safe)." Here the show presents its own instance of the global culture of consumer capitalism, transplanted intact and indistinguishably unaltered from the suburbs of America to a mountain top in some indefinable region of the post-partitioned Commonwealth nation of India, purely for the purpose of parodically criticizing the banality of quick-stop stores.

While America's insularity is often parodied through the use of ethnic stereotypes and cultural caricatures, in other words, anything "foreign" is thus relegated to the status of a stereotype or caricature in order for this parody to function. The critical gaze is turned outwards only in order that it may provide a clearer focus upon the familiar, an impasse effectively reinforcing the notion of the centrality of America and emphasizing the marginality of "Others." To put it another way, satire arises from and is directed towards what might be called a "home culture." While the notion of a home culture does involve such issues as foreign relations and the recognition of distinct international communities, this does not bestow upon it the mantle of "global culture," for it is still concerned with the issue of national identity, with addressing questions about the borders that distinguish "us" from "them." Perhaps this is why the show's representations of foreign characters, however humorous, seem so often to conjure up the specter of the security of national boundaries: an Albanian character spies on the United States, threatening the national defense capabilities of the nation at the same time as Bart is victimized by a duo of malevolent Frenchmen ("The Crepes of Wrath"); the obsessive work practices of the Japanese threaten the health of the inhabitants of Springfield when a batch of imported juicers is infected with the "Osaka flu" ("Marge in Chains"); and, at the end of "Bart vs. Australia," a renegade Koala, hanging on to the legs of a helicopter as the Simpson family flees the wrath of a bloodthirsty crowd of Australians, threatens the North American continent with ecological disaster.

While certain episodes, such as "Much Apu About Nothing," do provide incisive interrogations of the issues surrounding the representations of race and cultural difference, the presentations of Others that are made in passing seem to utilize cultural stereotypes much less critically. One need only witness other representations of foreigners on the show to realize that many of these stereotypes are adhered to with an almost monotonous regularity: the English are characterized as socially rigid "toffs" wearing bowler hats and tuxedos ("Lisa's Wedding"); the Italians as smooth-talking mobsters ("Bart the Murderer"); the Germans as hard-working, ruthlessly efficient corporate employers ("Burns Verkaufen der Kraftwerk"); the Albanians as obsessive political radicals, unilaterally involved in international espionage ("The Crepes of Wrath"), and so on. The degree to which these representations are problematized by elements of ambiguity and/or ambivalence in the show's satirical impulse is uncertain.

III

A great deal has been written about the instability of postmodern satire. Criticisms lodged against it usually address the problem of indeterminacy arising from the lack of a stable ground. Because postmodern satire does not conform to earlier definitions of satire, which maintain that satirical criticism must be based upon an implicit or explicit set of values, the relative and reflexive ground of postmodern satire rarely finds a positive voice of rejuvenation to provide alternative visions for situations that have been satirically criticized as unfavorable. Yet this is precisely how the satirical elements of *The Simpsons* operate, undermining media-generated stereotypes through an interrogatory utilization of these same stereotypes with subversively ironic intent. It is an act of satiric "defamiliarization" that is similar, but by no means identical, to that practiced by the literary critic Roland Barthes. Briefly stated, "defamiliarization" is the practice of consciously problematizing that which has come to be seen as "natural" or "normal" and hence unworthy of critical attention. Thus, the "problem" of postmodern satire: the radical indeterminacy and lack of textual stability actually form the very basis for the operation of satire within *The Simpsons*. It is precisely these qualities of probing instability and indeterminacy that permit the show to problematize the all-too-familiar stereotypes presented by the mass media, unveiling and laying open for question both their underlying ideological bases and their extended social effects.

The dilemma that we are faced with, then, seems less to revolve around the issue of the perceived instability of postmodern satire than it does the somewhat broader issue of the global exportation of texts whose satiric intent is locally directed. All satire comes from a home culture, it is impossible not to. The "problem" of postmodern satire results less from a quality unique to postmodern satire itself than the problem that arises when any form of satire is disseminated across the "postmodern" (read: culturally divergent) world by global systems of mass media. As John Gray points out in his work *False Dawn: The Delusions of Global Capitalism,* the spread of global communication does not produce anything resembling convergence among cultures. The American worldview, which is disseminated by the predominance of American forms of television on the global airwaves, is an ephemeral artifact of America's present lead in communications technologies, not a signpost on the road to global civilization. As Gray argues:

> By enabling practitioners of different cultures who are geographically scattered to interact through new communications media, globalization acts to express and to deepen cultural differences. The South Asian populations that are scattered across European countries reinforce their cultural ties when they watch satellite television channels that broadcast in their languages and embody their history and values. The Kurds exiled in European countries preserve their common culture through a Kurdish television channel. The universal proliferation of similar images is a surface effect of a global communications media. They break up common

cultures and replace them with traces and fragments. Yet modern communications media can also—as in Japan, Singapore, Malaysia and China—enable cultures to assert their identity and differences from western late modernity and from each other.[2]

The recurrent problem of the indeterminacy of satiric irony ultimately hinges on the particularities of audience reception. Just as irony is only effective if it can be recognized as such, defamiliarization is only effective if its target is recognizably familiar. Satire operates within specific cultural, political, and historical contexts and depends upon an understanding of these contexts in order to operate effectively. No text can be considered to be "essentially" satirical. For once the particular extra-textual elements that imbue a text with its particular meaning are removed, little potential for satire remains. Regardless of how *The Simpsons* is received in the United States (and it should be noted that this in itself is by no means a simple issue), "culture" in itself should not be seen as denoting homogeneity but rather a Wittgensteinian "family resemblance." An unavoidable transmutation of meaning occurs when the show is viewed by an audience whose cultural understanding is distinct from that of its originally intended audience. As has been stated, many Australian fans receive the show as a satire of the United States in general, rather than focusing upon very particular American social practices. This situation might be somewhat analogous to the variety of ways in which distinct groups of American viewers interpret the show. One can only imagine the differences in interpretation that might result from French, Finnish, German, Danish, Portuguese, Italian, and Spanish-speaking audiences.

What the satirical elements of *The Simpsons* are ultimately involved in is an analysis of American sociocultural practices and their relation to American notions of American identity. It is when viewed in this manner that its satire is at its most effective. Its interrogation of American identity assumes what is, for American audiences, an intuitive understanding of unspoken (and unspeakable) issues, primarily concerning what it means to be American. While overseas audiences may pay particular attention to the show's representations of foreigners, more often than not the primary function of these representations is as a background upon which to project and play out issues concerning America. *The Simpsons* is, despite widespread conjecture concerning the globalization of postmodern culture, an American television show.

IV

Here we seem to have been led to an impasse, a problematic puzzle centered on the possibility of teasing out the ramifications of the "globalization" of culture upon the localization of satire. To begin to address this problem, it must be recognized that *The Simpsons* should be considered relatively immune from hysterical charges of "cultural imperialism." However you interpret it, the conscious intentions of the show have never been to aid in the tyrannical spread of "American values" (if such a thing were indeed possible, for "American values" is a hazy notion in itself, heterogeneous and contested rather than homogeneous and consensual) but rather to critique and interrogate ideas of American national identity. This critique, in turn, leads us to recognize the impossibility of a truly inclusive and homogenous "global culture." Rather, with the spread of the heterogeneous voices of a globally encompassing mass media, what we now have is a manifold range of global cultures. What happens when the local context of a show such as *The Simpsons* does not travel well, when culturally divergent audiences recognize sources of conflict in the presentations of a particular show, is that the efficacy of the satiric mode threatens to degrade if not to disappear altogether. As an Australian viewer of *The Simpsons* might comment, "It takes the piss out of Americans. And *we* don't always get it." At times, this divergence in interpretations might lead to cross-cultural conflicts that are simply incommensurable, each party arguing from a different cultural foundation and in a differing symbolic language, like an Australian and an American arguing over whether a particular object is a "tap" or a "faucet," or whether that opening at the back of the car is a "trunk" or a "boot." What *The Simpsons* presents is not a form of global culture but of local culture with a global reach.

The extent to which satire that arises from and is directed towards a home culture can be discerned as satiric by global audiences, those innumerable peoples in their own home cultures, will always be a point of contention. Where *The Simpsons,* in particular, works best is in directing its satiric energies against the mass media that is so often seen as threatening us with an increasingly homogenized cultural experience. It is when *The Simpsons* satirizes the global presentations of the mass media that it is the most effective. For the wider the reach of the mass media, the more likely we are to recognize its subversive satiric shadow in the antics of a handful of animated characters, the more likely we are to recognize the voice of the mass media in the lilting tones of Kent Brockman, and the more likely we are to question our own particular cultural identities in the era of globalization. The more the mass media bring us together, the more we may learn to respect our own diversity.

Like it or not, we are all living in a post-humanist society. The former certainties of a bipolar political world have been overtaken by the erosion of notions of the homogeneity of national and cultural identity. We live in a world of global mass media in which ideas of stable identity have been so interpenetrated and networked with diverse other forms of community, culture, and business that we are forced to question that which we once thought of as solid and unchangeable. The way we understand the world is shaped not only by our language and social structures but also by our exposure to global mass media. What we make of this world is a by-product of the processes by which we set about understanding it. In the end, there is nothing stable about all of this. Each time we try and pin it down, we have already begun to change it.

NOTES

1. Stephen FitzGerald, *Is Australia An Asian Country? Can Australia Survive In An East Asian Future?* (St Leonards, NSW: Allen & Unwin, 1997).

2. John Gray, *False Dawn: The Delusions of Global Capitalism* (New York: New Press, 1998).

Bart Simpson:
Prince of Irreverence

DOUGLAS RUSHKOFF

*T*he *Simpsons* are the closest thing in America to a national media literacy program. By pretending to be a kids' cartoon, the show gets away with murder—that is, the virtual murder of our most coercive media iconography and techniques. What began as entertaining interstitial material for an alternative network variety show has revealed itself, in the 21st Century, as nothing short of a media revolution.

The marginality of the show's origins may be the very reason *The Simpsons* works so well. The Simpson characters were born to provide *The Tracey Ullman Show* with a way of cutting to commercial breaks. Their very function as a form of media was to bridge the discontinuity inherent to broadcast television. They existed to pave over the breaks. Rather than dampening the effects of these gaps in the broadcast stream, however, they heightened them. They acknowledged the jagged edges and recombinant forms behind the glossy patina of American television, and by doing so, initiated its deconstruction.

Consider, for a moment, the way we thought of media before this cartoon family satirized us into consciousness. Media used to be a top-down affair. A few rich guys in suits sat in offices at the tops of tall buildings and decided which stories would be in the headlines or on the evening news and how they would be told.

As a result, we came to think of information as something fed to us from above. We counted on the editors of the *New York Times* to deliver "all the news that's fit to print," and Walter Cronkite to tell us "that's way it was." We had no reason not to trust the editorial decisions of the media managers upon whom we depended to present, accurately, what was going on in the world around us. In fact, most of us did not even realize such decisions were being made at all. The television became America's unquestioned window to the world, as *The Simpsons*'s opening sequence—which shows each family member rushing home to gather at the television set—plainly acknowledges.

But we call the stuff on television "programming" for a reason. Television programmers are not programming television sets or evening schedules; they are programming the viewers. Whether they are convincing us to buy a product, vote for a candidate, adopt an ideology, or simply confirm a moral platitude, the underlying reason for making television is to hold onto our attention and then sell us a bill of goods. Since the time of the Bible and Aristotle through today's over-determined three-act action movies, the best tool at the programmer's disposal has been the story. However, thanks to interactive technologies such as the remote control and cynical attitudes such as Bart Simpson's, the story just does not hold together anymore.

For the most part, television stories program their audiences by bringing them into a state of tension. The author creates a character we like and identify with and then puts that character in some sort of jeopardy. As the character moves up the incline plane towards crisis, we follow him vicariously, while taking on his anxiety as our own. Helplessly we follow him into danger, disease, or divorce, and just when we cannot take any more tension without bursting, our hero discovers a way out. He finds a moral, a product, an agenda, or a strategy—the one preferred by the screenwriter or program sponsor, of course—that rescues him from danger and his audience from the awful vicarious anxiety. Then, everyone lives happily ever after. This is what it means to "enter-tain"—literally "to hold within"—and it only works on a captive audience.

In the old days of television, when characters would get into danger, the viewer had little choice but to submit. To change the channel would have required getting up out of the La-Z-Boy chair, walking up to the television set, and turning the dial. 50 calories of human effort; too much effort for a man of Homer's generation, anyway.

The remote control has changed all that. With an expenditure of, perhaps, .0001 calories, the anxious viewer is liberated from tortuous imprisonment and free to watch another program. Although most well-behaved adult viewers will soldier on through a story, children raised with remotes in their hands have much less reverence for well-crafted story arcs and zap away without a moment's hesitation. Instead of watching one program, they skim through ten at a time. They do not "watch TV," they watch the television itself, guiding their own paths through the entirety of media rather than following the prescribed course of any one programmer. No matter how much we complain about our children's short attention spans or even their Attention Deficit Disorders, their ability to disconnect from programming has released them from the hypnotic spell of even the best television mesmerizers.

The Nintendo-style joystick further empowered children while compounding the programmer's dilemma. In the old days, the television image was unchangeable, gospel truth piped into the home from the top of some glass building. Today, children have the experience of manipulating the image on the screen. This televisual interactivity has fundamentally altered their perception of and reverence for the television image. Just as the remote control allows viewers to deconstruct the television image, the joystick has demystified the pixel itself. The newsreader is just another middle-aged man manipulating his joystick. Hierarchy and authority are diminished, and the programmers' weapons neutralized. Sure, they might sit back and watch a program now and again—but they do so voluntarily, and with full knowledge of their complicity. It is not an involuntary surrender.

A person who is doing rather than receiving is much less easily provoked into a state of tension. The people I call "screenagers," those raised with interactive devices in their media arsenals, are natives in a media-space where even the best television producers are immigrants. Like Bart Simpson, they speak the media language better than their parents do and they see through clumsy attempts to program them into submission. They never forget for a moment that they are watching media and they resent those who try to draw them in and sell them something. They will not be part of a "target market," at least not without a fight.

What kind of television, then, appeals to such an audience? Programs that celebrate the screenager's irreverence for the image while providing a new sort of narrative arc for the sponsor-wary audience. It is the ethos and behavior embodied by screenager role model and anti-hero Bart Simpson.

His name intended as an anagram for "brat," Bart embodies youth culture's ironic distance from media and its willingness to disassemble and resplice even the most sacred cultural and ideological constructs. From within the plastic safety of his incarnation as an animated character, Bart can do much more than simply watch and comment on media iconography. Once a media figure has entered his animated world, Bart can interact with it, satirize it, or even become it. Although *The Simpsons* began as a sideshow, these animated tidbits became more popular than the live-action portion of *The Tracy Ullman Show,* and Fox Television decided to give the Simpson family their own series. It is not coincidental that what began as a bridging device between a show and its commercials—a media paste—developed into a self-similar media pastiche.

The Simpsons's creator, comic-strip artist Matt Groening, has long understood how to mask his countercultural agenda: "I find you can get away with all sorts of unusual ideas if you present them with a smile on your face," he said in an early 1990's interview.[1] In fact, the show's mischievous ten-year-old protagonist is really just the screen presence of Groening's inner nature. For his self-portrait in a *Spin* magazine article, Groening simply drew a picture of Bart and then scribbled the likeness of his own glasses and beard over it. Bart functions as Matt Groening's "smile," and the child permits him—and the show's young, Harvard-educated writing staff—to get away with a hell of a lot. *The Simpsons* takes place in a town called Springfield, named after the fictional location of *Father Knows Best,* making it clear that the Simpson family is meant as a contemporary answer to the media reality presented to us in the fifties and sixties. *The Simpsons* is the American media family turned on its head, told from the point of view of not the smartest member of the family, but the most ironic. Audiences delight in watching Bart effortlessly outwit his parents, teachers, and local institutions. This show is so irreverent that it provoked an attack from the first president Bush, who pleaded for the American family to be more like the Waltons than the Simpsons. The show's writers quickly responded, letting Bart say during one episode, "Hey, man, we're just like the Waltons. Both families are praying for an end to the depression." The show shares many of the viral features common in other programs from the nineties. Murphy Brown's office dartboard, for example, was used as a meme slot; in each episode it had a different satirical note pinned to it. *The Simpsons*'s writers also create little slots for the most attentive viewers to glean extra memes.[2] The opening credits always begin with Bart writing a different message on his classroom bulletin board and one of at least twenty-one different saxophone solos from his sister, Lisa.[3] Every episode has at least one film reenactment, usually from Hitchcock or Kubrick, to satirize an aspect of the modern cultural experience. In a spoof of modern American child care, writers re-created a scene from *The Birds,* except here, Homer Simpson rescued his baby daughter from a daycare center by passing through a playground of menacingly perched babies.

These media references form the basis for the show's role as a media literacy primer. The joy of traditional television storytelling is simply getting to the ending. The reward is making it through to the character's escape from danger. While most episodes of *The Simpsons* incorporate a dramatic nod to such storytelling convention, the screenagers watching the program could not care less about whether Principal Skinner gets married or if Homer finds his donut. These story arcs are there for the adult viewers only. No, the pleasure of watching *The Simpsons* for its media-literate (read: younger) viewers is the joy of pattern recognition. The show provides a succession of "aha" moments—those moments when we recognize which other forms of media are being parodied. We are rewarded with self-congratulatory laughter whenever we make a connection between the scene we are watching and the movie, commercial, or program on which it is based.

In this sense, *The Simpsons* deconstructs and informs the media soup of which it is a part. Rather than drawing us into the hypnotic spell of the traditional storyteller, the program invites us to make active and conscious comparisons of its own scenes with those of other, less transparent, media forms. By doing so, the show's writers help us in our efforts to develop immunity to their coercive effects.

The show's supervisors through *The Simpsons*'s golden years of the mid-1990's, Mike Reiss and Al Jean, were both *Harvard Lampoon* veterans. When I met with them on the Fox lot, they told me how they delighted in animation's ability to serve as a platform for sophisticated social and media satire. "About two thirds of the writers have been Harvard graduates," explained Jean, "so it's one of the most literate shows in TV."

"We take subjects on the show," added Reiss, who was Jean's classmate, "that we can parody. Homer goes to college or onto a game show. We'll take Super Bowl Sunday, and then parody the Bud Bowl, and how merchants capitalize on the event." Having been raised on media themselves, the Diet Coke-drinking, baseball-jacketed pair gravitated toward parodying the media aspects of the subjects they pick. They did not comment on social issues as much as they did the media imagery around a particular social issue.

"These days television in general seems to be feeding on itself. Parodying itself," Jean told me. "Some of the most creative stuff we write comes from just having the Simpsons watch TV." Which they do often. Many episodes are still about what happens on the Simpsons' own television set, allowing the characters to feed off television, which itself is feeding off other television. In this self-reflexive circus, it is Bart who is least likely to be fooled by anything. His father, Homer, represents an earlier generation and can easily be manipulated by television commercials and publicity stunts such as "clear beer." "Homer certainly falls for every trick," admitted Reiss, "even believing the Publishers Clearing House mailing that he is a winner." When Homer acquires an illegal cable television hookup, he became so addicted to the tube that he almost dies ("Homer vs. Lisa and the 8th Commandment"). Lisa, the brilliant member of the family, maintains a faith in the social institutions of her world, works hard to get good grades in school, and even entered and won a *Reader's Digest* essay contest about patriotism.

"But Lisa feels completely alienated by the media around her," Jean warned me. "The writers empathize with her more than any other character. She has a more intellectual reaction to how disquieting her life has become. When Homer believes he may die from a heart attack, he tells the children, 'I have some terrible news.' Lisa answers, 'Oh, we can take anything. We're the MTV generation. We feel neither highs nor lows.' Homer asks what it's like, and she just goes 'Eh.' It was right out there."

Bart's reaction to his cultural alienation, on the other hand, is much more of a lesson in Gen X strategy. Bart is a ten-year-old media strategist— or at least an unconscious media manipulator—and his exploits reveal the complexity of the current pop media from the inside out. In one episode ("Radio Bart")—the show that earned Reiss and Jean their first Emmy nomination—Homer sees a commercial for a product he feels will make a great birthday gift for Bart: a microphone that can be used to broadcast to a special radio from many feet away (a parody of a toy called Mr. Microphone). At first, Bart is bored with the gift and plays with a labeler he also received instead. Bart has fun renaming things and leaving messages like "property of Bart Simpson" on every object in his home; one such label on a beer in the fridge convinces Homer that the can is off limits. Bart's joy, clearly, is media . . . and subversive disinformation.

Homer plays with the radio instead, trying to get Bart's interest, but the boy knows the toy does not really send messages into the mediaspace; it only broadcasts to one little radio. Bart finally takes interest in the toy when he realizes its subversive value. After playing several smaller-scale pranks, he accidentally drops the radio down a well and gets the idea for his master plan. Co-opting a media event out of real history, when a little girl struggled for life at the bottom of a well as rescuers worked to save her and the world listened via radio, Bart uses his toy radio to fool the world and launch his own media virus.[4]

He creates a little boy named Timmy O'Toole, who cries for help from the bottom of the well. When police and rescuers prove too fat to get into the well to rescue the boy, a tremendous media event develops. News teams set up camp around the well, much in the fashion they gather around any real-world media event such as the OJ Trial or Waco standoff. They conduct interviews with the unseen Timmy—an opportunity Bart exploits to make political progress against his mean school principal. In Timmy's voice he tells reporters the story of how he came to fall into the well: he is an orphan, new to the neighborhood, and was rejected for admission to the local school by the principal because his clothes were too shabby. The next day, front-page stories calling for the principal's dismissal appear. Eventually, the virus grows to the point where the real-world pop musician, Sting, and Krusty the Klown, a television personality from within the world of *The Simpsons,* record an aid song and video to raise money for the Timmy O'Toole cause called "We're Sending Our Love Down the Well." The song hits number one on the charts.

So Bart, by unconsciously exploiting a do-it-yourself media toy to launch viruses, feeds back to mainstream culture. He does this both as a character in Springfield, USA, and as a media icon in our datasphere, satirizing the real Sting's charity recordings. The character Bart gets revenge against his principal and enjoys a terrific prank. The icon Bart conducts a lesson in advanced media activism. Most important, it is through Bart that the writers of *The Simpsons* are enabled to voice their own, more self-conscious comments on the media.

Finally, Bart remembers that he has put a label on his radio toy, earmarking it "property of Bart Simpson." He decides he better get the radio out of the well before it, and his own identity, are discovered. In his attempt to get the damning evidence out from the bottom of the well, however, Bart really does fall in. He calls for help, admitting what he has done. Once there is a real child in the well, however, and one who had attempted to play a prank on the media at that, everyone loses interest in the tragedy. The virus is blown. The Sting song plummets on the charts, and the television news crews pack up and leave. It is left to Bart's mom and dad to dig him out by hand. In our current self-fed media, according to the writers of *The Simpsons,* a real event can have much less impact than a constructed virus, especially when its intention is revealed.

No matter how activist the show appears, its creators insist that they have no particular agenda. Reiss insisted he promoted no point of view on any issue. In fact, he claimed to have picked the show's subjects and targets almost randomly: "The show eats up so much material that we're constantly just stoking it like a furnace when we parody a lot of movies and TV. And now so many of our writers are themselves the children of TV writers. There's already a second generation rolling in of people who not only watched TV but watched tons of it. And this is our mass culture. Where everyone used to know the catechism, now they all know episodes of *The Twilight Zone,* our common frame of reference."

Reiss was being deceptively casual. Even if he and the other writers claim to have no particular agenda—which is debatable—they readily admit to serving the media machine as a whole. As writers, they see themselves as "feeding" the show and using other media references as the fodder. It is as if the show is a living thing, consuming media culture, recombining it, and spitting it out as second-generation media, with a spin.

Even Bart is in on the gag. In one episode ("So It's Come to This: A Simpsons Clip Show"), when Homer is in the hospital, the family stands around his sick bed recalling incidents from the past, leading to a satire of the flashback format used by shows to create a new episode out of "greatest hit" scenes from old ones. As the family reminisces together about past events, Bart raises a seeming non sequitur. His mother, Marge, asks him, "Why did you bring that up?" "It was an amusing episode," replies Bart, half looking at the camera, before he quickly adds, "of our . . . lives." Bart knows he is on a television show and knows the kinds of tricks his own writers use to fill up airtime.

Such self-consciousness allows *The Simpsons* to serve as a lesson in modern media discontinuity. Bart skateboards through each episode, demonstrating the necessary ironic detachment needed to move through increasingly disorienting edits. "It's animation," explained Jean, who has since returned to writing for the program. "It's very segmented, so we just lift things in and out. If you watch an old episode of *I Love Lucy,* you'll find it laborious because they take so long to set something up. The thesis of *The Simpsons* is nihilism. There's nothing to believe in anymore once you assume that organized structures and institutions are out to get you."

"Right," chimed in Reiss, finally admitting to an agenda. "The overarching point is that the media's stupid and manipulative, TV is a narcotic, and all big institutions are corrupt and evil." These writers make their points both in the plots of the particular episodes and in the cut-and-paste style of the show. By deconstructing and reframing the images in our media, they allow us to see them more objectively, or at least with more ironic distance. They encourage us to question the ways institutional forces are presented to us through the media and urge us to see the fickle nature of our own responses. Figures from the television world are represented as cartoon characters not just to accentuate certain features, but also to allow for total recontextualization of their identities. These are not simple caricatures, but pop cultural samples, juxtaposed in order to illuminate the way they affect us.

As writers and producers, Reiss and Jean served almost as "channels" for the media as received through their own attitudinal filters. While they experience their function as simply to "stoke the furnace," the media images they choose to dissemble are the ones they feel *need* to be exposed and criticized.

Reiss admitted to me, "I feel that in this way *The Simpsons* is the ultimate of what you call a media virus. It sounds a little insidious because I have kids of my own, and the reason we're a hit is because so many kids watch us and make us a huge enterprise. But we're feeding them a lot of ideas and notions that they didn't sign on for. That's not what they're watching for. We all come from this background of comedy that has never been big and popular—it's this Letterman school or *Saturday Night Live, Harvard Lampoon, National Lampoon*. We used to be there, too."

The Simpsons provided its writers with a durable viral shell for their most irreverent memes: "It's as though we finally found a vehicle for this sensibility, where we can do the kind of humor and the attitudes, yet in a package that more people are willing to embrace. I think if it were a live-action show, it wouldn't be a hit," Reiss concluded quite accurately. Like a Trojan Horse, *The Simpsons* sneaks into our homes looking like one thing, before releasing something else, far different, into our lives.

NOTES

1. *Spin,* January 1993: 55.
2. "Memes" are the geneticist Richard Dawkin's term for bits of ideological and conceptual code within cultural systems analogous to the roles of genes in

the transmission and evolution of biological information. [ed. note] See Dawkins, "Universal Parasitism and the Co-Evolution of Extended Phenotypes," *Whole Earth Review* 62 (Spring 1989): 90–99.

3. Chad Lehman describes the solos on *The Simpsons Archive* website (April 15, 2002, http://www.snpp.com/guides/sololist.html). The solos are performed by saxophonist Terry Harrington [*The Simpsons Archive,* April 15, 2002, http://www.snpp.com/guides/lisa-4.html#4.1.7]) [ed. note].

4. "Media virus" refers to the central theoretical concept of the book from which this essay is derived. Rushkoff defines media viruses as "media events provoking real social change" by acting like biological viruses, which use the cover and protection of a protein shell to inject rogue DNA into the cells of the host organism. Similarly, media viruses use the "protein shell" of a media event, whether spontaneous or manufactured (examples range from Rodney King and OJ Simpson to *The Simpsons*) to inject "ideological code" into the media culture. As in a biological host, the media virus starts with a single media event but eventually affects the entire cultural system. See *Media Virus! Hidden Agendas in Popular Culture* (New York: Ballantine Books, 1996), 9 [ed. note].

LIST OF EPISODES CITED

"And Maggie Makes Three." 2F10. January 22, 1995. Written by Jennifer Crittenden. Directed by Swinton O. Scott III.

"Bart Gets Famous." 1F11. February 3, 1994. Written by John Swartzwelder. Directed by Susan Dietter.

"Bart Sells His Soul." 3F02. October 8, 1995. Written by Greg Daniels. Directed by Wesley Archer.

"Bart the Daredevil." 7F06. December 6, 1990. Written by Jay Kogen and Wallace Wolodarsky. Directed by Wesley Archer.

"Bart the General." 7G05. February 4, 1990. Written by John Swartzwelder. Directed by David Silverman.

"Bart the Mother." 5F22. September 27, 1998. Written by David S. Cohen. Directed by Steven Dean Moore.

"Bart the Murderer." 8F03. October 10, 1991. Written by John Swartzwelder. Directed by Rich Moore.

"Bart vs. Australia." 2F13. February 19, 1995. Written by Bill Oakley and Josh Weinstein. Directed by Wesley Archer.

"Bart vs. Thanksgiving." 7F07. November 22, 1990. Written by George Meyer. Directed by David Silverman.

"Bart's Comet." 2F11. February 5, 1995. Written by John Swartzwelder. Directed by Bob Anderson.

"Bart's Inner Child." 1F05. November 11, 1993. Written by George Meyer. Directed by Bob Anderson.

"Behind the Laughter." BABF19. May 21, 2000. Written by Tim Long, George Meyer, Mike Scully, and Matt Selman. Directed by Mark Kirkland.

"Black Widower." 8F20. April 9, 1992. Written by Jon Vitti, Thomas Chastain, and Sam Simon. Directed by David Silverman.

"Blood Feud." 7F22. July 11, 1991. Written by George Meyer. Directed by David Silverman.

"Boy-Scoutz N the Hood." 1F06. November 18, 1993. Written by Dan McGrath. Directed by Jeffrey Lynch.

"Burns Verkaufen der Kraftwerk." 8F09. December 5, 1991. Written by Jon Vitti. Directed by Matt Kirkland.

"Burns's Heir." 1F16. April 14, 1994. Written by Jack Richdale. Directed by Mark Kirkland.

"Cape Feare." 9F22. October 7, 1993. Written by Jon Vitti. Directed by Rich Moore.

"The Cartridge Family." 5F01. November 2, 1997. Written by John Swartzwelder. Directed by Pete Michels.

"The Crepes of Wrath." 7G13. April 15, 1990. Written by George Meyer, Sam Simon, John Swartzwelder, and Jon Vitti. Directed by Wesley Archer and Milton Gray.

"The Day the Violence Died." 3F16. March 17, 1996. Written by John Swartzwelder. Directed by Wesley Archer.

"D'oh-in' in the Wind." AABF02. November 15, 1998. Written by Donick Cary. Directed by Mark Kirkland and Matthew Nastuk.

"E-I-E-I (Annoyed Grunt)." AABF19. November 7, 1999. Written by Ian Maxtone-Graham. Directed by Bob Anderson.

"The Front." 9F16. April 15, 1993. Written by Adam I. Lapidus. Directed by Rich Moore.

"Grampa vs. Sexual Inadequacy." 2F07. December 4, 1994. Written by Bill Oakley and Josh Weinstein. Directed by Wesley Archer.

"Homer and Apu." 1F10. February 10, 1994. Written by Greg Daniels. Directed by Mark Kirkland.

"Homer Badman." 2F06. November 27, 1994. Written by Greg Daniels. Directed by Jeff Lynch.

"Homer Defined." 8F04. October 17, 1991. Written by Howard Gewirtz. Directed by Mark Kirkland.

"Homer Goes to College." 1F02. October 14, 1993. Written by Conan O'Brien. Directed by Jim Reardon.

"Homer Loves Flanders." 1F14. March 17, 1994. Written by David Richardson. Directed by Wesley Archer.

"Homer's Enemy." 4F19. May 4, 1997. Written by John Swartzwelder. Directed by Jim Reardon.

"Homer's Odyssey." 7G03. January 21, 1990. Written by Jay Kogen and Wallace Wolodarsky. Directed by Wesley Archer.

"Homer's Phobia." 4F11. February 16, 1997. Written by Ron Hauge. Directed by Mike B. Anderson.

"Homer the Heretic." 9F01. October 8, 1992. Written by George Meyer. Directed by Jim Reardon.

"Homer the Vigilante." 1F09. January 6, 1994. Written by John Swartzwelder. Directed by Jim Reardon.

"Homer to the Max." AABF09. February 7, 1999. Written by John Swartzwelder. Directed by Pete Michels.

"Homer's Triple Bypass." 9F09. December 17, 1992. Written by Gary Apple and Michael Carrington. Directed by David Silverman.

"Homer vs. Lisa and the 8th Commandment." 7F13. February 7, 1991. Written by Steve Pepoon. Directed by Rich Moore.

"In Marge We Trust." 4F18. April 27, 1997. Written by Donick Cary. Directed by Steve Moore.

"Itchy & Scratchy & Marge." 7F09. December 20, 1990. Written by John Swartzwelder. Directed by Jim Reardon.

"The Itchy & Scratchy & Poochie Show." 4F12. February 9, 1997. Written by David S. Cohen. Directed by Steven Dean Moore.

"Itchy & Scratchy Land." 2F01. October 2, 1994. Written by John Swartzwelder. Directed by Wesley Archer.

"Itchy & Scratchy: The Movie." 9F03. November 3, 1992. Written by John Swartzwelder. Directed by Rich Moore.

"Kamp Krusty." 8F24. September 24, 1992. Written by David M. Stern. Directed by Mark Kirkland.

"King Size Homer." 3F05. November 5, 1995. Written by Dan Greaney. Directed by Jim Reardon.

"Krusty Gets Busted." 7G12. March 29, 1990. Written by Jay Kogen and Wallace Wolodarsky. Directed by Brad Bird.

"Last Exit to Springfield." 9F15. March 11, 1993. Written by Jay Kogen and Wallace Wolodarsky. Directed by Mark Kirkland.

"Lisa's Pony." 8F06. November 7, 1991. Written by Al Jean and Mike Reiss. Directed by Carlos Baeza.

"Lisa's Rival." 1F17. September 11, 1994. Written by Mike Scully. Directed by Mark Kirkland.

"Lisa's Sax." 3G02. October 19, 1997. Written by Al Jean and Mike Reiss. Directed by Dominic Polcino.

"Lisa's Wedding." 2F15. April 9, 1995. Written by Mike Scully. Directed by Bob Anderson.

"Lisa the Iconoclast." 3F13. February 18, 1996. Written by Jonathan Collier. Directed by Mike B. Anderson.

"Lisa the Skeptic." 5F05. November 23, 1997. Written by David S. Cohen. Directed by Neil Affleck.

"Make Room for Lisa." AABF12. February 28, 1999. Written by Brian Scully. Directed by Matthew Nastik.

"Marge Gets a Job." 9F05. November 5, 1992. Written by Bill Oakley and Josh Weinstein. Directed by Jeff Lynch.

"Marge in Chains." 9F20. May 6, 1993. Written by Bill Oakley and Josh Weinstein. Directed by Jim Reardon.

"Marge on the Lam." 1F03. November 4, 1993. Written by Bill Canterbury. Directed by Mark Kirkland.

"Marge vs. the Monorail." 9F10. January 14, 1993. Written by Conan O'Brien. Directed by Rich Moore.

"Missionary Impossible." BABF11. February 20, 2000. Written by Ron Hauge. Directed by Steven Dean Moore.

"Mother Simpson." 3F06. November 19, 1995. Written by Richard Appel. Directed by David Silverman.

"Mr. Lisa Goes to Washington." 8F01. September 26, 1991. Written by George Meyer. Directed by Wesley Archer.

"Much Apu About Nothing." 3F20. May 5, 1996. Written by David S. Cohen. Directed by Susan Dietter.

"Oh, Brother, Where Art Thou?" 7F16. February 21, 1991. Written by Jeff Martin. Directed by. M. "Bud" Archer.

"One Fish, Two Fish, Blowfish, Blue Fish." 7F11. January 24, 1991. Written by Nell Scovell. Directed by Wesley Archer.

"The Pagans." *Tracy Ullman Show.* MG22. February 14, 1988. Written by Matt Groening.

"Radio Bart." 8F11. January 9, 1992. Written by John Vitti. Directed by Carlos Baeza.

"Radioactive Man." 2F17. September 24, 1995. Written by John Swartzwelder. Directed by Susan Dietter.

"Saddlesore Galactica." BABF09. February 6, 2000. Written by Tim Long. Directed by Lance Kramer.

"Scenes from the Class Struggle in Springfield." 3F11. February 4, 1996. Written by Jennifer Crittenden. Directed by Susan Dietter.

"Selma's Choice." 9F11. January 21, 1993. Written by David M. Stern. Directed by Carlos Baeza.

"Sideshow Bob Roberts." 2F02. October 9, 1994. Written by Bill Oakley and Josh Weinstein. Directed by Mark Kirkland.

"Sideshow Bob's Last Gleaming." 3F08. November 26, 1995. Written by Spike Ferensten. Directed by Dominic Polcino.

"Simpsoncalifragilisticexpiala[Annoyed Grunt]cious." 3G03. February 7, 1997. Written by Al Jean and Mike Reiss. Directed by Chuck Sheetz.

"Simpsons Bible Stories." Written by Tim Long, Larry Doyle, and Matt Selman. AABF14. April 4, 1999. Directed by Nancy Kruse.

"The Simpsons Spin-off Showcase." 4F20. May 11, 1997. Written by David S. Cohen, Dan Greaney, and Steve Tompkins. Directed by Neil Affleck.

"Simpson Tide." 3G04. March 29, 1998. Written by Joshua Sternin and Jeffrey Ventimilia. Directed by Milton Gray.

"So It's Come to This: A Simpsons Clip Show." 9F17. April 1, 1993. Written by Jon Vitti with contributions from Al Jean, Mike Reiss, Jay Kogen, Wallace Wolodarsky, John Swartzwelder, Jeff Martin, George Meyer, and Nell Scovell. Directed by Carlos Baeza.

"The Springfield Connection." 2F21. May 7, 1995. Written by Jonathan Collier. Directed by Mark Kirkland.

"The Springfield Files." 3G01. January 12, 1997. Written by Reid Harrison. Directed by Steven Dean Moore.

"$pringfield (or, How I Learned to Stop Worrying and Love Legalized Gambling)." 1F08. December 16, 1993. Written by Bill Oakley and Josh Weinstein. Directed by Wesley Archer.

"A Star Is Burns." 2F31. March 5, 1995. Written by Ken Keeler. Directed by Susan Dietter.

"Sunday, Cruddy Sunday." AABF08. January 31, 1999. Written by Tom Martin, George Meyer, Brian Scully, and Mike Scully. Directed by Steven Dean Moore.

"Trash of the Titans." 5F09. April 26, 1998. Written by Ian Maxtone-Graham. Directed by Jim Reardon.

"Treehouse of Horror." 7F04. October 25, 1990. Written by Jay Kogen, Wallace Wolodarsky, John Swartzwelder, Sam Simon, and Edgar Allan Poe. Directed by Wesley Archer, Rich Moore, and David Silverman.

"Treehouse of Horror VI." 3F04. October 29, 1995. Written by John Swartzwelder, Steve Tomkins, and David S. Cohen. Directed by Bob Anderson.

"Treehouse of Horror VIII." 5F02. October 26, 1997. Written by Mike Scully, David S. Cohen, and Ned Goldreyer. Directed by Mark Kirkland,

"Treehouse of Horror X." BABF01. October 31, 1999. Written by Donick Cary, Tim Long, and Ron Hague. Directed by Pete Michels.

"22 Short Films About Springfield." 3F18. April 14, 1996. Written by Richard Appel, David S. Cohen, Jonathan Collier, Jennifer Crittenden, Greg Daniels, Brent Forrester, Rachel Pulido, Steve Tompkins, Josh Weinstein, and Matt Groening. Directed by Jim Reardon.

"Two Bad Neighbors." 3F09. January 14, 1996. Written by Ken Keeler. Directed by Wes Archer.

"Two Cars in Every Garage, Three Eyes on Every Fish." 7F01. November 1, 1990. Written by Sam Simon and John Swartzwelder. Directed by Wesley Archer.

"The Two Mrs. Nahasapeemapetilons." 5F04. November 16, 1997. Written by Richard Appel. Directed by Steven Dean Moore.

"Whacking Day." 9F18. Apr. 29, 1993. Written by John Swartzwelder. Directed by Jeff Lynch.

"When You Dish Upon a Star." 5F19. November 8, 1998. Written by Richard Appel. Directed by Pete Michaels.

"Wild Barts Can't Be Broken." AABF07. January 17, 1999. Written by Larry Doyle. Directed by Mark Ervin.

"World War III." *Tracy Ullman Show.* MG20. November 22, 1987. Written by Matt Groening.

THE *SIMPSONS* COMPLETE EPISODE GUIDE, SEASONS 1–13

Each episode below is listed chronologically by title, production code, original airdate in the United States on the Fox network, writers, and directors. Detailed information about each episode can be found in The Simpsons: *A Complete Guide to Our Favorite Family,* ed. Ray Richmond and Antonia Coffman (New York: HarperPerennial, 1997) and The Simpsons *Forever: A Complete Guide to Our Favorite Family . . . Continued,* ed. Scott M. Gimple (New York: HarperPerennial, 1999). Regularly updated information can also be found at The Simpsons *Archive Episode Guide* <http://www.snpp.com/episodeguide.html>, which was begun by Mark Holtz and Dave Hall and is being maintained as of the publication of this book by Matt Rose, and at The Simpsons: *An Episode Guide* <http://www.epguides.com/Simpsons/>, currently maintained by Dennis Kytasaari and John Lavalie. The Fox network also provides episode information at The Simpsons *Web Site* <http://www.thesimpsons.com/episode_guide/0101.html>.

THE TRACEY ULLMAN SHOW

All short films by Matt Groening
Season 1 (1987)

"Good Night." MG01. April 19, 1987.
"Watching TV." MG02. May 3, 1987.
"Jumping Bart." MG03. May 10, 1987.
"Babysitting Maggie." MG04. May 31, 1987.
"The Pacifier." MG05. June 21, 1987.
"Burping Contest." MG06. June 28, 1987.
"Dinnertime." MG07. July 12, 1987.

Season 2 (1987–1988)

"Making Faces." MG09. September 22, 1987.
"The Funeral." MG14. October 4, 1987.

"What Maggie's Thinking." MG10. October 11, 1987.

"Football." MG08. October 18, 1987.

"House Of Cards." MG12. October 25, 1987.

"Bart and Homer's Dinner." MG15. November 1, 1987.

"Space Patrol." MG13. November 8, 1987.

"Bart's Haircut." MG18. November 15, 1987.

"World War III." MG20. November 22, 1987.

"The Perfect Crime." MG16. December 13, 1987.

"Scary Stories." MG17. December 20, 1987.

"Grampa and the Kids." MG19. January 10, 1988.

"Gone Fishin'." MG11. January 24, 1988.

"Skateboarding." MG21. February 7, 1988.

"The Pagans." MG22. February 14, 1988.

"Closeted." MG23. February 21, 1988.

"The Aquarium." MG24. February 28, 1988.

"Family Portrait." MG25. March 6, 1988.

"Bart's Hiccups." MG26. March 13, 1988.

"The Money Jar." MG27. March 20. 1988.

"The Art Museum." MG29. May 1, 1988.

"Zoo Story." MG28. May 8, 1988.

Season 3 (1988–1989)

"Shut Up, Simpsons." MG30. November 6, 1988.

"Shell Game." MG35. November 13, 1988.

"The Bart Simpson Show." MG38. November 20, 1988.

"Punching Bag." MG33. November 27, 1988.

"Simpson Christmas." MG40. December 18, 1988.

"The Krusty the Clown Show." MG39. January 15, 1989.

"Bart the Hero." MG34. January 29, 1989.

"Bart's Little Fantasy." MG41. February 5, 1989.

"Scary Movie." MG37. February 12, 1989.

"Home Hypnotism." MG32. February 19, 1989.

"Shoplifting." MG31. February 26, 1989.

"Echo Canyon." MG36. March 12, 1989.

"Bathtime." MG44. March 19, 1989.

"Bart's Nightmare." MG45. March 26, 1989.

"Bart of the Jungle." MG46. April 16, 1989.

"Family Therapy." MG47. April 23, 1989.

"Maggie in Peril (Chapter One)." MG42. April 30, 1989.

"Maggie in Peril (The Thrilling Conclusion)." MG43. May 7, 1989.

"TV Simpsons." MG48. May 14, 1989.

THE SIMPSONS

Season 1 (1989–1990)

"The Simpson's Christmas Special: Simpsons Roasting on an Open Fire." 7G08. December 17, 1989. Written by Mimi Pond. Directed by David Silverman.

"Bart the Genius." 7G02. January 14, 1990. Written by Jon Vitti. Directed by David Silverman.

"Homer's Odyssey." January 21, 1990. 7G03. Written by Jay Kogen and Wallace Wolodarsky. Directed by Wesley Archer.

"There's No Disgrace Like Home." 7G04. January 28, 1990. Written by Al Jean and Mike Reiss. Directed by Gregg Vanzo and Kent Butterworth.

"Bart the General." 7G05. February 4, 1990. Written by John Swartzwelder. Directed by David Silverman.

"Moaning Lisa." 7G06. February 11, 1990. Written by Al Jean and Mike Reiss. Directed by Wesley Archer.

"The Call of the Simpsons." 7G09. February 18, 1990. Written by John Swartzwelder. Directed by Wesley Archer.

"The Telltale Head." 7G07. February 25, 1990. Written by Al Jean, Mike Reiss, Sam Simon, and Matt Groening. Directed by Rich Moore.

"Life on the Fast Lane." 7G11. March 18, 1990. Written by John Swartzwelder. Directed by David Silverman.

"Homer's Night Out." 7G10. March 25, 1990. Written by Jon Vitti. Directed by Rich Moore.

"The Crepes of Wrath." 7G13. April 15, 1990. Written by Sam Simon, John Swartzwelder, Jon Vitti, and George Meyer. Directed by Wesley Archer and Milton Gray.

"Krusty Gets Busted." 7G12. April 29, 1990. Written by Jay Kogen and Wallace Wolodarsky. Directed by Brad Bird.

"Some Enchanted Evening." 7G01. May 13, 1990. Written by Matt Groening and Sam Simon. Directed by David Silverman and Kent Butterworth.

Season 2 (1990–1991)

"Bart Gets An F." 7F03. October 11, 1990. Written by David M. Stern. Directed by David Silverman.

"Simpson and Delilah." 7F02. October 18, 1990. Written by Jon Vitti. Directed by Rich Moore.

"The Simpsons Halloween Special: Treehouse of Horror." 7F04. October 25, 1990. Written by John Swartzwelder, Jay Kogen, Wallace Wolodarsky, Sam Simon, and Edgar Allan Poe. Directed by Wesley Archer, Rich Moore, and David Silverman.

"Two Cars in Every Garage and Three Eyes on Every Fish." 7F01. November 1, 1990. Written by John Swartzwelder and Sam Simon. Directed by Wesley Archer.

"Dancin' Homer." 7F05. November 8, 1990. Written by Ken Levine and David Isaacs. Directed by Matt Kirkland.

"Dead Putting Society." 7F08. November 15, 1990. Written by Jeff Martin. Directed by Rich Moore.

"Bart vs. Thanksgiving." 7F07. November 22, 1990. Written by George Martin. Directed by David Silverman.

"Bart the Daredevil." 7F06. December 6, 1990. Written by Jay Kogen and Wallace Wolodarsky. Directed by Wesley Archer.

"Itchy & Scratchy & Marge." 7F09. December 20, 1990. Written by John Swartzwelder. Directed by Jim Reardon.

"Bart Gets Hit by a Car." 7F10. January 10, 1991. Written by John Swartzwelder. Directed by Matt Kirkland.

"One Fish, Two Fish, Blowfish, Blue Fish." 7F11. January 24, 1991. Written by Nell Scovell. Directed by Wesley Archer.

"The Way We Was." 7F12. January 31, 1991. Written by Al Jean and Mike Reiss and Sam Simon. Directed by David Silverman.

"Homer vs. Lisa and the 8th Commandment." 7F13. February 7, 1991. Written by Steve Pepoon. Directed by Rich Moore.

"Principal Charming." 7F15. February 14, 1991. Written by David Stern. Directed by Matt Kirkland.

"Oh, Brother, Where Art Thou?" 7F16. February 21, 1991. Written by Jeff Martin. Directed by Wesley Archer.

"Bart's Dog Gets an F." 7F14. March 7, 1991. Written by Jon Vitti. Directed by Jim Reardon.

"Old Money." 7F17. March 28, 1991. Written by Jay Kogen and Wallace Wolodarsky. Directed by David Silverman.

"Brush with Greatness." 7F18. April 11, 1991. Written by Brian Roberts. Directed by Jim Reardon.

"Lisa's Substitute." 7F19. April 25, 1991. Written by Jon Vitti. Directed by Rich Moore.

"The War of the Simpsons." 7F20. May 2, 1991. Written by John Swartzwelder. Directed by Matt Kirkland.

"Three Men and a Comic Book." 7F21. May 9, 1991. Written by Jeff Martin. Directed by Wesley Archer.

"Blood Feud." 7F22. July 11, 1991. Written by George Meyer. Directed by David Silverman.

Season 3 (1991–1992)

"Stark Raving Dad." 7F24. September 19, 1991. Written by Al Jean and Mike Reiss. Directed by Rich Moore.

"Mr. Lisa Goes to Washington." 8F01. September 26, 1991. Written by George Meyer. Directed by Wesley Archer.

"When Flanders Failed." 7F23. October 3, 1991. Written by Jon Vitti. Directed by Jim Reardon.

"Bart the Murderer." 8F03. October 10, 1991. Written by John Swartzwelder. Directed by Rich Moore.

"Homer Defined." 8F04. October 17, 1991. Written by Howard Gewirtz. Directed by Matt Kirkland.

"Like Father, Like Clown." 8F05. October 24, 1991. Written by Jay Kogen and Wallace Wolodarsky. Directed by Jeffrey Lynch and Brad Bird.

"Treehouse of Horror II: A Simpsons Halloween." 8F02. October 31, 1991. Written by Al Jean, Mike Reiss, Jeff Martin, George Meyer, Sam Simon, and John Swartzwelder. Directed by Jim Reardon.

"Lisa's Pony." 8F06. November 7, 1991. Written by Al Jean and Mike Reiss. Directed by Carlos Baeza.

"Saturdays of Thunder." 8F07. November 14, 1991. Written by Ken Levine and David Isaacs. Directed by Jim Reardon.

"Flaming Moe's." 8F08. November 21, 1991. Written by Robert Cohen. Directed by Rich Moore and Alan Smart.

"Burns Verkaufen der Kraftwerk." 8F09. December 5, 1991. Written by Jon Vitti. Directed by Matt Kirkland.

"I Married Marge." 8F10. December 26, 1991. Written by Jeff Martin. Directed by Jeffrey Lynch.

"Radio Bart." 8F11. January 9 1992. Written by Jon Vitti. Directed by Carlos Baeza.

"Lisa the Greek." 8F12. January 23, 1992. Written by Jay Kogen and Wallace Wolodarsky. Directed by Rich Moore.

"Homer Alone." 8F14. February 6, 1992. Written by David Stern. Directed by Matt Kirkland.

"Bart the Lover." 8F16. February 13, 1992. Written by Jon Vitti. Directed by Carlos Baeza.

"Homer at the Bat." 8F13. February 20, 1992. Written by John Swartzwelder. Directed by Jim Reardon.

"Separate Vocations." 8F15. February 27, 1992. Written by George Meyer. Directed by Jeffrey Lynch.

"Dog of Death." 8F17. March 12, 1992. Written by John Swartzwelder. Directed by Jim Reardon.

"Colonel Homer." 8F19. March 26, 1992. Written by Matt Groening. Directed by Matt Kirkland.

"Black Widower." 8F20. April 9, 1992. Written by Jon Vitti. Directed by David Silverman.

"The Otto Show." 8F21. April 23, 1992. Written by Jeff Martin. Directed by Wesley Archer.

"Bart's Friend Falls in Love." 8F22. May 7, 1992. Written by Jay Kogen and Wallace Wolodarsky. Directed by Jim Reardon.

"Brother, Can You Spare Two Dimes?" 8F23. August 27, 1992. Written by John Swartzwelder. Directed by Rich Moore.

Season 4 (1992–1993)

"Kamp Krusty." 8F24. September 24, 1992. Written by David M. Stern. Directed by Mark Kirkland.

"A Streetcar Named Marge." 8F18. October 1, 1992. Written by Jeff Martin. Directed by Rich Moore.

"Homer the Heretic." 9F01. October 8, 1992. Written by George Meyer. Directed by Jim Reardon.

"Lisa the Beauty Queen." 9F02. October 15, 1992. Written by Jeff Martin. Directed by Matt Kirkland.

"Treehouse of Horror III." 9F04. October 29, 1992. Written by Al Jean, Mike Reiss, Johnny Kogen, Wallace Wolodarsky, Sam Simon, and Jack Vitti. Directed by Carlos Baeza.

"Itchy & Scratchy: The Movie." 9F03. November 3, 1992. Written by John Swartzwelder. Directed by Rich Moore.

"Marge Gets a Job." 9F05. November 5, 1992. Written by Bill Oakley and Josh Weinstein. Directed by Jeffrey Lynch.

"New Kid on the Block." 9F06. November 12, 1992. Written by Conan O'Brien. Directed by Wesley Archer.

"Mr. Plow." 9F07. November 19, 1992. Written by Jon Vitti. Directed by Jim Reardon.

"Lisa's First Word." 9F08. December 3, 1992. Written by Jeff Martin. Directed by Matt Kirkland.

"Homer's Triple Bypass." 9F09. December 17, 1992. Written by Gary Apple and Michael Carrington. Directed by David Silverman.

"Marge vs. the Monorail." 9F10. January 14, 1993. Written by Conan O'Brien. Directed by Rich Moore.

"Selma's Choice." 9F11. January 21, 1993. Written by David M. Stern. Directed by Carlos Baeza.

"Brother from the Same Planet." 9F12. February 4, 1993. Written by Jon Vitti. Directed by Jeffrey Lynch.

"I Love Lisa." 9F13. February 11, 1993. Written by Frank Mula. Directed by Wesley Archer.

"Duffless." 9F14. February 18, 1993. Written by David M. Stern. Directed by Jim Reardon.

"Last Exit to Springfield." 9F15. March 11, 1993. Written by Jay Kogen and Wallace Wolodarsky. Directed by Mark Kirkland.

"So It Has Come to This: A Simpsons Clip Show." 9F17. April 1, 1993. Written by Jon Vitti with contributions from Al Jean, Mike Reiss, Jay Kogen, Wallace Wolodarsky, John Swartzwelder, Jeff Martin, George Meyer, and Nell Scovell. Directed by Carlos Baeza.

"The Front." 9F16. April 15, 1993. Written by Adam I. Lapidus. Directed by Rich Moore.

"Whacking Day." 9F18. April 29, 1993. Written by John Swartzwelder. Directed by Jeffrey Lynch.

"Marge in Chains." 9F20. May 6, 1993. Written by Bill Oakley and Josh Weinstein. Directed by Jim Reardon.

"Krusty Gets Kancelled." 9F19. May 13, 1993. Written by John Swartzwelder. Directed by David Silverman.

Season 5 (1993–1994)

"Homer's Barbershop Quartet." 9F21. September 30, 1993. Written by Jeff Martin. Directed by Matt Kirkland.

"Cape Feare." 9F22. October 7, 1993. Written by Jon Vitti. Directed by Rich Moore.

"Homer Goes to College." 1F02. October 14, 1993. Written by Conan O'Brien. Directed by Jim Reardon.

"Rosebud." 1F01. October 21, 1993. Written by John Swartzwelder. Directed by Wesley Archer.

"Treehouse of Horror IV." 1F04. October 30, 1993. Written by Conan O'Brien, Bill Oakley, Josh Weinstein, Greg Daniels, Dan McGrath, and Bill Canterbury. Directed by David Silverman.

"Marge on the Lam." 1F03. November 4, 1993. Written by Bill Canterbury. Directed by Matt Kirkland.

"Bart's Inner Child." 1F05. November 11, 1993. Written by George Meyer. Directed by Bob Anderson.

"Boy-Scoutz N the Hood." 1F06. November 18, 1993. Written by Dan McGrath. Directed by Jeffrey Lynch.

"The Last Temptation of Homer." 1F07. December 9, 1993. Written by Frank Mula. Directed by Carlos Baeza.

"$pringfield (or, How I Learned to Stop Worrying and Love Legalized Gambling)." 1F08. December 16, 1993. Written by Bill Oakley and Josh Weinstein. Directed by Wesley Archer.

"Homer the Vigilante." 1F09. January 6, 1994. Written by John Swartzwelder. Directed by Rich Moore.

"Bart Gets Famous." 1F11. February 3, 1994. Written by John Swartzwelder. Directed by Susan Dietter.

"Homer and Apu." 1F10. February 10, 1994. Written by Greg Daniels. Directed by Mark Kirkland.

"Lisa vs. Malibu Stacy." 1F12. February 17, 1994. Written by Bill Oakley and Josh Weinstein. Directed by Jeffrey Lynch.

"Deep Space Homer." 1F13. February 24, 1994. Written by David Mirkin. Directed by Carlos Baeza.

"Homer Loves Flanders." 1F14. March 17, 1994. Written by David Richardson. Directed by Wesley Archer.

"Bart Gets an Elephant." 1F15. March 31, 1994. Written by John Swartzwelder. Directed by Jim Reardon.

"Burns' Heir." 1F16. April 14, 1994. Written by Jace Richdale. Directed by Mark Kirkland.

"Sweet Seymour Skinner's Baadasssss Song." 1F18. April 28, 1994. Written by Bill Oakley and Josh Weinstein. Directed by Bob Anderson.

"The Boy Who Knew Too Much." 1F19. May 5, 1994. Written by John Swartzwelder. Directed by Jeffrey Lynch.

"Lady Bouvier's Lover." 1F21. May 12, 1994. Written by Bill Oakley and Josh Weinstein. Directed by Wesley Archer.

"Secrets of a Successful Marriage." 1F20. May 19, 1994. Written by Greg Daniels. Directed by Carlos Baeza.

Season 6 (1994–1995)

"Bart of Darkness." 1F22. September 4, 1994. Written by Dan McGrath. Directed by Jim Reardon.

"Lisa's Rival." 1F17. September 11, 1994. Written by Mike Scully. Directed by Mark Kirkland.

"Another Simpsons Clip Show." 2F33. September 25, 1994. Written by Penny Wise with contributions from John Swartzwelder, Jon Vitti, Frank Mula, David Richardson, Jeff Martin, Bill Oakley, Josh Weinstein, Matt Groening, Sam Simon, Al Jean, Mike Reiss, Jay Kogen, Wallace Wolodarsky, Nell Scovell, David Stein, George Meyer, Conan O'Brien, Robert Cohen, Bill Canterbury, and Dan McGrath. Directed by David Silverman.

"Itchy & Scratchyland." 2F01. October 2, 1994. Written by John Swartzwelder. Directed by Wesley Archer.

"Sideshow Bob Roberts." 2F02. October 9, 1994. Written by Bill Oakley and Josh Weinstein. Directed by Mark Kirkland.

"Treehouse of Horror V." 2F03. October 30, 1994. Written by Greg Danula, Dan McGrath, David S. Cohen, and Bob Kushell. Directed by Jim Reardon.

"Bart's Girlfriend." 2F04. November 6, 1994. Written by Jonathan Collier. Directed by Susan Dietter.

"Lisa on Ice." 2F05. November 13, 1994. Written by Mike Scully. Directed by Bob Anderson.

"Homer Badman." 2F06. November 27, 1994. Written by Greg Daniels. Directed by Jeffrey Lynch.

"Grandpa vs. Sexual Inadequacy." 2F07. December 4, 1994. Written by Bill Oakley and Josh Weinstein. Directed by Wesley Archer.

"Fear of Flying." 2F08. December 18, 1994. Written by David Sacks. Directed by Mark Kirkland.

"Homer the Great." 2F09. January 8, 1995. Written by John Swartzwelder. Directed by Jim Reardon.

"And Maggie Makes Three." 2F10. January 22, 1995. Written by Jennifer Crittenden. Directed by Swinton O. Scott III.

"Bart's Comet." 2F11. February 5, 1995. Written by John Swartzwelder. Directed by Bob Anderson.

"Homie the Clown." 2F12. February 12, 1995. Written by John Swartzwelder. Directed by David Silverman.

"Bart vs. Australia." 2F13. February 19, 1995. Written by Bill Oakley and Josh Weinstein. Directed by Wesley Archer.

"Homer vs. Patty and Selma." 2F14. February 26, 1995. Written by Brent Forrester. Directed by Mark Kirkland.

"A Star Is Burns." 2F31. March 5, 1995. Written by Ken Keeler. Directed by Susan Dietter.

"Lisa's Wedding." 2F15. March 19, 1995. Written by Greg Daniels. Directed by Jim Reardon.

"Two Dozen and One Greyhounds." 2F18. April 9, 1995. Written by Mike Scully. Directed by Bob Anderson.

"The PTA Disbands." 2F19. April 16, 1995. Written by Jennifer Crittenden. Directed by Swinton O. Scott III.

"Round Springfield." 2F32. April 30, 1995. Written by Joshua Sternin and Jeffrey Ventimilia. Story by Mike Reiss and Al Jean. Directed by Steven Dean Moore.

"The Springfield Connection." 2F21. May 7, 1995. Written by Jonathan Collier. Directed by Mark Kirkland.

"Lemon of Troy." 2F22. May 14, 1995. Written by Brent Forrester. Directed by Jim Reardon.

"Who Shot Mr. Burns? (Part One)." 2F16. May 21, 1995. Written by Bill Oakley and Josh Weinstein. Directed by Jeffrey Lynch.

Season 7 (1995–1996)

"Who Shot Mr. Burns? (Part Two)." 2F20. September 17, 1995. Written by Bill Oakley and Josh Weinstein. Directed by Wesley Archer.

"Radioactive Man." 2F17. September 24, 1995. Written by John Swartzwelder. Directed by Susan Dietter.

"Home Sweet Homediddly-Dum-Doodily." 3F01. October 1, 1995. Written by Jon Vitti. Directed by Susan Dietter.

"Bart Sells His Soul." 3F02. October 8, 1995. Written by Greg Daniels. Directed by Wesley Archer.

"Lisa the Vegetarian." 3F03. October 15, 1995. Written by David S. Cohen. Directed by Mark Kirkland.

"Treehouse of Horror VI." 3F04. October 30, 1995. Written by John Swartzwelder, Steve Tompkins, and David S. Cohen. Directed by Bob Anderson.

"King Size Homer." 3F05. November 5, 1995. Written by Dan Greaney. Directed by Jim Reardon.

"Mother Simpson." 3F06. November 19, 1995. Written by Richard Appel. Directed by David Silverman.

"Sideshow Bob's Last Gleaming." 3F08. November 26, 1995. Written by Spike Feresten. Directed by Dominic Polcino.

"The Simpsons 138th Episode Spectacular." 3F31. December 3, 1995. Written by Penny Wise. Directed by Pound Foolish.

"Marge Be Not Proud." 3F07. December 17, 1995. Written by Mike Scully. Directed by Steven Moore.

"Team Homer." 3F10. January 6, 1996. Written by Mike Scully. Directed by Mark Kirkland.

"Two Bad Neighbors." January 14, 1996. 3F09. Written by Ken Keeler. Directed by Wesley Archer.

"Scenes From the Class Struggle in Springfield." 3F11. February 4, 1996. Written by Jennifer Crittenden. Directed by Susan Dietter.

"Bart the Fink." 3F12. February 11, 1996. Written by John Swartzwelder. Story by Bob Kushell. Directed by Jim Reardon.

"Lisa the Iconoclast." 3F13. February 18, 1996. Written by Jonathan Collier. Directed by Mike B. Anderson.

"Homer the Smithers." 3F14. February 25, 1996. Written by John Swartzwelder. Directed by Steven Dean Moore.

"The Day the Violence Died." 3F16. March 17, 1996. Written by John Swartzwelder. Directed by Wesley Archer.

"A Fish Called Selma." 3F15. March 24, 1996. Written by Jack Barth. Directed by Mark Kirkland.

"Bart on the Road." 3F17. March 31, 1996. Written by Richard Appel. Directed by Swinton O. Scott III.

"22 Short Films About Springfield." 3F18. April 14, 1996. Written by Greg Daniels, Richard Appel, David S. Cohen, Jonathan Collier, Jennifer Crittenden, Greg Daniels, Brent Forrester, Rachel Pulido, Steve Tompkins, Josh Weinstein, and Matt Groening. Directed by Jim Reardon.

"Raging Abe Simpson and His Grumbling Grandson in 'The Curse of the Flying Hellfish.' " 3F19. April 28, 1996. Written by Jonathan Collier. Directed by Jeffrey Lynch.

"Much Apu About Nothing." 3F20. May 5, 1996. Written by David S. Cohen. Directed by Susan Dietter.

"Homerpalooza." 3F21. May 19, 1996. Written by Brent Forrester. Directed by Wesley Archer.

"Summer of 4 Ft. 2." 3F22. May 19, 1996. Written by Dan Greaney. Directed by Mark Kirkland.

Season 8 (1996–1997)

"Treehouse of Horror VII." 4F02. October 27, 1996. Written by Ken Keeler, Dan Greaney, and David S. Cohen. Directed by Mike Anderson.

"You Only Move Twice." 3F23. November 3, 1996. Written by John Swartzwelder. Directed by Mike Anderson.

"The Homer They Fall." 4F03. November 10, 1996. Written by Jonathan Collier. Directed by Mark Kirkland.

"Burns, Baby Burns." 4F05. November 17, 1996. Written by Ian Maxtone-Graham. Directed by Jim Reardon.

"Bart After Dark." 4F06. November 24, 1996. Written by Richard Appel. Directed by Dominic Polcino.

"A Milhouse Divided." 4F04. December 1, 1996. Written by Steve Tompkins. Directed by Steven Moore.

"Lisa's Date with Density." 4F01. December 15, 1996. Written by Mike Scully. Directed by Susan Dietter.

"Hurricane Neddy." 4F07. December 29, 1996. Written by Steve Young. Directed by Bob Anderson.

"El Viaje Misterioso de Nuestro Jomer (The Mysterious Voyage of Homer)." 3F24. January 5, 1997. Written by Ken Keeler. Directed by Jim Reardon.

"The Springfield Files." 3G01. January 12, 1997. Written by Reid Harrison. Directed by Steven Dean Moore.

"The Twisted World of Marge Simpson." 4F08. January 19, 1997. Written by Jennifer Crittenden. Directed by Chuck Sheetz.

"Mountain of Madness." 4F10. February 2, 1997. Written by John Swartzwelder. Directed by Mark Kirkland.

"Simpsoncalifragilisticexpiala(Annoyed Grunt)cious." 3G03. February 7, 1997. Written by Al Jean and Mike Reiss. Directed by Chuck Sheetz.

"The Itchy & Scratchy & Poochie Show." 4F12. February 9, 1997. Written by David S. Cohen. Directed by Steven Dean Moore.

"Homer's Phobia." 4F11. February 16, 1997. Written by Ron Hauge. Directed by Mike Anderson.

"Brother from Another Series." 4F14. February 23, 1997. Written by Ken Keeler. Directed by Pete Michels.

"My Sister, My Sitter." 4F13. March 2, 1997. Written by Dan Greaney. Directed by Jim Reardon.

"Homer vs. the Eighteenth Amendment." 4F15. March 16, 1997. Written by John Swartzwelder. Directed by Bob Anderson.

"Grade School Confidential." 4F09. April 6, 1997. Written by Rachel Pulido. Directed by Susan Dietter.

"The Canine Mutiny." 4F16. April 13, 1997. Written by Ron Hauge. Directed by Dominic Polcino.

"The Old Man and the Lisa." 4F17. April 20, 1997. Written by John Swartzwelder. Directed by Mark Kirkland.

"In Marge We Trust." 4F18. April 27, 1997. Written by Donick Cary. Directed by Steven Dean Moore.

"Homer's Enemy." 4F19. May 4, 1997. Written by John Swartzwelder. Directed by Jim Reardon.

"The Simpsons Spin-off Showcase." 4F20. May 11, 1997. Written by David S. Cohen, Dan Greaney, and Steve Tompkins. Story by Ken Keeler. Directed by Neil Affleck.

"The Secret War of Lisa Simpson." 4F21. May 18, 1997. Written by Richard Appel. Directed by Mike B. Anderson.

Season 9 (1997–1998)

"The City of New York vs. Homer Simpson." 4F22. September 21, 1997. Written by Ian Maxtone-Graham. Directed by Jim Reardon.

"The Principal and the Pauper." 4F23. September 28, 1997. Written by Ken Keeler. Directed by Steve Moore.

"Lisa's Sax." 3G02. October 19, 1997. Written by Al Jean. Directed by Dominic Polcino.

"Treehouse of Horror VIII." 5F02. October 26, 1997. Written by Mike Scully, David S. Cohen, and Ned Goldreyer. Directed by Mark Kirkland.

"The Cartridge Family." 5F01. November 2, 1997. Written by John Swartzwelder. Directed by Pete Michels.

"Bart Star." 5F03. November 9, 1997. Written by David M. Stern. Directed by Mark Kirkland.

"The Two Mrs. Nahasapeemapetilons." 5F04. November 16, 1997. Written by Richard Appel. Directed by Steven Dean Moore.

"Lisa the Skeptic." 5F05. November 23, 1997. Written by David S. Cohen. Directed by Neil Affleck.

"Realty Bites." 5F06. December 7, 1997. Written by Dan Greaney. Directed by Swinton O. Scott III.

"Miracle on Evergreen Terrace." 5F07. December 21, 1997. Written by Ron Hauge. Directed by Bob Anderson.

"All Singing, All Dancing." 5F24. January 4, 1998. Written by Steve O'Donnell. Directed by Mark Ervin.

"Bart Carny." 5F08. January 11, 1998. Written by John Swartzwelder. Directed by Mark Kirkland.

"The Joy of Sect." 5F23. February 8, 1998. Written by Steve O'Donnell. Directed by Steven Dean Moore.

"Das Bus." 5F11. February 15, 1998. Written by David S. Cohen. Directed by Pete Michels.

"The Last Temptation of Krust." 5F10. February 22, 1998. Written by Donick Cary. Directed by Mike B. Anderson.

"Dumbbell Indemnity." 5F12. March 1, 1998. Written by Ron Hauge. Directed by Dominic Polcino.

"Lisa the Simpson." 4F24. March 8, 1998. Written by Ned Goldreyer. Directed by Susan Dietter.

"This Little Wiggy." 5F13. March 22, 1998. Written by Dan Greaney. Directed by Neil Affleck.

"Simpson Tide." 3G04. March 29, 1998. Written by Joshua Sternin and Jeffrey Ventimilia. Directed by Milton Gray.

"The Trouble With Trillions." 5F14. April 5, 1998. Written by Ian Maxtone-Graham. Directed by Swinton O. Scott III.

"Girlie Edition." 5F15. April 19, 1998. Written by Larry Doyle. Directed by Mark Kirkland.

"Trash of the Titans." 5F09. April 26, 1998. Written by Ian Maxtone-Graham. Directed by Jim Reardon.

"King of the Hill." 5F16. May 3, 1998. Written by John Swartzwelder. Directed by Steven Dean Moore.

"Lost Our Lisa." 5F17. May 10, 1998. Written by Brian Scully. Directed by Pete Michels.

"Natural Born Kissers." 5F18. May 17, 1998. Written by Matt Selman. Directed by Klay Hall.

Season 10 (1998–1999)

"Lard of the Dance." 5F20. August 23, 1998. Written by Jane O'Brien. Directed by Dominic Polcino.

"The Wizard of Evergreen Terrace." 5F21. September 20, 1998. Written by John Swartzwelder. Directed by Mark Kirkland.

"Bart the Mother." 5F22. September 27, 1998. Written by David S. Cohen. Directed by Steven Dean Moore.

"Treehouse of Horror IX." AABF01. October 25, 1998. Written by Donick Cary, Larry Doyle, and David S. Cohen. Directed by Steven Dean Moore.

"When You Dish Upon a Star." 5F19. November 8, 1998. Written by Richard Appel. Directed by Pete Michels.

"D'oh-in' in the Wind." AABF02. November 15, 1998. Written by Donick Cary. Directed by Mark Kirkland and Matthew Nastuk.

"Lisa Gets an A." AABF03. November 22, 1998. Written by Ian Maxtone-Graham. Directed by Bob Anderson.

"Homer Simpson in 'Kidney Trouble.' " AABF04. December 6, 1998. Written by John Swartzwelder. Directed by Mike B. Anderson.

"Mayored to the Mob." AABF05. December 20, 1998. Written by Ron Hauge. Directed by Swinton O. Scott III.

"Viva Ned Flanders." AABF06. January 10, 1999. Written by David M. Stern. Directed by Neil Affleck.

"Wild Barts Can't Be Broken." AABF07. January 17, 1999. Written by Larry Doyle. Directed by Mark Ervin.

"Sunday, Cruddy Sunday." AABF08. January 31, 1999. Written by Tom Martin, George Meyer, Brian Scully, and Mike Scully. Directed by Steven Dean Moore.

"Homer to the Max." AABF09. February 7, 1999. Written by John Swartzwelder. Directed by Pete Michels.

"I'm with Cupid." AABF11. February 14, 1999. Written by Dan Greaney. Directed by Bob Anderson.

"Marge Simpson in: 'Screaming Yellow Honkers.' " AABF10. February 21, 1999. Written by David M. Stern. Directed by Mark Kirkland.

"Make Room For Lisa." AABF12. February 28, 1999. Written by Brian Scully. Directed by Matthew Nastuk.

"Maximum Homerdrive." AABF13. March 28, 1999. Written by John Swartzwelder. Directed by Swinton O. Scott III.

"Simpsons Bible Stories." AABF14. April 4, 1999. Written by Tim Long, Larry Doyle, and Matt Selman. Directed by Nancy Kruse.

"Mom and Pop Art." AABF15. April 11, 1999. Written by Al Jean. Directed by Steven Dean Moore.

"The Old Man and the 'C' Student." AABF16. April 25, 1999. Written by Julie Thacker. Directed by Mark Kirkland.

"Monty Can't Buy Me Love." AABF17. May 2, 1999. Written by John Swartzwelder. Directed by Mark Ervin.

"They Saved Lisa's Brain." AABF18. May 9, 1999. Written by Matt Selman. Directed by Pete Michels.

"Thirty Minutes over Tokyo." AABF20. May 16, 1999. Written by Donick Cary and Dan Greaney. Directed by Jim Reardon.

Season 11 (1999–2000)

"Beyond Blunderdome." AABF23. September 26, 1999. Written by Mike Scully. Directed by Steven Dean Moore.

"Brother's Little Helper." AABF22. October 3, 1999. Written by George Meyer. Directed by Mark Kirkland.

"Guess Who's Coming to Criticize Dinner." AABF21. October 24, 1999. Written by Al Jean. Directed by Nancy Kruse.

"Treehouse of Horror X." BABF22. October 31 1999. Written by Donick Cary, Tim Long, and Ron Hauge. Directed by Pete Michels.

"E-I-E-I-(Annoyed Grunt)." AABF19. November 7, 1999. Written by Ian Maxtone-Graham. Directed by Bob Anderson.

"Hello Gutter, Hello Fadder." BABF02. November 14, 1999. Written by Al Jean. Directed by Mike B. Anderson.

"Eight Misbehavin'." BABF03. November 21, 1999. Written by Matt Selman. Directed by Steven Dean Moore.

"Take My Wife, Sleaze." BABF05. November 28, 1999. Written by John Swartzwelder. Directed by Neil Affleck.

"Grift of the Magi." BABF07. December 19, 1999. Written by Tom Martin. Directed by Matthew Nastuk.

"Little Big Mom." BABF04. January 9, 2000. Written by Carolyn Omine. Directed by Mark Kirkland.

"Faith Off." BABF06. January 16, 2000. Written by Frank Mula. Directed by Nancy Kruse.

"The Mansion Family." BABF08. January 23, 2000. Written by John Swartzwelder. Directed by Michael Polcino.

"Saddlesore Galactica." BABF09. February 6, 2000. Written by Tim Long. Directed by Lance Kramer.

"Alone Again Natura-Diddly." BABF10. February 13, 2000. Written by Ian Maxtone-Graham. Directed by Jim Reardon.

"Missionary: Impossible." BABF11. February 20, 2000. Written by Ron Hauge. Directed by Steven Dean Moore.

"Pygmoelian." BABF12. February 27, 2000. Written by Larry Doyle. Directed by Mark Kirkland.

"Bart to the Future." BABF13. March 19, 2000. Written by Dan Greaney. Directed by Michael Marcantel.

"Days of Wine and D'Ohses." BABF14. April 9, 2000. Written by Deb Lacusta and Dan Castellaneta. Directed by Neil Affleck.

"Kill the Alligator and Run." BABF16. April 30, 2000. Written by John Swartzwelder. Directed by Jen Kamerman.

"Last Tap Dance in Springfield." BABF15. May 7, 2000. Written by Julie Thacker. Directed by Nancy Kruse.

"It's a Mad, Mad, Mad, Mad Marge." BABF16. May 14, 2000. Written by Larry Doyle. Directed by Steven Dean Moore.

"Behind the Laughter." BABF17. May 21, 2000. Written by Tim Long and George Meyer and Mike Scully and Matt Selman. Directed by Mark Kirkland.

Season 12 (2000–2001)

"Treehouse of Horror XI." BABF21. November 1, 2000. Written by Rob LaZebnik and John Frink and Don Payne and Carolyn Omine. Directed by Matthew Nastuk.

"A Tale of Two Springfields." BABF20. November 5, 2000. Written by John Swartzwelder. Directed by Shaun Cashman.

"Insane Clown Poppy." BABF17. November 12, 2000. Written by John Frink and Don Payne. Directed by Bob Anderson.

"Lisa the Treehugger." CABF01. November 19, 2000, Written by Matt Selman, Directed by Steven Dean Moore,

"Homer vs. Dignity." CABF04. November 26, 2000. Written by Rob LaZebnik. Directed by Neil Affleck.

"The Computer Wore Menace Shoes." CABF02. December 3, 2000. Written by John Swartzwelder. Directed by Mark Kirkland.

"The Great Money Caper." CABF03. December 10, 2000. Written by Carolyn Omine. Directed by Michael Polcino.

"Skinner's Sense of Snow." CABF06. December 17, 2000. Written by Tim Long. Directed by Lance Kramer.

"HOMR." CABF22. December 24, 2000. Written by Al Jean. Directed by Mike Anderson.

"Pokeymom." CABF05. January 14, 2001. Written by Tom Martin. Directed by Bob Anderson.

"Worst Episode Ever." CABF08. February 4, 2001. Written by Larry Doyle. Directed by Matthew Nastuk.

"Tennis the Menace." CABF07. February 11, 2001. Written by Ian Maxtone-Graham. Directed by Jen Kamerman.

"Day of the Jackanapes." CABF10. February 18, 2001. Written by Al Jean. Directed by Michael Marcantel.

"New Kids on the Blecch." CABF12. February 25, 2001. Written by Tim Long. Directed by Steven Dean Moore.

"Hungry Hungry Homer." CABF09. March 4, 2001. Written by John Swartzwelder. Directed by Nancy Kruse.

"Bye Bye Nerdy." CABF11. March 11, 2001. Written by John Frink and Don Payne. Directed by Lauren MacMullan.

"Simpsons Safari." CABF13. April 1, 2001. Written by John Swartzwelder. Directed by Mark Kirkland.

"Trilogy of Error." CABF14. April 29, 2001. Written by Matt Selman. Directed by Mike B. Anderson.

"I'm Goin' to Praise Land." CABF15. May 6, 2001. Written by Julie Thacker. Directed by Chuck Sheetz.

"Children of a Lesser Clod." CABF16. May 13, 2001. Written by Al Jean. Directed by Mike Polcino.

"Simpsons Tall Tales." CABF17. May 20, 2001. Written by John Frink, Don Payne, Bob Bendetson, and Matt Selman. Directed by Bob Anderson.

Season 13 (2001–2002)

"Treehouse of Horror XII." CABF19. November 6, 2001. Written by Joel H. Cohen, John Frink, Don Payne, and Carolyn Omine. Directed by Jim Reardon.

"The Parent Rap." CABF22. November 9, 2001. Written by George Meyer and Mike Scully. Directed by Mark Kirkland.

"Homer the Moe." CABF20. November 18, 2001. Written by Dana Gould. Directed by Jen Kamerman.

"Hunka Hunka Burns in Love." CABF18. December 2, 2001. Written by John Swartzwelder. Directed by Lance Kramer.

"The Blunder Years." CABF21. December 9, 2001. Written by Ian Maxtone-Graham. Directed by Steven Dean Moore.

"She of Little Faith." DABF02. December 16, 2001. Written by Bill Freiberger. Directed by Steven Dean Moore.

"Brawl in the Family." DABF01. January 6, 2002. Written by Joel H. Cohen. Directed by Matthew Nastuk.

"Sweets and Sour Marge." DABF03. January 20, 2002. Written by Carolyn Omine. Directed by Mark Kirkland.

"Jaws Wired Shut." DABF05. January 27, 2002. Written by Matt Selman. Directed by Nancy Kruse.

"Half-Decent Proposal." DABF04. February 10, 2002. Written by Tim Long. Directed by Lauren MacMullan.

"The Bart Wants What It Wants." DABF06. February 17, 2002. Written by John Frink and Don Payne.

"The Lastest Gun in the West." DABF07. February 24, 2002. Written by John Swartzwelder. Directed by Bob Anderson.

"The Old Man and the Key." DABF09. March 10, 2002. Written by Jon Vitti. Directed by Lance Kramer.

"Tales from the Public Domain." DABF08. March 17, 2002. Written by Andrew Kreisberg, Josh Lieb, and Matt Warburton. Directed by Mike B. Anderson.

"Blame it On Lisa." DABF10. March 31, 2002. Written by Bob Bendetson. Directed by Steven Dean Moore.

"Weekend at Burnsie's." DABF11. April 7, 2002. Written by Jon Vitti. Directed by Michael Marcantel.

"Gump Roast." DABF12. April 21, 2002. Written by Deb Lacusta and Dan Castellaneta. Directed by Mark Kirkland.

"I Am Furious Yellow." DABF13. April 28, 2002. Written by John Swartzwelder. Directed by Chuck Sheetz.

"The Sweetest Apu." DABF14. May 5, 2002. Written by John Swartzwelder. Directed by Matthew Nastuk.

"Little Girl in the Big Ten." DABF15. May 12, 2002. Written by Jon Vitti. Directed by Lauren MacMullan.

"The Frying Game." DABF16. May 19, 2002. Written by John Swartzwelder. Directed by Michael Polcino.

"Papa's Got a Brand New Badge." DABF17. May 22, 2002. Written by Dana Gould. Directed by Pete Michels.

ABOUT THE CONTRIBUTORS

John Alberti is an associate professor of English at Northern Kentucky University, where he teaches American literature, critical theory, film studies, and composition. He has published essays on the teaching of race and class in American literature, the role of working class universities in higher education, and rock and roll.

David L. G. Arnold teaches English at the University of Wisconsin-Stevens Point. Besides *The Simpsons* and popular culture his interests include Faulkner and modern literature and also crime fiction. It is one of his chief goals to become famous as the author of tacky crime novels of the type found in supermarkets.

Duncan Stuart Beard has completed a Ph.D. in English Literature at The Australian National University. During this time he was involved in tutoring and lecturing, organized a postgraduate conference, and edited the work *Impossible Selves: Cultural Readings of Identity* (published by Australian Scholarly Press). Until recently he was the webmaster of the International Association for Commonwealth Literature website. He has also performed as an associate editor of the internationally distributed Asian Studies magazine *AMIDA*. Dr. Beard has more recently worked at the Research School of Pacific and Asian Studies in an eclectic variety of roles associated with publishing, including graphic design, advertising, editing, print production, marketing, and warehouse management. He is currently production coordinator within Pandanus Books.

Mick Broderick teaches Media Analysis at Murdoch University, Western Australia, and is Associate Director of the Centre for Millennial Studies at the University of Sydney. He is the author of *Nuclear Movies* (Jefferson: McFarland & Co, 1991) and *Hibakusha Cinema: Hiroshima, Nagasaki and the Nuclear Image in Japanese Film* (London: Kegan Paul International, 1996; trans. Gendai Shokan, Tokyo, 1999).

Vincent Brook is a former film editor and screenwriter and current adjunct professor of film and television at California State University, Los Angeles, and at Pierce College. Articles of his have appeared in *Cinema Journal, Journal of Film and Video, Quarterly Review of Film and Video, Television and New Media, Velvet Light Trap,* and *Emergences.* His book on "Jewish" sitcoms is due out from Rutgers University Press.

Valerie Weilunn Chow is on permanent leave from the Ph.D. program in English Literature at the University of California Irvine, having completed her master's degree. She is now a television producer with the Discovery Channel.

Kevin J. H. Dettmar is professor of English at Southern Illinois University Carbondale. He has written on James Joyce, Modernist literature, the relationship between artistic and commodity capital, and rock and roll. He serves as co-editor of the twentieth-century materials for the *Longman Anthology of British Literature.*

Matthew Henry is currently a full-time faculty member of the English Department at Richland College in Dallas, Texas, where he teaches courses in composition, American popular culture, African American literature, and independent cinema. He earned both a bachelor's and a master's degree in English at the State University of New York at Brockport, and he has completed coursework in the doctoral program in English at Syracuse University. He has published critical essays in *The Griot, Critique, Teaching English in the Two-Year College,* and *Studies in Popular Culture.* An essay on the *Shaft* films and contemporary black masculinity appears in the Summer 2002 issue of *The Journal of Popular Film and Television.*

Kurt Koenigsberger is an assistant professor of English at Case Western Reserve University, where he teaches courses in twentieth-century British literature and in post-colonial literature and theory. He has published essays on Henry James, Virginia Woolf, and William Hazlitt, and serves as associate director of the Society for Critical Exchange. He also directs the Globalization and the Image project for the SCE.

Megan Mullen is Associate Professor of Communication and director of the Humanities Program at University of Wisconsin-Parkside. She teaches courses in media history and analysis. She is the author of *"The Revolution Now in Sight": Cable Television Programming in the United States, 1948–1995.*

Douglas Rushkoff   is author of eight books about media, technology, and culture, which have been translated into seventeen languages so far. They include *Coercion, Media Virus!, Playing the Future, Cyberia,* and the interactive novel, *Exit Strategy.* His novel *Ecstasy Club* is being made into a motion picture and he is developing a feature-length animation. Rushkoff is a Markle Foundation fellow and on the board of the Media Ecology Association. He is currently working on a new book about "Open Source Judaism" called *Nothing Sacred,* teaching at New York University, and delivering commentaries on National Public Radio.

William J. Savage, Jr.   earned his Ph.D. in American literature and interpretive theory at Northwestern University, where he currently teaches in the English Department. He is co-editor (with Daniel Simon) of Nelson Algren's *The Man with the Golden Arm: 50th Anniversary Critical Edition* (New York: Seven Stories Press, 1999) as well as (with David Schmittgens) Algren's *Chicago: City on the Make: 50th Anniversary Edition, Newly Annotated* (Chicago: University of Chicago Press, 2002).

Robert Sloane   is a Ph.D. candidate in the Institute of Communications Research at the University of Illinois Urbana-Champaign. He is writing a dissertation on the production of genre in the music industry.

INDEX

CPSIA information can be obtained
at www.ICGtesting.com
Printed in the USA
LVHW020404031220
673227LV00017B/3068